How
COLLEGE
AFFECTS
STUDENTS

Ernest T. Pascarella
Patrick T. Terenzini

Foreword by Kenneth A. Feldman

How

COLLEGE

AFFECTS

STUDENTS

*Findings and Insights
from Twenty Years of Research*

 Jossey-Bass Publishers
San Francisco

Substantial discounts on bulk quantities of Jossey-Bass books are available to corporations, professional associations, and other organizations. For details and discount information, contact the special sales department at Jossey-Bass Inc., Publishers (415) 433-1740; Fax (800) 605-2665.

For sales outside the United States, please contact your local Simon & Schuster International Office.

Jossey-Bass Web address: http://www.josseybass.com

Manufactured in the United States of America

JACKET DESIGN BY WILLI BAUM

Library of Congress Cataloging-in-Publication Data

Pascarella, Ernest T.
    How college affects students : findings and insights from twenty years of research / Ernest T. Pascarella, Patrick T. Terenzini; foreword by Kenneth A. Feldman.
        p.   cm.—(The Jossey-Bass higher and adult education series)
    Includes bibliographical references and index.
    ISBN 1-55542-304-3
    ISBN 1-55542-338-8 (paperback)
    1. College students—United States.   I. Terenzini, Patrick T.   II. Title.   III. Series.
    LA229.P34   1991
    378.1'98'0973—dc20   90-46068

FIRST EDITION
HB Printing   10 9 8 7 6 5 4 3 2 1
PB Printing   10 9 8 7 6

The Jossey-Bass
Higher and Adult Education Series

Consulting Editor

Kenneth A. Feldman
State University of New York, Stony Brook

Contents

Foreword   xi
   by Kenneth A. Feldman

Preface   xv

The Authors   xxiii

1. Studying College Outcomes: Overview and Organization
    of the Research   1

2. Theories and Models of Student Change in College   15

3. Development of Verbal, Quantitative, and Subject
    Matter Competence   62

4. Cognitive Skills and Intellectual Growth   114

5. Psychosocial Changes: Identity, Self-Concept, and Self-Esteem   162

6. Psychosocial Changes: Relating to Others and the
    External World   214

7. Attitudes and Values   269

8. Moral Development   335

9. Educational Attainment   369

10. Career Choice and Development   424

11. Economic Benefits of College   500

12. Quality of Life After College   538

13. How College Makes a Difference: A Summary   556

14. Implications of the Research for Policy and Practice   636

     Appendix: Methodological and Analytical Issues in
     Assessing the Influence of College   657

     References   693

     Name Index   849

     Subject Index   877

Foreword

Some fifty-five years ago, Stephen M. Corey (1936) published a ten-page article entitled "Attitude Differences Between College Classes: A Summary and Criticism" in the *Journal of Educational Psychology*. Reviewing seventeen studies published between 1925 and 1935, Corey found that many of them showed students in upper-level college classes to be somewhat more socially, politically, or religiously liberal than students in lower-level classes. He had only one methodological comment to make, but it was an important one. Because each of the studies collected cross-sectional data rather than longitudinal data, Corey warned that the results of the various bodies of research did not necessarily show that the colleges under study had actually produced changes in their students. Rather, differences between upper- and lowerclassmen might have resulted merely from selective attrition of students: "To conclude, from a comparison of scores made by freshmen, sophomores, juniors, and seniors, that education either has or has not been effective in engendering or qualifying certain attitudes is to overlook the very obvious fact that the differences between these scores, or for that matter, the absence of differences, might quite possibly be due to selection brought about by academic mortality" (p. 327). There may have been earlier studies of college impacts on students' attitudes and earlier reviews of these studies; Corey did not mention any, however.

To go from this early review (with its exclusive focus on student attitudes, its summary of a mere handful of studies, and its one methodological comment) to the present book (with its consideration of roughly 2,600 pieces of research, its ten chapters on different student characteristics potentially influenceable by college, its chapter reviewing relevant theoretical models, its appendix on methodological concerns, and its chapter on policy implications) is to make a vast jump, perhaps even a quantum leap. Of course, there have been other reviews and syntheses along the way. One thinks of Philip Jacob's *Changing Values in College* (1957), my own work with Theodore Newcomb (*The Impact of College on Students*, 1969), and Howard Bowen's *Investment in Learning* (1977), to name only three of the more comprehensive efforts. None of these, however, is on quite the same scale as the present volume.

In synthesizing the research of the late sixties through the seventies and eighties, Pascarella and Terenzini have cast an especially wide net in selecting for review the student characteristics potentially affected by the college experience. They consider the following sets of student outcomes: verbal skills, quantitative skills, and knowledge of specific subject matter; general cognitive competence and cognitive skills; self-conceptions and self-evaluations; psychosocial characteristics and personality traits; attitudes and values; moral reasoning, moral judgment, and moral behavior; educational attainment; career choice and career attainment; economic returns and benefits; and nonmonetary benefits, life satisfaction, and quality of life. Whenever possible, for each of these sets of characteristics, the research summarized is subdivided into the separate considerations of overall change and stability during college, net effects of college, between-college effects, within-college effects, conditional effects of college, and long-term effects of college. This particular arrangement, besides helping to systematize and clarify an otherwise confusing array of studies, enhances one of the main benefits of reviews or syntheses: The amount of research that has or has not been done in an area is clearly highlighted, thereby making evident which topics of interest have been the object of little or no research and which bear a surfeit.

How College Affects Students may be monumental, but it is also accessible. The authors have made sure it will appeal to readers of differing involvement. Even the most casual of readers can learn much by reading no more than the book's summary chapter (Chapter Thirteen), although such readers may also want to look at the introductory chapter and the chapter on implications for policy and practice (Chapters One and Fourteen). The somewhat more invested reader may want to add the thorough summaries at the end of each substantive chapter (Chapters Three through Twelve). The most avid readers, of course, will enjoy delving into the details of these substantive chapters.

The serious reader will also want to examine Chapter Two, which offers an elegant distillation and comparison of various psychological and sociological models of student development and collegiate impact. In this chapter, the authors note that most of the prominent contributors to theory development and to research into the impact of college on students have been psychologists. The authors note further that "as a consequence, the study of college students and the training of many higher educational researchers and administrators for the last quarter-century have been based largely on one theoretical genre." This genre has been challenged and modified by alternative approaches (primarily sociological) for studying student change and for planning educational programs and services. A psychological orientation—in particular, a developmental perspective—is an important aspect of Pascarella and Terenzini's own view of the interplay between student and college and subtly underlies their analysis of college student change and stability. Yet they are anything but doctrinaire or one-sided in their analysis. Indeed, their psychological approach is heavily tempered by considerations of the nature of interpersonal settings of colleges, the structural and organizational features of colleges' social environments, and the institutional characteristics of college. Incidentally, I might note that Newcomb and I essentially took the reverse tack in synthesizing the research on college impacts: We heavily tempered our more sociological approach with psychological considerations. To put the matter in its briefest formulation, whereas Pascarella and Terenzini lean toward *psychological* social psychology, we leaned toward *sociological* social psychology (compare House, 1977).

The authors have been most shrewd in handling methodological considerations; they are careful not to overwhelm those readers less than expert in their knowledge of research design and data analysis. As the authors themselves state in Chapter One, "Throughout our synthesis of the evidence, we attempt to deal with issues and problems of research design, measurement, and data analysis as they arise and then as simply and benignly as possible." They have also written a technical appendix that addresses in considerable detail the major methodological and analytical issues in assessing the influence of college on students. Even this section makes only minimal assumptions about the reader's statistical or mathematical knowledge and is both readable and lucid.

Pascarella and Terenzini are to be applauded for skillfully drawing out the implications of their synthesis for public policy and institutional practice. They are stalwart in raising policy issues concerning equality and inequality in postsecondary educational outcomes, institutional tolerance of individual student differences, and tensions between educational effectiveness and economic efficiency. Moreover, they use their findings to spell out how the faculty and administrators on individual campuses might best shape the educational and interpersonal settings of their campuses to promote learning and achievement of each institution's goals as well as to induce more students to become involved in the activities of these settings and thus benefit from the proffered opportunities.

How College Affects Students will be of enormous value to researchers, educators, administrators, and others interested in higher education. Its publication is indisputably a milestone in the analysis of college effects on students. More than ever before, we now know how students change at college and understand why they change as they do. At the same time, we are also more aware of *exactly* what we do *not* know about college impacts on students and of *precisely* what gaps in knowledge need filling in. With respect, then, to the influence on students that colleges do have and could have, the present book helps set the research and policy agenda for this, the last decade of the twentieth century.

February 1991

Kenneth A. Feldman
State University of New York, Stony Brook

We dedicate this book to the memory of
Lance Corporal Michael Doane
United States Marine Corps
Killed in action, Republic of Vietnam, spring 1968
In gratitude for the life of Ernest T. Pascarella

Preface

"If one believes in the cumulative nature of science, then periodic stock-taking becomes essential for any particular arena of scientific endeavor. The cumulation of knowledge in an area may, of course, occur more or less haphazardly—but this does not and should not preclude more systematic attempts by laborers in the field to determine where they have arrived and where they might go." With these words, Kenneth Feldman and Theodore Newcomb (1969) opened the preface to their landmark work, *The Impact of College on Students,* in which they reviewed and synthesized the findings of more than 1,500 studies conducted over four decades on the influence of college on students. They succeeded not only in providing the first comprehensive conceptual map of generally uncharted terrain but also in generating a number of interesting hypotheses about the ways in which college influences students. Moreover, along with the earlier pioneering empirical work of such scholars as Astin (1961, 1962, 1963a, 1963c); Dressel and Mayhew (1954); Eddy (1959); Jacob (1957); Newcomb, Koenig, Flacks, and Warwick (1967); Pace and Stern (1958); Sanford (1956), and Thistlethwaite (1959a, 1959b, 1960, 1962), Feldman and Newcomb were instrumental in precipitating a virtual torrent of studies on the characteristics of collegiate institutions and their students and how students change and benefit during and after their college years from college attendance.

The Impact of College on Students is now a classic, a standard text in graduate courses dealing with college students, as well as a standard and frequently cited reference for scholars, students, and administrators of higher education. Much of what those in the field of higher education currently understand about the developmental influence of college is based on the work of Feldman and Newcomb.

More than twenty years have now passed since the publication of the *Impact of College on Students.* In the intervening decades, the number of empirical studies added to the literature has surpassed the number produced in the preceding four decades reviewed by Feldman and Newcomb. Moreover, major areas of inquiry, such as the effects of college on learning, cognitive development, moral reasoning, and various indexes of status attainment, have reached maturity largely since the late 1960s. These facts in themselves suggest the need for a current synthesis of what we have learned about the influence of college on student development in the last twenty years.

The warrant for this book, however, lies in more than the publication of the many hundreds of studies on the influence of college on students conducted since Feldman and Newcomb's review. The impact of college on students as an area of inquiry has grown qualitatively as well as quantitatively since 1969, in both theory and method. Theories of student development and change have emerged in sometimes daunting number and variety. Multivariate statistical procedures, necessary for testing and extending these emergent theories, have become increasingly accessible to scholars (a development that has yielded mixed blessings). History-altering progress in both mainframe and microcomputing hardware and software has been the handmaiden of these advances, facilitating both the complex statistical analyses needed for testing complex theories and the analysis of large, nationally representative data bases. This happy, phenomenally productive conjunction of theory development, increased design and statistical sophistication, and data management capabilities has produced a research environment and resources that twenty years ago would have been well beyond the reach of all but a handful of well-funded scholars. Today, they are within reach of virtually anyone with interest, talent, and modest support.

Over the last decade, the increasing costs of college attendance and operation, plus mounting criticism of the quality of undergraduate education in the United States, have also spurred research on college outcomes. As computing equipment and management information systems have given college and university administrators and state and federal policymakers greater understanding of and control over college operating budgets and expenditures, the character of the questions asked of higher education has also changed. Questions about cost have increasingly been followed by questions about worth and value, education's "return on investment" in both economic and noneconomic terms. "Assessment" of undergraduate student learning has gained in popularity as a vehicle for a public accounting of an institution's stewardship of its resources and as a mechanism for improving the quality of the education offered.

Increases in all of these areas—in theory, methodological sophistication, computing, cost, criticism, and external oversight—have contributed to the burgeoning literature on the effects of college on students. What have we learned from this enormous volume of research? *Does* college make a difference? In all its simplicity and all its complexity, that is the question we have tried to answer.

The appeal of its straightforwardness notwithstanding, the question is really a naive one. In fact, we have tried to answer six questions. These are discussed more fully in the introductory chapter, but they are reducible to three: Do students change in various ways during the college years? To what extent are changes attributable to the collegiate experience and not to other influences (like growing up)? And finally, what college characteristics and experiences tend to produce changes? Our interest in this last question focuses particularly on institutionally manipulable influences on student change: those sources of change that are amenable to systematic institutional intervention through programmatic and policy decision making.

Audience

We believe our findings will be useful to a wide spectrum of people involved in or responsible for higher education. The full range of academic and student affairs administrators and staff—from middle-level administrators to vice-presidents and presidents—will find the current empirical foundations (or lack thereof) for many of their institutions' student-related activities, programs, and policies. Graduate students preparing for administrative or research positions in higher education, as well as researchers in such fields as psychology, sociology, anthropology, economics, public administration, and business administration who have an interest in the effects of college on students, will find a comprehensive analysis of the literature for a wide variety of student outcome areas, identification of areas in this literature where research is most needed, a conceptual framework (provided by the six questions we pose) for thinking about college effects, and a comprehensive bibliography. State and federal policymakers and their staffs—perhaps better able than we to extract the policy significance of this literature—will gain insight into the sources of influence on student change and what we consider to be the major implications of this body of evidence for administrative practice and public and institutional policy. Anyone interested in higher education in America and its effects on students will, we hope, find here a useful reference book and guide to understanding one of America's most important social institutions.

Overview of the Contents

The introductory chapter (Chapter One) provides a detailed discussion of the evolution of research on college outcomes as an area of study and outlines the conceptual framework that guided our review. Each of the six questions we pose in each college impact area is explained. These questions, we believe, provide a useful way to think about college effects, whether retrospectively (as we have done) or in planning future research. This first chapter also describes our search and review methods and defines key terms used throughout the book.

Chapter Two summarizes the major theoretical models of college effects on student change. These include the "developmental" models of Chickering, Kohlberg, and Perry and the college "impact" models of Astin,

Pascarella, Tinto, and Weidman. A number of less prominent theories and models of student change are also identified.

Chapters Three and Four address the influence of college on learning and cognitive development. Chapter Three focuses on the academic subject matter and skills learned during college, while Chapter Four is concerned with the development of more generalizable intellectual skills and analytical competencies.

Chapters Five through Eight deal with the influence of college on various dimensions of personal growth and change. Chapters Five and Six focus primarily on psychosocial changes, with Chapter Five examining changes in students' self systems (for example, their sense of identity and their self-evaluation), while Chapter Six reviews the research on changes in students' relational systems (for example, the ways they relate to people and institutions outside themselves). Included in the latter chapter are such topics as autonomy, locus of control, authoritarianism, interpersonal relations, personal adjustment, and maturity. Chapter Seven examines changes in students' cultural, aesthetic, and intellectual values; educational and occupational values; political and social attitudes and values; religious values and activities; and gender role orientations. Chapter Eight assesses the impact of college on moral development.

Chapters Nine through Eleven deal with the influence of college on the socioeconomic attainment process, primarily for educational, occupational, and economic attainments. Chapter Nine examines the impact of college on educational attainment. The focus here is on factors that influence educational aspirations, persistence, completion of college, and attainment of graduate and professional degrees. Chapter Ten reviews the contributions of college to career choice and the noneconomic aspects of career achievement and career progression. Here the focus is on factors that influence choice of a career and the various noneconomic dimensions of career success (for example, occupational status, rate and level of promotion, job productivity, and job satisfaction). Chapter Eleven summarizes the various economic returns of college attendance and different collegiate experiences.

Chapter Twelve synthesizes what is known about the long-term impact of college on the quality of life. Included are such factors as subjective well-being, health, marriage, family planning and child nurturance, consumer behavior, savings and investment behavior, and leisure.

Chapter Thirteen summarizes the total body of evidence pertaining to what we know about the impact of college. In the process, the chapter emphasizes the extent to which the evidence corroborates or amplifies the earlier syntheses of Feldman and Newcomb (1969) and Bowen (1977). The chapter also delineates a few of the ways in which certain evidence supports theoretical models of student development and the impact of college.

Chapter Fourteen discusses implications of the evidence for institutional practice and public policy. With regard to institutional practice, we review the findings of our synthesis that have implications for academic and student affairs policy formulation, program and service development, and program evaluation at the level of the individual campus. The key focus is on how the impact of college can be enhanced by administrative action at the campus level. With regard to public policy, we discuss and analyze the implications of the major findings for state and federal policy. Emphasis is on directions the evidence indicates should be taken in state and federal legislation and governmental program development and evaluation.

Following Chapter Fourteen is a technical appendix that addresses in considerable detail some of the major methodological and analytical issues in assessing the influence of college on students. Included is a discussion of such factors as research design, problems in attributing causality, statistical control, residual analysis, regression procedures, commonality analysis, causal modeling and path analysis, unit of analysis, change scores, and conditional versus general effects. This section is intended to be didactic and makes only minimal assumptions about the reader's statistical or mathematical knowledge. It is something of a primer for the nonquantitatively inclined.

Levels of Detail Within Each Chapter

Chapters devoted to a synthesis of the evidence (that is, Chapters Three through Twelve) are written on two levels as far as detail is concerned. On one level, we review the literature within the framework of our six guiding questions, giving attention to theoretical and methodological considerations that often determine the reliability and validity of findings. This detailed presentation of the evidence constitutes the major portion of each chapter. On a second level, we provide a comprehensive summary of our conclusions about the evidence, generally purged of methodological discussion. Such a summary appears at the end of each chapter.

Although many readers will approach each chapter by reading first the detailed synthesis of studies and then the summary, that is by no means the only effective way to digest the large amount of information in the book. Some may find that they gain more from reading the detailed discussion of studies *after* they read the comprehensive summary. We also recognize that a considerable number of readers may be most interested in the comprehensive summary and will use the detailed discussion of evidence in each chapter primarily as an elaborative selective reference. For this group of readers, we have taken pains to ensure that the summary section is in fact a comprehensive rather than a cursory review of our conclusions.

Acknowledgments

Publication of this volume is the culmination of some eight person-years of work, but its completion would have been impossible altogether without the assistance of a large number of people. We cannot possibly acknowledge our indebtedness to everyone who helped us in one way or another, such as the millions of students who agreed to participate in the more than 2,600 studies we reviewed, our graduate students who understood what we were about and respected our need for time and privacy, and the many scholars in the field who supplied us with fugitive conference papers, technical reports, unpublished papers, and original data for our review.

There are some, however, whose contributions to our work require special recognition. We are most deeply indebted to the College of Education at the University of Illinois, Chicago, and to the Institute of Higher Education at the University of Georgia, particularly to Cameron Fincher, for their sustained financial support of our efforts over the last four years. We highly value and appreciate the exceptional quality of the staff they made available to us at various times and in various capacities. Mary Sue Love of the University of Georgia's Institute of Higher Education patiently typed the original text and numerous changes for half of the chapters and made extensive revisions on five more. Yolanda Doyle and Aurelia Jones of the University of Illinois, Chicago, typed and maintained our bibliography, perhaps the most ponderous and cumbersome of its kind anywhere in captivity, as if it were their own. Joyce Placek, Susan Sheffield, and Mary Snyder, all from the University of Georgia, provided various kinds of technical support, from dealing with balky word processors to overseeing institute budgets and ensuring that we had what we needed when we needed it.

We are also deeply grateful to our graduate research assistants: Leslie Herzog of the University of Illinois, Chicago, and Ronald Core, Frances Rauschenberg, and Betty Watts-Warren of the University of Georgia. Collectively, they spent thousands of hours locating, copying, and abstracting journal articles, setting up computerized bibliographic systems, verifying references, and doing countless other tasks that attract little attention but without which competent library research is impossible. We appreciate their enthusiasm for our project and their good humor as much as their competence and attention to detail.

As these young scholars supported our efforts, so were they themselves (and through them were we) supported by the outstanding reference and interlibrary loan librarians and higher education bibliographers of the University of Illinois, Chicago, and University of Georgia libraries. The higher education collections of these two fine research libraries are exceeded only by the competence and patience of their librarians, and on behalf of our graduate assistants and for ourselves, we thank and applaud them.

A literature review of this magnitude requires about equal measures of dedication, hubris, and foolhardiness, and we are indebted to numerous colleagues who encouraged and supported our efforts over the period of the study. From the start, Gale Erlandson, higher education editor for Jossey-Bass, was as enthusiastic about the idea for this volume as we were.

She gave us valuable advice and encouragement throughout the project. We are particularly appreciative of the conscientious and constructive reviews of various chapters that we received from John P. Bean, John M. Braxton, Sven Groennings, Patricia M. King, George D. Kuh, Marcia Baxter Magolda, Theodore K. Miller, James L. Ratcliff, James R. Rest, John C. Smart, Daryl G. Smith, Herbert J. Walberg, and Roger B. Winston, Jr. Their knowledge of their scholarly areas, their thoughtfulness, and their insights contributed substantially to our thinking and writing. Any major oversights or analytical failures we will (good-naturedly, of course) attribute to them.

Special thanks are due to Leonard Baird and Oscar Lenning, who reviewed all chapters and made numerous important suggestions for revisions and improvements in the manuscript. We expected no less from these two meticulous scholars, and we certainly were not disappointed.

We are particularly grateful to Kenneth Feldman. His and Theodore Newcomb's prescience, their dedication to the study of college impacts on students, and their courage in taking on the tasks that produced *The Impact of College on Students* were inspirational in many ways. Our volume, of course, owes its intellectual genesis to theirs. Although there are some fundamental differences between the two books, together they contain a comprehensive analysis and history of the research on college students from its inception to the present. Ken Feldman read all our chapters and made numerous substantive and editorial suggestions that improved both the quality of our thinking and the tightness of our prose. On many occasions we benefited from the insights he had gained from producing his own review, from his encyclopedic knowledge of the research on college students, from his good humor and encouragement when our intellectual reach seemed to exceed our grasp, and from the example of the almost unattainably high standards his work has set for reviews of the literature.

Finally, we are most deeply indebted to our families for the sacrifices they have made. Our wives, Diana Pascarella and Caroline Terenzini, know better than all others what has gone into the preparation of this manuscript. Through it all, they were unfailingly supportive, understanding, and patient. Our children—Andy, Allison, and Emily Pascarella and Eden, John, and Drew Terenzini—made their own special contributions. Although they may not have fully understood what their absentee fathers were up to, their patience and enthusiasm for seeing what came to be called simply "the Book" provided a kind of encouragement that can come only from one's children.

To all these people we extend heartfelt thanks.

February 1991

Ernest T. Pascarella
Chicago, Illinois

Patrick T. Terenzini
State College, Pennsylvania

The Authors

Ernest T. Pascarella is professor of educational psychology at the University of Illinois, Chicago. Previously, he was associate director for research at the Center for Instructional Development at Syracuse University, where he received his Ph.D. degree (1973) in higher education. He received his A.B. degree (1965) in religion from Princeton University and his M.S. degree (1970) in psychological measurement from the University of Pennsylvania.

For the past seventeen years, Pascarella has focused his research and writing on student persistence in higher education and the impact of college on students. He has received awards for outstanding research from the International Reading Association (1981), the Association for Institutional Research (1987), the National Association of Student Personnel Administrators (1988), and the American Educational Research Association, Division J (1989). In 1986 he received the Distinguished Scholar-Teacher Award from the College of Education at Illinois and in 1989–90 served as president of the Association for the Study of Higher Education.

Patrick T. Terenzini is professor of higher education and senior scientist at the Center for the Study of Higher Education at The Pennsylvania State University. During most of the writing of this volume (1986–1989), he was professor of higher education at the Institute of Higher Education of the University of Georgia. Previously, he was assistant to the president for planning (1984–1986) and director of institutional research (1978–1984) at the State University of New York, Albany. Terenzini received his A.B. degree (1964) in English from Dartmouth College, his M.A.T. degree (1965) in English education from Harvard University, and his Ph.D. degree (1972) in higher education from Syracuse University.

Terenzini has received both the Sidney Suslow Award and two Forum Best Paper Awards from the Association for Institutional Research. He is editor-in-chief of *New Directions for Institutional Research,* associate editor of *Higher Education: Handbook of Theory and Research,* and a consulting editor for *Research in Higher Education.*

stricts opportunities for participation, impact is diminished); (3) curriculum, teaching, and evaluation (curricular flexibility, variety in instructional styles and modes, student participation in learning, and learning-oriented evaluation promote impact); (4) residence hall arrangements (the close friendships and reference groups that develop can promote or inhibit personal development, depending upon the diversity, attitudes, and values of the occupants); (5) faculty and administration (frequent, friendly contact in diverse settings with psychologically accessible adults will promote development); and (6) friends, groups, and student culture (student cultures amplify or attenuate other institutional influences on development, depending upon the degree of congruence between student and institutional values).

While a detailed critique of this theory, as well as others to follow, is beyond the scope of this chapter, critics have tended to focus on the theory's failure to treat cognitive or intellectual development in greater detail than as simply one subtask of the "developing competence" vector. Critics have also noted the absence of any detailed consideration of the underlying processes relating to change on each vector. Indeed, some individuals believe Chickering's vectors constitute not so much a theory (with the attendant specification of the systemic relations between and among variables and outcomes) as a description of what ideally happens to students during the college years. (Chickering, it should be noted, readily acknowledges the origins of his framework in the then-extant research literature.) Critics have also noted the lack of sufficient specificity in Chickering's model for easy application in research and administrative programming. These and other limitations (and strengths) of the theory are discussed in greater detail elsewhere (Ellison & Simon, 1973, pp. 50–53; Rodgers, 1980, pp. 51–52; Thomas & Chickering, 1984; Knefelkamp, Widick, & Parker, 1978, pp. 27–28).

Other Psychosocial Theories and Models

While Chickering's work has attracted greater attention and inspired more research and administrative programming than other psychosocial theories or models, several others merit attention. Space precludes detailed discussion of them, however.

Marcia's Model of Ego Identity Status. Building on Erikson's (1956, 1963, 1968) proposition that the definition of one's identity constitutes the central "crisis" of adolescence, James Marcia (1965, 1966) reasoned that "ego identity status" formation is a dynamic process that involves the resolution of two psychosocial tasks. The first is the experience of "crisis," understood in its Eriksonian sense as the engagement of and choice among meaningful but competing alternatives. The second task involves the making of occupational and ideological (that is, religious and political) commitments. *Commitment* refers to the level of the individual's personal investment in each of the three areas. Shortly after the model's initial explication and early testing, a fourth area—sexual values—was added so that its theoretical and operational forms would be as applicable to women as to men (Marcia, 1980; Marcia & Friedman, 1970; Schenkel & Marcia, 1972). Crisis is presumed to lead to differentiation and individualization, while commitment is assumed to result in stability, continuity, and comfort (Prager, 1986).

In his juxtaposition of these two psychosocial tasks, Marcia identifies four different responses to the need for identity and the process of identity formation. "Identity-diffused" individuals have neither experienced the crisis of the search for an identity nor made commitments to an identity in any of the occupational or value areas. Such people tend either to be uninterested in occupational or ideological matters or to accept all positions as more or less equal. "Foreclosed" individuals have not undergone any crisis, but they have made commitments. The commitments upon which their identities rest, however, tend to be those of their parents and have been accepted without question or examination. People in "moratorium" status are actively involved in a crisis period, searching for a defining identity, evaluating possible alternatives. These individuals are distinguished from identity-diffused people by the presence of their conscious search, but their commitments remain unformed or, at best, emergent. "Identity-achieved" individuals have both successfully weathered a crisis and made personal occupational, religious, political, and sex role commitments. These commitments have been independently arrived at, may be at variance with those of parents or others, and form a basis for independent action. Marcia (1976) notes, however, that identity achievement probably is not a permanent state. Rather, he suggests that individuals may shift through various statuses as they accommodate changes associated with the life cycle. Bourne (1978b) gives a conceptual and methodological critique of Marcia's model. The research on it relating to college effects is reviewed in Chapter Five of this volume (see also Bourne, 1978a; Marcia, 1980; Matteson, 1975; Waterman, 1982). Josselson (1987) offers a research-based discussion of Marcia's theory as it applies specifically to women.

Cross's Model of Black Identity Formation. Current research and theory on college student change and development appear quite clearly to assume that the nature and processes of identity development among black and other nonwhite students are essentially the same as those for whites. Others have reached a similar conclusion (Carter & Helms, 1987; Semmes, 1985; Stikes, 1984; Taylor, 1976; Wright, 1987). In the last two decades, however, a literature specifically addressing the characteristics of black identity and proposing models of its development has begun to emerge. Helms (1990b, p. 5) identifies three components of racial identity: (1) a personal identity (consisting of "one's attitudes and feelings about oneself"), (2) a reference group orientation (the extent to which one uses a particular racial group to define one's personal identity; it is reflected in one's values, attitudes, and behaviors), and (3) an ascribed identity ("the individual's deliberate affiliation or commitment to a particular racial group"). Racial identity is presumed to derive from the particular weightings the individual assigns to these three components. The possible variations in weightings give rise to different models, or racial identity "resolutions" (Helms, 1990b).

Helms (1990c) identifies two theoretical racial identity strands running through the variety of potential "resolutions." The first is a "type" perspective that consists of essentially taxonomic models that seek to classify individuals according to their characteristic racial beliefs, attitudes, feelings, and behaviors. Models in this category tend to focus on the implications of identity status for counseling and psychotherapeutic purposes. Because of this tendency and because these models have attracted virtually no attention in the study of the fact or process of identity development among black college students, we do not consider such models further. Helms labels the second theoretical strand the "Nigrescence or racial identity development (NRID) perspective," which seeks to describe "the developmental process by which a person 'becomes Black' where Black is defined in terms of one's manner of thinking about and evaluating oneself and one's reference groups rather than in terms of skin color per se" (p. 17). Most models fall into this second, stage category of black identity formation (Baldwin, 1980, 1981, 1984; Banks, 1981; Cross, 1971a, 1971b, 1978, 1980, 1985; Gay, 1984; Hauser & Kassendorf, 1983; Jackson, 1975; Sherif & Sherif, 1970; Taylor, 1976, 1977; Thomas, 1971; Toldson & Pasteur, 1975; White & Burke, 1987; see also Wyne, White, & Coop, 1974, for a discussion of black self-concept formation in the childhood and early adolescent years).

Of these, Cross's model has attracted more research attention than any other. According to Cross (1971a, pp. 100–107), individuals pass through five stages as their personal black identity takes shape. In Stage 1, "Preencounter" (or prediscovery), the individual's worldview is dominated by Euro-American determinants, with the emphasis in life on being assimilated or integrated into the dominant, white world. Stage 2, "Encounter," involves some experience (for example, the assassination of Martin Luther King, Jr.) that confronts the individual's understanding of blacks' place in the world and triggers a reinterpretation of initial views and beliefs. In Stage 3, "Immersion-Emersion," the individual searches for a new understanding of self as black. The immersion in "the world of Blackness" (p. 102) involves a turning inward and the view that everything of value must be black. In the emersion phase, the individual emerges from "the dead-end, either/or, racist, oversimplified aspects of the immersion experience . . . [and] begins to 'level off' and control his experiences" (p. 104). In Stage 4, "Internalization," four outcomes are possible: (1) continuation and rejection; (2) continuation and fixation at Stage 3; (3) internalization that brings an inner security and satisfaction with self but involves only a receptivity to discussions and plans for action, but no commitment to action; and (4) movement to what is actually Stage 5, "Internalization-Commitment." This is the most desirable outcome of the process and differs from Stage 4 in that the individual has a plan for participation in the reformation of the black community. While the individual's values may yet be Western, the individual now "represents a 'relevant' as opposed to a 'token' reformer" (p. 106). Because of measurement difficulties in differentiating Stage 5 from earlier states, however, doubts have been raised about whether Stage 5 constitutes a discrete identity level (Helms, 1990c). The research based on Cross's model is summarized in Chapter Five.

Descriptions and models relating to the psychosocial development of other minority groups have been offered, including ones specific to Asian Americans (for example, Sue & Sue, 1971), Hispanics (for example, Martinez, 1988), and Native Americans (for example, Johnson & Lashley, 1988), as well as several dealing with development in racial or ethnic groups more broadly defined (for example, Atkinson, Morten, & Sue, 1983; Ho, 1987). Moore (1990) provides a review of recent theories of student development that relate specifically to groups based on gender, age, sexual orientation, and ethnicity. Much of this thinking and writing focuses heavily on counseling and psychotherapeutic applications, although some attention is also given to the programmatic implications of group-specific student development models. Their utility for research on the psychosocial development of students over time remains unexamined.

Heath's Maturity Model. Douglas Heath (1968, 1978) offers a "dimensional" (as opposed to "stage") model of student development similar in many ways to Chickering's (1969) theory. Heath (1965) reviewed "clinical, theoretical, and empirical literature" in biology, psychoanalysis, psychology, anthropology, education, and mental health "for the traits describing mentally healthy, psychologically sound, optimally functioning, self-actualizing, fulfilled, emotionally mature, 'ideal' persons" (Heath, 1978, pp. 193–194). His review of this literature, his synthesis of what twenty-five educational philosophers throughout history have suggested are the goals of a liberal education, and his research led him to construct a model of the person as "a maturing system who can be described in terms of five interdependent dimensions in the four principal sectors of his life" (1977b, p. 7).

The five dimensions of maturing include becoming (1) more able to symbolize one's experiences (for example, through writing, speech, art, music, mathematics), (2) more allocentric (or "other centered"), (3) more integrated, (4) more stable, and (5) more autonomous. Maturing along each of these dimensions occurs in four "self system" (Widick, Knefelkamp, & Parker, 1980, pp. 99–100) sectors or structures: cognitive skills, values, self-concept, and interpersonal relations. Heath's emphasis is clearly on "becoming," or, as he prefers, "maturing." Maturing, as Heath sees it, is an organismic, systemic, reciprocal, and unending process. His theory "assumes that the development of one structure is not independent of the development of others" (1968, p. 5). Indeed, extreme development or lag along one dimension or in one structure will eventually inhibit development along other dimensions or in other sectors.

A distinctive feature of Heath's (1965, 1968, 1978) work is his persistent efforts to relate his model's constructs to the tenets of a liberal education as he discerns them in the writings of major educational philosophers and thinkers since Plato. Heath believes a liberal education is a powerful force toward maturity, and he offers a detailed analysis of his model with specific reference to various philosophers over the centuries (see Heath, 1968, appendix A). He also sets forth three conditions that define "a particularly powerful liberally educating environment: the educability of its students, its communal educative conditions, and the coherence of its purposes and means" (1968, p. 264). (The research evidence on Heath's model is reviewed in Chapter Six.)

Heath & liberal education

The last two decades have seen both an explosive growth in the number of older people returning to (or beginning) college and the emergence of life-span theories of psychosocial development. The focus of this book and space limitations preclude discussion of these theories. Interested readers should consult Chickering and Havighurst (1981), Gould (1972), Levinson (1978), Neugarten (1964, 1968, 1975), Sheehy (1974), and Vaillant (1977).

Cognitive-Structural Theories

Whereas Erik Erikson is a significant progenitor of psychosocial theories and models, virtually all cognitive-structural theories of student development owe their origins to Jean Piaget (1964). Whereas psychosocial theorists focus on the content of development (for example, vectors, identity statuses, dimensions), cognitive-structural theorists seek to describe the process of change, concentrating on the cognitive structures individuals construct in order to give meaning to their worlds. Indeed, the psychosocial and cognitive-structural families appear to be complementary. "One describes what students will be concerned about and what decisions will be primary; the other suggests how students will think about those issues and what shifts in reasoning will occur" (Knefelkamp, Widick, & Parker, 1978, p. xii).

Cognitive-structural theories have several things in common. They all posit a series of stages through which an individual passes in the developmental process. In most theories, these stages are hierarchical, the successful attainment of one being a prerequisite to movement on to the next, and in most the progression is irreversible. Because of their foundations in cognition, one simply cannot "go home again" because one now perceives, structures, and gives meaning to one's world in a way that is fundamentally different from what it was at earlier stages. Because of this fundamental character of "making meaning," the stages of development are believed to be universal and transcultural, and some evidence exists to support that belief. All focus on *how* meaning is structured, not on what is known or believed.

Finally, as with psychosocial theories, cognitive-structural theories assume that developmental change involves a chain of stimulus (challenge) and response. As individuals develop, they encounter new information or experiences that conflict with or challenge the validity of their current cognitive structure. Adaptive responses to conflict or challenge may involve either of two processes: assimilation or accommodation. In assimilation, the individual perceptually reorders or reinterprets the source of conflict to make it consistent with current knowledge, belief, or value structures. In accommodation, the individual changes presently held cognitive or belief structures to admit or be consistent with the new experience presenting the conflict. The developmental process is seen as a series of constructions and reconstructions. "Healthy" responses to cognitive or affective conflict are presumed to lead to a reformation of existing structures that incorporates new and old knowledge, attitudes, values, and self-concepts in revised, coherent, integrated perceptual structures at the next, more advanced stage or developmental condition.

William Perry and Lawrence Kohlberg, the other two members of the "Triumvirate" or "Gang of Three," are both cognitive-structural developmentalists. Because of their prominence in the research literature, their theories are examined at some length.

Perry's Scheme of Intellectual and Ethical Development

On the basis of an extensive series of interviews with Harvard College students, William Perry (1970, 1981) sought to map conceptually the development he observed clinically in the "structures which the students explicitly or implicitly impute to the world, especially those structures in which they construe the nature and origins of knowledge, of value, and of responsibility" (1970, p. 1). Perry maintains that such structures transcend content and thus are less likely to be socially, culturally, or otherwise temporally dependent. His theory is clearly a stage model, although he prefers the term *position* because it implies no assumptions about duration and is "happily appropriate to the image of 'point of outlook' or 'position from which a person views his world' " (1970, p. 48).

Perry's model, or "scheme," asserts that the developmental sequence of forms "manifests a logical order—an order in which one form leads to another through differentiations and reorganizations required for the meaningful interpretation of increasingly complex experience" (1970, p. 3). Perry (1970) identified nine positions. At the broadest conceptual level, he has suggested that development can be conceived as comprising two major parts, with the pivotal stage (his Position 5) being the perception of all knowledge and values (including authority's) as relative.

Prior to the attainment of Position 5, cognitive structures or ways of perceiving one's world are dominated by a dualistic perception: Things are either right or wrong, good or bad, and knowledge of which is which is derived from "Authority." The dichotomous categories include knowledge, values, and people, and they are absolute. At Position 5, the individual begins to perceive not only the presence of multiple points of view but the indeterminacies of "Truth." The relative character of knowledge and values is recognized. Following this recognition, the individual follows a progression through the last four positions, moving toward higher developmental levels according to the extent to which the individual can cope with a relativistic world and begin to develop personal commitments (1970, p. 57). Perry (1981, p. 79) grouped his original nine positions into the following three clusters (King, 1978, offers four clusters).

Dualism Modified (Positions 1–3). In the early positions, students order their worlds in dualistic, dichotomous, and absolute categories. Knowledge is presumed to be absolute and known to authorities. Alternative views or different perspectives on the same phenomenon create discomfort and confusion. To students at these levels, learning means catching whatever the instructor pitches. By Position 3, however, "Multiplicity," the existence of multiple perspectives on any given issue, is recognized, and others holding an opinion contrary to one's own are no longer seen as simply wrong, but as entitled to their views. Indeed, all opinions are seen as having comparable claims on correctness.

Relativism Discovered (Positions 4–6). Recognition of multiplicity in the world leads to understanding that "knowledge is contextual and relative" (King, 1978, p. 38). Analytical thinking skills emerge, and students are able to critique their own ideas and those of others. They recognize that not all positions are equally valid. This stage can be problematic, however, since the discovery of relativism in ideas and values can lead to a resistance to choose among presumably equal alternatives. Subsequent development may be delayed at this stage.

Commitments in Relativism Developed (Positions 7–9). Students moving through Positions 7 through 9 "have made an active affirmation of themselves and their responsibilities in a pluralistic world, establishing their identities in the process" (King, 1978, p. 39). Commitments are made to ideas, to values, to behaviors, to other people (for example, in marriage and careers). According to Perry (1970), perhaps 75 percent of the students in his studies had reached the level of commitment denoted by Positions 7 and 8 by their senior year. Subsequent research, however, has found virtually no students scoring at these levels (P. M. King, letter to one of the authors, October 10, 1988).

Like students' cognitive structures, their commitments must be seen as dynamic and changeable, not in any capricious, fast-paced fashion but as a series of constructions and reconstructions, "differentiations and reorganizations" (Perry, 1970, p. 3). Commitments are modifiable, subject to new evidence and understanding about who one is and how the world is. Commitments may be made, but they are not immutable; they are alterable in the face of new evidence about the world. This process of construction and reconstruction does not end with college. Indeed, it may be a lifelong process (Perry, 1981).

More recently, Perry (1981) appears to attach greater significance to the transitions between positions: "Positions are by definition static, and development is by definition movement" (p. 78). He stresses that each position "both includes and transcends earlier positions, as the earlier ones cannot do with the later [ones]. This fact defines the movement as *development* rather than mere changes or 'phases' " (p. 78). Perry also suggests that development is recurrent: The discovery and reconstruction of "forms" that characterize the development of college students can also be experienced at later points in the life span. He concludes: "Perhaps the best model for growth is neither the straight line nor the circle, but a helix, perhaps with an expanding radius to show that when we face the 'same' old issues we do so from a different and broader perspective" (p. 97).

A persistent criticism of Perry's scheme has been the difficulty of operationalizing and measuring position change, particularly with large samples, although a number of different approaches have been attempted (King, 1978). The shift in the scheme's focus between Positions 5 and 6, from cognitive and intellectual growth to identity formation, has also been noted (see the discussion of Kitchener and King's reflective judgment model below). Studies of change during college based on Perry's scheme are reviewed in Chapter Four.

Kohlberg's Theory of Moral Development

Whereas Perry's theory seeks to explain cognitive and ethical growth, Lawrence Kohlberg's theory focuses somewhat more narrowly on moral development (Kohlberg, 1969, 1972, 1975, 1981a, 1981b, 1984; Kohlberg, Levine, & Hewer, 1983). Kohlberg sought to delineate the nature and sequence of progressive changes in individuals' cognitive structures and rules for processing information on the basis of which moral judgments are made. His principal concern, however, was not with the content of moral choice (which may be socially or culturally determined) but with modes of reasoning, with the cognitive *processes* (thought to be universal) by which moral choices are made.

Kohlberg's is a cognitive "stage" theory that identifies three general levels of moral reasoning, with two stages at each level, for a total of six stages, although in his later writings the sixth stage has been dropped from the formal model because of the absence of empirical evidence to support its existence as a distinct stage (Kohlberg, Levine, & Hewer, 1983). At each stage, the primary concern is with the principle of justice. Kohlberg (1972, p. 14) distinguishes between a "rule," which prescribes action, and a "principle," which affords "a guide for choosing among behaviors." Passage through the presumably invariant sequence of stages involves an increasingly refined, differentiated set of principles and sense of justice. At the earlier stages, this sense is based on considerations of self-interest and material advantage. At the opposite end of the moral development continuum, an internalized, conscience-based set of moral principles guides an individual's actions. A more detailed summary of the levels and component stages follows.

Level I: Preconventional. At Stage 1 ("Obedience and Punishment Orientation"), the physical consequences determine whether behavior is "good" or "bad." The individual recognizes and defers to superior physical strength out of self-interest. Any concern for laws or rules is based on the consequences of violations of those rules. At Stage 2 ("Naively Egoistic Orientation"), "right" actions are those that satisfy one's needs, but signs of an emerging relativism are apparent. The needs of others might be acknowledged, but any reciprocity is based not on a sense of the rights of others but on a "You-scratch-my-back-and-I'll-scratch-yours" bargain.

Level II: Conventional. At Stage 3 ("The 'Good Boy' Orientation"), the expectations of others are recognized as valuable in their own right, not merely for what obedience to them will return to the individual. Behavior is guided by a need for approval and to please others, particularly those closest to the individual (for example, parents and peer groups). The "intention" behind an action is considered important. At Stage 4 (which Kohlberg [1975] terms the "Authority and Social-Order Maintaining Orientation"), respect for authority as a social obligation emerges. "Moral judgments are based on concerns to maintain the social order and to meet the expectations of others. Law is seen . . . as necessary to protect and maintain the group as a whole" (Nucci & Pascarella, 1987, p. 273). Kohlberg (1975, p. 571) has characterized this stage as the " 'Law and Order' Orientation."

Level III: Postconventional. At Stage 5 ("Contractual Legalistic Orientation"), duty is seen as a social contract, which is acknowledged to have an arbitrary starting point, with an emphasis on democratically agreed upon, mutual obligations. Violations of the rights of others or the will of the majority are avoided. Because of the emphasis given at this third level of development to "equality and mutual obligation within a democratically established order," Kohlberg (1972, p. 15) has referred to the morality of this stage as "the morality of the American Constitution." Behavior at Stage 6 ("Conscience or Principle Orientation"), the highest level, is guided not by social rules but by principles thought to be logical and universal. "Highest value [is] placed on human life, equality, and dignity" (Kohlberg, 1972, p. 15). Right action is guided by personally chosen ethical principles and the dictates of conscience. As noted earlier, however, this stage has been dropped from more recent formal statements of the theory because of the lack of empirical evidence of its existence. (Studies of change in moral development during college, most of which are based on Kohlberg's theory, are reviewed in Chapter Eight.)

Other Cognitive-Structural Theories

As one might expect, both Perry's and Kohlberg's work have their critics. In some instances, critiques have spawned new theoretical statements that merit attention, although space constraints prohibit detailed discussion.

Kitchener and King's Reflective Judgment Model. Kitchener and King (1981, 1990; see also King, 1977; King, Kitchener, Davison, Parker, & Wood, 1983; Kitchener, 1978, 1986; Kitchener, King, Wood, & Davison, 1989) have argued that the Perry (1970) scheme shifts its focus between Positions 5 and 6 from cognitive or intellectual growth to identity development, leaving unspecified the nature and processes of any cognitive growth beyond that point. Rodgers (1989) has noted that this confounding of cognitive-structural and psychosocial development leaves two questions unanswered: "What does the psychosocial development of college students look like prior to Perry's Stage 6? What does their intellectual cognitive-structural development look like after Perry's Stage 5?" (p. 142). Rodgers suggests that Chickering's (1969) vectors answer the first question, and Kitchener and King's theory deals with the second.

Kitchener and King (1981) offer a model of "reflective judgment," defining a hierarchical, seven-stage sequence of increasingly complex stages relating to what people "know" or believe and how they justify their knowledge claims and beliefs. "Each stage represents a logically coherent network of assumptions and corresponding concepts that are used to justify beliefs" (p. 91). Each stage consists of a set of assumptions about reality and knowledge that the individual "uses to perceive and organize available information and to make judgments about an issue. The process of forming judgments becomes increasingly complex, sophisticated, and comprehensive from lower to higher stages" (p. 92).

The lowest three stages of Kitchener and King's model appear to coincide rather closely with Perry's first three positions (Rodgers, 1989). For example, in both models truth is seen as coming from authorities and is accepted without inspection by the individual. For Kitchener and King, individual beliefs are justified in terms of their conformity to an authority's truths. At Perry's Position 4, however, differences between the two frameworks begin to appear, with Kitchener and King continuing to focus on cognitive-structural changes (Rodgers, 1989). At the highest stage of Kitchener and King's model, "reality is understood as existing objectively" (Kitchener & King, 1981, p. 92). Knowledge statements are understood to have varying degrees of accuracy, and those with the highest claims on acceptance are those that are based on "a rational process of conjecture that demonstrates the use of evidence and rules of inquiry appropriate for the issue at hand" (Kitchener & King, 1981, p. 92). Knowledge claims must be evaluated and open to scrutiny by others. Rodgers (1989, pp. 142–146) compares and contrasts these two theories in greater detail, but he is unable to conclude whether they represent two distinct theories or one theory (Perry's) clarified by the other (Kitchener and King's).

Gilligan's "Different Voice" Model. Kohlberg's (1969) theory has also attracted critical attention that has led to a refined, if not an alternative, theoretical formulation. For some time, when interviews have been analyzed by means of instruments operationalizing Kohlberg's theory of moral development, women have consistently been scored at lower stages of development than men. This finding has typically been interpreted as evidence of a problem in women's development. Carol Gilligan in her research, however (1977, 1982a, 1982b, 1986a, 1986b), observed persistent discrepancies between women's concepts of self and morality and the major theories of human and moral development, including those of Piaget, Erikson, Kohlberg, and others, but particularly that of Kohlberg. Gilligan suggests the problem lies not with women but with conceptually biased theories, all of which emerged from studies of the moral development of male subjects. While these accepted theories purport to explain a universal developmental sequence, Gilligan argues that they do not accurately describe the experience of women, their sense of self, or the bases of their moral reasoning.

Gilligan's (1977) critique of Kohlberg's theory focuses on its "subordination of the interpersonal to the societal definition of the good" (p. 489). The problem, says Gilligan, is that for women the perception of the self is "tenaciously embedded in relationships with others" and women's judgments of what is moral are "insistently contextual" (1977, p. 482). The values of justice and autonomy that are given center stage in Kohlberg's theory "imply a view of the individual as separate and of relationships as either hierarchical or contractual, bound by the alternatives of constraint and cooperation. In contrast, the values of care and connection that emerge saliently in women's thinking imply a view of self and others as interdependent and of relationships as networks sustained by activities of care-giving and response" (1986a, p. 40). For Gilligan, women's concern with the well-being of others constitutes a "different voice" from that used by males: Women's moral reasoning is in the "care voice," while men tend to reason in the "justice voice." Similar observations of the central importance of interpersonal relations in women's sense of themselves are reported by Douvan and Adelson (1966) and Josselson (1987).

Gilligan's own model resembles other social development theories, with developmental movement "from an egocentric through a societal to a universal perspective" (1977, p. 483). Her first level ("Orientation to Individual Survival") focuses squarely and clearly on the self. As development occurs, there is a transition period ("From Selfishness to Responsibility"), characterized by the discovery of responsibility as a new basis for defining relations between self and others. The second level ("Goodness as Self-Sacrifice") focuses on the incorporation of a maternal concept of morality that involves the perception of the importance of protecting "the dependent and unequal." At this stage, "the feminine voice" emerges clearly, and "the good is equated with caring for others" (p. 492). The inequality inherent in this stage leads to a second transition ("From Goodness to Truth"), which seeks to resolve the conflict between selfishness and responsibility. Resolution is achieved at the third level ("The Morality of Nonviolence"), when an equilibrium is found between the expectations of conformity and caring in conventional notions of womanhood and individual needs. That equilibrium is found in nonviolence as a moral principle and a basis for decision making. "Judgment remains psychological in its concern with the intention and consequences of action, but it now becomes universal in its condemnation of exploitation and hurt" (Gilligan, 1977, p. 492).

The differences between Kohlberg and Gilligan are the differences between the morality of rights and the morality of responsibility, between concepts of autonomy and separation and concepts of connectedness and relationships. Gilligan, however, does not see these differences as reflecting any conflict; it is not a case of one theory being more or less adequate than the other. Rather, she believes they represent two different ways of viewing the world. Moreover, despite her focus on women, she asserts that both voices are inherent in the life cycle, constituting alternative grounds on which to evaluate the moral. She believes all individuals reason in both voices, although one is preferred and tends to dominate. Some men will tend to use the feminine "care" voice, while some women will prefer the "justice" voice. The care voice, however, is more frequently found among women and the justice voice among men. Gilligan's point is that by emphasizing one dimension, the other is neglected, leading "to the casting of all problems as problems of dominance and subordination" (Gilligan, 1986a, p. 54).

Kohlberg (1984) has responded by asserting that there is no need for two structures, that differences in the two voices merely constitute different styles of moral reasoning. Brabeck (1983b) and Walker (1984) present evidence in support of Kohlberg's position, whereas Baumrind (1986) supports Gilligan's position. While the issue remains unresolved (see Kerber et al., 1986), the possibility that the differences are substantive has implications for academic and student affairs programs (see Rodgers, 1989, p. 141; 1990b).[4]

Jane Loevinger's Theory of Ego Development. Loevinger (1976), focusing on ego development, offers a theory that is more comprehensive than Perry's or Kohlberg's. Loevinger does not offer any detailed definition of ego development, something she believes may not be possible, but her theory subsumes moral growth and interpersonal relations, as well as cognitive development. She sees the ego as a general organizing framework by means of which individuals view themselves and their worlds, and "ego development" connotes "the course of character development within individuals" (1976, p. 3).

Loevinger (1976) postulates nine stages, the first three of which ("Symbiotic," "Impulsive," and "Self-Protective") are generally found in individuals of precollege age. The three middle stages are the most frequently observed ones among traditional-age college students (see Chapter Five). Most new freshmen are at the "Conformist" stage, wherein individual behavior is largely determined by group behaviors, values, and attitudes. The need for acceptance and approval is high, and individual differences are not recognized. The developing individual then passes through the "Self-Aware" level in a transition from the the "Conformist" to the "Conscientious" stage. The transition's salient characteristics are "an increase in self-awareness and the appreciation of multiple possibilities in situations" (Loevinger, 1976, p. 19). It is a precursor of movement from the unexamined assumptions of the "Conformist" level toward the more complex reasoning required by the "Conscientious" level. At the "Conscientious" stage, rules and values have been internalized, and the individual has attained the capacity for detachment and empathy. Reasoning is more complex, and responsibility for one's actions is recognized. Our review identified no research that found college students at any of the final three stages of Loevinger's model (the "Individualistic" level [another transition] and the "Autonomous" and "Integrated" stages).

Loevinger (1976) sees the individual throughout as a unified but dynamic whole. Each of the nine stages has distinctive manifestations in terms of impulse control and character development, interpersonal style, conscious preoccupations, and cognitive style, although she sees these four components as really "four facets of a single coherent process" (p. 26). Chapter Five reviews the research using Loevinger's theory in the study of change among college students, and Hauser (1976) provides a critique of both Loevinger's theory and its measurement with the Sentence Completion Test (SCT). Loevinger (1979) also reviews the literature on the SCT's construct validity.

Other Models. Still other cognitive-structural theories or models have been developed. Harvey, Hunt, and Schroder (1961), with subsequent refinements by Hunt (1966, 1970), view cognitive development in terms of "conceptual levels" or stages based on cognitive complexity. The stages relate to the complexity of the information the individual can process and to the flexibility and sophistication of the processing itself. Hunt emphasizes ways in which instructional environments can be tailored to the level of the individual's conceptual functioning (see Hunt, 1976). Kegan (1979, 1980, 1982) offers a "constructive-developmental" framework for ego development that focuses on the processes by means of which individuals simultaneously "make meaning" of their world and define themselves in subject-object relationships. For Kegan, developmental stages are less interesting than the often painful and disorienting transitions that separate them, marking the terminus of one stage and the origin of the next. Stages mark developments in "the process of the restless, creative *activity* of personality, which is first of all about the making of meaning" (Kegan, 1980, p. 374). Kegan's model was developed more with counseling and psychotherapeutic applications than with research applications in mind.

Typological Models

Whereas psychosocial and cognitive-structural theories focus on the nature and processes of change (respectively), a third family of theories or models emphasizes distinctive but relatively *stable* differences among individuals. These models categorize individuals into groups based on these distinctive characteristics and thus are considered typological models. Typically, they focus on characteristic differences in the ways individuals perceive their world or respond to conditions in it. They may focus on cognitive style (Witkin, 1962, 1976), learning style (Kolb, 1976, 1984; see Claxton & Murrell, 1987, for a review of these models), maturity level and personal style (Heath, 1964, 1973), personality (Myers, 1980a, 1980b; Myers & McCaulley, 1985), or sociodemographic characteristics (Cross, 1971, 1981).

Type models have several characteristics in common (Rodgers, 1989). First, the styles or preferences that characterize people of a given type and differentiate them from people of another type are believed to develop relatively early and to be comparatively stable (although not unchanging) over time. Second, an individual may have or demonstrate characteristics indicative of other types within the taxonomy, but that individual tends to think, choose, or behave in ways consistent with the distinctive characteristics or preferences of the dominant type. Third, type categories describe areas of tendencies or preferences that people have in common. They do not explain idiosyncratic differences among individuals. They constitute "various tracks to wholeness, 'zip code' areas within which we grow and develop" (Rodgers, 1989, p. 153). Finally, these models generally do not attempt to explain either the content or processes of change (developmental or otherwise) in students. If change is treated at all, it is not central to the typology.

Nonetheless, typological models can be useful in understanding differences among college students and in illuminating why students respond differently to their college experiences. Indeed, as will be seen in subsequent chapters in this book, we still know comparatively little about the conditional effects of college, that is, how similar interpersonal and organizational experiences have varying effects related to differences in students' personal characteristics (for example, sex, race, aptitude, or psychological type). Because individual differences shape both cognitive and affective learning, typological models serve as a reminder of the need to take these differences into account in academic and nonacademic policies and practices. Because typological models do not seek to explain changes in students, however, we do not discuss them in any detail. Here, we briefly describe one such typology that has been particularly prominent in the college student research literature, that of Isabel Briggs Myers.

The Myers-Briggs typology follows the work of Carl Jung, as interpreted and given operational expression by Isabel Briggs Myers and her mother, Katharine Cooke Briggs (Myers, 1980a, 1980b; Myers & McCaulley, 1985; see also Lawrence, 1982, 1984). Jung believed that apparently random behaviors are, in fact, attributable to orderly and observable differences in mental functioning. Differences originate in the ways individuals prefer to receive information (the perception functions) and to reach conclusions or make decisions (the judgment functions). Within each of these functional areas are two preferences. In using the perception functions, one may prefer "sensing," or using the five senses, or alternatively, one may prefer "intuition," involving insight and unconscious associations. In exercising the judgment functions, an individual may prefer either "thinking" (that is, logic) or "feeling" (that is, affective values) as a basis for choosing or making decisions.

Type is presumed to be dynamic, not static. An individual may use all four functions at different times. Each individual, however, has a preference for using one or the other perception function and one or the other judgment function. Writers in this area sometimes use the analogy of handedness to illustrate the point: While an individual is capable of using both hands, one or the other tends to be preferred for certain functions, such as writing. "The favorite function is called *dominant* and will be either a perception process, Sensing (S) or Intuition (N), or a judgment process, Thinking (T) or Feeling (F). The dominant function is the unifying process in one's life" (Lynch, 1987, p. 7). The auxiliary function is not forgotten, however; it supplements the dominant.

The Myers-Briggs typology also includes two additional dimensions, called attitudes or orientations (Lynch, 1987). These attitudes reflect which function is dominant and which auxiliary, as well as where they are used. The first attitude, Extraversion (E) or Introversion (I), describes the individual's focus of attention and source of energy in the world, whether outward toward people, objects, and actions or inward toward ideas and concepts. The second attitude, Judgment (J) or Perception (P), reflects the individual's preferences for interacting with the external world. A Judgment orientation is toward organization, planning, and control of one's world, while a Perception orientation is toward openness, flexibility, and spontaneous reactions to events.

Knowledge of an individual's preferences within each of the two functions (perception and judgment), as well as his or her preferences on the two attitudinal dimensions, permits classification of that individual into one of sixteen types. These types can be used for research purposes or in the design of academic and nonacademic programs and activities. Provost and Anchors (1987) discuss some of the higher educational applications of the Myers-Briggs Type Indicator (MBTI), an instrument for operationalizing the theory. Lynch (1987) discusses type development and student development. Lawrence (1982) discusses use of the MBTI in instructional settings, and Lawrence (1984) and Claxton and Murrell (1987) review the MBTI-based research in this area.

Person-Environment Interaction Theories

Strictly speaking, person-environment theories[5] are not developmental in the sense that they do not attempt to explain in detail either the nature or specific processes of student "development" or growth. They are included here, however, because they do attempt to explain human behavior and provide frameworks for thinking about student change and college effects.

To varying degrees, all the theories and models discussed to this point acknowledge the role of the individual's environment in shaping human behavior and development. Certain theories and models, however, focus specifically and in detail on the environment and how it, through its interactions with characteristics of the individual, influences behavior. The extent to which person and environment receive equal attention in these theories varies, sometimes substantially. Within this general family of models, several subcategories are identifiable (Baird, 1988; Huebner, 1980, 1989;

Strange & King, 1990). Some of their differences derive from writers' decisions about whether the environment should be defined objectively, as a reality external to the individual, or perceptually, reality being whatever the individual perceives and believes it to be. Baird (1988) provides an extensive discussion and critique of a number of models that fall into this general category, as well as of some of the important theoretical and technical issues involved in measuring person-environment interactions and their effects.

Physical Models

Physical theories and models focus on the external, physical environment, whether natural or man-made, and how it shapes behavior by permitting certain kinds of activities while limiting or making impossible other kinds. The physical environment may be conceived rather specifically, as in the architectural features of residence halls (for example, Heilweil, 1973; Schroeder, 1980a), or quite broadly, as in urban settings (Michelson, 1970; Sommer, 1969).

Perhaps the most fully developed theory in this category is Barker's (1968; Barker & Associates, 1978) theory of "behavior settings." According to Barker, environments select and shape the behavior of the people occupying any given setting, tending to influence them in similar ways despite their individual differences. Behavior settings are bounded, "standing patterns of behavior . . . [such as] a basketball game, a worship service, a piano lesson . . . that persist when the participants change" (1968, p. 18). Such settings also have a "milieu [that is] an intricate complex of times, places, and things" (1968, p. 19) that surrounds or encloses the behavior and that exists independently of the standing pattern of behavior and of anyone's perception of the setting. Wicker (1973) and Wicker and Kirmeyer (1976) report evidence indicating that a setting's influence is to some extent dependent upon the balance between the number of people in the setting, the activities to be performed, and the physical size of the setting. In this refinement of Barker's ideas, a setting can be "undermanned" or "overmanned," depending on the number of people the setting's activities and physical space can accommodate. Behavior is shaped accordingly.

Human Aggregate Models

Authors of human aggregate models describe an environment and its influences in terms of the aggregate characteristics (for example, sociodemographic characteristics, goals, values, attitudes) of the people who inhabit it. Astin (1968b) and Holland (1966, 1985) are examples, but Holland's work on vocational choice has attracted the most attention and underpins a substantial body of research on college students.

Holland (1966, 1985) argues that choosing a vocation is also a manifestation of personality: "The choice of an occupation is an expressive act which reflects the person's motivation, knowledge, personality, and ability" (1966, p. 4). His theory rests on four "working assumptions" (1985, pp. 2–4). First, most people can be categorized into one of six theoretical "types": realistic, investigative, artistic, social, enterprising, or conventional.[6] Each type reflects a distinctive constellation of preferences, activities, interests, and dispositions, and each corresponds to a given category of vocations. The types are derived from observation of the characteristics of individuals in those occupations, and "each type has a characteristic repertoire of attitudes and skills for coping with environmental problems and tasks. Different types select and process information in different ways, but all types seek fulfillment by exercising characteristic activities, skills, and talents and by striving to achieve special goals" (1985, p. 3). An individual may have certain of the characteristics of more than one type, and while one type is likely to be more prominent than the others, an individual's personality pattern is one of similarity and dissimilarity with each of the six types.

Second, six "model environments" correspond to the six individual types. Environments are determined by the personality types of the individuals who dominate them (for example, "Realistic" environments are dominated by Realistic type people, "Investigative" environments are dominated by Investigative types, and so on). According to Holland, "where people congregate, they create an environment that reflects the types they are, and it becomes possible to assess the environment in the same terms as we assess people individually" (1985, p. 4).

Third, people seek out those environments that permit them to use their skills, exercise their attitudes and values, and play desirable roles. Through their particular constellation of characteristics and friendship networks, environments also recruit and select individuals for membership.

Finally, the interaction of personality and environment determines behavior. Where the individual's personality pattern is similar to the pattern of others who define the environment, stability is likely. Where there are inconsistencies, some sort of change can be forecast, either in the individual or, more likely, in the setting as the individual withdraws from an incompatible setting in search of one more congruent with his or her type pattern. Theoretically, then, given knowledge of an individual's pattern and environment, certain occupational, social, personal, and educational outcomes are predictable.

Perceptual Models

In perceptual models, definitions of the environment are related in some fashion to the individual student's perception and interpretation of the external world, whether behavioral or psychosocial. While each student's perceptions are subjective and particular to that individual, in the

the residual score. Such residual scores have two properties. First, they are statistically independent of the predictor variables. Thus, the investigators had a measure of institutional achievement that was statistically purged of the influence of the aptitude and academic major of the students enrolled. Second, despite problems in the reliability of residual scores, they can nevertheless be used as an estimate of institutional productivity or value added. Positive residual scores indicate higher institutional achievement than would be expected on the basis of student aptitude and major, while negative residuals would indicate lower than expected achievement. (A fuller discussion of residual scores is found in the Appendix.)

Rock, Centra, and Linn (1970) used a sophisticated grouping procedure to relate the three residual GRE scores to a battery of college characteristics traditionally associated with institutional "quality" (for example, number of books in the library, faculty-student ratio, proportion of faculty with doctoral degrees). Only two institutional factors, however, college income per student and proportion of faculty with a doctorate, tended consistently to identify colleges with high residual achievement scores. This tendency was somewhat stronger for achievement in the natural sciences and humanities than it was for achievement in the social sciences.

Centra and Rock (1971) used the same three dependent variables and much the same analytical procedures as Rock, Centra, and Linn (1970) but focused on measures of the institutional environment rather than on traditional indexes of institutional "quality." The investigators used a subsample of the larger sample described above, which consisted of 1,064 students from twenty-seven small liberal arts colleges with enrollments of less than 1,500. Measures of the college environment were five factors from the Questionnaire on Student and College Characteristics completed by students in the sample: faculty-student interaction, curriculum flexibility, cultural facilities, student activism, and degree of academic challenge. The residual GRE scores for each institution were related to the five environmental factors. Faculty-student interaction tended to be linearly related to residual achievement in that colleges with high scores on this dimension tended to overachieve (that is, to have positive achievement residuals) on the humanities and natural science tests, while institutions with low levels of faculty-student interaction tended to underachieve (that is, to have negative residuals) on all three GRE area tests. This finding is consistent with an ancillary finding reported by Astin (1968c). Using multiple regression to control salient student precollege characteristics, Astin found that a variable termed "familiarity with the instructor" had a statistically significant (and positive) partial regression coefficient with the humanities score of the GRE. (The "familiarity with the instructor" scale was a measure of the degree of student-faculty informal interaction at the institution.)

Centra and Rock (1971), too, found that curriculum flexibility was further related to higher than predicted institutional achievement on the natural science and social science tests. (This finding was also consistent with the positive partial correlations reported between flexibility of the curriculum and the GRE area tests by Astin [1968c].) Colleges with relatively high scores on the cultural facilities scale tended to overachieve on the humanities test but had lower than predicted scores on the natural science test. Finally, institutions with relatively high levels of challenge in their academic course work tended to overachieve on the humanities test. Thus, based on Centra and Rock's findings, a college environment particularly effective in fostering learning is one with the following characteristics: frequent student-faculty interaction, with faculty perceived as being interested in teaching and treating students as individuals; a relatively flexible curriculum in which students have freedom in choosing courses and can experiment before selecting a major; an intellectually challenging academic program with a stress on intellectual rather than social matters; and strong cultural facilities (for example, lectures, concerts, plays).

The final analysis of the sample of the ninety-five liberal arts colleges was conducted by Rock (1972) and Rock, Baird, and Linn (1972). With initial academic ability of students controlled, colleges were clustered by means of a taxonomic technique. Discriminant analysis was then used to determine the institutional characteristics that best distinguished the groups on GRE achievement. It was found that in all three achievement areas one group or cluster of colleges could be identified as being more effective than the remaining groups of colleges. Perhaps the most important finding of the study, however, was the fact that there was no one group of colleges that was highest in all three GRE area tests. Moreover, the institutional characteristics associated with high net achievement in one area test were not necessarily the same ones associated with high net achievement in another area. For example, on the humanities area test the most effective group of colleges was characterized by a higher proportion of faculty with doctorates, greater selectivity (average SAT scores in the student body), and a larger total budget. On the social science test, however, the most effective group (of four groups of colleges) had the second lowest student body selectivity and proportion of faculty with a doctorate. Budget did not discriminate among the groups. On both the social science and natural science tests the proportion of social science and natural science majors, respectively, was the characteristic that best discriminated the most effective from the least effective institutions. These particular effects were small, however, as indeed were all effects in the study.

To date, the most recent research focusing on institutional characteristics and student learning was conducted by Ayres and Bennett (1983), who used a sample of 2,229 students from fifteen public institutions in North Carolina, ten predominantly white and five predominantly black. Institutions were the unit of analysis, which meant that the analyses had relatively little chance of finding statistically significant trends because of the extremely small sample size. Unlike previous studies, which employed various forms of the Graduate Record Examination, the dependent variable Ayres and Bennett used was the National Teacher Examination (NTE). The NTE is designed to measure college achievement in professional education, English expression, science, mathematics, social studies, literature, and fine arts. Thus, the investigators judged it to be a reasonable outcome estimate of a general undergraduate education program.

A regression equation that included the average SAT score of each institution, average number of credit hours taken in general education, average educational attainment of the faculty, average faculty salary, institutional age, library size, and institutional size explained 88 percent of the variance in NTE achievement. Net of the influence of all other variables, the average educational attainment of faculty accounted for the largest percentage of unique variance in NTE achievement of all institutional variables. Using the statistics reported by Ayres and Bennett, we calculated the unique variance explained by the faculty degree index at 4.8 percent, which was marginally significant at $p < .14$. No other institutional variable in the equation approached statistical significance. Although the institutional sample size of the Ayres and Bennett study was quite small ($n = 15$), their study does have the advantage of a relatively large sample of individual students from each institution (233 students per campus). More important, perhaps, is the fact that the major finding of the study is consistent with the earlier results reported by Rock, Centra, and Linn (1970), that a greater proportion of faculty with a doctorate tended to identify institutions that overachieved on the three area scores of the Graduate Record Examination.

The weight of evidence from investigations designed to estimate the effects of different institutional characteristics on student learning clearly suggests that for four-year institutions at least, such effects are both small and inconsistent. Regardless of whether individual students or institutions were the unit of analysis, when student precollege traits were controlled statistically, measures of institutional "quality" or environmental characteristics accounted for a relatively minor percentage of the variance in standardized measures of learning. Furthermore, if one considers only those findings consistent across studies based on independent samples, only measures of student-faculty interaction, degree of curricular flexibility, and faculty formal education (that is, percentage with a doctorate) had significant associations with learning when salient student precollege traits were taken into account. The magnitude of these associations was small, however, perhaps even trivial in terms of a meaningful impact on learning.

One obvious interpretation of such evidence is that when statistical controls are made for the capabilities of the students enrolled, different kinds of four-year postsecondary institutions appear to have essentially the same general influence on student knowledge acquisition. That is, two students of equal academic aptitude, one attending a high "quality" institution (for example, selective admission, large library, abundant financial resources) and the other attending a college of lesser "quality," might not generally differ in how much they learned during college. One implication of this interpretation is that indexes of an institution's "quality"—or perhaps more accurately, its stock of human, educational, and financial resources—tend to have a diminishing return rather than a linear relationship with student learning. A library of one million volumes, for example, may be adequate to support effectively nearly any undergraduate curriculum. While the addition of another two million volumes is unlikely to be detrimental, the incremental benefits it provides for student learning beyond the first one million volumes may be relatively small. Thus, substantial differences in "quality" indexes or resources among colleges may not be matched by similar differences in measures of student learning.

In a related sense, the absence of important net differences in student learning among different colleges tends to confirm Pace's (1974) findings of increasing homogeneity and conformity among American four-year postsecondary institutions. If one assumes diminishing diversity and distinctiveness in the nation's four-year colleges and universities, it follows that institutional effects on student learning (or other areas of development, for that matter) will also become increasingly indistinguishable (Birnbaum, 1983; Bowen, 1980, 1981; Chickering, McDowell, & Campagna, 1969; Newman, 1971; Stadtman, 1980).

Alternative Explanations for the Absence of Between-College Effects

There is a certain appeal to the conclusion that differences in institutional characteristics or environments have few independent effects on student learning during college, most notably in that it agrees with existing evidence. On the other hand, given the fact that such a conclusion is based on studies from only five different samples carried out over a period of nearly two decades, it is worth at least positing several alternative explanations or hypotheses for the results. Most of these alternative hypotheses are bound up in the methodological problems of existing investigations. One of the most obvious is the restricted range of the samples used. In the Nichols (1964) and the Astin (1968c) and Astin and Panos (1969) investigations (which used students as the unit of analysis), the sample was either National Merit Scholarship finalists or students who took the Merit Scholarship Qualifying Test in secondary school. Selectivity of this sort in a sample will typically attenuate the correlations in any analysis (Cohen & Cohen, 1975). Thus, even if these students attend very different kinds of institutions, environmental effects on individual outcomes are likely to be suppressed by the relatively restricted range of aptitude represented. In short, analyses of samples consisting largely of the most academically able students may mask important institutional effects that might be discernible in a sample representing a broader range of talent.

An analogous problem exists in those studies that use the institution as the unit of analysis. The ninety-five institutions in the Rock, Centra, and Linn (1970) and the Rock, Baird, and Linn (1972) studies were really all small, private liberal arts colleges, as were the twenty-seven institutions employed by Centra and Rock (1971). Restricting the range of institutions sampled may have the same masking tendency on environmental effects as does restricting the range of students sampled.

A second potential methodological problem in existing research concerns the analytical approaches used. When student precollege characteristics are not independent of the type of institution attended, a considerable part of the explained variance in achievement or learning is likely to be the result of the *joint* influence of student precollege traits and the institutional environment. This joint influence cannot be uniquely attributed either to the college environment or to student precollege traits. However, the analytical approaches used in nearly all existing studies tend either to disregard joint effects or to attribute them to student precollege traits. This is understandable because the studies reviewed were primarily interested in estimating the unique or net effects of college environments on learning. Unfortunately, and perhaps unavoidably, this approach produces a somewhat conservative estimate of institutional effects. Because of this methodological problem, for which there is no easy or simple remedy, the existing body of evidence may be underestimating the extent and magnitude of institutional effects on learning. In short, the existing evidence may be reporting a lower-bounds estimate of between-college effects. (For a fuller discussion of this issue, see the Appendix.)

A third methodological problem concerns the level of organizational specificity on which existing studies focus in attempting to estimate the effects of institutional or environmental factors on student learning. Given evidence to suggest that a substantial number of distinguishable subenvironments exist in many institutions (for example, Feldman & Newcomb, 1969; Lacy, 1978; Pascarella, 1976; Phelan, 1979; Weidman, 1979), one might legitimately question the sensitivity of existing studies that assess the effects of environmental dimensions or other characteristics at the institutional level. This level of aggregation may simply be too gross to capture the influence of differential subenvironments or subcultures in the institution. It seems reasonable that if students have more intensive exposure to these subenvironments or subcultures, they are more likely to be influenced by them than they are by the total campus environment (Baird, 1974, 1988; Newcomb, 1968; Newcomb & Wilson, 1966). Indeed, at many institutions the "average" or "typical" environmental stimuli may have little to do with the reality impinging on students in different campus subenvironments (different academic majors, residential arrangements, and so forth).

Thus, another alternative explanation for the general absence of consistent institutional effects on student learning is that the institution is simply too general a level of aggregation. Evidence for this is offered by Hartnett (1976) and Hartnett and Centra (1977). Their study estimated the effects of academic departments (rather than entire colleges) and employed as a criterion standardized measures of achievement tests appropriate for individual departments. The dependent variables were field test scores of the Educational Testing Service Undergraduate Assessment Program. The achievement tests for each department were residualized on SAT scores, and departments were the unit of analysis. The findings revealed substantial between-department variation in net achievement within the same institution. For example, many institutions that had departments with achievement in the top 20 percent of positive residuals (that is, better than predicted departmental achievement based on students' SAT scores) also had departments in the lower 20 percent of negative residuals. It is likely that such marked differences within institutions would have been masked in studies where mean institutional score on characteristics such as student body selectivity and educational resources per student was employed as the unit of analysis. Even within institutions that are most advantaged in terms of overall human, educational, and financial resources, there are likely to be distinguishable differences in the effectiveness with which individual departments foster learning.

Similarly, it is unclear that many colleges, particularly large research institutions, provide much of a common learning experience for their students. With hundreds of courses available, few students may really have a common curricular experience that lasts throughout college. Evidence for this is provided by Ratcliff and Associates (1988) in their analysis of the course transcripts of a sample of graduating seniors at a large, urban, doctorate-granting university. These investigators examined the transcripts of 151 graduating seniors and found that they had collectively enrolled in 1,358 unduplicated courses during college. Of these 1,358 courses, there were only 282 (20.8 percent) in which five or more of the students had enrolled. If students have such different formal academic experiences within the same institution, it seems reasonable that this would produce differential effects on knowledge acquisition. A similar case might be made for the influence of different student subcultures within the same institution. Thus, another plausible explanation for why between-college effects on learning are so small is that important influences on learning within any particular college may be quite heterogeneous (J. Ratcliff, personal communication, July 24, 1988).

A final problem with existing research may stem from the instruments used to assess the learning outcomes of college. Typically, these have been standardized measures of rather broad academic achievement (for example, Graduate Record Examination verbal and quantitative tests, Na-

tional Teacher Examination) or level of knowledge in somewhat more focused subject matter or curricular areas (for example, Graduate Record
Examination area tests in the natural sciences, social sciences, and humanities). While such instruments tend to be strong in terms of psychometric
reliability and content validity, one might question whether they are sensitive or focused enough to capture those aspects of environmentally induced
impacts on learning that may be unique to some institutions. It may well be
that the GRE and related standardized achievement tests used in the studies
reviewed above are measuring a relatively common body of knowledge and
academic skills; and there may not be a great deal of variation among preparation programs at the four-year institutions sampled in terms of the effectiveness with which they impart this body of knowledge and skills. This
may, in part at least, account for the relative absence of substantial and
consistent institutional differences in GRE (or NTE) performance when
student precollege aptitude is controlled. Existing studies may have simply
focused on a "common core" of subject matter knowledge and skill outcomes in which we should expect only minimal differences among institutions.

Related to this notion is the argument that some institutions, most
notably those with highly selective student bodies, are capable of inducing
levels of intellectual development that are qualitatively different from those
fostered by less selective institutions. Warren (1984) has argued that the
learning achievements of poorly prepared students in unselective institutions cannot be compared with the accomplishments of well-prepared students in selective institutions as though they were distances each group of
students has moved along the same dimension. The content, objectives, and
activities of upper-division courses in selective institutions, he argues, are
often *qualitatively* different from any encountered in unselective institutions.
(Braxton and Nordvall [1985] provide evidence from liberal arts colleges to
support this argument.) These qualitative differences in the types of knowledge or learning fostered by highly selective institutions may not be adequately captured by standardized indicators such as the GRE area scores or
subscores. Some recent evidence in this regard suggests that item-type scores
within the GRE (for example, quantitative comparisons, analytical reasoning, data interpretation) may capture discrete forms of learning that the
GRE subscores do not effectively differentiate (Ratcliff & Associates, 1988;
Wilson, 1985).

Within-College Effects

In commenting on the body of research on the college environment
conducted in the early and mid-1960s, Berdie (1967) made a particularly
cogent point in a paper entitled "A University Is a Many Faceted Thing."
He argued that most institutions are not monolithic organizations with a

single uniform set of environmental stimuli impinging equally on all members. Rather, individuals are members of different subenvironments within the same institution that may have substantially different influences on growth and development. In terms of the acquisition of subject matter knowledge and skills, the academic program is perhaps the most salient of these subenvironments. Obviously, not all learning occurs as a result of the academic program or in classroom settings. Students clearly learn a range of valuable skills from peers, work, and extracurricular and athletic involvements, to name only a few. Yet it is undeniably the college's academic program, with its courses, classroom, laboratory, library, and related experiences, that is the major vehicle through which subject matter knowledge and skills are transmitted (for example, Bisconti, 1987; Bisconti & Kessler, 1980). This section will focus primarily on ways in which differences in the individual student's academic experience influence learning in college. Emphasis will be placed on the influence of differences in patterns of course work, the teaching/learning context, instructional approaches, teaching behavior, and the extent of student involvement or engagement in academic and related experiences. Although there are other conceptual schemes for organizing the effects of college experiences on learning (for example, Bergquist, Gould, & Greenberg, 1981), we think these categories most accurately reflect both where the preponderance of evidence exists and how it is clustered.

Patterns of Course Work

It seems reasonable to expect that what a student learns during college will depend largely on the nature of the courses he or she takes. Different patterns of courses taken should lead to the development of different kinds of knowledge and skills. The hypothesis that differential course work accounts for much of the differences in learned abilities has had considerable attention in research on the impact of secondary education (for example, Fennema & Sherman, 1977; Pallas & Alexander, 1983; Steel & Wise, 1979). While there has been a growing interest in course work patterns in postsecondary education, the bulk of inquiry has been descriptive (for example, Beeken, 1982; Blackburn, Armstrong, Conrad, Didham, & McKune, 1976; Dressel & DeLisle, 1969; Prather, Williams, & Wadley, 1976; Warren, 1975). Comparatively little attention has been devoted to determining whether differential course work leads to differential learning.

One notable exception to this is the work of Ratcliff and Associates (1988) on a single-institution sample. These researchers first residualized the nine item types of the Graduate Record Examination on student Scholastic Aptitude Test scores to produce measures of senior-year learning statistically independent of precollege academic ability. They then cluster analyzed courses on student transcripts by the residual scores on the nine item types of the GRE: quantitative comparison, antonyms, regular mathematics, analytical reasoning, sentence completion, analogies, data interpretation, reading comprehension, and logical reasoning.

The results yielded two major findings. First, high residual GRE achievement generally did not appear to be associated with course work taken in any one year. Rather, a spread of course work taken from the freshman to the senior year was most consistently associated with high GRE residuals on seven of the nine item types. This further supports the notion that significant academic learning is not concentrated in any one period during college but instead occurs over the entire span of the college years.

The second major finding of the Ratcliff and Associates (1988) study was that high residual scores on specific GRE item types were associated with specific sets of course work differing by discipline, level (that is, freshman, sophomore, junior, senior), and sequence. One course work cluster consisted primarily of lower-division courses in the arts and sciences and was associated with high residual achievement on antonyms and low achievement in analytical reasoning. A second cluster consisted primarily of business courses evenly distributed between lower and upper divisions. This group was associated with high performance in analytical reasoning and quantitative comparisons and low performance on antonym items. A third cluster consisted primarily of upper-division business and social science courses and was associated with high achievement on analytical reasoning and regular mathematics items. The fourth cluster was defined primarily by lower-division course work in mathematics and the natural sciences and was linked to high residual performance in regular mathematics. A final cluster was largely made up of lower- and upper-division courses in journalism, English, and mathematics and was associated with strong performance in regular mathematics and weak performance in analytical reasoning.

Ratcliff and Associates' (1988) findings are preliminary, and although there is some evidence of their generalizability across institutions (Ratcliff, 1988), they await more definitive replication before any but the most tentative conclusion can be made. They nevertheless provide support for a differential course work hypothesis at the postsecondary level. While a consistent pattern may not necessarily emerge, the results clearly suggest that the pattern of course work taken during college may have important implications for the types of learning that occur, independent of student academic ability.

The Teaching/Learning Context

Perhaps the most obvious contextual difference in the academic experience of students within the same institution is one's major field of study. The vast majority of colleges and universities require students to select a primary field of study, and this represents a significant portion of the student's total formal course work. Although the extent of requirements for majors varies, it is generally quite substantial: 30 to 40 percent of the total undergraduate course load for the typical B.A. degree and from 40 to 50 percent of the total load for the B.S. degree (Levine, 1978; Jacobs, 1986). As such, the academic major represents an important social and intellectual subenvironment for the student. For example, the major facilitates frequent contact between peers with similar academic and career interests, thus shaping acquaintance networks and reinforcing initial interests (Jacobs, 1986; Feldman & Newcomb, 1969). Moreover, it would appear that majors form somewhat distinctive instructional environments in terms of classroom environments (Astin, 1965a), the nature of the interaction between students and faculty (Gamson, 1966; Hearn & Olzak, 1981; Vreeland & Bidwell, 1966), the effort devoted to instruction (Stark & Morstain, 1978; Trow, 1977), and students' cognitive preferences and strategies for meeting course demands (Barrall & Hill, 1977; Goldman & Hudson, 1973; Goldman & Warren, 1973; Tamir & Kempa, 1977).

Given this evidence, it would seem reasonable to anticipate that one's major would provide distinctive learning outcomes during college. However, beyond the rather obvious and unsurprising finding (cited earlier) that students demonstrate the highest levels of proficiency on subject matter tests most congruent with their academic major, there is little to suggest that students become *generally* more knowledgeable during college *because* of what they major in. Again, the problem is one of separating the socialization effect of different major fields of study from the recruitment effect of students with different characteristics entering different majors to begin with. Unfortunately, in terms of estimating effects on knowledge acquisition, the few existing studies have generally not addressed this issue. In a single-institution study, for example, Dumont and Troelstrup (1981) found no statistically significant differences in average freshman-to-senior gains on the ACT achievement test composite score across five broad academic fields of study. Since amount of change is a function of a group's initial score, however, it is somewhat difficult to interpret these findings, particularly in the absence of some control for initial score.

Perhaps the most extensive evidence concerning major field of study and academic learning is provided by Adelman (1984). Adelman conducted a secondary analysis of student performance between 1964 and 1982 on the Graduate Record Examination, the Graduate Management Admission Test, the Medical College Admission Test, the Law School Admission Test, and fifteen tests of advanced achievement in specific subject areas. With the exception of engineering, students majoring in professional or occupational fields consistently had lower scores on these tests than did those majoring in traditional arts and science fields. Students majoring in engineering, science, and mathematics consistently scored the highest of all major fields. Since Adelman was unable to adjust for initial academic aptitude, however, it is difficult to causally attribute these differences to the effect of one's academic major. If not totally, then at least to a great extent, they probably reflect initial differences in academic aptitude or proficiency among students entering different major fields of study.

If there is little solid evidence one way or the other to suggest that one's academic major has a significant impact on what is generally learned in college outside of one's major field, this should not be construed as indicating that major is unimportant. As we shall see throughout the remainder of this book, one's academic major has a set of influences that extends beyond the college experience to such salient outcomes as one's career choice and income.

Class Size

A somewhat narrower context for teaching and learning than academic major is class size. Here there has been a substantial amount of research over the last sixty years concerning the influence of class size on learning in college (for example, Edmonson & Mulder, 1924; Mueller, 1924; Hudelson, 1928; Cheydleur, 1945; Nachman & Opochinsky, 1958; Simmons, 1959; Siegel, Adams, & Macomber, 1960; Hoover, Baumann, & Schafer, 1970; Attiyeh & Lumsden, 1972; Karp & Yoels, 1976; Williams, Cook, Quinn, & Jensen, 1985). In addition to the body of empirical evidence, there have been a number of reviews of the research on class size and learning (Dubin & Taveggia, 1968; Laughlin, 1976; McKeachie, 1978, 1980; Milton, 1972; Witmer & Wallhaus, 1975). The consensus of these reviews—and of our own synthesis of the existing evidence—is that class size is not a particularly important factor when the goal of instruction is the acquisition of subject matter knowledge and academic skills. Moreover, this finding appears to hold across class type (for example, lecture, discussion) and when measures of learning were standardized across content areas (Williams, Cook, & Jensen, 1984). It is probably the case, however, that smaller classes are somewhat more effective than larger ones when the goals of instruction are motivational, attitudinal, or higher-level cognitive processes (McKeachie, 1980).

Instructional Approaches

Not surprisingly, the question of the effects of different instructional approaches on academic learning and skill acquisition has been the focus of much research. This large body of research is as diverse as it is extensive. Indeed, it may well merit a book-length synthesis in and of itself. Fortunately, however, a number of scholars have undertaken syntheses of different segments of this evidence, upon which our own analysis substantially relies.

Lecture Versus Discussion. One of the initial areas of inquiry into the effects of different instructional approaches on learning is that of lecturing versus discussion. It is reasonably clear that lecturing is the overwhelming method of choice for undergraduate teaching in most institutions. Pollio (1984), for example, estimates that teachers in the typical classroom spend about 80 percent of their time lecturing to students, who in turn are attentive to what is being said about 50 percent of the time. Even so, there is little consistent evidence to suggest that lecturing is any less efficient in imparting subject matter knowledge to students than is instruction that emphasizes class discussion (Dunkin & Barnes, 1985; Kulik & Kulik, 1979; McKeachie, 1962; Ryan, 1969). The weight of evidence, as well as the findings of most literature reviews, tends to converge on this conclusion. The evidence also appears to be consistent in indicating that lecturing is a somewhat less effective instructional approach than classroom discussion when the goal of instruction is higher-order cognitive skills (critical thinking, problem solving, and the like) rather than the transmission of factual information.

Here we see a conclusion quite similar to that of the cognitive benefits of large versus small classes. Since instructional approach is not independent of class size (that is, small classes are more conducive to discussion than large classes), it is likely that these two conclusions are mutually confounding. Nevertheless, the weight of evidence makes it reasonably clear that in postsecondary education neither large or small classes nor lecture or discussion formats are more effective than the other in fostering the mastery of factual subject matter material.

Team Teaching. Another instructional approach that has received some attention in postsecondary education has been that of team teaching. By team teaching we mean the use of two or more people assigned to the same class *at the same time* for instructional purposes. Schustereit (1980) conducted a synthesis of studies pertaining to the influence of team teaching on subject matter achievement. He divided the studies reviewed into two types, those comparing classes taught by a team and those taught by one teacher and studies comparing different teaching techniques, including team teaching. Using the box score method of synthesizing research, he found inconsistent results from the studies reviewed. There were generally as many studies favoring team teaching as favoring solitary teaching. Thus, any generalization about team teaching being a consistently superior or inferior instructional technique for enhancing subject matter learning appears unwarranted.

Individualized Instruction. One characteristic of most traditional lecture or discussion instructional approaches (whether individually or team taught) has been that the pace at which instruction is provided tends to be a constant for all students, while level of achievement or subject matter proficiency tends to vary among students (Cross, 1976, 1981). In the early 1960s, however, Carroll (1963) developed a learning model that essentially reversed the relationship between what is constant and what varies in instruction. In brief, he argued that learners will succeed in learning a given task to the extent that they receive proper instruction and that they spend the amount of time they individually need to learn it. Therefore, according to Carroll, virtually all students can achieve mastery of any learning task if each is given enough time and receives competent instruction.

Although Carroll's (1963) model was developed primarily to address elementary and secondary school learning, it and the closely related mastery concepts of Bloom (1968) have significantly influenced collegiate instruction during the last two decades. Indeed, it is probably safe to say that one important strand of the intellectual heritage of Carroll and Bloom has been the development of various approaches to individualized instruction in postsecondary education. These approaches have taken various forms and are exemplified, though not necessarily exhausted, by the following:

1. *Audio-tutorial instruction (AT):* This instructional method, as developed by Postlethwaite (Postlethwaite, Novak, & Murray, 1972), involves three main components. The independent study session is the primary activity in audio-tutorial instruction. Students work independently on learning tasks in a learning center equipped with laboratory materials, audio tapes, and visual aids. The small assembly session is a weekly meeting of six to ten students and an instructor for the purpose of discussion and quizzing. A weekly meeting, the general assembly session, is used for motivational lectures, films, and major examinations.

2. *Computer-based instruction (CBI):* This approach involves the interactive use of a computer. Programmed instruction, drill and practice, and/or tutorial exercises are frequently implemented in CBI.

3. *Personalized system of instruction (PSI):* This approach was first described by Keller (1968) and has frequently been termed the Keller Plan. PSI involves the following components: (1) small modularized units of instruction, (2) study guides, (3) mastery orientation and immediate feedback on unit tests, (4) self-pacing through the material, (5) student proctors to help with individual problems, and (6) occasional lectures for motivation.

4. *Programmed instruction (PI):* This approach involves the presentation of material in a step-by-step sequential manner. It is a procedure employed in many types of individualized instructional methods.

5. *Visual-based instruction (VI):* This approach relies heavily on visually based materials (for example, slide tapes, films, and other visual instructional technology) as the main instructional vehicle for a course.

While these instructional methods or approaches differ from each other in some specific respects, they have many similarities. Perhaps the primary one is the acknowledgment of individual differences among students coupled with a concern for adapting instruction to the individual learner (Goldschmid & Goldschmid, 1974). Second, the different methods tend to modularize the course content into reasonably small, self-contained units (Dunkin & Barnes, 1985). Third, most of the methods tend to require mastery of material presented in the small units and typically provide immediate (or at least timely) feedback to students concerning their performance on mastery tests (Aiello & Wolfle, 1980; Rowe & Deture, 1975). Finally, the different methods all appear to emphasize active individual student involvement in the learning process, a feature consistent with what is known about effective learning environments (for example, McKeachie, Pintrich, Lin, & Smith, 1986; Rosenshine, 1982). Consequently, there is often less emphasis on employing the teacher in formal or traditional teaching situations such as lectures (Dunkin & Barnes, 1985).

It is our view that these and related attempts to individualize instruction constitute the single most dramatic shift in college teaching over the last two decades. Moreover, the weight of evidence from experimental studies would suggest that such approaches are reasonably effective in improving the acquisition of subject matter content (at least as measured by course-specific tests) over more traditional instructional approaches such as lecture, discussion, and combinations of lecture and discussion. The magnitude of the improvement, however, is not uniform across the different implementations of individualized instruction.

Kulik, Kulik, and Cohen (1979b) and Kulik (1983) summarized the results of forty-two studies employing the audio-tutorial (AT) method in college courses. The major criterion for a study's inclusion in this synthesis was that it had a control group taught by more traditional methods (for example, lecture, discussion) and reported the results of a common course examination. Although there was considerable variation across studies in the magnitude of the effect size (that is, the average of the AT group minus the average of the conventional group divided by the pooled standard deviation of both groups), the average effect size was .20 of a standard deviation favoring the AT group. This effect size was statistically significant (that is, non-zero) and represented an achievement advantage attributable to the AT approach of 8 percentile points. In other words, if the conventionally taught group was achieving at the 50th percentile, the AT group was, on the average, at the 58th percentile. Quite similar results have been reported by Mintzes (1975) in a narrative review of research on the audio-tutorial method and by Aiello and Wolfle (1980) in another meta-analysis based on twenty-seven studies. Aiello and Wolfle report an effect size favoring the AT group of .21, almost exactly the same as that found by Kulik and colleagues. It is also important to note that Kulik, Kulik, and Cohen (1979b) found no statistically significant differences between AT and conventional methods in the attitudes of students toward instruction or their rates of withdrawal from the course. Thus, the modest learning advantages associated with the audio-tutorial approach do not appear to come at the cost of increased course withdrawal rates or negative student attitudes toward the instruction received.

Aiello and Wolfle (1980) and Kulik, Kulik, and Cohen (1980) conducted independent meta-analyses of the effects of computer-based instruction (CBI). The former synthesis was based on eleven studies, while the latter was based on fifty-nine studies. This may account for the substantial difference in effect sizes reported: .42 for Aiello and Wolfle and .25 for Kulik, Kulik, and Cohen. Because the Kulik, Kulik, and Cohen synthesis is based on nearly five times as many studies as the Aiello and Wolfle synthesis, we are inclined to have greater faith in the representativeness of its findings. The statistically significant effect size of .25, favoring CBI over conventional instruction, represents an advantage of 10 percentile points in course achievement. Furthermore, across those studies that address the questions, computer-based instruction showed a positive and significant effect on student attitudes toward instruction and a significant reduction in the hours per week needed for instruction.

Meta-analyses of research on programmed instruction (PI) have been conducted by Aiello and Wolfle (1980) on the basis of twenty-eight studies and by Kulik, Cohen, and Ebeling (1980) on the basis of fifty-seven studies. The results of these two independent syntheses are remarkably similar. The effect size favoring PI over conventional instruction reported by Aiello and Wolfle is .27 of a standard deviation, while that reported by Kulik, Cohen, and Ebeling is .26. Again, this represents an achievement advantage attributable to the PI approach of 10 percentile points. Kulik, Cohen, and Ebeling also report the same achievement advantage for both immediate and delayed measures of achievement and no statistically significant differences between PI and conventional approaches in attitudes toward instruction, course withdrawal rates, and hours per week required for instruction.

Evidence from sixty-five studies that focused on the effects of visual-based instruction (VI) on subject matter learning has been synthesized by Cohen, Ebeling, and Kulik (1981). They report a statistically significant effect size of .15, favoring VI over conventional instructional approaches. While the typical student in the conventional approach functioned at the 50th percentile in learning, the typical student exposed to visual-based instruction was functioning at the 56th percentile (an advantage of 6 percentile points in learning). Cohen, Ebeling, and Kulik also report no significant differences between VI and conventional methods across studies in course withdrawal rate or attitudes toward the instruction received.

Finally, a substantial amount of interest has focused on synthesizing evidence that addresses the effectiveness of the Keller Plan, or personalized system of instruction (PSI), on subject matter learning (for example, Aiello & Wolfle, 1980; Block & Burns, 1976; Johnson & Ruskin, 1977; Kulik, 1982; Kulik, Kulik, & Carmichael, 1974; Kulik, Kulik, & Cohen, 1979a; Robin, 1976). This is probably due to the fact that with the possible exception of the audio-tutorial approach, PSI tends to be the most fully developed and elaborated system of instruction. Thus, it is perhaps the easiest to implement and has the added advantage of not being overly dependent on instructional hardware. Whatever the reason, there is striking consensus in each individual synthesis we reviewed to suggest that PSI is effective in fostering improved subject matter mastery over more conventional instructional approaches. This is true regardless of whether the synthesis is quantitative or narrative.

The meta-analytical syntheses of PSI and learning have been conducted by Aiello and Wolfle (1980) on the basis of nineteen studies and by Kulik, Kulik, and Cohen (1979a) on the basis of sixty-one studies. The former report an effect size of .42, favoring PSI over conventional instruction, while the latter report an effect size of .49. Because of Kulik, Kulik, and Cohen's more extensive sampling of the evidence, we are inclined to have somewhat more faith in the effect that they report (although the difference in effect sizes between the two syntheses is probably trivial). Kulik, Kulik, and Cohen's statistically significant effect size translates into an achievement advantage of 19 percentile points attributable to the personalized system of instruction. They also found that across relevant studies, PSI was associated with a statistically significant advantage of 18 percentile points over conventional methods in students' attitudes toward the instruction received. No statistically significant differences were found between PSI and conventional methods in terms of course withdrawal rates or time required for instruction. (It is noted a recent synthesis by Kulik, Kulik, and Bangert-Drowns (1990) suggests a reconsideration of this conclusion.)

In addition to analyses of the overall effects of the personalized system of instruction on subject matter learning, there has been at least some interest in discovering which particular components of PSI contribute most to its effectiveness (Kulik, 1982; Kulik, Jaksa, & Kulik, 1978; Robin, 1976). The studies cited tend to agree that the most salient aspects of PSI in terms of enhancing learning are the mastery requirement and immediate feedback on tests and quizzes. Thus, students in PSI approaches may perform better on common final examinations than students in conventional instruction, in part, at least, because they are forced to study more and have more opportunities to practice the criterion behavior (for example, Cline & Michael, 1978). There is less support for the idea that PSI features such as self-pacing and optional lectures are essential for improving learning, although they may have indirect effects by fostering greater motivation or satisfaction with instruction.

One can conclude from the extensive syntheses of research on the various forms of individualized instruction that each appears to enhance subject matter learning over traditional approaches such as lectures and/or discussion sections. Moreover, this learning advantage appears to occur without giving rise to undesirable side effects in terms of negative student attitudes toward instruction, increased course withdrawal rates, or increased time required to meet course demands. It is also clear, however, that the relative magnitude of the learning advantages attributable to individualized instruction varies quite markedly across its different implementations. Four of the five approaches reviewed (audio-tutorial, computer-based, programmed instruction, and visual-based) provide learning advantages over conventional instruction that are consistent but modest, ranging from 6 to 10 percentile points. In comparison, the learning advantage attributable to the personalized system of instruction (19 percentile points) is twice as great as any of the other approaches.[2]

A second conclusion is that the magnitude of the estimated advantage for each of the different implementations of individualized instruction is essentially independent of study characteristics. Typically, this is determined by regressing effect size on certain design characteristics of the studies included (for example, subject self-selection, randomized assignment to conditions, pretreatment equivalence of experimental and control groups). When this was done, the study design characteristics contributed little to explaining differences in study outcomes (Aiello & Wolfle, 1980; Kulik, Kulik, & Cohen, 1979a, 1979b, 1980). Consequently, one can reasonably conclude that the effects of the different forms of individualized instruction on subject matter learning are not generally biased in their direction by the methodological rigor of the research.

There is one possibly important exception to this conclusion in the research on computer-based instruction, visual-based instruction, and the personalized system of instruction. In these areas student achievement results somewhat more favorable to individualized approaches were found if different instructors implemented individualized and conventional approaches than if the same instructor implemented both. Dunkin and Barnes (1985) argue that this suggests the possibility of an instructor self-selection effect, with individualized approaches tending to attract the most motivated or effective instructors.

A final conclusion about the effects of individualized instructional approaches on student learning is that they tend to be essentially independent of the teaching/learning context. There is little evidence from any of the syntheses that individualized approaches tend to be more effective in some content areas than in others. The one exception to this is that the personalized system of instruction appeared to have stronger positive effects on learning in mathematics, engineering, and psychology than in other social sciences or the natural sciences (Dunkin & Barnes, 1985; Kulik, Kulik, & Cohen, 1979a). Of course, there is a caveat to this conclusion: Individualized instructional approaches are, by their very nature, more likely to be implemented in some content areas and/or course levels than in others.

It is probably much more likely, for example, that PSI would be implemented in an introductory calculus course than in a literature course on modern European writers. Indeed, the evidence from most reviews suggests this. Consequently, although it is safe to conclude that individualized instructional approaches are equally effective across nearly all content areas *where they have been implemented,* it is also important to acknowledge that they have not been implemented equally across all possible content areas in the curriculum.

Teacher Behavior

Do differences in teaching behavior systematically influence the acquisition of subject matter knowledge by students? The answer to this question appears to be yes; and it is based on a substantial body of evidence. By and large, this evidence has focused on answering two related questions. First, what are the dimensions of more effective (versus less effective) teaching behavior? Second, how are these various dimensions of teaching behavior related to subject matter learning?

Given the concerns of this book, the first question is perhaps less important than the second. Suffice it to say that reviews of the factor-analytical studies of the dimensions of student evaluations of teaching yield about six general dimensions (Cohen, 1981; Doyle, 1975; Feldman, 1976; Kulik & McKeachie, 1975; Marsh, 1984, 1986a). While different studies employ different names for what may be the same construct, the taxonomy offered by Cohen (1981) is useful and parsimonious. His labels for the dimensions are as follows:

1. *Skill:* This dimension represents the instructor's overall pedagogical adroitness. Typical items are "the instructor has good command of subject matter"; "the instructor gives clear explanations."
2. *Rapport:* This dimension assesses the instructor's empathy, accessibility, and friendliness; for example, "the instructor is available to talk with students outside of class."
3. *Structure:* This dimension measures how well the instructor planned and organized the course; for example, "the instructor uses class time well."
4. *Difficulty:* This dimension assesses the amount and difficulty of work expected in the course; for example, "the instructor assigns difficult reading."
5. *Interaction:* This dimension measures the extent to which students are encouraged to become actively involved in class sessions; for example, "the instructor facilitates classroom discussion."
6. *Feedback:* This dimension measures the extent to which the instructor

provides feedback on the quality of a student's work; for example, "the instructor keeps students informed of their progress."

In terms of the second question, the evidence suggests that while these dimensions of students' perceptions of teaching behavior are largely independent of class size (Feldman, 1984), they have statistically significant positive correlations with course achievement (for example, Benton, 1982; Centra, 1977, 1979; Cohen, 1972; Costin, Greenough, & Menges, 1971; Follman, 1974; Frey, Leonard, & Beatty, 1975; Gage, 1974; Marsh, 1984; Marsh, Fleiner, & Thomas, 1975; McKeachie & Lin, 1978; Mintzes, 1982; Murray, 1985; Sullivan, 1985; Sullivan & Skanes, 1974). Cohen (1981) conducted a meta-analytical synthesis of much of the research on the relationship between student perceptions of teaching behavior and subject matter achievement. His overall synthesis was based on forty-one independent validity studies reporting data from sixty-eight separate multisectional courses. Of the six dimensions of teaching behavior named above, only instructor skill and course structure or organization had statistically significant mean correlations with course achievement, .50 and .47, respectively. More modest correlations were found for such dimensions of teacher behavior as rapport (average correlation = .31), feedback (r = .31), and interaction (r = .22). Cohen also reports statistically significant mean correlations between course achievement and overall student ratings of the course instructor (r = .43) and the course (r = .43).

Additional analysis by Cohen (1981) suggests that the magnitude of the association between student perceptions of instructor proficiency and course achievement is influenced by a number of study characteristics. (In this analysis only overall rating of instructor was employed as a measure of instructor proficiency.) Most notably, correlations between instructor rating and achievement were larger for full-time (versus part-time) faculty,[3] when an external evaluator (not an instructor) graded students' course achievement, and when students knew their final grades before rating the instructor. The last finding, in particular, suggests that knowledge of one's grade may bias perceptions of the quality of instruction received. Additional study characteristics such as statistical control for ability, course level, institutional setting, and a measure of the overall quality of the study had only trivial influences on the magnitude of the correlation between rating of instructor proficiency and subject matter achievement.[4]

Despite the suggestion in Cohen's (1981) synthesis that knowledge of one's grade may bias perceptions of the quality of instruction received, the body of evidence clearly suggests that subject matter learning has a nontrivial relationship with the quality of instruction received. Two dimensions of teacher behavior stand out as being particularly salient in terms of potential influence on learning. These are skill, the general classroom adroitness and pedagogical clarity of the teacher, and structure, the degree of clear organization in the course. Other factors such as instructor rapport, interpersonal accessibility, and feedback to students also appear to be positively associated with achievement but less strongly than instructor skill and course structure.

A recent synthesis of an expanded data base of studies by Feldman (1989, in press) provides an important refinement to the above conclusion regarding instructor skill and course structure. Feldman's analyses suggest that the positive association found between instructor skill and student learning depends more on instructor clarity and understandability than on other constituent factors such as instructor subject matter knowledge or sensitivity to class level and progress. Likewise, the positive association between course structure and learning is more dependent on instructor preparation and organization than on clarity of course objectives and requirements.

Teacher Clarity. Research on student evaluations of teaching is only one source of evidence on the relationship between variations in teaching behavior and variations in achievement. Other researchers have come at the issue from a somewhat different perspective. Interestingly, however, the findings from this research are in rather close agreement with the evidence just reviewed.

One perspective is to take a very micro view of teaching and focus on the effects of specific, observable behaviors on subject matter learning. One of the most developed lines of research in this area is that concerned with teacher clarity. Most of the original work on the influence of teacher clarity and achievement was conducted by Land and Smith and their colleagues (Denham & Land, 1981; Land, 1979, 1980, 1981a, 1981b; Land & Smith, 1979a, 1979b, 1981; L. Smith, 1977, 1982; Smith & Edmonds, 1978; Smith & Land, 1980). They have attempted to identify specific teacher behaviors that present clear and unambiguous learning stimuli to students versus behaviors that lead to ambiguity and confusion. Examples of the former are using examples to illustrate concepts, identifying key points, and clearly signaling topic transitions. Examples of the latter are using "vagueness terms" and "mazes." Vagueness terms are imprecise terms that confuse the learner, such as *basically, you know, so to speak, usually, kind of, I'm not sure,* and so on (Hiller, Fisher, & Kaess, 1969). Mazes are units of discourse that do not make sense, such as starts or halts in speech, redundantly spoken words, and complex tangles of words (L. Smith, 1977).

Land and Smith have attempted to estimate the effects of teacher clarity (versus vagueness or lack of clarity) on subject matter achievement through the series of experimental studies just cited. In the typical study the same instructional content was purposefully taught under different levels of teacher clarity. The basic results of this body of research suggest that independent of other influences, degree of teacher clarity has a statistically significant positive effect on subject matter achievement. Conversely, high frequencies of teacher vagueness terms and mazes, in particular, appear to inhibit learning by college students.

More recent research on teacher clarity by Hines, Cruickshank, and Kennedy (1982, 1985) has broadened the operational definition of the term to include twenty-nine different low-inference (observable) variables thought to comprise clarity in instruction. To determine the independent effect of these variables on subject matter learning, the researchers conducted a complex experiment in which thirty-two student teachers were randomly assigned to classes to teach a twenty-five-minute lesson in matrix multiplication to peers. The teachers were free to select any instructional strategy they believed effective, and all instructional sessions were videotaped so that the teacher clarity behaviors could be recorded by independent observers. Net of student perceptions of teacher clarity and student satisfaction with the instruction, observer ratings of teacher clarity accounted for a statistically significant 52 percent of the variance in mean class achievement on a common posttest. Individual teacher behaviors most strongly and positively related to achievement were using relevant examples during explanation, reviewing material, asking questions to find out if students understood, teaching in a step-by-step manner, explaining things and then stopping so that students could think about the explanation, presenting the lesson in a logical manner, and informing students of lesson objectives or what they were expected to be able to do on completion of instruction. Such behaviors, as well as those uncovered by Land and Smith, are quite consistent with student perceptions of faculty behaviors (for example, skill, structure) that are also positively associated with student learning.[5] Moreover, given the fact that many of the teaching behaviors found to be associated with enhanced subject matter learning are themselves learnable, the research on teacher clarity may have potentially important implications for the pedagogical training of college faculty. Dalgaard (1982), for example, has experimentally demonstrated that teaching-training interventions can significantly improve the classroom effectiveness of graduate teaching assistants.

Student-Faculty Informal Interaction and Effective Teaching. Another perspective on the relationship between teacher behavior and student learning takes a somewhat more macro view. Typical of this approach is the research on the relationship between student-faculty informal interaction and effective teaching conducted by Wilson, Wood, and Gaff (1974) and Wilson, Gaff, Dienst, Wood, and Bavry (1975). In a comprehensive multi-institutional study the researchers had faculty and students identify faculty members whom they (faculty and students) regarded as having a particularly significant impact on students. These "effective teachers" were then compared with other faculty not so identified on a number of teaching dimensions.[6] Aside from factors such as using examples and analogies in teaching and efforts to make courses interesting, effective teachers were also characterized by accessibility to students outside of class. Thus, not only were the effective teachers the most skillful and interesting in the classroom; they also tended to extend their contact with students to nonclassroom situations. Moreover, faculty who interacted frequently with students outside of class tended to give cues as to their "social-psychological accessibility" for such interaction through their in-class teaching behaviors.

Such teaching behaviors and personal traits are not restricted to effective teachers in four-year institutions. Guskey and Easton (1983) report markedly similar behaviors and traits as also characterizing effective teachers in urban community colleges.

Student Involvement

Several recent models of learning and student development have suggested the importance of student involvement or engagement as a key determinant of the outcomes of education (for example, Astin, 1984; Friedlander, 1980; Pace, 1976, 1984; Parker & Schmidt, 1982; Rosenshine, 1982). Not surprisingly, perhaps, a substantial body of evidence exists to suggest that the greater the student's involvement in academic work or in the academic experience of college, the greater his or her level of knowledge acquisition. This evidence is consistent whether extent of involvement is measured at the class level or in terms of broader-based types of involvement.

At the class level, for example, substantial experimental evidence suggests that students are more attentive and involved in what transpires in class when they are required to take notes, and in turn note taking has positive effects on course subject matter achievement (for example, Hult, Cohn, & Potter, 1984; Kiewra, 1983; King, Biggs, & Lipsky, 1984; Locke, 1977; Weiland & Kingsbury, 1979). Similarly, evidence reported by Johnson (1981) and Johnson and Butts (1983) suggests that the greater the proportion of time in which the student is actually engaged in learning activities (taking notes, engaging in discussion, answering questions, and the like), the greater the level of content acquisition.

Peer Teaching or Tutoring. One method by which faculty have sought to increase students' active involvement or engagement in learning is through peer teaching or tutoring (Goldschmid and Goldschmid, 1976). Most of the recent research has suggested that peer teaching and peer tutorial programs have a positive impact on learning. Bargh and Schul (1980) conducted an experiment in which one group of undergraduates studied verbal material to learn it themselves while another group studied the material for the purpose of teaching it to another person. When pretest scores were controlled statistically, students who were preparing to teach scored significantly higher on a subsequent test of content retention than their counterparts who studied only to learn it for themselves. Similar results have been reported by Annis (1983), who compared comprehension knowledge in history among randomly assigned groups of sophomore women who differed in whether they read a passage for the purpose of teaching it to another student or not. With initial reading comprehension scores controlled statistically, students who read the passage with the purpose of teaching it or who actually taught it to another student scored significantly higher on a test of comprehension than students who merely read the passage or who read it and were taught.

Perhaps the most comprehensive study in this area of research was conducted by Benware and Deci (1984). They hypothesized that learning in order to teach facilitates greater intrinsic motivational processes than simply learning to be tested and that intrinsically motivated learning is more active and results in greater conceptual learning. In order to create an intrinsic or active orientation, randomly assigned students in an introductory psychology course were asked to learn material with the purpose of teaching it to another student, while the passive orientation asked students merely to learn material in order to be tested. The results indicated significantly higher conceptual learning of the material read for the group learning to teach but no statistically significant differences in rote learning between the group learning to teach and the group learning to be tested. The group learning to teach also perceived themselves to be more actively engaged in the course than the group learning to be tested, even though they spent equal time with the material.

The experimental research on peer teaching provides reasonably strong evidence that learning material in order to teach it not only increases student involvement in the process of learning but also enhances mastery of the material itself, particularly at the conceptual level. A possible explanation suggested by Bargh and Schul (1980) is that the cognitive benefits of learning to teach result from the use of a different and more comprehensive method of study than that employed when one is merely learning material in order to be tested. This may, in part, account for the finding that tutors in PSI courses benefit even more in terms of content mastery from these courses than do students who take them (Johnson, Sulzer-Azaroff, & Mass, 1977; McKeachie, Pintrich, Lin, & Smith, 1986).

Extent and Quality of Student Effort. A somewhat more broadly based perspective on student involvement and learning has been taken by Pace (1980, 1984). A basic assumption of Pace's work is that what a student gets out of college is dependent not only upon what the college does or does not do but also on the extent and quality of effort that the student puts into college. Thus, extent of subject matter learning, as well as other outcomes of college, is a function of what the institution offers and what the student does with those offerings. To assess involvement Pace has developed fourteen "quality of effort" scales that estimate a student's use of an institution's facilities and opportunities. The scales consist of items that vary according to complexity or "quality of effort" involved in a specific activity; and the respondent indicates level of involvement on a "never" to "very often" continuum. For example, items on the classroom involvement scale range from relatively simple activities such as taking notes or underlining to more complex or higher-level cognitive activities such as efforts to explain, organize, and go beyond assignments. The fourteen scales cluster into three factors: (1) academic and intellectual experiences (for example, library, faculty, classrooms), (2) personal and interpersonal experiences (for example, student acquaintances, conversation topics), and (3) group facilities and opportunities (for example, student union, clubs).

Pace (1980) administered the quality of effort scales to a sample of more than 4,000 students at all class levels at thirteen institutions. He also attempted to assess student knowledge acquisition by means of self-reported gains on two scales: general education (gaining broad general knowledge and cultural awareness) and academic and intellectual outcomes (acquiring field-specific knowledge and intellectual skills). (While there are assessment problems with such self-reports, most evidence suggests that they have moderately positive correlations, $r = .25$ to $r = .65$, with objective measures of knowledge [for example, Baird, 1976a; Berdie, 1971; Dumont & Troelstrup, 1980; McMorris & Ambrosino, 1973; Pohlmann & Beggs, 1974].) Pace found that the quality of effort students put into the academic or intellectual aspects of the college experience had statistically significant correlations of .39 with both the general education and the academic (intellectual) outcome scales. It was also the case, however, that the student's quality of effort in personal and interpersonal experiences and group facilities and opportunities had statistically significant positive correlations with the same two outcomes (ranging from $r = .19$ to $r = .40$).

To Pace, such findings suggest a basic wholeness about the college experience. In addition to academic and intellectual effort, involvement in personal and social experiences in college may contribute to learning and the development of intellectual skills. An alternative hypothesis, of course, is that involvement in personal and social experiences is associated with learning and intellectual skill development only because students who are highly involved in the academic and intellectual experience of college tend also to be involved in the personal and social experience of college (for example, Pace, 1987; Pascarella, 1985c; Pascarella & Terenzini, 1980a; Stage, 1987). Thus, if academic and intellectual efforts directly influence learning, personal and social involvements are also likely to correlate with learning but not necessarily in a causal sense.

Despite this alternate hypothesis, Pace's findings on quality of effort and learning are important, particularly since they have been supported by other studies. For example, a series of single-institution, longitudinal analyses by Terenzini and colleagues (Terenzini, Pascarella, & Lorang, 1982; Terenzini, Theophilides, & Lorang, 1984a; Terenzini & Wright, 1987a; Volkwein, King, & Terenzini, 1986) sought to determine the kinds of college experiences that were related to student self-reports of progress in academic and intellectual skill development. Using regression analysis to control statistically for salient background characteristics (for example, race, gender, secondary school achievement) and personal goals, the investigators found that a measure of classroom involvement had generally consistent, positive associations with the academic and intellectual progress measure. The classroom involvement scale measures such factors as how frequently students express their ideas in class and are intellectually stimulated by material covered in class.

Student Interactions with Faculty. Related to the concept of classroom involvement and effort is that of students' interactions and relationships with faculty. If one is willing to assume that faculty generally attach substantial value to student behaviors and attitudes that increase effort and learning (for example, Wallace, 1963, 1967a, 1967b; Pascarella, 1980) and that faculty influence on student values, behaviors, and attitudes is enhanced through informal contact beyond the classroom, it would seem to follow that student interaction with faculty is a potentially important influence on learning. A number of studies tend to confirm this notion, although the evidence is not totally consistent. Endo and Harpel (1982, 1983) conducted two longitudinal studies that looked at the influence of different measures of student-faculty interaction on self-report measures of knowledge acquisition in the senior and freshman years, respectively. Controlling for student precollege characteristics and expectations of college, Endo and Harpel (1982) found that frequency of informal contact with faculty had statistically significant positive associations with seniors' self-reports of adequacy of general knowledge and adequacy of mathematics skills. With similar statistical controls, Endo and Harpel (1983) found that frequency of informal contact with faculty also had a statistically significant positive association with freshmen's reports of their knowledge of basic facts. The researchers also found that perceived quality of relationships with faculty was significantly associated with this outcome.

In terms of the influence of *frequency* of student-faculty informal contact on self-reports of progress in/academic and intellectual skill development, similar results have been reported in the longitudinal investigations of Terenzini, Theophilides, and Lorang (1984a) and Terenzini and Wright (1987a). Less supportive evidence, however, has been reported by Terenzini, Pascarella, and Lorang (1982) and Volkwein, King, and Terenzini (1986). In terms of the *quality* of students' relationships with faculty, the findings of Terenzini and colleagues are quite consistent with those of Endo and Harpel (1982, 1983). Controlling for student precollege characteristics,

Terenzini and colleagues found that a measure of the extent to which a student had developed a friendly, informal, influential relationship with at least one faculty member was a statistically significant positive predictor of perceived gains in academic skill development.

In addition to the possible problems of reliability and validity of student self-reports (discussed previously), much of the research on student involvement or quality of effort and learning is plagued by potential ambiguity in causal direction. This is particularly evident in those studies that find statistically significant associations between frequency of student-faculty informal interaction and various measures of gains in academic knowledge and skills. Do frequency and quality of informal interaction with faculty enhance students' academic competence, or do initial perceptions of gains in academic knowledge and skills eventually lead students to seek informal contact with faculty beyond the classroom? Unfortunately, the designs of existing studies make it difficult, if not impossible, to answer this question.

Despite this and related methodological problems, the research that links broad-based student involvement or quality of effort during college and increases in academic knowledge and skills opens a potentially significant new area of inquiry. This is particularly true if we can gain a better understanding of those institutional policies, practices, and organizational structures that facilitate involvement or quality of effort. Some evidence does exist to suggest two important influences: living on campus (versus commuting to college) and both institutional and major department size. The former tends to facilitate involvement (for example, Astin, 1973b; Chickering, 1974a; Chickering & Kuper, 1971; Pace, 1980; Pascarella, 1984b), while the latter factors tend to inhibit it (for example, Hearn, 1987; Pascarella, 1985c; Stoecker, Pascarella, & Wolfle, 1988). Moreover, evidence from Pascarella (1985d) suggests that the effect of place of residence on student involvement during college persists irrespective of institutional size, while the inhibiting effect of attending a large institution holds even when place of residence is held constant. Chapman and Pascarella (1983) have suggested that the factors that influence different types of student involvement during college depend on a complex pattern of interactions (conditional effects) between student precollege characteristics and the type of institution attended (four-year residential, four-year commuter, two-year commuter). It is difficult, however, to draw any clear generalizations from their findings.

Conditional Effects of College

Student-by-Institution Effects

We found little consistent evidence to suggest the presence of conditional effects in the influence of college on student subject matter learning.

A study by Robertshaw and Wolfle (1982), reviewed earlier, found that with secondary school achievement controlled, white students derived greater verbal and mathematics knowledge from attendance at two-year colleges than did black students. This finding, however, has not been replicated.

Another investigation by Ayres (1982, 1983) suggests that black students may not benefit the same amount from attendance at different kinds of institutions. Using the same sample as Ayres and Bennett (1983) but with students (n = 3,426 from fifteen institutions) rather than the institutions as the unit of analysis, Ayres sought to determine whether the racial composition of a college influences achievement on the National Teacher Examination. Using analysis of covariance to control for differences in entering aptitude (SAT scores), black students at predominantly white institutions tended to score higher on the NTE than students of similar aptitude at predominantly black institutions. This finding is only partially supported by Davis (1977) with samples of black physical education majors at predominantly black and predominantly white colleges. Controlling for entrance examination scores, Davis found that blacks at predominantly white institutions had significantly higher NTE scores on competencies necessary for effective teaching. However, no statistically significant differences were found between blacks at predominantly black and predominantly white institutions with respect to NTE area (physical education) scores.

The study by Rock, Baird, and Linn (1972) reviewed earlier presents evidence to suggest that students initially highest in precollege academic aptitude may benefit slightly more in terms of GRE achievement from attending an academically selective rather than a nonselective liberal arts college. (Selectivity here is operationally defined as the average SAT score of the institution's student body.) Astin (1968c), however, found no evidence to suggest that the academically most capable student benefited more in terms of GRE achievement from attending a selective rather than a nonselective college. Since Astin's study used students rather than institutions as the unit of analysis, his test for conditional effects is probably more definitive than that of Rock, Baird, and Linn.

Student-by-Instructional Approach Effects

One area that has received considerable attention with respect to the possibility of conditional effects is that of instructional approach, particularly for various forms of individualized instruction. Since a major characteristic of much individualized instruction is to ensure subject matter mastery irrespective of student ability, one plausible hypothesis is that the academically least well prepared students will benefit relatively more from individualized instruction than the better prepared. There is some support for this hypothesis from individual studies. For example, Pascarella (1977a, 1978) compared calculus achievement between similar students in a personalized system of instruction versus a traditional lecture and recitation format. While PSI generally outperformed the traditional approach, the greatest advantage was for the mathematically least well prepared student. As level of precourse mathematics preparation increased, the relative advantage of PSI tended to decrease. Similar findings are reported by Born, Gledhill, and Davis (1972); Gay (1986); Ross and Rakow (1981); Stinard and Dolphin (1981).

Despite the findings of these selected individual studies, the weight of evidence nevertheless suggests that the generally positive effects of individualized instruction on subject matter learning do not vary significantly with student aptitude or prior subject matter preparation. In each of the five meta-analyses of various forms of individualized instruction previously reviewed, effect sizes for conditional effects based on prior aptitude on subject matter achievement were computed. In all cases the effect sizes were statistically nonsignificant and trivial. This indicates that the magnitude of the effect of each of the five forms of individualized instruction reviewed does not depend on student aptitude or prior subject matter preparation (Cohen, Ebeling, & Kulik, 1981; Kulik, Cohen, & Ebeling, 1980; Kulik, Kulik, & Cohen, 1979a, 1979b, 1980). Overall, the best- and least-prepared students apparently derive equal learning benefits from individualized instruction.

Some evidence does suggest that different instructional approaches may be differentially effective for students with different personality characteristics. Most of the consistent findings in this area have focused on the degree to which the student is characterized as independent, internally motivated, flexible, or having a high need for achievement. The weight of evidence would appear to indicate that students who come to a course high on any or all of these characteristics tend to derive greater achievement benefits when the instructional approach stresses learner self-direction and participation. Conversely, students who score low on such traits tend to have higher achievement under more structured or teacher-directed approaches. Experimental evidence reported by Domino (1968, 1971) and Peterson (1979), for example, shows that students high in need for achievement via independence demonstrate greater subject matter achievement in instructional conditions that stress student self-direction and participation than in more structured or teacher-directed formats. Conversely, students high in need for achievement via conformity have higher achievement in structured rather than more independent instructional approaches. With the exception of Goldberg (1972), strikingly consistent results have been reported by Daniels and Stevens (1976); Horak and Horak (1982); Parent, Forward, Canter, and Mohling (1975); and Van Damme and Masui (1980) using learner internal versus external locus of control, by Pascarella (1977b) using a motivation construct, and by Charkins, O'Toole, and Wetzel (1985) using students' preferences for dependent, collaborative, or independent learning style.

Though not extensive, the body of research on the interaction of student personality traits and instructional approaches underscores the importance of being sensitive to individual differences in college instruction. Not all students may benefit equally from the same instructional format. The research further suggests that it may be possible to enhance subject matter learning by adapting instruction to individual differences among learners.[7]

Long-Term Effects of College

A substantial part of the evidence pertaining to the long-term effects of college on knowledge acquisition is based on surveys of college graduates. Typically, graduates are asked to indicate the extent to which their undergraduate experience influenced a number of educational objectives, including knowledge acquisition. The use of retrospective self-reports of college impact on learning is a strategy employed in national surveys of college graduates by Bisconti and Solmon (1976), Pace (1974), and Spaeth and Greeley (1970). All three studies report evidence indicating that college alumni attribute their undergraduate experience with substantially increasing the acquisition of both general and specific knowledge. In 1968 Spaeth and Greeley (1970), for example, surveyed nearly 5,000 alumni who graduated from 135 colleges or universities in 1961. Of those surveyed, 41 percent said that college "greatly affected" and 46 percent said that it "somewhat affected" their ability to think and express themselves. Similarly, 35 percent reported that college "greatly affected" and 42 percent reported that it "somewhat affected" the development of a broad knowledge of the arts and sciences.

Consistent findings are reported by Pace (1974) in a nineteen-year follow-up study of alumni from seventy-nine institutions. In his study the percentage of alumni who reported deriving "very much" or "quite a bit" of benefit from college in different areas of development was as follows: 79 percent for vocabulary, terminology, and facts in various fields of knowledge; 64 percent for awareness of different philosophies, cultures, and ways of life; 62 percent for broadened literary acquaintance and appreciation; and 54 percent for understanding and appreciating science and technology.

The study by Bisconti and Solmon (1976) followed up more than 4,000 individuals approximately fourteen years after they had entered college in 1961. The authors report that 73 percent of those surveyed said that their college experiences were "very useful" in increasing their general knowledge.

Such consistent evidence from national surveys is, of course, encouraging. The possibility nevertheless exists that equally capable individuals who did not go to college would feel equally influenced by their various noncollegiate experiences. This issue was addressed, at least to some extent, in a massive secondary analysis by Hyman, Wright and Reed (1975). Using data on Caucasian individuals, aged thirty-seven to forty-eight, from fifty-four Gallup, National Opinion Research Center, and Institute for Social Research samples covering twenty-two years (1949–1971), Hyman, Wright, and Reed analyzed individuals' responses to a battery of factual questions in three general areas. These areas measured each individual's ability to (1) identify correctly prominent public figures and major public events; (2) answer correctly questions on vocabulary, humanities, history, civics and government, geography, science, and so on; and (3) respond correctly to questions on popular culture and sports. On nearly all questions in these areas, correct responses were closely related to formal education, with differences between college and high school graduates being substantial. For example, the advantage in percentage correct for college versus high school graduates was 20 percent in history, 32 percent in humanities, 24 percent in geography, and 34 percent in civics. More important, these differences remained even after statistical or design controls were made for race, gender, religion, native or foreign born, geographical origin, age, socioeconomic origin, and current socioeconomic status. Unfortunately, not all controls could be made on the same surveys.

The Hyman, Wright, and Reed (1975) analyses also report two additional findings. First, while the differences in knowledge between college and high school graduates continued into the oldest age brackets, they were somewhat more pronounced for the younger respondents than for the older ones. This perhaps suggests that the influence of college on knowledge acquisition is partially diluted over time in the general population by intervening life experiences. How much this occurs for individuals, or whether it occurs at all, however, may depend to a great extent on the nature of those intervening experiences. Second, although the differences in knowledge between college and high school graduates held for all levels of current socioeconomic status, they tended to be greatest for the highest levels. To Hyman, Wright, and Reed this suggests that the effects of education on knowledge are frequently enhanced among those whose social and economic circumstances are advantaged. Such individuals may be in the best position to engage in cultural, intellectual, and artistic activities that both further enhance interests and tastes developed in college and expand their knowledge base.

There is, of course, an important potential limitation to the findings of Hyman, Wright, and Reed (1975). It is not apparent that the most important confounding variables are controlled in their analyses. In the absence of controls for potentially confounding background factors such as intelligence, motivation, and aspiration, strict attribution of differences in knowledge to level of formal education is somewhat risky. The results might

(though not exclusive) criterion measure used was the Watson-Glaser Critical Thinking Appraisal, a very broad-based, general measure of critical thinking that is not tied to academic content. In terms of specific instructional variables, six studies found no statistically significant differences, three reported mixed findings, and four found statistically significant differences favoring a particular instructional variable. However, no single instructional variable was found consistently to enhance critical thinking. Similarly, in terms of course interventions, three studies found no significant effects, three found mixed effects, and only one found significant effects.

One conclusion that can be drawn from the McMillan (1987) review is that specific instructional and course interventions have little consistent impact on the development of critical thinking. The major reason for this may be that a one-quarter or one-semester instructional experience is simply too brief and isolated to have a discernible impact on a general cognitive skill such as critical thinking. This may be particularly true as the instrument of choice for assessing critical thinking in these studies is the Watson-Glaser CTA, a measure that is oriented toward critical thinking in everyday matters rather than in academic matters.

The McMillan (1987) synthesis takes a box score approach (that is, number of studies showing significant results, number showing mixed results, and number showing no significant differences). It therefore tends to be conservative in that studies with statistically nonsignificant findings are considered to indicate a zero effect for the experimental intervention. A meta-analysis, on the other hand, would take a more liberal (Bayesian) approach and consider the size of an intervention's effect even if it were not significantly different from zero. McKeachie, Pintrich, Lin, and Smith (1986) reconsidered an unpublished version of McMillian's review from this perspective and concluded that instruction that stresses student discussion and/or places explicit emphasis on problem-solving procedures and methods may enhance critical thinking. Additional studies not included in McMillian's synthesis would lend at least some support for this position (for example, Holloway, 1976; Moll & Allen, 1982).

There has been less research on the influence of purposeful curricular interventions on critical thinking. In their second-year evaluation of the ADAPT curriculum, Tomlinson-Keasey and Eisert (1978b) compared freshman-year change scores on the Watson-Glaser CTA between students in the ADAPT program and control groups of regular university freshmen. The ADAPT students showed a statistically significant gain of more than one standard deviation, while the gains for the control groups were essentially trivial and statistically nonsignificant, averaging only about .05 of a standard deviation. Unfortunately, the pretest of the ADAPT group was more than a full standard deviation lower than that of the control groups. Consequently, the greater improvement in critical thinking for the ADAPT students may have been, in large part, the result of regression artifacts.

Somewhat more impressive evidence concerning the effects of curricular interventions on critical thinking is presented by Winter, McClelland, and Stewart (1981). They hypothesized that a curriculum experience that requires the integration of ideas, courses, and disciplines would enhance critical thinking over the more typical curriculum, which merely provides a checklist of requirements without any integrative rationale. To test this hypothesis, they compared students in two different curricula within the same institution on gains on the Test of Thematic Analysis. (Recall that the TTA is an essay measure of critical thinking.) The experimental curriculum was a joint humanities program in which students took a group of two or more courses from different but complementary subject areas. The courses focused on an integrative theme relevant to the different disciplines. The control group was made up of students in the regular courses in the same general area, covering the same material, over the same period of time. While students in the integrative program started out on the TTA higher than the controls (1.66 versus 1.22), they also showed significantly greater gains (average increase of .50 versus .08 for the controls). This is the opposite of what one would expect from regression artifacts and represents reasonably impressive evidence of a real effect, despite the absence of an equivalent control group. Winter, McClelland, and Stewart conclude from this evidence that the experience of having to integrate two or more disciplines at the same time elicits greater cognitive growth than does simply studying the same material in separate courses without a consciously integrative structure. This is consistent with the evidence reported by Dressel and Mayhew (1954) and Forrest (1982) concerning the marked effects on critical thinking and reasoning skills of colleges that stress integrative general education in their curricula.

Postformal Reasoning. A small body of evidence suggests that college instruction can be designed to facilitate development along Perry's (1970) scheme of intellectual development. (Recall that this scheme views intellectual development as advancing through three basic stages: a dualistic right-versus-wrong stage, a relativistic stage in which facts are seen in terms of their context, and a stage in which the individual can make intellectual commitments within a context of relative knowledge.) Stephenson and Hunt (1977) report the results of a course-based intervention founded on a theory of cognitive developmental instruction. This type of instruction assumes that intellectual development occurs as a result of "cognitive conflict or dissonance which forces individuals to alter the constructs they have used to reason about certain situations" (Widick, Knefelkamp, and Parker, 1975, p. 291). The experimental intervention was a freshman social science course that focused on human identity within the context of literature and psychology (readings were from such authors as Edward Albee, James Baldwin, Arthur Miller, and Sylvia Plath). The method of instruction was specifically intended to advance dualistic students toward the relativistic stage of the Perry continuum. As such, the instruction emphasized challenges to the students' values and cognitive constructs within a supportive teaching paradigm. The control groups were made up of students in a humanities class and an English class that focused on similar course content but did not include cognitive developmental instruction.

Students in both instructional conditions were pre- and posttested with an instrument developed specifically to measure position on the Perry continuum. Even though the groups were generally equal to begin with, the experimental group exhibited substantially greater stage movement (mean change of +.85 stage) than the control groups (mean change of +.25 stage). Since students self-selected themselves into both the experimental and control conditions, however, there is still the possibility that the findings may be confounded by the interaction of selection and change (that is, the reason why an individual chooses a particular mode of instruction may be a determinant of the degree of change).

Findings generally consistent with those of Stephenson and Hunt (1977) have been reported in two additional course interventions described by Knefelkamp, (1974); Widick, Knefelkamp, and Parker (1975); and Widick and Simpson (1978). As with the Stephenson and Hunt study, the two course interventions sought to determine whether cognitive developmental instruction matched to the student's initial stage on the Perry scheme could facilitate progress along the continuum. Once again the instruction emphasized challenges to the students' cognitive and value structure within an overall supportive learning environment. In one intervention, without a control group, there was a pre- to postcourse gain of slightly more than .75 of a stage in the Perry continuum.[5] In the second intervention study, a greater percentage of those exposed to cognitive developmental instruction exhibited progress on the Perry continuum (63 percent) than those in the control sections (51.5 percent). The second study, however, was unclear as to how students were placed in the experimental and control sections. More recent findings similar to those of Knefelkamp (1974); Widick, Knefelkamp, and Parker (1975); and Widick and Simpson (1978) have been reported for an application of cognitive developmental instruction in an introductory course on educational foundations (Mortensen & Moreland, 1985, as reviewed in Kurfiss, 1988).

Conceptual Complexity. We uncovered only one study that dealt with the effects of instructional interventions on conceptual complexity, and that involved the ADAPT curriculum described earlier in the chapter. Tomlinson-Keasey and Eisert (1978a) compared changes in freshman-year scores on the Test of Conceptual Complexity for students in the ADAPT curriculum and regular freshmen. The Test of Conceptual Complexity appears to be a version of the Paragraph Completion Method. (Recall that conceptual complexity assessed in this manner measures the extent to which a person is capable of conceptualizing complex issues on increasingly abstract levels.) Although the ADAPT and control groups were not significantly different on the pretest, the ADAPT students increased approximately .50 of a standard deviation during the freshman year, while the control group actually decreased. The difference in the change in scores was statistically significant. Again, however, these results may be confounded by the fact that students selected the ADAPT or control curriculum. Although students in both groups were similar in conceptual complexity at the beginning of the freshman year, the reasons for their selection of one curriculum rather than the other could have been a determinant of differential change.

Teacher Behavior

As indicated in Chapter Three, there is a considerable body of research on teacher behavior and its relationship to students' learning of subject matter content. In contrast, there has been surprisingly little inquiry concerning the influence of teacher behavior on general cognitive skills. Perhaps the most useful research in this area has been conducted by D. Smith (1977, 1981), who employed a correlational design to assess the relationship between college classroom interactions and critical thinking. Critical thinking was measured by the Watson-Glaser CTA and Chickering's (1972) self-report index of critical thinking behavior. The Flanders (1970) Interaction Analysis System was used to assess four dimensions of classroom interactions. These interactions were related to changes between precourse and postcourse scores on the critical thinking appraisal and to postcourse scores on the six dimensions of the self-report index of critical thinking by means of canonical correlation (akin to multiple regression analysis with more than one dependent variable). The sample included twelve classes (138 students) distributed across disciplines, with analyses conducted at both individual and classroom levels of aggregation. The results suggest that at both levels three types of instructor-influenced classroom interactions were consistently and positively related to gains in critical thinking and to the analysis and synthesis dimensions of critical thinking behavior: the degree to which faculty encouraged, praised, or used student ideas; the degree to which students participated in class and the cognitive level of that participation; and the extent of peer-to-peer interaction in the class.

Clearly, the D. Smith (1977, 1981) research has an important methodological limitation, namely, the absence of controls for possible confounding differences in student precourse levels of critical thinking. (Indeed, research with samples of medical students suggests that student classroom participation is significantly and positively associated with precourse levels of critical thinking [Foster, 1981, 1983].) Nevertheless, the results do suggest that student critical thinking may be enhanced by teacher classroom behaviors that foster active student involvement in the learning process at a rather high level of interchange between student and teacher and between student and student. In this sense Smith's findings are quite consistent with earlier research suggesting that student-initiated discussions or verbal interactions in the classroom enhance the development of higher-order problem-solving skills over more traditional lecture approaches (for example, Beach, 1968; Romig, 1972; C. Smith, 1970). In fact, it may well be that increased student participation is an important causal mechanism underlying the positive association found between small classes and the development of higher-order cognitive processes (Dunkin & Barnes, 1985; McKeachie, 1978, 1980). Other factors being equal, student discussion is probably more likely in a class of 15 to 20 than in one of 250. The D. Smith findings, however, further suggest that amount of student-faculty and student-student interchange may not be particularly influential unless that interchange is at a reasonably high cognitive level.

Student Involvement

Consistent with the theoretical propositions of Astin (1984) and Pace (1980), as well as with the findings of studies synthesized in Chapter Three, a considerable body of evidence suggests that a student's quality of effort or level of involvement in college has a significant and positive influence on various dimensions of general cognitive development. Much of this research uses student self-reports of intellectual or cognitive development during college. As we suggested in Chapter Three, there are some psychometric problems with this approach; yet there also tend to be moderate positive correlations between self-reports and more objective measures of growth during college. Consequently, student self-reports provide a reasonable, if not totally adequate, indicator of cognitive growth.

Self-reports were used in an eight-institution study of college impact reported by Gaff, Wilson, and their colleagues (Gaff, 1973; Wilson, Wood, & Gaff, 1974; Wilson, Gaff, Dienst, Wood, & Bavry, 1975). Seniors at the eight institutions were asked to indicate both the extent of their campus involvement in nine different activities (intellectual, vocational, athletic, political, social, and so on) and the extent of their progress during college on a number of different dimensions of cognitive growth (for example, learning abstractions, applying principles, evaluating materials and methods). Degree of involvement was found to be significantly associated with cognitive growth but in a somewhat selective way. Specifically, perceived growth tended to be commensurate with involvement in activities that were consistent with it and supported it. For example, regardless of academic or vocational interests, students who were most involved in the pursuit of intellectual activities reported the most progress in learning abstractions, comprehending ideas, and applying principles. Conversely, students who had become the most deeply involved in social and athletic activities reported the least cognitive growth.

Similar results have been reported by Volkwein, King, and Terenzini (1986) in a single-institution study of students who transferred to a large state university and were followed over their first year of attendance. The study assessed student background characteristics (for example, age, socioeconomic status, secondary school achievement, intended major, and educational/vocational goals) and campus experiences (classroom involvement, relations with peers, extracurricular activities, social involvement, and so forth). The dependent measure was termed intellectual skill development and was a self-report scale of progress that focused on cognitive skills (for example, thinking analytically, critically evaluating ideas). Statistically controlling for background characteristics, the researchers found that a measure of classroom involvement had the strongest statistically significant association with the scale of intellectual skill development. The net association of other campus experiences such as social involvement or extracurricular activities was generally much smaller and statistically nonsignificant. Additional evidence from a related series of single-institution studies (Terenzini, Theophilides, & Lorang, 1984a; Volkwein, Wright, & Agrotes, 1987) and a study based on a national sample (Anaya, 1989) tend to support this finding. Each of these investigations relies on similar self-report measures of cognitive development.

Less supportive evidence concerning the role of student involvement in facilitating the development of cognitive skills has been reported by Hood (1984) in a study of freshman-to-senior gains in cognitive complexity (assessed with the paragraph completion method). Gain in cognitive complexity for each student was examined in relation to involvement in various undergraduate experiences such as major, type of residence, work experience, and participation in various campus activities. None of the specific college experiences, however, had a statistically significant correlation with the gain scores.

At first glance, results similar to those of Hood's (1984) investigation are apparently reported by Pascarella (1989) in a study of growth in critical thinking during the freshman year. (Critical thinking was measured by the Watson-Glaser CTA.) Nine individual measures of the undergraduate academic or social experience—residence arrangement, time spent studying, extracurricular activities, number of intellectually focused interactions with faculty and peers, and the like—had only trivial and statistically nonsignificant relationships with critical thinking at the end of the freshman year when the initial level of critical thinking was taken into account. However, when Pascarella combined the individual experience variables into a composite estimate of student social and intellectual involvement, it yielded a statistically significant positive association (partial $r = .34$) between involvement and critical thinking at the end of the freshman year. This association remained significant even when precollege critical thinking, academic aptitude, socioeconomic status, and college selectivity were controlled statistically. These findings, like those of Pace (1980, 1984) reported in Chapter Three, suggest a certain wholeness to student involvement or quality of effort in terms of its impact on cognitive development.

Pascarella's (1989) findings are also similar to those of Ory and Braskamp (1988) and Pace (1987, 1990). In these three studies level of student involvement or effort in both academic (intellectual) and interpersonal experiences had significant positive correlations with a measure of intellectual skill development (analysis, synthesis, and so on) that were markedly similar in magnitude. Thus, while it may well be, as indicated by the work of Wilson, Volkwein, Terenzini, and their colleagues, that a student's academic involvement holds the greatest potential for fostering growth in intellectual skills, it is also the case that the student is a member of a larger social system in which interpersonal interactions with the major agents of socialization (faculty and student peers) may provide an important influence on student intellectual growth in their own right. This influence may have both direct and indirect components. In the case of the latter, interpersonal interactions with faculty and peers may indirectly influence intellectual growth by influencing students' levels of involvement in academic or intellectual experiences.

Substantial evidence exists to suggest that interactions with major socializing agents (faculty and peers) are, in fact, significantly linked to the development of general cognitive skills during college. In an eight-institution study, for example, Wilson, Gaff, Dienst, Wood, and Bavry (1975) found that seniors who reported the greatest gains in such areas as ability to comprehend, interpret, or extrapolate; ability to evaluate materials and methods; and ability to apply abstractions or principles also had the highest amount of informal, nonclassroom interaction with faculty. This relationship appears to hold even when controls are made for differences among students in salient precollege characteristics. Pascarella and Terenzini (1978) controlled for fourteen such precollege characteristics (academic ability, secondary school achievement, race, socioeconomic status, personality characteristics, and the like) and found that frequency of student nonclass contact with faculty to discuss intellectual matters had a statistically significant positive association with reported gains in intellectual development during the freshman year. (The measure of intellectual development included such items as critical evaluation of ideas and applying abstractions or principles in problem solving.) This finding, replicated on an independent sample by Terenzini and Pascarella (1980a), and generally consistent findings with respect to the association between informal contact with faculty and perceived gains in cognitive development have also been reported in longitudinal studies by Endo and Harpel (1982, 1983); Elfner, McLaughlin, Williamsen, and Hardy (1985); and Spady (1971). Each of these studies attempted to control for important confounding variables (including academic ability, aspirations, major) in estimating the association in question.

A related line of longitudinal inquiry has focused primarily on the relationship between the *quality* of interactions between students and major agents of socialization on campus and perceived growth in cognitive skills (Endo & Harpel, 1983; Pascarella, Duby, Terenzini, & Iverson, 1983; Terenzini & Pascarella, 1980a; Volkwein, King, & Terenzini, 1986). The analytical designs of these studies typically regress measures of perceived student cognitive growth (thinking critically, thinking analytically, evaluating ideas, and so forth) on student precollege characteristics and measures of the quality of interaction with faculty and student peers. This permits statistical control of important confounding influences when estimating the association between the measures of interaction and measures of development. The general results of this body of evidence suggest that net of the effects of confounding variables, students who reported the greatest cognitive development were also most likely to (1) perceive faculty as being concerned with teaching and student development, (2) report developing a close, influential relationship with at least one faculty member, and (3) find their interactions with peers to have had an important influence on their development.

The potential impact of developing a close relationship with a faculty member is further suggested by Baxter Magolda (1987b) in an analysis of student intellectual development on the Perry scheme as assessed by the Measure of Epistemological Reflection. Students at the highest level of complexity in intellectual development preferred a relationship with faculty that emphasized working together as colleagues. In contrast, students at the lowest level preferred the relationship to be comfortable and relaxed but not too personal.

As suggested in Chapter Three, there are problems in drawing conclusions from this body of evidence because of ambiguities in the direction of causal influence. Do the extent and quality of student-faculty informal interactions influence cognitive growth, or do increases in cognitive skills lead to closer relationships and more frequent interactions with faculty? It is also possible that the causal linkages could be circular or reciprocal—interaction influencing growth, which in turn fosters even more interaction. Despite this ambiguity, the evidence does underscore the potential importance of the collegiate social environment and the extent and focus of interactions within that environment as an influence on student cognitive development.

One area in which colleges have at least some reasonable policy control over the student social environment is in residence halls. Indeed, a substantial amount of research has addressed ways in which residence halls might be structured to enhance the normative press for academic values and academic achievement.[6] Surprisingly little inquiry, however, has addressed the influence of residential living on the development of more general cognitive skills. As reported earlier in this chapter, Winter, McClelland, and Stewart (1981) found statistically significant freshman-to-senior changes on the Test of Thematic Analysis at a selective liberal arts college. To determine the institutional experiences that accounted for those changes, the researchers regressed student TTA gain scores on seven different scales derived from a factor analysis of a seventy-item measure of college experiences. Net of the other influences, a scale measuring the students' involvement in dormitory-sponsored activities (the dormitory-centered life scale) had a statistically significant negative association with gains on the TTA. Winter, McClelland, and Stewart suggest that one explanation for this finding is that a college's dormitories may often be a constraining influence that prolongs an overly protective, quasi-familial living atmosphere (for instance, residence staff *in loco parentis*). Thus, rather than providing an intellectually challenging environment, many dormitory activities may simply provide an insulated, comfortable, and unchallenging niche for students.

With respect to Winter, McClelland, and Stewart's (1981) findings, it is important to point out that residence arrangements within the same institution can differ substantially in the extent of their intellectual or traditional collegiate press (for example, Moos, 1976, 1979). Thus, some residential environments may be more conducive than others to the kinds of experiences and interactions that foster intellectual growth. Pascarella and Terenzini (1980b) addressed this issue in a quasi-experimental study that compared freshmen in traditional residence hall settings with those in a "living-learning" residence on self-reported gains in applying abstractions and principles in problem solving, critical evaluation of ideas, and other aspects of cognitive development. The living-learning residence was structured to integrate the students' academic and residential life and to enhance the intellectual impact of interactions between students and faculty and between students and their peers. Because of self-selection of freshmen into the traditional and living-learning residences, statistical controls were made for fifteen precollege variables (including academic aptitude, socioeconomic status, secondary school academic and social achievement, expectations of college). Net of these influences, students in the living-learning residence rated the institutional environment significantly stronger in intellectual press and sense of community and also reported significantly greater freshman-year gains on the measure of cognitive development.

A final piece of evidence on student involvement and cognitive development during college concerns the potential role of athletic participation. Winter, McClelland, and Stewart (1981), in their investigation of gains in critical thinking (as measured by the Test of Thematic Analysis) at a selective liberal arts college, also found that increases on the TTA were positively associated with varsity athletic participation, particularly for men. They explain this finding as follows (p. 134): "Success in athletics [requires] at least two qualities of mind: disciplined, thorough practice and adaptability to complex and rapidly changing circumstances. Applied to mental life, this practice and adaptability should enhance a person's ability to form and articulate abstract cognitive concepts to organize complex experience. (Thus coaches in many sports, for example, speak of a player's ability to diagnose or 'read' the other team's intentions or the course of the game.)"

This would seem to suggest that the student-athlete has a set of experiences during college that are particularly rich in terms of their potential for impact on adaptive and critical thinking processes. It is likely, however, that the institutional ethos, particularly with respect to the importance of athletics in the total scheme of things, may be a significant moderator of this impact. At the particular college in which these analyses were conducted, the varsity athletes did not receive athletic scholarships, live in special dormitories, or take special academic programs. Indeed, they were a representative cross section of the entire student body and, as such, were likely to be active participants in the academic as well as the athletic life of the institution. Whether varsity sports participation would have a similar impact on the cognitive development of student-athletes at institutions where varsity athletics are emphasized at the price of the individual's academic life is problematic.

Conditional Effects of College

We uncovered almost no evidence to suggest that the effects of college on the development of general cognitive skills differ for different kinds of students. The one study that made a concerted effort to investigate conditional effects found none. In a quasi-expermental study of the effect of the first year of college on critical thinking, Pascarella (1989) also attempted to determine whether different students benefited differentially from attending versus not attending college, from attending colleges of different selectivity, and from involvement in various social and academic activities in college. The magnitude of the influence of these factors on the development of critical thinking did not differ for students of different races or genders or for students with different levels of secondary school critical thinking, academic aptitude, academic achievement, family socioeconomic status, or educational aspirations. In short, the effects were the same for all students. It is important to point out, however, that this study had a very small, matched sample ($n = 47$) that did not afford it great statistical power to detect conditional effects. Because of this constraint, the Pascarella study may have failed to detect statistically significant conditional effects that were in fact present, if perhaps modest in magnitude.

Some scattered evidence concerning the impact of different instructional approaches suggests the possibility that certain kinds of students may benefit more than others from these approaches. For example, in a quasi-experimental investigation to estimate the comparative effects on Piagetian formal reasoning of a learning cycle–inquiry approach versus a traditional lecture/demonstration approach, Renner and Paske (1977) found that less advanced (concrete) reasoners benefited more from learning cycle instruction while students with some initial expertise in formal reasoning made greater progress in the traditional approach. In short, students advanced most in instruction matched to their initial level of reasoning. Similar if not totally parallel findings have been reported by Lawrenz (1985) in an experimental study of the use of student groupings in a learning cycle–inquiry type of science instruction. In each phase of instruction students worked and interacted in small groups. All students tended to make statistically significant gains in formal reasoning during the instruction. Greater gains were made, however, when students were homogeneously grouped by initial reasoning ability than when the reasoning ability in the small group was heterogeneous.

Long-Term Effects of College

In attempting to synthesize the evidence on the long-term effects of college on the development of general cognitive skills, we must rely almost totally on surveys that ask alumni about their retrospective perception of the influence or benefits of college. The sheer weight of evidence from this research suggests that college alumni perceive their undergraduate experience as having an important influence on their general cognitive development. Pace (1979), for example, reviewed the results of five surveys (three of which were based on national samples) of college alumni conducted from 1948 through 1976. The percentage of alumni in these surveys who reported that college affected them "greatly" or "somewhat" in critical thinking and analytical skills ranged from 72 to 96 percent. Similarly, the percentage reporting that college helped them "very much" or "quite a bit" in written and oral communication varied from 63 to 85 percent. Our own further analysis of this data suggests no statistically significant relationship between the perceived effect of college on these competencies and how long it had been since the various samples graduated from college, a time period ranging from about six to twenty years.

If alumni do not appear to differ significantly in their perceptions of the effectiveness of college on cognitive development on the basis of the time period since graduation (at least between six and twenty years since graduation), there are nevertheless some modest differences based on the student body selectivity of the college attended. Pace (1974), for example, found that 74 percent of alumni from selective universities and 77 percent from selective liberal arts colleges indicated that their institution provided "very much" or "quite a bit of " benefit in the development of critical thinking compared to a national baseline of 72 percent for all institutions in the sample. Similarly, in a ten-year follow-up of a national sample of college graduates, Bisconti and Solmon (1976) found that 51 percent of those graduating from highly selective institutions felt their undergraduate experience had been "very useful" in increasing their ability to think clearly. This compared to 42 percent of those graduating from less selective institutions. This relationship remained statistically significant even after controls were made for the individual's family background, gender, college grades, and academic major. Such statistical controls notwithstanding, it would be hazardous to attribute the differences in alumni perceptions to environmental differences between selective and less selective colleges. A plausible alternative explanation is that selective colleges simply recruit and enroll academically able students who are more open to the intellectual impacts of college to begin with. Thus, the findings could be the result of differential student recruitment rather than differential environmental or socialization effects.

Although the evidence from alumni surveys is impressive, at least in terms of how these individuals retrospectively perceive the impact of college on their cognitive development and thinking skills, it is not clear that it fully captures the total effect of college. As stressed in Chapter Three, a major if often ignored impact of college is transmitted through its influence on the graduate's postcollege experiences (further schooling, occupation, leisure activities, continuing intellectual interests). A large part of the long-term impact of college on cognitive development may take this indirect path of college influencing the nature of postcollege experiences, experiences that have a continuing influence on cognitive growth. For example, consider the evidence reported by Kohn and Schooler (1978, 1983) that intellectually and socially stimulating work makes an independent contribution to continued cognitive development in adult life. One important indirect effect of college on cognitive development, then, may be through the channeling of its graduates into occupations with relatively high ideational content, demanding social interaction and substantial self-direction (Beaton, 1975; Lindsay & Knox, 1984). Indeed, as we shall see in a subsequent chapter, a college degree may be the crucial entry criterion for many such jobs (for example, Bowen, 1977; Jencks et al., 1979; Sewell, Haller, & Portes, 1969; Sewell & Hauser, 1975).

This channeling effect perhaps helps to explain the findings of Heath (1976c). In his follow-up of male graduates of a liberal arts college who were in their early thirties, Heath discovered that the most important enduring effect of the institution (from a graduate's perspective) was its impact on intellectual maturation (relating ideas to each other at increasingly abstract levels, thinking logically, and the like). Even so, the undergraduate experience was ranked behind other factors (such as wife, graduate or professional school, occupation) in terms of its relative impact on intellectual maturation. It is likely, however, that graduation from college (or perhaps even that particular college) enhanced the likelihood of postgraduate educational and occupational experiences that in turn had an accentuating effect on trends in intellectual development initiated during the undergraduate years.

Summary

Change During College

Our synthesis suggests that students make statistically significant gains during the college years on a number of dimensions of general cognitive capabilities and skills. Compared to freshmen, seniors have better oral and written communication skills, are better abstract reasoners or critical thinkers, are more skilled at using reason and evidence to address ill-structured problems for which there are no verifiably correct answers, have greater intellectual flexibility in that they are better able to understand more than one side of a complex issue, and can develop more sophisticated abstract frameworks to deal with complexity. Since not all the studies we reviewed provided the necessary statistical data (for example, standard deviations), estimates of the magnitude of these freshman-to-senior gains are tenuous at best. Nevertheless, our best estimate is that the magnitude of the gains made are as follows: oral communication, .60 SD (an improvement of 22 percentile points); written communication, .50 SD (an improvement of 19 percentile points); Piagetian formal (abstract) reasoning, .33 SD (an improvement of 13 percentile points); critical thinking, 1 SD (an improvement of 34 percentile points); using reason and evidence to address ill-structured problems, 1 SD (an improvement of 34 percentile points); and ability to deal with conceptual complexity, 1.2 SD (an improvement of 38 percentile points). It is also our best estimate that about 50 percent or more of the gains made in abstract reasoning, critical thinking, and ability to conceptualize complexity occur during the freshman and sophomore years of college. One must keep in mind, however, that only a portion of these gains can be attributed to the influence of college.

Net Effects of College

The body of evidence concerning the net effects of college on the development of general cognitive skills is small and limited in scope. From this evidence, however, we offer the following conclusions.

1. When both age and academic ability are taken into account, seniors still have significantly better written and oral communication skills than freshmen. Similarly, graduates of community colleges score higher than incoming freshmen on a measure of general intellectual and analytical

skill development, even when age, verbal ability, and mathematical ability are held constant.

2. There is reasonably sound and consistent evidence to suggest that college has a net positive influence on diverse measures of critical thinking that cannot be explained away by differences among those who attend and do not attend college in initial critical thinking, academic aptitude, maturation, socioeconomic status, or aspirations. The effect of college on critical thinking, however, seems to be selective. It appears to enhance one's ability to weigh evidence, to determine the validity of data-based generalizations or conclusions, and to distinguish between strong and weak arguments. There is less support for the claims that college has a unique effect on one's ability to discriminate the truth or falsity of inferences, recognize assumptions, or determine whether stated conclusions follow from information provided.

3. The weight of evidence suggests that attending college has a stronger influence than normal maturation on reflective judgment, one's ability to use reason and evidence in making judgments about controversial issues. It would appear that those who attend college not only make greater gains in reflective judgment than those who do not but also that these gains cannot be explained away by differences in initial academic ability between those who attend college and those who do not.

4. Net of age, intelligence, and academic aptitude, attending college appears to influence one's intellectual flexibility (ability to comprehend and effectively argue both sides of a complex or controversial issue) positively and significantly.

The research on the net effects of college sheds little light on *why* college attendance fosters greater average growth in general cognitive skills than other post–high school experiences. One reasonable explanation, however, is that of all the experiences a student could have after secondary school, college is the one that most typically provides an overall environment where the potential for intellectual growth is maximized. To be sure, a diverse array of noncollege experiences might exert substantial impact on an individual's intellectual growth. The advantage of college, however, is that salient intellectual, cultural, and interpersonal influences (for example, courses, libraries, laboratories, faculty, and other similarly engaged peers) tend to be concentrated in one place. Given this concentration of influences, evidence supporting a net positive impact of college on a range of general cognitive competencies and skills may not be particularly surprising.

Between-College Effects

We found only a limited amount of consistent evidence to suggest that institutional characteristics have an important influence on the development of general cognitive skills. A number of studies indicate that general cognitive growth is maximally enhanced at institutions with selective undergraduate student bodies, particularly when cognitive growth is assessed by student or alumni self-reports of gains made during college. However, more methodologically sound studies, using objective measures and/or controlling for important precollege characteristics, have found little relationship between institutional selectivity and objective measures of cognitive development. It may be that selectivity only has a discernible impact on student cognitive development when it is combined with other factors such as small size and an institutional ethos that encourages a high level of student effort and involvement. Certain selective liberal arts colleges tend to combine these traits, though methodologically sound and replicated findings concerning their direct impact on cognitive development are sparse. It does appear that selective liberal arts colleges tend to give examinations that stress more higher-order cognitive skills than do less selective liberal arts colleges. Whether this reflects actual differences in the level at which courses are taught or simply professorial perceptions of students' capabilities, however, is still unclear.

There is some evidence that institutions with a strong emphasis on fraternity or sorority life tend to inhibit growth in critical thinking. Nevertheless, the apparent absence in this evidence of controls for freshman-cohort differences within and among institutions makes any firm conclusions difficult. Similarly, there is cross-sectional evidence, paired with appropriate cohort statistical controls, to suggest that black students demonstrate greater development in critical thinking and concept attainment at predominantly black institutions than at predominantly white ones. This finding awaits replication, however.

The only area where we found consistent evidence with respect to between-college effects (and it is based on only two studies) was in the influence of institutional curricular emphasis. Despite some methodological problems, it would appear that students at institutions with a strong and balanced curricular commitment to general education show particularly large gains in measures of critical thinking and adult reasoning skills. The two studies that provide this evidence were conducted nearly thirty years apart.

Within-College Effects

The weight of evidence would suggest that one's major course of study influences the development of general cognitive skills but that the influence is selective. A student's cognitive growth is greatest on measures where the content is most consistent with his or her academic major or course work emphasis. Thus, for example, science majors tend to outperform others on measures of formal reasoning and critical thinking when these skills are applied to sciencelike tasks or problems. In contrast, when the tasks or problems are presented in the form of social science content, social science majors tend to perform best. On general measures of critical thinking (for example, the Watson-Glaser Critical Thinking Appraisal) or postformal reasoning (for example, reflective judgment), one's academic major has little consistent relationship with gains.

A reasonably consistent body of experimental evidence suggests that the learning cycle–inquiry approach to science instruction is effective in moving students from concrete to formal (abstract) operational reasoning. This approach stresses an inductive learning process that is geared to concrete reasoning and in which actual experiments or other concrete activities are used to introduce concepts and abstractions. The learning cycle–inquiry approach has also been shown to enhance the development of formal reasoning and conceptual complexity when implemented in a general freshman-year curriculum not restricted to science courses.

Whether one concludes that there are instructional approaches that consistently enhance critical thinking depends on how one reads the evidence. From a conservative perspective, where statistically nonsignificant findings equal a zero treatment effect, no one instructional or curricular approach appears consistently to facilitate the growth of critical thinking, particularly when critical thinking is measured by general, nonacademic instruments such as the Watson-Glaser Critical Thinking Appraisal. A more liberal perspective, which considers experimental control differences as being non-zero even if the differences are not statistically significant, would suggest that instruction that stresses student discussion at a relatively high level of cognitive activity and/or instruction that places emphasis on problem-solving procedures and methods may enhance critical thinking.

There is evidence that a curriculum experience that requires the integration of ideas and themes across courses and disciplines enhances critical thinking over simply taking a distribution of courses without an integrative rationale or theme. Although this evidence is based on only one study, it is nevertheless of some importance because of its consistency with evidence suggesting that colleges stressing integrative general education in their overall curriculum are particularly effective in promoting growth in critical thinking.

A small body of research suggests that specially structured course interventions may enhance the development of postformal reasoning, specifically, stage movement on the Perry continuum. These interventions, which have been termed cognitive developmental instruction, focus on providing challenges to the individual's initial cognitive and value structures paired with instructional supports appropriate for the individual's initial level of cognitive development. The internal validity of experiments that assess the influence of these interventions, however, is not particularly strong. Thus, causal attribution is tenuous.

It is important to point out that the estimated magnitude of instructional or curricular effects on measures of general cognitive skills tends to be smaller than that of the effect of the overall college experience. This would suggest that growth in many areas of cognitive development may be a gradual process characterized by a period of rapid advancement followed by a period of consolidation (Kitchener, 1982). Fundamental shifts in thought processes may proceed slowly and irregularly. Thus, a single instructional or curricular experience over a limited period may not provide the developmental impact of a cumulative set of mutually reinforcing experiences over an extended period of time (Kitchener, 1983; White, 1980).

Consistent with theoretical expectations, extent of growth in general cognitive skills during college appears to be a direct result of a student's quality of effort or level of psychological and social involvement in college. Involvement in intellectual and cultural activities may be more important to general cognitive development than other types of involvement (social, athletic, and so on). Yet it also appears that the nature and quality of social interactions with faculty members and student peers play a role of some consequence in one's cognitive growth. These interactions are of particular salience if they focus on ideas or intellectual matters. The weight of evidence, we believe, suggests that the more one's social experience reflects and reinforces one's academic experience, the greater will be the possibilities for intellectual development. Put another way, the more complete the integration between a student's academic life and social life during college, the greater the likelihood of his or her general cognitive and intellectual growth.

One place where some institutions can influence this integration is student residence facilities. What evidence does exist suggests that when this academic and social integration is purposefully and successfully implemented in a residence hall environment, student cognitive growth can be facilitated. To the extent that residential life simply functions as a comfortable, protective, anti-intellectual niche for students, however, it may actually inhibit cognitive growth.

Conditional Effects

We found little consistent evidence to indicate that the effects of college on general cognitive skills differ for different kinds of students. Similarly, little evidence exists to suggest that the characteristics of the college attended have a differential influence on general cognitive skills for different kinds of students. There is, nonetheless, a small body of evidence suggesting that learning cycle–inquiry instruction has its most pronounced influence on the development of Piagetian formal reasoning either for students who are initially at the concrete reasoning stage or for students grouped with others at the same initial Piagetian reasoning level.

Long-term Effects

Although the evidence (from national samples) on long-term effects of college is based largely on alumni perceptions, its clear weight indicates that the undergraduate experience is seen as having an important influence on general cognitive development and thinking skills. These perceptions do not appear to be a function of time elapsed since graduation, but there is a slight trend for alumni from academically selective institutions to report greater impact than alumni from less selective institutions. The latter finding is consistent with differences in retrospective reports of seniors or other upperclassmen from selective and less selective institutions. It should be underscored that this modest association between self-reports of impact and college selectivity may not be due to environmental or socialization differences between selective and less selective colleges. The nature of the evidence makes differential student recruitment by selective and less selective colleges as plausible an explanation for these findings as any differential socialization that might take place in colleges of varying selectivity.

Finally, there is evidence to suggest that intellectually and socially stimulating work environments make an independent contribution to cognitive development in adult life. We have suggested that a major, though indirect, long-term effect of college on cognitive development comes through its power to position graduates in intellectually and socially demanding employment.

Notes

1. There is also evidence to suggest that students make statistically significant gains in purely verbal measures of abstract reasoning during college. Welfel and Davison (1986) found that engineering majors and humanities and social science majors made statistically significant freshman-to-senior gains on the Concept Mastery Test of about one standard deviation. The Concept Mastery Test is a measure of verbal abstract reasoning that consists of synonyms and antonyms and the completion of analogies.

2. There is also corroborating evidence from self-reports to suggest that students make nontrivial gains in the general ability to think critically. Heath (1968), in an extensive analysis of student maturation during college, suggests that increasing integration of intellectual skills (a broad notion of intellectual development that includes critical thinking) was one of the major and most significant maturing effects of college as perceived by students. Similarly, in a longitudinal study of 311 students, Endo and Harpel (1980) found that seniors were significantly more likely than freshmen to indicate capabilities typically associated with critical thinking (for example, recognizing assumptions, detecting

faulty reasoning, examining statements critically). (See also Bisconti & Solmon, 1976; Coles, 1983; Gaff, 1973; Hesse-Biber, 1985.)

3. We also found several studies that suggested that such approaches as remedial instruction in natural science and mathematics (Reif, 1984), practice in Piagetian tasks (Thomas & Grouws, 1984), modeling principles of formal thought (Wilson, 1987), and instruction in logic (Enyeart, 1981) enhanced progress from concrete to formal reasoning. However, these studies lacked the independent replication that characterized the evidence on the learning cycle–inquiry approach.

4. See Bailey (1979); Beckman (1956); Coscarelli and Schwen (1979); Gressler (1976); Hancock (1981); Hancock, Coscarelli, and White (1983); Hardin (1977); Hayden (1978); Jackson (1961); Jones (1974); Logan (1976); Lyle (1958); Moll and Allen (1982); Shuch (1975); Tomlinson-Keasey and Eisert (1978b). See also Kurfiss (1988) for an excellent discussion of different instructional strategies designed to improve problem solving and critical thinking in various disciplines.

5. Similar results are also reported by Stonewater and Daniels (1983) for a course based on psychosocial theory and designed to help students understand the process of career decision making and acquire skills useful in making appropriate career decisions. There were statistically significant advances on the Perry scheme, but there was no control group for comparative purposes.

6. See Ainsworth and Maynard (1976); Blai (1971); Blimling and Hample (1979); Brown (1968); Centra (1968); DeCoster (1968, 1979); Duncan and Stoner (1977); Gifford (1974); Gerst and Moos (1972); Golden and Smith (1983); McIntire (1973); Magnarella (1975); Moos, DeYoung, and Van Dort (1976); Pugh and Chamberlain (1976); Scott (1975); Schrager (1986); Schroeder (1980b); Snead and Caple (1971); Taylor and Hanson (1971); Williams and Reilly (1972); Winston, Hutson, and McCaffrey (1980).

5

Psychosocial Changes: Identity, Self-Concept, and Self-Esteem

Historically, America's colleges and universities have had an educational and social mission to "educate" in a sense that extends beyond the cognitive and intellectual development of students. That broader mission has defined education to include increased self-understanding; expansion of personal, intellectual, cultural, and social horizons and interests; liberation from dogma, prejudice, and narrow-mindedness; development of personal moral and ethical standards; preparation for useful and productive employment and membership in a democratic society; and the general enhancement of the quality of graduates' postcollege lives. In this and the next three chapters, we focus on the changes college students experience in the psychosocial, attitudinal, and moral areas sometimes referred to as the affective or non-cognitive domains.

Our understanding of these phases and processes of student change may be in transition. Keniston (1970, 1971a, 1971b), for example, believes that social and cultural transformations have produced a new phase that he calls *youth* to characterize "a growing minority of post-adolescents today . . . [who] have not settled the questions whose answers once defined adulthood: questions of relationship to the existing society, questions of vocation, questions of social role and life-style" (1970, p. 634). Others (Sanford, 1962; Chickering, 1969; Freedman, 1965; Goldscheider and Da Vanzo, 1986; Miller & Winston, 1990) share Keniston's view of a distinctive and evolving developmental period between adolescence and young adulthood. Holt (1980, p. 919) offers some supportive empirical evidence. Parsons and Platt (1970, chap. 4), witnessing the same phenomenon through the eyes of sociologists, believe that mass higher education has created a social situation in which colleges and universities are the primary vehicles of a newly emergent phase ("studentry") in the socialization process.

The literature on college students comes from diverse and evolving disciplinary and theoretical origins (Kitchener, 1982) that have produced varying conceptions of change or growth in human dimensions given varying names. Methodological problems also abound, including (among oththe way of significant college effects on students' self systems. These studies generally indicate that after holding constant various relevant student background characteristics, the discernible direct effects of college attendance tend to be small. Much of the evidence simply will not sustain claims of substantial and direct collegiate effects. At the same time, however, reasonably consistent evidence indicates that college attendance does make a difference, albeit small. But its effects appear to be more indirect than direct, being mediated largely by the academic and social interactions students have with one another and with faculty members.

Finally, it is neither unreasonable nor novel to argue that it may be unrealistic to expect the college experience to have an effect much greater than that revealed by the available research. Self systems are complex, poorly understood, and generally believed to reach deeply into an individual's being. As such, they are not likely to be easily touched, changed, or measured, especially over comparatively short periods of time. If this is so, then we ought not to be too surprised by the apparently modest effects of college in these areas. It may also be, however, that as this general area of inquiry matures, as theories are tested, clarified, and refined, as more psychometrically sound instruments and more rigorous designs and analytical procedures are adopted, the effects of college attendance will be more clearly discernible than they are at present.

Notes

1. Other authors have suggested taxonomies consistent with Inkeles's (1966) model and the focus on self and relational systems in this chapter and the next. See Drum (1980); Heath (1968); Kuh, Krehbiel, and MacKay (1988, p. 94); and Trent and Medsker (1968, p. 9).

2. Indeed, the authors of several studies of psychosocial change specifically comment on the *absence* of crisis in the sense of a psychological emergency, noting the comparatively smooth transition from one condition or phase to another (Freedman, 1967; Katz & Associates, 1968; King, 1973; Offer & Offer, 1975).

3. Matteson (1975), Bourne (1978a, 1978b), Marcia (1980), and Waterman (1982) review the literature on Marcia's (1965, 1966) model. Bourne (1978b) also provides a conceptual and methodological critique.

4. The bulk of this research examines the relationships between identity status and self-esteem (Fannin, 1977; Marcia, 1967; Marcia & Friedman, 1970; Orlofsky, 1977; Prager, 1982; Schenkel & Marcia, 1972). However, a number of researchers have studied the relation between identity status and a considerable variety of other variables, including anxiety (Schenkel & Marcia, 1972), authoritarianism (Marcia, 1967; Marcia & Friedman, 1970; Schenkel & Marcia, 1972), autonomy and

conformity (Toder & Marcia, 1973; Waterman, Buebel, & Waterman, 1970), decision-making style (Waterman & Waterman, 1974), expressive writing (Waterman & Archer, 1979; Waterman, Kohutis, & Pulone, 1977), intimacy and isolation (Orlofsky, Marcia, & Lesser, 1973), locus of control (Adams & Shea, 1979; Waterman, Buebel, & Waterman, 1970), academic major (Marcia & Friedman, 1970; Fannin, 1977; Waterman & Waterman, 1972), moral development (Podd, 1972), sex role orientation (Orlofsky, 1977), and work role salience (Fannin, 1977).

5. A considerable literature examines the undergraduate experience of black students at both black and white institutions (for example, Allen, 1986, 1987; Astin, 1982; Beckham, 1987; Burbach & Thompson, 1971; Centra, 1970; Davis & Borders-Patterson, 1973; Edwards, 1970; Epps, 1972; Fleming, 1981, 1984; Gibbs, 1973, 1974, 1975; Gurin & Epps, 1975; Hedegard & Brown, 1969; Kiernan & Daniels, 1967; Loo & Rolison, 1986; McSwine, 1971; Monroe, 1973; Moore, 1972; Semmes, 1985; Sowell, 1972; Stikes, 1984; Thomas, 1981a; Willie & Levy, 1972; Willie & McCord, 1972). Several reviews of the research literature on black students in higher education are available (Fleming, 1981; Harper, 1975; Ramseur, 1975; Sedlacek, 1987; Stikes, 1975; Willie & Cunnigen, 1981). See Duncan (1976) for a discussion of psychosocial conditions for minority graduate students. Several sources discuss the particular needs of various minority group students, including black students (Pounds, 1987; Sedlacek, 1987), Hispanic students (Olivas, 1986; Quevedo-Garcia, 1987), Asian Americans (Chew & Ogi, 1987), and Native Americans (LaCounte, 1987). This list is not exhaustive.

6. Freedman (1965) reached this conclusion on the basis of the timing of change along various dimensions of "personality."

7. Wylie (1974) offers an extensive critique of the various research methodologies employed in the study of self-esteem, or what she frequently refers to as self-regard. Wylie (1979) has also given a comprehensive review of studies of the self-concept or self-esteem of people six through fifty years of age, with particular emphasis on self-concept/esteem as a function of age and developmental level. See also Wells and Marwell (1976) and Dickstein (1977).

8. Astin (1977a) reports similar findings and reaches similar conclusions. His evidence tends to be somewhat indirect, however, being based on positive relations between senior-year self-concepts (net of precollege levels and a host of other background variables) and such variables as involvement in college (greater change among students who were also more involved in college is presumed to indicate college effects) and persistence (higher self-concepts among persisters than dropouts, implying college effects). Because Astin does not report a relation between increases in academic and/or social self-concept and some specific measure of educational attainment (for example, number of years

enrolled, highest degree earned), however, we do not discuss his results in detail. Astin does report finding no relation between changes
in academic or social self-concept and age, which argues against a
"maturation" explanation (and strengthens the "college effects" explanation) of the observed changes. Thus, while Astin does not report
specific tests of a relation between educational attainment and positive
changes in self-concepts, his data tend to support a conclusion of college effects net of other variables.

9. While this study was competently conducted, Knox, Lindsay, and Kolb
   consider their findings preliminary and expect to report additional
   analyses in a forthcoming book entitled *The Way Up: The Long-Term
   Effects of Higher Education on Students.*

10. See Marsh (1986b), Marsh and Parker (1984), and other references in
    those papers for related studies based on elementary and high school
    students.

11. The only other study identified that deals with between-college effects
    on self-esteem as defined here (Edwards & Tuckman, 1972) con-
    trasted community college and university liberal arts students after
    two years. Initially, community college students had lower self-esteem
    than the university students, but after two years, these differences dis-
    appeared as community college students showed marked increases and
    the university students remained unchanged.

12. A considerable number of studies examine the effects of what Thrasher
    and Bloland (1989) call intentional interventions, specially developed
    courses or programs intended (or perhaps implicitly expected) to alter
    in some fashion students' psychosocial development. Because these in-
    terventions take such diverse, often idiosyncratic forms (see below),
    are often of very brief duration, frequently employ opportunity sam-
    ples of questionable representativeness for any larger population, and
    use widely varied designs and analytical procedures, no attempt is made
    here to summarize their findings. Overall, our review leads us to agree
    with Thrasher and Bloland, who reviewed the literature on such in-
    tervention programs published between 1973 and 1987 and con-
    cluded that while program effects were found, they tended to be small,
    perhaps because most studies examined change over a short period
    of time. Studies of the effects of interventions on various dimensions
    of students' identity or ego development, academic and/or social self-
    concept, and self-esteem fall into the following general categories (ref-
    erences are not exhaustive within categories): formal courses (Brush,
    Gold, & White, 1978; Kammer, 1984; King, Walder, & Pavey, 1970;
    Loeffler & Feidler, 1979; McClaran & Sarris, 1985; Parish, 1988b;
    Plummer & Koh, 1987; Stake & Gerner, 1985; Tracy, 1975; West &
    Kirkland, 1986), periods of study abroad (Barnhart & Groth, 1987;
    Carsello & Creaser, 1976; Hensley & Sell, 1979; Hull & Lemke, 1975;

Hull, Lemke, & Houang, 1977; Juhasz & Walker, 1988; Kuh & Kauff-
man, 1985; McEvoy, 1986; Morgan, 1972, 1975; Nash, 1976; Stauf-
fer, 1973), various forms of personal counseling (Cooker & Caffey,
1984; Guller, 1969; Heppner & Krause, 1979; Locke & Zimmerman,
1987; McWilliams, 1979; Terranova, 1976), marathon and encounter
group sessions (Culbert, Clark, & Bobele, 1968; Foulds, 1971; Guinan
& Foulds, 1970; Kimball & Gelso, 1974; Lieberman, Yalom, & Miles,
1973; Meador, 1971; Treppa & Fricke, 1972; University of Massachusetts Counseling Center, 1972; Young & Jacobson, 1970), remediation
or compensatory programs (Fennimore, 1968; Leib & Snyder, 1967;
Olsen, 1972; Peterson, 1973), generalized psychosocial development
programs (Loeffler & Feidler, 1979; Ohlde & Vinitsky, 1976; Parrott
& Hewitt, 1978; Walsh, 1985), cooperative education or community
work experiences (Hursh & Borzak, 1979), student exchange programs within the United States (Hull, Lemke, & Houang, 1977; Wor-
ley, 1978), and wilderness training programs (Heaps & Thorstenson,
1972; Lambert, Segger, Staley, Spencer, & Nelson, 1978; Robbins, 1976;
Vander Wilt & Klocke, 1971). McHugo and Jernstedt (1979) review
the literature on field experiences (including study abroad and wilderness training).

13.   It should be noted that Smart (1985) and Pascarella, Smart, Ethington, and Nettles (1987) examined academic self-concept nine years
after matriculation. They also controlled for postcollege educational
attainment (highest degree earned) and employment (job status). Thus,
while some of these results may be influenced to an unknown degree
by postcollege activities, two important sources of bias—postbaccalaureate education and employment—have been at least partially controlled.

14.   This finding is inferred from the absence of any mention by Astin
(1977a) of finding a statistically significant relation between residence
and change in academic self-concept (Astin uses the term *intellectual
self-esteem,* but the operational form of this term is equivalent to what
we have labeled *academic self-concept*). The correctness of this inference
was confirmed in a telephone conversation with Astin on April 9, 1990.

15.   A number of studies of college students have explored differences
between the sexes in various facets of identity formation and ego development but do not directly test differences between the sexes in
the amount of change over time. Because this volume is concerned
with the fact and determinants of college student changes in a number of areas, these studies are only tangentially related to the question
of differential change conditional on sex. However, readers interested
in questions relating to sex-based differences in identity status and
ego stage development might find one or more of the following studies of use: Alishio and Schilling (1984); Allen (1986); Belenky, Clin-

chy, Goldberger, and Tarule (1986); Douvan and Adelson (1966); Gilligan (1982a); Hodgson and Fischer (1979); Rodgers (1990b); Stark and Traxler (1974); W. Stewart (1977); and Waterman and Nevid (1977). This listing is neither an exhaustive nor a comprehensive collection of such studies. See also the sections on conditional effects in Chapters Three, Four, Six, Seven and Eight of this volume.

16.   The findings of these studies may appear to conflict with those of large, national studies of self-concept change over four years by Astin (1977a) and over nine years by Astin and Kent (1983), both of which suggest that men increase their positive academic self-concepts more than women. The discrepancies, however, are due to different analytical strategies. Astin (1977a) appears to have tested the main effect of sex on senior-year self-concepts (both academic and social) after holding constant the effects of numerous other background variables on the follow-up measure. It is not clear whether he included in this particular analysis some measure of educational attainment (for example, number of years enrolled, whether a degree had been earned). Astin and Kent (1983) base their conclusions on a comparison of changes in the percentage of respondents rating themselves "above average" on a variety of items relating to academic and social self-concept. Thus, based on his report, it appears doubtful that Astin specifically tested the significance of any differences in the *rates* of change between the sexes (the years of education × sex interaction term). It is clear that Astin and Kent did not.

17.   Bragg (1976) summarizes the literature on socializing processes related to identity development. While her review concentrates on the development of professional identities in graduate education programs, it has some generalizability to undergraduate settings and identity more broadly conceived.

6

Psychosocial Changes:
Relating to Others
and the External World

Whereas Chapter Five deals with changes in students' conscious and unconscious conceptions and evaluations of themselves, this chapter examines changes in what Inkeles (1966) referred to as individuals' "relational systems." These include changes in students' relationships with other students and in their orientations to authority figures, intimates, peers, and collectivities. In short, this chapter deals with changes in the ways students relate to their external world.

The literature on these changes is both extensive and varied in the particular aspects of psychosocial development that are the object(s) of study. Moreover, the research is based on varying theoretical or conceptual perspectives that in turn beget different constructs, terminologies, and instrumentation. Much of this research is also based on pencil and paper tests, the construct validity of which is frequently unestablished. In addition, the connections between the psychosocial characteristics presumably measured by these instruments and actual student behaviors have frequently not been shown.

Our review indicates that the research concerning relational systems falls into six categories, dealing with issues of (1) autonomy, independence, and locus of control; (2) authoritarianism, dogmatism, and ethnocentricism; (3) intellectual orientation (considered part of the relational system because of its generally external thrust); (4) interpersonal relations; (5) personal adjustment and psychological well-being; and (6) maturity and general personal development.

Change During College

Autonomy, Independence, and Locus of Control

Studies in autonomy, independence, and locus of control examine the extent to which students change in their susceptibility to external influ-

214

ences, whether human or institutional. Most studies focus on changes in students' levels of autonomy and/or independence, that is, their degree of freedom from the influence of others in their choices of attitudes, values, and behaviors. (Note that the emphasis here is on students' general orientation, not on specific areas of belief, which are reviewed in Chapter Seven.) Agents of outside influence might be parents, peers, and institutions, with their formal rules, regulations, and laws. The terms *autonomy* and *independence* are subject to some ambiguity. For example, taken to their logical extreme, they could denote antisocial behavior. For Chickering (1969), however, autonomy, in its highest form, is synonymous with interdependence, which involves not simply one's freedom to choose or act free of outside influences but rather a freedom that also recognizes one's dependence on and obligations to others, both individuals and societal collectivities and conventions.

Other studies examine locus of control, a concept based on social learning theory and referring to the extent to which one is self-directed or believes oneself to be the determiner of one's own fate. Internally directed people tend to believe that they can control what happens to them, while externally directed individuals believe that their destiny is determined more by luck, chance, or fate (Rotter, 1966, 1975; Phares, 1973, 1976).

For centuries, independence of thought and action has been considered an important characteristic in most conceptions of adulthood and psychosocial health. As such, independence has long been an educational goal. Changes in the extent to which students think and behave in ways that reflect independence of the influence of others have been an object of study for more than thirty years. Few psychosocial traits have received more attention, and the evidence—from whichever decade—consistently indicates changes along this personal dimension during the college years.

Wolfle and Robertshaw (1982), Knox, Lindsay, and Kolb (1988),[1] and Nichols (1967), all drawing on large, national data bases, have provided the most persuasive evidence on changes in students' autonomy, independence, or locus of control. Wolfle and Robertshaw studied some 8,650 white males who participated in the National Longitudinal Study of the High School Class of 1972 (NLS-72) and who were tested again in 1976 with a short form of Rotter's (1966) locus of control scale. About 60 percent of the respondents had had some postsecondary schooling. Wolfle and Robertshaw found a statistically significant (but slight) shift from external to internal locus of control, indicating an increase in students' sense of control over what happens to them and a decline in their sense that their world is controlled by luck, fate, chance, or other external forces. Kanouse and colleagues (Kanouse et al., 1980), Knox, Lindsay, and Kolb (1988), Behuniak and Gable (1981), and Smart, Ethington, and McLaughlin (undated), who all used NLS-72 data, report findings consistent with those of Wolfle and Robertshaw, although they employ somewhat different samples, designs, and analytical approaches. Nichols (1967), who studied more than 600 National Merit Scholarship finalists in more than 100 colleges, also reports evidence consistent with these findings.

With some exceptions (for example, Adams & Shea, 1979; Watkins, 1987; Whiteley, 1982), single-institution or small-scale studies of students' locus of control status generally report increases in internality during the college years that are consistent both with the studies reported above and within this set of studies (Finnie, 1970; Goldman & Olczak, 1976, 1980; King, 1970; Knoop, 1981; Leon, 1974; Linder, 1986; Olczak & Goldman, 1975; Priest, Prince, & Vitters, 1978; Schroeder, 1973; Schroeder & Lemay, 1973; Scott, 1975).[2]

Our analysis of data reported by Wolfle and Robertshaw (1982) indicates an increase in internality of .26 of a standard deviation (10 percentile points). However, this estimate includes nonstudents as well as students. It was not possible to estimate the effect sizes for the two groups separately. Nichols's (1967) data, on the other hand, do indicate four-year declines on a measure of "dependence" of .28 and .29 of a standard deviation (−11 percentile points) among male and female National Merit finalists, respectively, accompanied by gains of .25 and .49 of a standard deviation (10 and 19 percentile points) for men and women, respectively, on a measure of "self-sufficiency." Thus, it appears that during the college years, students experience statistically significant but relatively small gains in internality.

With respect to changes in autonomy, the second edition of the Student Developmental Task Inventory, or SDTI-2 (Winston, Miller, & Prince, 1979), is designed to operationalize three of Chickering's (1969) seven vectors: achieving autonomy, freeing interpersonal relations, and developing purpose. Our synthesis of results from four studies (Greeley & Tinsley, 1988; Jordan-Cox, 1987; Straub & Rodgers, 1986; Winston, Miller, & Prince, 1979) that used the autonomy scale of the SDTI-2, as well as the autonomy scale norms of the Student Developmental Task and Lifestyle Inventory, a major revision of the SDTI-2 (Winston & Miller, 1987), indicates average freshman-to-senior differences of .59 of a standard deviation (22 percentile points). Other studies that used the SDTI-2 consistently indicate gains in autonomy during the college years, but the information needed to estimate effect sizes is not given (Itzkowitz & Petrie, 1986, 1988; Polkosnik & Winston, 1989). Still other single-institution studies that employed quite varied instruments and methodologies support the conclusion that students gain in their freedom from the influence of others during the college years (Chickering, 1967; Constantinople, 1967, 1970; Fry, 1976, 1977; Graffam, 1967; Heath, 1968; Hood & Jackson, 1986c; Lokitz & Sprandel, 1976; Matteson, 1977; Montgomery, McLaughlin, Fawcett, Pedigo, & Ward, 1975; Offer & Offer, 1975; Stikes, 1984; Straub, 1987; Pemberton, as cited in Williams & Reilly, 1972).

While the concept of autonomy implies a freedom from the influence of various individual and institutional sources (parents, peers, friends, teachers, schools, governments), most studies treat autonomy, independence, or locus of control as a global construct. Only a small group of studies, all of which used the College Student Questionnaire's (Peterson, 1968) peer independence and family independence scales, differentiate changes in students' degree of independence from parents as well as from peers. The psychological separation from parents is a common theme in the theoretical literature on adolescence. On the basis of various theories of identity development discussed in Chapter Two and the research on that topic reviewed in Chapter Five, one might predict that students would gain their independence from family before they would from peers. As the psychological (and sometimes physical) distance between the individual and parents increases, the individual turns increasingly to people outside the home (primarily but not exclusively peers) as psychosocial referents. Indeed, the departure from home experienced by many (but by no means all) students and the socialization processes of the college years provide ample opportunities for students to begin, if not consummate, the emotional and psychological separation from family. Whether that is, in fact, what happens, however, remains something of an open question.

Of the nine studies identified that spoke directly to the issue of change in level of independence from family and peers, six report statistically significant increases in family independence. Changes with respect to peers were smaller and either statistically nonsignificant or ignored in the presentation of results, thereby suggesting statistical nonsignificance (Hatch, 1970; Miller, 1973; Newcomb, Brown, Kulik, Reimer, & Revelle, 1970; Peterson, 1968; Wilder, Hoyt, Doren, Hauck, & Zettle, 1978; Wilder, Hoyt, Surbeck, Wilder, & Carney, 1986). Newcomb and his colleagues, as well as Heath (1968), report a decline in peer independence scores among freshmen. Hatch found this to be true only among women, while the men in her study increased in peer independence. Fry (1974) reports statistically significant increases in family independence among students from rural but not urban backgrounds. The remaining two studies (Nelsen & Johnson, 1971; Nelsen & Uhl, 1977) found statistically significant increases on both the family and peer independence scales, although in both studies the increases in independence from family exceeded those relating to peers. Across the few studies reporting data that can be used to estimate magnitudes, it appears that students gain in independence from family on the order of .60 of a standard deviation (29 percentile points) and from peers by about .20 of a standard deviation (8 percentile points). With one exception (Wilson, Anderson, & Fleming, 1987), studies based on other measures also report freshman-senior increases in autonomy in students' interpersonal relations with their parents (Heath, 1968; Lokitz & Sprandel, 1976).

Thus, the weight of evidence tends to support the proposition that students gain greater independence from parents than from peers during the college years. The research on this point is not yet conclusive, however.

Authoritarianism, Dogmatism, and Ethnocentricism

The studies reviewed in this section deal with one or another form of narrow-mindedness. Definitions of *authoritarianism* generally include such personal descriptors as an undemocratic orientation, obedience and submissiveness toward authority, rigid adherence to rules, intolerance of ambiguity and points of view contrary to one's own, and general anti-intellectualism.[3] *Dogmatism* (see Rokeach, 1960) is a somewhat broader term that reflects the closed character of an individual's belief systems, nonreceptivity to relevant information, and inability to evaluate and act on the inherent merits of information, unaffected by irrelevant considerations originating inside or outside the individual. The term *ethnocentricism* typically denotes an individual's tendency to view social interactions in terms of in-groups and out-groups, where in-groups are seen as dominant and perceptions of individuals' characteristics are determined on the basis of stereotypic positive or negative images of the groups to which they belong. The ethnocentric individual tends to be submissive to the in-group and hostile to the out-group.

As will become evident shortly, a significant amount of the research conducted in these areas has focused on changes in authoritarianism and employed the Omnibus Personality Inventory (OPI) (Heist & Yonge, 1968), particularly the autonomy and social maturity scales. "High scorers [on the autonomy scale] show a tendency to be independent of authority as traditionally imposed through social institutions" (Heist & Yonge, 1968, p. 4). They also tend to "feel that disobedience to government is sometimes justified, and do not favor strict enforcement of all laws no matter what the consequences" (Heist & Yonge, 1968, p. 6). "High scorers [on the social maturity scale] tend to be uncompulsive, nonpunitive, independent, and not subject to feelings of victimization. . . . Low scorers tend to be more judgmental, intolerant, and conventional in their thinking" (Trent & Medsker, 1968, p. 149). Because of the substantive similarity between the content of these scales and generally accepted definitions of authoritarianism described above and for other empirical reasons,[4] results obtained by means of the OPI autonomy and social maturity scales are reviewed here as reflecting students' authoritarian orientations despite the fact that the scales' labels imply that somewhat different traits are being measured.

The only multi-institutional (or otherwise large-scale) studies to investigate four-year changes in students' levels of authoritarianism are those of Chickering and his colleagues (Chickering, 1969, 1971b, 1974b; Chickering & Kuper, 1971; Chickering & McCormick, 1973; Chickering, McDowell, & Campagna, 1969); Clark, Heist, McConnell, Trow, and Yonge (1972); and Trent and Medsker (1968). (See also Trent & Craise, 1967; Walizer & Herriott, 1971.) Chickering's analyses are based primarily on longitudinal data from thirteen institutions (or subsets of them) that were part of his Project on Student Development, a five-year research project begun in 1965 (Chickering, 1969). Those of Clark and his colleagues draw on cross-sectional data from eight institutions (also studied in the late 1960s). Although these institutions were not chosen to be representative of higher educational institutions in America, they are quite diverse with respect to student and institutional characteristics. Trent and Medsker followed some 10,000 1959 high school graduates from sixteen communities throughout the United States over a five-year period. All three of these projects used the Omnibus Personality Inventory.

Virtually without exception, the analyses from these three projects found statistically significant changes away from authoritarian thinking from freshman to senior year. Our synthesis of data reported by Clark, Heist, McConnell, Trow, and Yonge (1972) and by Chickering (1974b) indicates that the average magnitudes of the four-year increases on the autonomy scale (indicating gains in nonauthoritarianism) were .72 of a standard deviation (26 percentile points) in the Chickering data and .80 of a standard deviation (29 percentile points) among the students studied by Clark and his colleagues. Evidence from several single-institution studies of four-year change, also based on the OPI's autonomy scale, suggests that increases in autonomy may even be somewhat higher (Bennett & Hunter, 1985; Kuh, 1976; Yonge & Regan, 1975). The average four-year increase in OPI autonomy scores across five studies, regardless of sample size or number of institutions, was .88 of a standard deviation (31 percentile points), with the range from .51 to 1.52 standard deviations (19 to 43 percentile points).

Similar results, both in direction and in magnitude, are reported in studies that used OPI social maturity scores (Korn, 1968; Ellis, 1968; Levin, 1967; Trent & Golds, 1967; Trent & Medsker, 1968).[5] Our synthesis of data reported in these studies indicates an average increase in nonauthoritarianism (across eight groups) of .90 of a standard deviation (about 32 percentile points). Except for Levin, these same studies gathered data on four-year change on the California F-scale measure of authoritarianism. Our synthesis of these changes (averaged across eleven groups) indicates a decrease in authoritarianism of .73 of a standard deviation (-27 percentile points). Caution is warranted, however, since the Trent and Golds and Trent and Medsker studies in some instances drew on the same data base. Nonetheless, the similarities of the magnitudes of the four-year changes on these scales and across multiple samples are striking.

Our synthesis of Korn's (1968, p. 167) and Ellis's (1968, pp. 327–330) data on four-year changes on the E (ethnocentricism) scale among men and women attending the University of California, Berkeley, and Stanford University indicates a drop (averaged across the four groups) of .45 SD (−17 percentile points). No studies were identified that would permit responsible estimation of the magnitudes of the changes in dogmatism. Although data to estimate effect sizes were not reported, a number of single-institution or small-scale studies that used the OPI's autonomy and/or social maturity scales, the California F scale or E scale, or other measures report evidence substantially consistent in their indications of declines (over varying periods of time) from freshman-year scores in authoritarianism, dogmatism, and/or ethnocentricism (Alfert & Suczek, 1971; Ayers & Turck, 1976; Baker, 1976a, 1976b; Brawer, 1973; Cade, 1979; Elton, 1969, 1971; Elton & Rose, 1969; Feldman & Weiler, 1976; Finnie, 1970; Freedman, 1967; Katz & Associates, 1968; Lacy, 1978; Newcomb, Brown, Kulik, Reimer, & Revelle, 1971; Ogle & Dodder, 1978; Rich & Jolicoeur, 1978; Schmidt, 1970, 1971; Suczek, 1972).

Regrettably, there is little evidence upon which to base a firm conclusion concerning the timing of changes in these general areas. Feldman and Newcomb (1969, pp. 96–104) concluded that there was more evidence for gradual change over the college years than for greater changes in some years than in others. The research completed in the last twenty years sheds little light on this question. Most studies in this and other areas of student change did not examine variations in the rate of change over the college years. Some evidence does *suggest* that changes may be greater in the first two years of college than in the later years. Data reported by Chickering, McDowell, and Campagna (1969) and by Newcomb, Brown, Kulik, Reimer, and Revelle (1971) on the degree of change in these areas over two years (gains of .73 and .68 SD in OPI autonomy scores and a decline of .66 SD on an "authoritarian cluster" of scales), when compared to the estimates of four-year change in authoritarianism reported earlier, suggest that most or all of the change away from authoritarianism occurs in the first two years of college. Clearly, however, two studies do not constitute conclusive evidence, and more extensive and current research will be needed before this proposition can be accepted with confidence.

Intellectual Orientation

In Chapter Four, we reviewed studies that examined changes in students' general cognitive skills (communication skills, Piagetian formal reasoning, critical thinking, postformal reasoning, and so on). In this section, we examine another dimension of intellectual change, that which deals more with students' general intellectual orientation to their world. The term *intellectual orientation* is used here to characterize students' intellectual approaches to their world, including their intellectual curiosity, inclination to be skeptical and critical of information, analytical orientation, and intellectual flexibility and complexity. The studies reviewed here examined students' general disposition to be inquisitive, reflective, rational, logical, analytical, critical, and skeptical.

As in the preceding section, much of the research in this area has relied on the use of several scales from the Omnibus Personality Inventory (Heist & Yonge, 1968). Such studies typically involve one or more of six OPI scales: thinking introversion (TI), theoretical orientation (TO), estheticism (Es), complexity (Co), autonomy (Au), and religious orientation (RO). Because of these scales' content, the evidence from the autonomy scale is discussed in this chapter with other measures of authoritarianism (see note 4), and evidence from the aestheticism and religious orientation scales is reviewed in Chapter Seven. In this section we focus on the evidence from the remaining three OPI scales and other sources.

Before doing so, however, it may be helpful to briefly describe the general content of these three OPI scales.

Thinking Introversion (TI): [High scorers] are characterized by a liking for reflective thought and academic activities. . . . Their thinking is less dominated by immediate conditions and situations, or by commonly accepted ideas, than that of thinking extroverts [low scorers]. Most thinking extroverts show a preference for overt action and tend to evaluate ideas on the basis of their practical, immediate applications, or to entirely reject or avoid dealing with ideas and abstractions.
Theoretical Orientation (TO): This scale measures an interest in, or orientation to, a more restricted range of ideas than is true of TI. High scorers indicate a preference for dealing with theoretical concerns and problems and for using the scientific method in thinking; . . . High scorers are generally logical, analytical, and critical in their approach to problems and situations.
Complexity (Co): This measure reflects an experimental and flexible orientation rather than a fixed way of viewing and organizing phenomena. High scorers are tolerant of ambiguities and uncertainties; they are fond of novel situations and ideas. Most persons high on this dimension prefer to deal with complexity, as opposed to simplicity, and very high scorers are disposed to seek out and to enjoy diversity and ambiguity [Heist & Yonge, 1968, p. 4].

As with the research on authoritarianism, dogmatism, and ethnocentricism, the best evidence on changes in students' general intellectual orientations comes from four major sources: Chickering and colleagues' thirteen-college study (Chickering, 1974b; Chickering & Kuper, 1971; Chickering & McCormick, 1973; Chickering, McDowell, & Campagna, 1969), the eight-college study done at the University of California, Berkeley's Center for Research and Development in Higher Education (Clark, Heist, McConnell, Trow, & Yonge, 1972; McConnell, 1972; Wilson, Gaff, Dienst, Wood, & Bavry, 1975), Trent and Medsker's (1968) classic five-year longitudinal study of high school seniors who graduated in 1959 (see also Trent & Craise, 1967), and samples of "West Coast" institutions and National Merit Scholars analyzed and reported by Trent and Golds (1967). Excepting Trent and Medsker (1968), we identified no nationally representative study of general intellectual disposition conducted in the last two decades.

Virtually without exception, the OPI-based evidence indicates consistent but modest increases in students' intellectual orientations during the college years. On the basis of change estimates averaged across ten groups in four national studies (Chickering, 1974b; Clark, Heist, McConnell, Trow, & Yonge, 1972; Trent & Golds, 1967; Trent & Medsker, 1968), our analyses indicate four-year average increases of .34 of a standard deviation (13 percentile points) in thinking introversion and .36 of a standard deviation (14 percentile points) in complexity. Interestingly, the gains in thinking orientation tended with reasonable consistency to be only one-half to one-third the size of the gains on the other two scales: an average increase of only .19 of a standard deviation (8 percentile points) across the groups in these studies. No particular reason for these differences in scale results is readily apparent.

Whatever the reason, it is clear that students as a group consistently increase modestly in their general intellectual orientations during the college years when tested by means of these three OPI scales. McConnell (1972) and Wilson, Gaff, Dienst, Wood, and Bavry (1975) report similar and consistent evidence based on these and other OPI scales aggregated to form "Intellectual Disposition Categories" (IDCs). Wilson and his colleagues found that of the 1,033 students in their sample, 47 percent increased one IDC or more over the four years, but 53 percent remained the same or declined. With some exceptions (Brawer, 1973; Snyder, 1968), results from a number of smaller-scale investigations, also based on these OPI scales, provide evidence substantially consistent with that of the large-scale studies (Bennett & Hunter, 1985; Elton, 1969, 1971; Feldman & Weiler, 1976; Kuh, 1976; Lacy, 1978; Newcomb, Brown, Kulik, Reimer, & Revelle, 1971; Welty, 1976; Yonge & Regan, 1975). Similarly consistent evidence (with the exception of Tomlinson-Keasey, Williams, & Eisert, 1978; and Schmidt, 1970, 1971) is provided by additional studies that examined change over varying periods of time using measures of intellectual disposition other than the OPI (Barton, Cattell, & Vaughan, 1973; Burton & Polmantier, 1973; Eisert & Tomlinson-Keasey, 1978; Friedlander & Pace, 1981; Hummel-Rossi, 1976; Magnarella, 1975; Regan, 1969; Schmidt, 1971; Smith, 1971).[6]

We identified only one study that shed any light on the timing of change in intellectual disposition over the traditional four-year period of college. Our analysis of data in Chickering, McDowell, and Campagna (1969) indicates one-year increases of .12 and .18 of a standard deviation (5 and 7 percentile points) in thinking introversion and complexity, respectively, with gains of .18 and .24 of a standard deviation (7 and 9 points) over a two-year period. Comparing these effect sizes with the four-year change estimates of .34 and .36 SD reported earlier, one might speculate that perhaps half to two-thirds of the gains occur in the first two years. While this finding is consistent with that of Lehmann (1963) in terms of changes in students' critical thinking abilities, the body of evidence on this point can hardly be characterized as convincing. Although there is little on the point, it is entirely possible that these rather modest group gains mask more substantial individual changes, both upward and downward.

Interpersonal Relations

Changes in individuals' self and relational systems such as those discussed in Chapter Five and here are complex and interconnected. The self is not defined in isolation but at least partially by one's interactions with others. Perceptions of self and beliefs about others' perceptions of oneself shape not only individuals' internal, psychological structures but also their responses to and interactions with their external social world. In this section, we review the research literature that deals with changes in students' social adjustment and interpersonal relations.

Only Chickering (1974b) reports evidence from a large-scale study of four-year changes in students' social and interpersonal interactions. His study of thirteen small colleges relied heavily on the Omnibus Personality Scale, and his evidence on interpersonal relations comes from that measure's social extroversion (SE) scale. High SE scores indicate a preference for being with people, seeking social activities, and deriving satisfaction from them, while the low-scoring introvert tends to withdraw from such social interaction. The students in the institutions studied by Chickering showed no freshman-senior change in their interest in being with people or in seeking out and deriving pleasure from social activities. Indeed, our analyses of data in two single-institution studies (Kuh, 1976; Yonge & Regan, 1975) indicate a *drop* in social extroversion of about .20 of a standard deviation (−8 percentile points) across the two studies. Brawer (1973) and Hatch (1970) also report declines in social extroversion during the early college years.

The meaning of such stability (possibly even declines) on this psychosocial dimension is difficult to interpret with confidence. Stability or small declines might suggest a certain developmental regression or withdrawal from other people and social activities in general, a withdrawal into oneself, and possibly greater self-centeredness rather than the social and interpersonal expansion often expected in the college years (for example, Chickering, 1969). At the same time, one might reasonably argue that the scores reflect not so much a shift toward introversion as an increase in students' interpersonal maturity, in their selectivity of friends, and in increased intimacy with that smaller circle of close friends. This latter interpretation, of course, is consistent with the successful resolution of Erikson's (1956, 1963) "intimacy versus isolation" crisis, and with Chickering's (1969) "freeing interpersonal relationships" vector, particularly the component relating to changes in the quality of intimate relations with others. It is also possible that the college experience may be anchoring these dimensions, preventing regression or decline.

Possible answers to the nature of the changes reflected by the OPI's social extroversion scores are suggested in a series of small-scale studies based on the SDTI-2 (Winston, Miller, & Prince, 1979), which constitutes another body of research dealing with freshman-senior changes in students' interpersonal relations. Of interest here is the SDTI-2's "developing mature interpersonal relations" (MIR) scale, which characterizes students' relationships with the opposite sex, mature relationships with peers, and tolerance (the capacity to respond to others as individuals rather than stereotypes). Our analyses of MIR data in four studies of freshman-to-senior changes (Greeley & Tinsley, 1988; Itzkowitz & Petrie, 1986; Jordan-Cox, 1987; Winston, Miller, & Prince, 1979) indicate average increases in developing mature interpersonal relations on the order of .16 of a standard deviation (6 percentile points). It is worth noting that the Winston, Miller, and Prince study was the only one reporting a four-year decline ($-.04$ SD) on this scale, while the estimated gains in the other three studies (each of which used a sample rather different from the others) ranged from .17 to .26 of a standard deviation. Freshman-senior increases on the MIR scale in a revised version of the SDTI-2, the Student Developmental Task and Lifestyle Inventory, or SDTLI, mentioned earlier, averaged .57 of a standard deviation (22 percentile points) among undergraduates at twenty different colleges in the United States and Canada (Winston & Miller, 1987). Still other studies, based on a considerable variety of samples and instruments and covering varying periods of time, give generally consistent evidence of increases in students' capacities for more mature interactions with their peers and others (Fisher, 1981; George & Marshall, 1972; Hanson, 1988; Hood & Mines, 1986; J. Katz, 1974; King, 1970, 1973; McArthur, 1970; Reid, 1974; Riahinejad & Hood, 1984; Rich & Jolicoeur, 1978; Schmidt, 1970, 1971; Spaeth & Greeley, 1970; Theophilides, Terenzini, & Lorang, 1984b; Withey, 1971).

When the stability of or small declines in students' OPI social extroversion scale scores are considered with the increases reported by more numerous (if smaller) studies that used other measures of students' interpersonal relations, the evidence (some of which is examined below) leads us to conclude that changes in students' interpersonal relations probably involve shifts toward more mature relations with peers and others. Fleming (1984) is a notable exception to this pattern. In her study of black students at predominantly black and predominantly white institutions, she found that the nature and degree of change depended largely upon the social context in which it occurred.

Personal Adjustment and Psychological Well-Being

As with other dimensions of students' "relational systems," a substantial portion of the literature relating to changes in students' personal adjustment and general psychological well-being during the college years is based on the Omnibus Personality Inventory, particularly the impulse expression (IE), anxiety level (AL), schizoid functioning (SF), and personal integration (PI) scales. The general conceptual relatedness of these scales has been suggested by Yonge and Regan (1975), and generally moderate correlations among the scales are given in the OPI's technical manual (Heist & Yonge, 1968, p. 50).

Only two large-scale research projects (neither of which can be considered nationally representative) dealt with changes in students' emotional adjustment: Clark and his colleagues' (1972) study of students at eight diverse institutions and Chickering and his associates' studies of thirteen small colleges (Chickering, 1969, 1971b, 1974b; Chickering & Kuper, 1971; Chickering & McCormick, 1973; Chickering, McDowell, & Campagna, 1969). Our analyses of data reported in Clark, Heist, McConnell, Trow, and Yonge, (1972) and in Chickering (1974b; Chickering & McCormick, 1973) indicate average increases on the impulse expression scale of .40 of a standard deviation (16 percentile points). High scores on this scale reflect a "readiness to express impulses and to seek gratification in thought and action . . . have an active imagination, [and] value sensual reactions and feelings"; very high scores indicate a tendency toward aggression (Heist & Yonge, 1968, p. 5). Although there is considerable variability among individual estimates, our synthesis of increases (no declines were found) in impulse expression across nine samples in five single-institution studies indicates average four-year gains of .37 of a standard deviation (14 percentile points). A comparison of these estimates of four-year change with estimated shifts of +.25 and +.41 of a standard deviation on the same scale over a one- and a two-year period, respectively (Chickering, McDowell, & Campagna, 1969), suggests the possibility that half or more of any shift in impulse expression may occur in the first two years of college, stabilizing in the latter two years. Evidence consistent with this possibility is reported by Newcomb, Brown, Kulik, Reimer, and Revelle (1971).

With some exceptions (such as Brawer, 1973), smaller-scale studies, covering varying periods of time, also report evidence of increases in students' willingness to express impulses (Bennett & Hunter, 1985; Cade, 1979; Freedman, 1967; Offer & Offer, 1975; Snyder, 1968; Suczek, 1972). Nichols (1967), in a study of National Merit Scholarship finalists, also reports declines on measures of superego strength (.26 and .38 of a standard deviation [−10 and −15 percentile points] among males and females, respectively) and deferred gratification (.36 and .33 of a standard deviation; −14 and −13 percentile points among males and females, respectively).

As with social extroversion, however, the interpretation of these changes is ambiguous. Gains might reflect a general increase in students' comfort with normal and natural feelings and concomitant gains in self-confidence, spontaneity, and self-esteem, as well as an emergent personal identity. Conversely, one might infer that observed gains reflect declines in self-control and a shift toward aggressiveness, disruptiveness, rebellion, hostility, or other form of social deviancy. Indeed, the IE scale correlates negatively with the self-control, socialization, responsibility, and good impression scales of the California Psychological Inventory (Heist & Yonge, 1968, p. 31). The antisocial tendencies tapped by this scale are apparent primarily in people who score two or more standard deviations above the mean. Thus, caution is advised in inferring developmentally or socially desirable changes from the results summarized above.[7]

Some insight into the nature of these psychological changes may also be gained by considering the shifts in scores on other, related scales. Freshman-senior changes in score on the OPI's schizoid functioning scale averaged across eight samples on ten campuses (Clark, Heist, McConnell, Trow, & Yonge, 1972; Korn, 1968; Ellis, 1968), according to our estimates, indicate declines of about .41 and .45 of a standard deviation (-16 and -17 percentile points) among men and women, respectively. Higher scores indicate social alienation, with feelings of isolation, loneliness, hostility, and aggression. Chickering's (1974b) data, however, indicate much more modest freshman-senior declines in students' sense of isolation, tension, and difficulty in adjusting to their social environment, as reflected on the OPI's anxiety level scale. (Higher scores on this scale reflect *less* anxiety, nervousness, or difficulty in adjusting to one's social environment.) Our synthesis indicates an increase of only .10 of a standard deviation. Three studies that used the anxiety level scale indicate somewhat larger reductions in anxiety levels over the four years of college (Bennett & Hunter, 1985; Kuh, 1976; Yonge & Regan, 1975), although only the Yonge and Regan study was based on a sample of more than 175 students.

Consistent with the above findings, Chickering's (1974b) data on the OPI's personal integration scale (on which high scorers admit to *few* behaviors or attitudes that characterize socially alienated or emotionally disturbed individuals) suggest an average increase of .41 of a standard deviation (16 percentile points). Studies by Kuh (1976) and Yonge and Regan (1975) also reflected freshman-senior gains, but these increases were about half the size of those indicated by Chickering's (1974b) data. Taken together, these estimates of average change in impulse expression ($+.37$ SD), schizoid functioning ($-.43$ SD), and personal integration ($+.41$ SD) are strikingly similar to the estimated overall change in psychological well-being ($+.40$ SD) reported by Bowen (1977, p. 134). With one exception (Cade, 1979), other smaller-scale studies that used the personal integration scale or other similar scale scores over varying periods of time also report increases in students' self-understanding and control of emotions and gains in personal integration over varying periods of time (Brawer, 1973; Bennett & Hunter, 1985; Heath, 1968; Hood & Jackson, 1986b; King, 1970, 1973; Newcomb, Brown, Kulik, Reimer, & Revelle, 1971).

Our analyses of one- and two-year changes in personal integration scale data from Chickering, McDowell, and Campagna (1969) suggest, as they did with the impulse expression scale, that perhaps half to two-thirds of these changes may occur in the first two years of college (+.24 and +.31 standard deviations after one and two years, respectively). This speculation, however, awaits more rigorous verification.

Glenn and Weaver (1981) and Witter, Okun, Stock, and Haring (1984) provide strong evidence of educational-related increases in generalized psychological well-being. However, because their data were collected primarily in the postcollege years, these studies are discussed in detail in Chapter Twelve. Several single-institution studies (Hearn, 1980; Martin & Light, 1984; Schubert, 1975b) also provide evidence of increases in students' general psychological well-being during the college years.

Given this evidence, let us now return to the question of whether the freshman-senior increases in impulsivity reported earlier reflect developmentally and socially desirable change. From the gains on the OPI's impulse expression scale, together with the evidence of declines in seniors' social alienation (for example, schizoid functioning) and increases in general psychological well-being, we conclude that the weight of evidence suggests general increases in areas most people would consider desirable psychosocial change during the college years. The inverse relation between impulse expression and schizoid functioning, together with the decline in anxiety levels and gains in personal integration and general psychological well-being, is, we believe, generally indicative of healthy impulsivity, spontaneity, and individual emotional expression. It is worth recalling, however, that changes in this area during college may vary considerably, depending upon the context and the characteristics of the individuals involved (see the discussion of black identity formation in Chapter Five and Lamont, 1979).

Maturity and General Personal Development

Several studies have examined students' psychosocial development not in specific areas but as more globally conceived. In the only "national" study of students' more generalized personal development, Pace (1990) analyzed data from a nonrandom (but probably reasonably representative) 25,427 undergraduates at seventy-four colleges and universities between 1983 and 1986. The data were accumulated from responses to his College Student Experience Questionnaire (CSEQ). Pace found that between 62 and 81 percent of his respondents (depending upon the kind of institution they attended) reported making "substantial progress" in "developing [their] own values and ethical standards," in "understanding [themselves]—[their] abilities, interests, and personality," and in "understanding other people and [in] the ability to get along with different kinds of people" (p. 58).

Pascarella, Terenzini, and their associates report a series of studies based on data from three large research universities (two residential and one commuter) conducted over nearly a decade with a half-dozen independent samples of students who were followed up over varying periods of time. The dependent measure in these studies, with minor variations, was a factorially derived measure of "personal development," consisting of items that ask respondents to report the amount of progress (on a 1–4 scale, from "none" to "a great deal") they believe they have made during the academic year just ending. Progress is reported in such areas as developing a clearer understanding of oneself, developing interpersonal skills, increased openness to new ideas, a growing sense of self-reliance and personal discipline, and a clearer idea of abilities and career goals. Without exception, students in these studies reported gains on this measure of personal change over varying periods of time (Pascarella & Terenzini, 1978, 1980b, 1981; Pascarella, Duby, Terenzini, & Iverson, 1983; Terenzini & Pascarella, 1980a; Terenzini, Pascarella, & Lorang, 1982; Terenzini, Theophilides, & Lorang, 1984b; Terenzini & Wright, 1987b, 1987c). The magnitudes of these changes, however, cannot be estimated in a way that would be meaningfully comparable to those reported elsewhere in this book. Similar evidence of increases in perceived maturity are reported in other single-institution studies, such as Benezet (1976), Shields (1972), and Zirkle and Hudson (1975).

Perhaps the best known and most sustained series of studies of changes in students' "maturity" are those of Douglas Heath. On the basis of an earlier study (Heath, 1965) and a synthesis of what twenty-five educational philosophers throughout history have said about the goals of a liberal education, Heath (1968, 1977b, 1978) developed a comprehensive, dimensional model of college student "maturity." For Heath, maturing is a process that takes place in four major "personality sectors" (cognitive skills, self-concept, values, and interpersonal relations) and, within each of these sectors, along five interdependent dimensions: symbolization, allocentricism, integration, stability, and autonomy. (See Chapter Two for a more detailed description of Heath's model.)

Heath's (1968) most important report of research on maturity during the college years was based on a cross-sectional study of 25 percent samples of two Haverford College graduating classes ($n = 24$ each) and a 20 percent sample ($n = 25$) of freshmen, who were followed up one year later. His data collections have all been multifaceted, based on standard psychological tests, projective and semiprojective measures, and measures and questionnaires specially designed to examine change in the twenty specific sectors of his model. Heath drew three general conclusions from his intensive analyses: (1) seniors were more mature than freshmen, and both groups were more mature than they were upon entry to Haverford; (2) seniors reported greater advances toward maturity after four years than did the freshmen after one year; and (3) the rate of maturing varies across the different sectors of the personality. Interestingly, students believed themselves to have matured even more than Heath's objective data indicated. Unfortunately, data that would permit estimation of the magnitude of the increases in maturity were not reported.

Heath's students matured most in their attitudes about themselves, their interpersonal relations, and their values and least in cognitive and intellective skills. This finding is consistent with the relative magnitudes of changes reviewed earlier in this chapter in intellectual orientation and, say, autonomy and independence or authoritarianism and dogmatism. However, the finding is contrary to findings reported by studies reviewed in Chapters Three and Four of this volume. The differences in these findings may be related to the specificity of the cognitive skills measured and reviewed in the earlier chapters. Seniors ranked gains in the integration of intellectual skills, awareness and understanding of themselves and the development of a more conscious self-concept, and integration and other-centered maturation of interpersonal skills as the three areas of greatest change during their college years. Heath (1968, p. 133) identified the progressive psychosocial integration of both seniors and freshmen as "the most important maturational change in college," a process that affected all other sectors of the personality in different but important ways. Maturation occurred "more in one sector of [the students'] personality than in another at different times, depending upon the demands of the environment and their readiness to respond to those demands" (p. 118).

Heath (1968) concluded that the freshman year was particularly important, a conclusion reached by Lehmann (1963) and consistent with the evidence reported in several areas above. The pattern of subsequent growth, Heath found, was set in the freshman year, possibly even the first few months of college. He considered much of the later growth a movement toward greater stabilization and integration of growth patterns established in the earlier college years.

Because Heath's (1968) research was based on a small sample of men from a single, highly selective liberal arts college and because his freshman-senior comparisons were cross-sectional rather than longitudinal, care must be taken not to overgeneralize his findings to college students at large. His results are, however, generally consistent with those of other researchers who have studied larger samples on different campuses around the country. Regrettably, we identified only two studies by other authors who used Heath's model in dealing with change in college students (Erwin, 1983; Jones, 1987). Jones concluded from his review of the published literature "that no one has independently tested the model empirically" (p. 206). The systemic complexity of Heath's model, some of its terminology, and the multiple measures needed to operationalize it may have deterred other researchers from adopting it.

Net Effects of College

Autonomy, Independence, and Locus of Control

Whether the observed gains in personal independence and autonomy are in fact due to the college experience, to normal maturation, or to other influences remains an open question. We identified no studies of net college effects based on anything resembling a nationally representative sample. In the largest study in this area, Barton, Cattell, and Vaughan (1973) focused on 573 subjects recruited from high schools in three major New Zealand cities. Of these subjects, 355 went on to college and 218 went directly to work. Both groups had a mean age of eighteen years at the time of the first testing in 1965. At this time there were no differences between the groups on a measure of independence. Five years later, however, respondents who went on to college showed no change, while those who went straight into a job showed a significant drop from their original scores. The authors speculate that these findings may reflect employed respondents' increased marital obligations or the nature of their low-status jobs. If this is the case, then the effect of college attendance on postsecondary school levels of autonomy and independence would appear to be an anchoring one, while high school graduates who do not go on to college decline in these areas. In any event, it is not possible to attribute these findings to educational attainment with great confidence inasmuch as various alternative explanations (socioeconomic status, cognitive development, or other personality traits) were untested or uncontrolled.

Several studies that used the SDTI-2 found generally consistent, significant, and positive relationships between academic class level and scores on overall and subtask scales of that measure's developing autonomy scale (Greeley & Tinsley, 1988; Itzkowitz & Petrie, 1986, 1988; Straub & Rodgers, 1986; Winston, Miller, & Prince, 1979). All of these studies, however, were cross-sectional, employed simple one-way analysis of variance, and controlled neither for precollege autonomy levels nor for other factors that might be associated with changes in autonomy scores. Winston, Miller, and Prince (1979) found autonomy scores unrelated to age, but Straub and Rodgers (1986) and Hood and Jackson (1986c) report contrary evidence. Hood and Jackson used the Iowa Developing Autonomy Inventory and found that autonomy scores correlated .50 and .43 with age and academic class, respectively. In none of these three studies, however, was class or age controlled while the relation between autonomy and the other variable was being tested.

The evidence on the effects of college on students' locus of control, net of other possible influences, is much more conclusive than that dealing with autonomy and independence. With one exception (Kanouse et al., 1980), studies of net college effects on locus of control indicate that college attendance has a statistically significant and positive effect on students' internality, but education's direct effect is probably quite small.

The most definitive evidence comes from Wolfle and Robertshaw (1982), who analyzed data from a subsample of 8,650 white males randomly drawn from the NLS-72 data base of seniors at 1,318 public and private high schools who were tested in 1972 and again in 1976. Wolfle and Robertshaw used a short form of Rotter's (1966) locus of control scale as a dependent measure and dichotomized postsecondary educational attainment into one category of respondents who had had no schooling beyond high school and another group who had had any postsecondary schooling from a four-year college or university or from a two-year college or vocational or technical school. Using LISREL (a sophisticated analytical procedure that controls for a variety of statistical artifacts commonly left uncontrolled), Wolfle and Robertshaw also held constant students' precollege vocabulary, reading, and math ability; socioeconomic status; and 1972 locus of control status. They found that postsecondary attendance and 1976 locus of control correlated .252, but only about one-fifth (.054) of this was the direct effect of college attendance on locus of control. The remainder was due to other sources—particularly 1972 level of locus of control—upon which educational attainment and 1976 locus of control were mutually dependent. Results consistent with these are reported by Smart, Ethington, and McLaughlin (undated) and by Knox, Lindsay, and Kolb (1988). These studies also used NLS-72 data but followed subjects over seven and fourteen years, respectively. Knox, Lindsay, and Kolb report regression coefficients (estimated effect sizes net of several background characteristics) for different levels of postsecondary educational attainment ranging from .028 for less than two years to .070 for holding an advanced degree. After fourteen years, having two or more years of postsecondary education had the largest impact (.083) on locus of control. While all of these studies left occupational variables uncontrolled, their inclusion could only have reduced the already small educational effect sizes. Thus, it would appear that while college may have a statistically significant positive impact on internal locus of control, the magnitude of that impact is small.

Smart, Ethington, and McLaughlin (undated) also found that the pattern of change was not the same across groups that varied by postsecondary educational attainment. For respondents with no postsecondary education, the rate of increase in locus of control[8] was greater than that of all others in the first (post–high school) interval. Yet four to seven years later, their rate of increase in internality was the lowest of all groups.

It is noteworthy that these changes toward internality, net of other salient variables, were consistent (if small) across the two-decade period covered by this review. Moreover, during the first of those decades, the intra-individual shifts appear to have occurred simultaneously with an inter-individual trend in scores on Rotter's (1966) I-E scale among successive cohorts in the general student population toward greater *external* control. This phenomenon is perhaps related to a sense of loss of control associated with the war in Vietnam and with Watergate (Phares, 1976; Schneider, 1971). Given the ambiguous evidence on whether age and locus of control are related (Lefcourt, 1982), these contrary intra- and inter-individual shifts, taken together, constitute strong evidence of the presence of college effects independent of changes in the population.

Authoritarianism, Dogmatism, and Ethnocentrism

In the late 1950s and early 1960s, Walter Plant and his colleagues conducted an extended series of what have become classic studies of the net effects of college on changes in students' levels of authoritarianism, dogmatism, and ethnocentrism (Plant, 1958a, 1965; Plant & Telford, 1966; Telford & Plant, 1968; for related studies, see McCullers & Plant, 1964; Plant, 1958b; Plant & Minium, 1967). The substantive significance of these studies is that except for Plant (1958a), they indicate that the declines consistently reported in other studies of students' levels of authoritarianism, dogmatism, and/or ethnocentrism were also observable among groups of age-mates who did *not* go to college. Plant concluded that the reported changes were probably due to general personality changes under way among college-age individuals and were independent of educational attainment level.

As Trent and Medsker (1968, p. 156) have pointed out, however, Plant's conclusion rests on tests of pre- and posttest differences *within* groups that differed in educational attainment. While all groups showed statistically significant declines (Plant, 1965; Plant & Telford, 1966; Telford & Plant, 1968), leading to the conclusion of general maturational changes, the differences in the *amounts* of change across groups were never tested, despite their sometimes substantial size and the general tendency for the amount of change to have been positively related to educational attainment.

Only the Trent and Medsker (1968) study addressed the net effects of college on changes in authoritarianism and dogmatism using a nationally representative sample. Analyzing the responses of 1959 high school graduates to the Omnibus Personality Inventory's nonauthoritarianism and social maturity scales, Trent and Medsker compared the changes among 1,301 respondents who persisted in college throughout the four-year period with those of 922 continuously employed individuals. College men and women were significantly more nonauthoritarian than their employed counterparts in 1959 (by 3.2 and 3.7 standard score points for men and women, respectively). Moreover, four years later the differences between the groups were even greater: more than 10 and 12 points, over a full standard deviation (34 and 38 percentile points), respectively. While the college groups had increased their scores by 6 and 8 points (for men and women, respectively) over the period, their employed peers' scores had decreased ($-.99$ and $-.32$ standard score points, both nonsignificant) (see also Trent & Craise, 1967). Similar differences were observed in the groups' social maturity scores: Although both groups increased at statistically significant levels, the rate of increase for the college group was significantly greater than that of the employed group. These differences were observed after controlling for academic ability and socioeconomic status, although initial OPI scores were not controlled. Given that the college students' scores were initially higher than the scores of their employed peers, these findings are at odds with any expectations of regression to the mean, providing further support for the hypothesis of net college effects. Evidence consistent with the net college effect hypothesis is also found in the twelve-institution study conducted by Rich and Jolicoeur (1978).

Intellectual Orientation

Trent and Medsker (1968), using the thinking introversion (TI) and complexity (Co) scales of the OPI, also provide the most definitive evidence of net college impact on students' intellectual orientation. The TI scale reflects an interest in reflective and abstract thinking and in thought that is less dominated by immediate conditions or practical considerations. High scores on the Co scale reflect an experimental and flexible orientation toward reality rather than a fixed way of viewing and organizing phenomena. Trent and Medsker contrasted the scores on these two scales of 1,300 individuals who had persisted in college for four years after high school graduation with those of age-mates who had been employed full-time since graduation. Persisting college men and women showed statistically significant, if modest, gains (.31 and .35 of a standard deviation, or 12 and 14 percentile points, for men and women, respectively) in reflective thinking (TI). The college women also gained significantly over four years in their interest in inquiry and tolerance for ambiguity (Co), although the college men showed no changes on this scale. By comparison and with one exception, those who were continuously employed full-time over the four years after high school showed statistically significant declines (a range of $-.07$ to $-.29$ across sexes) in their intellectual dispositions. The exception was employed men, who gained in their interest in reflective thinking over the period at a rate only slightly lower than that of their male college counterparts (.23 versus .31 of a standard deviation, or 9 versus 12 percentile points). The declines among employed individuals were particularly sharp on the complexity scale ($-.29$ and $-.20$ of a standard deviation, or -11 and -8 percentile points, for males and females, respectively). Declines on both scales among women who became homemakers and had had no outside work experience were greater than those of any other group of women (including groups who had any combination of college, work, and/or homemaking).

Thus, over a four-year period, those who went on to college, as a group, increased in their intellectual dispositions, while those who went to work tended to show less tolerance for ambiguity and less interest in intellectual inquiry. Statistical tests indicate that these differences in change rates (with the exception of the males on the TI scale) are all statistically significant. Other tests indicate that these difference tend to persist even when intellectual disposition scores at time of high school graduation, socioeconomic status, and ability are taken into account. Analyses of students who attended college for varying amounts of time produced results consistent with those described above, indicating positive net college effects on intellectual disposition. Generally similar results are reported by Barton, Cattell, and Vaughan (1973) and by Friedlander and Pace (1981).

Interpersonal Relations

The evidence on the net effects of college on student abilities to interact in mature ways with their peers and others is mixed, methodologically weak, and thus inconclusive. A dozen studies contain evidence germane to this point. Six of them suggest a positive relation between academic class level and increases in the maturity of students' interpersonal relationships (Friedlander & Pace, 1981; George & Marshall, 1972; Hood, 1984; Hood & Jackson, 1986a; Itzkowitz & Petrie, 1988; Jordan-Cox, 1987). Three reports found no relationship (Greeley & Tinsley, 1988; Straub & Rodgers, 1986; Winston, Miller, & Prince, 1979). The other three studies (one based on our own analyses of data reported) produced mixed results (Itzkowitz & Petrie, 1986; Kuh, 1976; Yonge & Regan, 1975). More important in determining the presence (or absence) of college effects net of other student characteristics, none of these studies controlled for any precollege student traits, leaving amount of postsecondary education confounded with age and normal maturation. Moreover, many of these studies were based on relatively small samples, and all were conducted at single institutions, from which generalizations to a national population would be tenuous at best. Thus, little is known with any degree of confidence about the net effects of college on students' development of mature interpersonal relations.

Personal Adjustment and Psychological Well-Being

A substantial body of evidence based on national samples indicates that educational attainment is positively related to psychological well-being, although the magnitude of education's effects appears to be slight, if statistically significant. Because these studies examined psychological well-being during the postcollege years, however, they are discussed in Chapter Twelve. Only a handful of single-institution studies have addressed the question of net college effects. With one exception (Hood & Jackson, 1986b), these studies also lend support to the conclusion that education is reliably, if modestly, related to general psychological well-being (Martin & Light, 1984; Schubert, 1975b), although the studies were not based on rigorous designs or analytical procedures.

Maturity and General Personal Development

No studies were identified with samples or designs strong enough to support even tentative conclusions about the effects of educational attainment on students' personal development or changes in levels of maturity net of normal maturation or other potentially confounding influences. Most studies dealing with change in this area employed longitudinal, freshman-senior designs in which all subjects received equal exposure to the influences of college.

Between-College Effects

Autonomy, Independence, and Locus of Control

We identified only one study that used a national data base and dealt with the effects of institutional characteristics on students' independence from parents or peers. Knox, Lindsay, and Kolb (1988) analyzed data from 7,500 participants in the NLS-72 study who had attended some type of postsecondary institution and were followed up periodically over the next fourteen years. Net of race, sex, parental socioeconomic status, academic abilities, and precollege locus of control, the 1986 internality level was found to be positively and significantly related to institutional cohesion (a factorially derived measure based on the proportion of freshmen on campus, the "full-timeness" of the student body, and the proportion of out-of-state freshmen), the proportion of freshmen working, and institutional selectivity (median SAT score). The magnitudes of these effects were quite modest, however, with beta weights ranging from .077 to .103.

In a separate analysis, Knox, Lindsay, and Kolb (1988) also examined differential institutional effects by means of the nine-category Carnegie Foundation typology of colleges and universities. Controlling for the same student characteristics as in their other analysis, these investigators found internal locus of control to be higher among individuals who attended most types of postsecondary institutions than among high school graduates, but no one type showed any distinctive amount of influence over the others. Only attendance at (Carnegie classification type) Comprehensive Colleges and Universities-II (those that enroll 1,500–2,500 full-time students, more than half of whom graduate in occupational or professional disciplines) or, interestingly, Liberal Arts I (highly selective) institutions was *un*related to higher internality when compared to those whose formal education ended with high school.

Authoritarianism, Dogmatism, and Ethnocentrism

The evidence on between-college effects in the areas of authoritarianism, dogmatism, and ethnocentrism comes from three major research projects: Trent and Medsker's (1968), Clark, Heist, McConnell, Trow, and Yonge's (1972), and Chickering's study of thirteen small colleges (Chickering, 1969, 1971b, 1974b; Chickering, McDowell, & Campagna, 1969; Chickering & McCormick, 1973). These studies are virtually unanimous in finding statistically significant declines in measures of authoritarianism (largely OPI based) at all kinds of institutions over varying periods of time. There is less agreement, however, on whether differences exist among institutions.

Trent and Medsker (1968), while controlling academic ability and socioeconomic status, found only minor variations in freshman-senior increases on the social maturity scale across the six different types of institutions (public, nonsectarian, and church-related colleges and universities). These researchers report somewhat larger variations across institutional types on the nonauthoritarianism scale. They also found some evidence of less positive effects being associated among women (but not men) with attendance at Catholic colleges. Trent and Golds (1967) even found some evidence of increases in authoritarianism among students at Catholic colleges. Trent and Medsker, however, concluded that changes in nonauthoritarian attitudes were more closely related to the type of institution chosen and to persistence in that institution than to changes associated with the experiences at a particular kind of institution.

Clark, Heist, McConnell, Trow, and Yonge (1972) report findings essentially consistent with Trent and Medsker's (1968). However, Clark and his colleagues also report evidence suggesting some variations across institutions, depending on the liberal or conservative climate of the school. This association between institutional environment and impact on students' levels of authoritarianism is also reported by Chickering (1974b). Despite the differences among his thirteen small liberal arts colleges in their educational missions, institutional characteristics, and kinds of students enrolled, Chickering found few substantial differences in the amount or nature of change for a majority of the students across institutions (Chickering, 1974b; Chickering, McDowell, & Campagna, 1969). When students' precollege autonomy levels were controlled, however, Chickering found evidence of institutional effects on the amount of student change over both two- and four-year periods. Larger increases in autonomy were discovered on campuses with a higher proportion of nonconformist students with already high autonomy scores and where teaching practices that give ample time for classroom discussions and course assignments that require complex mental activities were more likely to be found. Increases on the autonomy scale are less likely at institutions with a practical, instrumental orientation; with a mannerly, "proper" atmosphere; and with a heavy reliance on lectures, memorization, and extrinsic motivations (Chickering, 1974b). Rich and Jolicoeur (1978) found some suggestion that declines in dogmatism were more likely on small than on large campuses, but otherwise they uncovered little evidence of any effects related to selectivity or type of control.[9]

Intellectual Orientation

It is clear that different kinds of institutions attract and enroll students with widely varying intellectual orientations. It is equally clear that there are substantial differences among institutions in the intellectual dispositions of their graduates. The limited existing evidence on change indicates quite consistently, however, that net of students' precollege intellectual orientations, the *rates* of increase in this area are approximately the same across kinds of institutions. For example, Trent and Golds (1967) found few statistically significant differences in the amount of changes in three OPI measures of intellectualism (thinking introversion, theoretical orientation, and complexity) among students attending Catholic institutions, Catholics at secular institutions, and non-Catholics at public institutions. These findings persisted when Trent and Golds corrected for ability and were observable in three independent samples, one consisting of five West Coast Catholic colleges plus one public college and one public university. The second of these was the national data base developed by Trent and Medsker (1968). The third was a sample of National Merit Scholarship winners. In virtually all instances, students at Catholic colleges matriculated with lower levels of intellectual curiosity than their Catholic and non-Catholic peers at nondenominational institutions. Four years later they were still below their peers, with the size of the differences among them having changed little, if at all.

Clark and his colleagues (Clark, Heist, McConnell, Trow, & Yonge, 1972), in their study of eight disparate institutions, and Chickering and his colleagues (Chickering, 1974b; Chickering, McDowell, & Campagna, 1969), in their thirteen-college study, report essentially the same findings. Clark and his associates also found no evidence that relatively small group gains were masking more substantial, though counterbalancing, individual changes over the college years. Moreover, between-institution differences in the percentages decreasing in intellectual curiosity disappeared when freshman-year levels were controlled.

Interpersonal Relations

Several studies report evidence gathered from multiple institutions relating to changes in the nature or maturity of students' interpersonal relations with their peers and others. For various reasons, however, most provide little evidence that can be generalized to college students en masse (Brawer, 1973; Cheatham, Slaney, & Coleman, 1990; Fleming, 1984; Itzkowitz & Petrie, 1986, 1988; Jordan-Cox, 1987; McLeish, 1970). The only national evidence is provided by Nichols (1967), who analyzed data from 297 men entering 104 different colleges and 128 women entering 86 colleges. All were National Merit Scholarship finalists. After controlling for students' precollege personality characteristics, high school rank, academic aptitude (SAT scores), and parents' education, Nichols found few college characteristics significantly related to freshman-senior changes in students' scores on a measure of dominance or extraversion (the latter reflecting sociability and some degree of status seeking). Institutional affluence was positively related to larger than predicted gains in extroversion (given precollege characteristics) among both sexes and larger than predicted gains in dominance among the women. Attending a university (private for men, public for women), in contrast to other types of institutions, was positively associated with gains in extroversion. Among women, coed liberal arts college attendance was negatively related to extroversion. Other structural characteristics (size and ability level of the study body and so on), however, were largely unrelated to changes in either sex. Certain other variables characterizing the environment of a campus appeared to have an influence net of students' background characteristics, but no clear pattern was apparent. Chickering and his associates (Chickering, 1974b; Chickering, McDowell, & Campagna, 1969) found little change in students' scores on the OPI's social extraversion scale over one-, two-, or four-year periods and only minor variations across the thirteen small colleges studied. No clear pattern was discernible. Rich and Jolicoeur (1978), in a study of twelve California colleges and universities, found no relation between the degree of change in students' interpersonal skills and institutional size, type, or selectivity.

Thus, limited evidence indicates little if any between-institution effects on students' development of mature interpersonal relations. It may well be that the development of such relations is highly individualistic and responsive to an individual's specific circumstances rather than to more global conditions or influences.

Personal Adjustment and Psychological Well-Being

A relatively small but consistent body of evidence indicates that net of various precollege characteristics, where one goes to college probably does have a differential effect upon one's personal adjustment and general psychological well-being. The literature in this area relies more on environmental characterizations of institutions, however, than on the more global structural variables typically used to differentiate among institutions.

In the largest and best-controlled study in this area, Nichols (1967) residualized National Merit Scholarship finalists' senior-year OPI scores on thirty-eight personality scales, mothers' and fathers' education, high school rank, and SAT scores. With these influences controlled, he found that the scores of both men and women on a factorially derived measure of anxiety increased at colleges where many students majored in "realistic" or intellectually oriented subjects (for example, engineering and the sciences). Men's anxiety scores decreased at institutions where majors in artistic and social fields were more dominant. Women's scores decreased at institutions with an "enterprising orientation" (those with many majors in law, political science, or history). Nichols found *no* statistically significant correlations between residualized change scores and such conventional characteristics of institutions as student body ability, size, or type of control.

Similar evidence suggesting that institutional environment or ambience is related to changes in various measures of personal adjustment or psychological well-being is reported by Chickering (1974b; Chickering & McCormick, 1973), Clark, Heist, McConnell, Trow, and Yonge (1972), and Winter, McClelland, and Stewart (1981). Chickering found that (over both a two- and a four-year period) students' OPI impulse expression (IE) scale scores were likely to increase at colleges where a large proportion of students already score high on the IE scale, where students often participate in class discussions and decisions about course content and procedures, where the amount of time invested in more complex study activities is relatively high, and where intrinsic reasons for study predominate. Taken together, the results of all these studies indicate that there probably are between-college differences in personal adjustment and psychological well-being. However, contrary to what one might expect, the differences are more likely due to environmental differences than to structural or organizational ones. Nevertheless, little can be said with confidence about which sorts of environments promote adjustment and which impede it.

Maturity and General Personal Development

Only two studies (Ewell, 1989; Pace, 1990) were identified that examined differential institutional effects on students' general personal development or maturity. Without exception, all other studies identified in this area were conducted on a single campus.

Pace (1990) analyzed aggregated (1983–1986) College Student Experience Questionnaire (CSEQ) data from more than 25,000 students at seventy-four colleges and universities, grouped into five types of institutions: research universities, doctoral universities, comprehensive colleges and universities, general liberal arts colleges, and selective liberal arts colleges. Three of his outcome measures dealt with students' reported progress in their personal development. With the exception of the selective liberal arts colleges (which had the largest percentage of students reporting "substantial progress" on all three items), Pace found virtually no differences among the other four types of institutions. He did find considerable variability in the amount of progress students reported *within* category types, indicating that *which* institution a student attends may indeed make a difference, although the *type* of institution attended probably does not.

Ewell (1989) explored the influences of four sets of institutional variables on faculty and administrators' perceptions of their institution's effectiveness in enhancing students' personal development: (1) institutional characteristics (for example, size, type of control, selectivity, curricular emphasis); (2) mission (identity, distinctiveness, degree of consensus on mission, and so forth); (3) institutional culture or environment; and (4) "institutional functioning" (degree of trust, student-faculty contact, information flow, and the like). Ewell conducted a secondary analysis of 320 four-year institutions using data from the Assessment of Performance of Colleges and Universities (APCU) survey and from the U.S. Department of Education's 1983 Higher Education General Information Survey (HEGIS). He found that both public control and the percentage of part-time students were consistently important—and negative—sources of influence on each of three one-item indicators of institutional effectiveness in promoting students' general personal development (or providing opportunities for same). The presence of a "clan" (or extended familylike) culture was also associated with each outcome measure, but on only one item did the effect persist in the presence of various "institutional functioning" variables, such as high student-faculty contact and high levels of organizational information and feedback (the sense of being kept informed). The latter two variables were identified as important mediators of perceptions of institutional effectiveness. Each set of "nonmaterial" variables (mission direction and specificity, clanlike versus hierarchical culture, organizational feedback, and student-faculty interaction) made statistically significant and unique contributions to perceptions of institutional effectiveness above and beyond such structural characteristics as size, control, selectivity, and curricular emphasis. Although the validity of Ewell's findings is open to challenge as evidence of between-college effects on students' personal development, the findings are consistent with Pace's (1990) and with the evidence in other areas of psychosocial development that suggests the importance of interpersonal contacts and institutional environments in psychosocial change among students.

Within-College Effects

With a few exceptions, studies of the within-college sources of change in students' relational systems fall into two categories: one dealing with the effects of academic majors or curricular programs or experiences and the other focusing on the effects of place of residence. Several studies examined the effects of "living-learning" centers, thus combining curricular and residential effects. In a few areas, some attention was also focused on the effects of students' membership in fraternities or sororities and students' interpersonal experiences with faculty and peers.

Autonomy, Independence, and Locus of Control

Studies that examine academic program or curricular experiences are few in number and disparate in focus. Behuniak and Gable (1981) analyzed freshman-to-senior locus of control data from more than 5,600 NLS-72 participants, but they did so without controls of any kind. They found that across six major fields, most groups showed freshman-senior increases in internality (ranging from $-.01$ to $+.18$ of a standard deviation, or 0 to 7 percentile points). Business majors showed the largest gains, and students majoring in the natural and physical sciences, mathematics, and the social sciences recorded the smallest gains. Surprisingly, however, no tests were conducted on the significance of the differences in the amount of change across the major fields. King (1973) reports that increases in internal locus of control were greater among honors program participants than among regular curriculum students, but Graffam (1967) concluded that increases in independence, net of age, were due more to the general institutional environment than to degree program (A.B. versus B.S.). Neither study controlled initial levels of autonomy or independence, however, and given the heterogeneity of these studies, little can be concluded with any confidence.

Somewhat greater clarity exists among studies that examined the effects of experimental, living-learning programs on changes in student autonomy and independence, but the picture is somewhat ambiguous. Evidence from 197 freshmen who entered the University of Michigan's Residential College (RC) in 1967 and from 410 freshmen in three different control groups indicates that while the scores of all groups on the College Student Questionnaire's family independence scale increased, gains among the RC students were more substantial, although they fell narrowly short of statistical significance after adjustment for initial level of family independence. On the peer independence scale, scores for all groups decreased, but there were no appreciable differences in adjusted scores among the groups in the amount of change. In this area, as in others, there were indications that the experimental college had a slight accentuation effect—initial differences becoming greater over time (Newcomb, Brown, Kulik, Reimer, & Revelle, 1970, 1971). Pemberton (cited in Williams & Reilly, 1972) found small increases in peer independence among the residents of a living-learning center compared to those in a conventional residence hall.

In two studies (the second a replication of the first), Goldman and Olczak (1976, 1980) found that freshmen in a living-learning center showed smaller gains (or no gains at all) on Shostrom's (1966) inner-directedness scale. It is quite possible, however, that the differences between these studies and those just discussed are artifactual, due to sample and contextual differences among the studies.[10]

We identified only two studies that specifically examined differences in changes in independence among residential and commuting students. Sullivan and Sullivan (1980) and Scott (1975) found that increases in inner-directedness occurred more often among residence hall students than among commuters or students living off campus. Straub's (1987) study of critical incidents related to the development of autonomy produced evidence consistent with this finding: Moving away from home was a prominent factor for many. None of these studies, however, controlled for precollege independence levels of other potential confounding variables (Sullivan and Sullivan controlled only for SAT scores).[11]

A small body of research has examined the effects over time of Greek fraternity and/or sorority membership on autonomy (Hughes & Winston, 1987; Miller, 1973; Wilder, Hoyt, Doren, Hauch, & Zettle, 1978; Wilder, Hoyt, Surbeck, Wilder, & Carney, 1986). The most convincing evidence is presented in the two studies of Bucknell University students by Wilder and his associates (the second study a replication of the first). In each of the seven cohorts of entering freshmen studied over the period from 1965 to 1981, Greeks were significantly lower than non-Greeks upon entry to college in both family and peer independence, as measured by the Educational Testing Service's College Student Questionnaire (CSQ). Moreover, both investigations found significantly larger freshman-senior gains among non-Greeks than among Greeks on the family independence scale. Neither study, however, recorded statistically significant differences between the groups in the amount of change on the CSQ's peer independence scale.

In the more recent Bucknell study (Wilder, Hoyt, Surbeck, Wilder, & Carney, 1986), a third group, ex-Greeks (students who had joined but then withdrew from the organization or became inactive), did show significantly greater increases in peer independence than either Greeks or non-Greeks and significantly greater gains than Greeks on the family independence scale. Wilder and his colleagues concluded that the impact of Greek membership was modest and to a large extent dependent upon how one defined "Greek membership."[12]

Caution is warranted in interpreting these and similar findings (for the conventional level of moral reasoning (for example, Keniston, 1969; Kohlberg, 1969, 1981a, 1981b; Kramer, 1968; Rest, 1979a, 1986c). If college contributes significantly to moral development beyond general age-typical experience (that is, beyond simply growing older), it should be evidenced by a greater upward shift in moral stage or by a greater proportion of postconventional (principled) reasoners among college upperclassmen than among either entering freshmen or same-age peers in the general population.

Measuring Growth in Moral Reasoning

The concept of developmental stages of moral growth as explicated by Kohlberg is a complex one and has been the subject of considerable debate (Gilligan, 1982a; Nucci & Pascarella, 1987; Shweder, Mahaptra, & Miller, 1987; Sullivan, 1977; Walker, 1984). No less complex are the problems inherent in assessing moral development. Since two instruments dominate the assessment of moral development, we will briefly describe each before turning to a review of the evidence on the influence of college. The two basic instruments used are the Moral Judgment Interview (MJI) (Colby et al., 1982; Colby, Kohlberg, Gibbs, & Lieberman, 1983) and the Defining Issues Test (DIT) (Rest, 1975, 1979c, 1983a, 1983b).

The Moral Judgment Interview that is now in use has undergone progressive revision and development over the past twenty-five years. The interview has three parallel forms. Each form consists of three hypothetical moral dilemmas followed by a series of standardized questions designed to elicit justifications for the subject's moral judgments. Scoring of the interview follows a standardized classification system designed to permit an analysis of the structure of the subject's reasoning independent of any dilemma-specific content. This scoring system yields either a global interview score in terms of estimated stage of development or a continuous scale "moral maturity" score, which is a weighted average of the total scored responses to the interview. The interrater reliability—that is, the extent to which two independent raters of the same interview arrive at the same score—is in the .84 to .98 range, while the test-retest correlations range from .96 to .99 (Colby, Kohlberg, Gibbs, & Lieberman, 1983).

In contrast to the interview format of the MJI, the Defining Issues Test is a paper and pencil test that can be group administered and quickly and objectively scored. The DIT, like the MJI, asks subjects to respond to moral dilemmas. Accompanying each dilemma are twelve issue statements that represent ways in which subjects at Levels I through III might respond. The subject is asked to indicate on a five-point scale how important each issue statement is in making a decision regarding the dilemma. On the basis of these responses, several scores are produced. The most widely used is the P-index, which is a measure of the relative importance subjects give to postconventional or principled justifications. The higher the P-index (which is expressed as a percentage), presumably the more developed the individual. As reported in Rest (1979c), average DIT reliabilities range from .78 to .81.

As perhaps indicated by the brief descriptions above, both the MJI and the DIT assess moral development in terms of one's level of moral reasoning. They are not, in and of themselves, measures of one's actual moral behavior. Nevertheless, while inconsistencies between reasoning and behavior have been found in some investigations, comprehensive reviews or discussions by Blasi (1980, 1983), Kohlberg (1981a, 1981b), Rest (1983a, 1983b), Turiel and Smetana (1984), and Turiel (1983) suggest a significant link between moral reasoning score and such behaviors as resistance to cheating, helping behavior, and civil disobedience. Evidence regarding this relationship as it applies to college students is presented in more detail later in the chapter.

Change During College

It is unlikely that increased sensitivity to moral issues develops in isolation from other cognitive and affective changes in students coinciding with college attendance. Rather, moral reasoning is perhaps most appropriately seen as an integral part of an interconnected and often mutually reinforcing network of developmental trends that characterize changes that tend to occur in college students. For example, as we have seen in earlier chapters, there is abundant evidence to suggest that students make statistically significant gains in their abilities to reason critically, flexibly, and abstractly during college. There is also a clear though modest correlation between various measures of cognitive development and level of moral reasoning (for example, de Vries & Walker, 1986; Doherty & Corsini, 1976; King, Kitchener, Wood, & Davison, 1985; Lutwak, 1984; P. Meyer, 1977; Rowe & Marcia, 1980; Smith, 1978). Some of this research has even suggested that the development of Piagetian formal (abstract) reasoning is a necessary condition for the development of principled moral judgment (Cauble, 1976; Rowe & Marcia, 1980).

Similarly, as we have seen in preceding chapters, there is substantial evidence to suggest a clear association between college attendance and a general liberalization of personality and value structures. In the vast majority of studies conducted, upperclassmen, as compared to freshmen, tend to be less authoritarian or dogmatic and more open and flexible in their perceptual processes, more autonomous and independent of authority imposed through social institutions, more tolerant and understanding of others, and more interpersonally sensitive and skilled (for example, Chickering, 1974b; Chickering & McCormick, 1973; Clark, Heist, McConnell, Trow, & Yonge, 1972; Feldman & Newcomb, 1969; Lehmann & Dressel, 1962, 1963;

Pace, 1974; Spaeth & Greeley, 1970; Trent & Medsker, 1968; Withey, 1971). As with increases in cognitive capabilities, there is also evidence to suggest that level of moral reasoning in college samples tends to have modest positive correlations with these and similar dimensions of personality and value development (for example, Clouse, 1985; Czapski & Gates, 1981; de Vries & Walker, 1986; Fishkin, Keniston, & MacKinnon, 1973; Hogan & Dickstein, 1972; Hult, 1979; Liberman, Gaa, & Frankiewicz, 1983; Lupfer, Cohn, & Brown, 1982; Parish, Rosenblatt, & Kappes, 1979; Polovy, 1980; Sullivan, McCullough, & Stager, 1970).

Given such supportive developmental trends in the cognitive or intellectual and the personal or value orientations of college students, it seems reasonable to hypothesize that increases in principled moral reasoning might also accompany the experience of college. The evidence to support this hypothesis is impressive, not only in terms of the sheer number of studies conducted but also in terms of the extensive diversity of samples employed. Since the Defining Issues Test has the advantage of being a paper and pencil, group-administered measure, it is not surprising that it is the most frequently employed instrument in cross-sectional as well as longitudinal studies of moral development.

Studies That Use the Defining Issues Test

With few exceptions (for example, P. Meyer, 1977; White, 1973), the cross-sectional studies that employ the DIT P-index (which, again, measures the relative importance one gives to principled moral considerations in making a moral decision) show statistically significant age-education trends in moral judgment. Rest (1976, 1979a, 1979c) and Rest, Davison, and Robbins (1978) have synthesized data from more than fifty published and unpublished cross-sectional studies in the United States that used the DIT. Represented in these studies were 5,714 subjects and 136 different samples. When the P-scores were aggregated across samples, Rest found that average P-scores tended to increase about ten points at each level of education as a student progressed from junior high (average P-score of 21.9 percent) to senior high (average P-score of 31.8 percent) to college (average P-score of 42.3 percent) to graduate or professional school (average P-score of 53.8 percent). Grouping the samples by these age-education categories accounted for about 38 percent of the variations or differences in P-scores. Remarkably similar results have been reported in other cross-sectional studies with the DIT (Cohen, 1982; Guldhammer, 1983; Martin, Shafto, & Van Deinse, 1977; Mentowski & Strait, 1983; Ponsford, Alloway, & Mhoon, 1986; Yussen, 1976). In all of these studies, upperclassmen or seniors tended to give greater preference to principled moral considerations in making moral decisions than did underclassmen or freshmen.

The strong age-education trends in DIT P-scores are not confined to

American samples. Moon (1985) reviewed and synthesized a number of studies of moral judgment development using samples from Hong Kong (Hau, 1983), Korea (Park & Johnson, 1983), Iceland (Thornlidsson, 1978), the Philippines (Villanueva, 1982), and Australia (Watson, 1983). Nearly all of these studies also showed clear developmental trends in principled thinking. Subjects who were older and who had completed higher levels of formal education (through college) tended to attribute more importance to principled moral considerations on the DIT than subjects who were younger and not as well educated. Thus, the pronounced developmental trends in principled thinking as measured by the P-index of the DIT appear to be reasonably independent of national and cultural settings.

While longitudinal studies following the same sample of subjects over time are less numerous than cross-sectional investigations, there is nevertheless considerable evidence to suggest that students tend to have significantly higher DIT P-scores as end-of-year freshmen or upperclassmen than they did as entering freshmen. Moreover, exposure to postsecondary education appears to be linked with marked increases in principled thinking even when subjects are followed beyond the typical four-year period of college.

Shaver (1985) found statistically significant freshman-to-senior P-score gains of 10.85 points for students in a conservative, religious liberal arts college. The magnitude of this freshman-to-senior increase in principled moral judgment is markedly similar to that found with other college samples. Whiteley (1982) reports modest but statistically significant increases in P-scores from the beginning to the end of the freshman year for three cohorts of students at a state university. The average P-score increase during the freshman year for all three classes was 4.08 points. When these same three samples were followed from freshman to senior year the significant P-score gain was approximately 11.14 points (Loxley & Whiteley, 1986). Thus, while the magnitude of the overall freshman-to-senior gain was quite consistent with that of Shaver (1985), about 36 to 37 percent of the gain in principled moral judgment that occurred during the four years of college did so during the freshman year. A similar pattern of change is reported by Mentkowski and Strait (1983) for two cohorts of entering freshmen who were followed up during their sophomore, junior, and senior years. Statistically significant freshman-to-sophomore and sophomore-to-senior P-score increases were found for the combined samples. The total freshman-to-senior P-score increase was 9.7 points. Of this, the freshman-to-sophomore increase was 7.37 points, while the sophomore-to-senior gain was considerably smaller (2.33 points).

Other longitudinal studies have tended to support the overall statistically significant increase in principled moral reasoning from freshman to upperclassman year or from freshman to senior year (Broadhurst, 1980; Gorman, Duffy, & Heffernan, undated; Hood, 1984; Janos, Robinson, &

Lunneborg, 1987; Kaseman, 1980; Towers, 1984). The magnitude of this increase, however, is often difficult to determine from the data presented.

Perhaps the most ambitious longitudinal investigation of changes in principled moral reasoning associated with college attendance is that conducted by Rest and his colleagues (Rest, 1986c; Rest & Thoma, 1985; Deemer, 1985). They report the findings of research that followed three cohorts of high school graduates over six and ten years, respectively. For students who had completed at least three years of college, the six-year increase in P-score was 14 points (Rest, 1986c; Rest & Thoma, 1985). Similarly, when followed up after ten years, students with at least some college had an average P-score increase of approximately 11 points (Deemer, 1985).

The only longitudinal evidence inconsistent with the general trend of increases in principled moral judgment during college is reported by McGeorge (1976) and Shaver (1987). McGeorge found positive but statistically nonsignificant gains in P-scores over a two-year period for a sample of New Zealand Teachers College students. Shaver considered changes in P-scores at a Bible college and found that from the freshman to senior year they changed little. However, this absence of an overall statistically significant freshman-to-senior gain masked the fact that P-scores actually increased significantly through the end of the sophomore year but decreased thereafter.

Studies That Use the Moral Judgment Interview

Research that has relied on Kohlberg's Moral Judgment Interview (MJI) has also shown a positive association between level of formal education and moral development with both cross-sectional data (Lei, 1981; Lei & Cheng, 1984; Mentkowski and Strait, 1983; Whitla, 1978) and longitudinal data (Colby, Kohlberg, Gibbs, & Lieberman, 1983; Loxley & Whiteley, 1986; Mentkowski & Strait, 1983). Lei and Cheng found that Taiwanese college students had higher average scores on the MJI than did secondary school students, and graduate students had higher scores than college students. The difference between college and high school students was three and one-half times as large as the difference between graduate students and college students. Further, while 70 percent of the graduate students and 34.8 percent of the college students were functioning at the higher or more principled stages of moral maturity (Kohlberg's Stages 4 and 4/5), only 17.1 percent of the secondary school students were reasoning at these stages. Mentkowski and Strait (1983) found that graduating seniors at an American institution had significantly higher moral maturity scores on the MJI than did entering freshmen. Compared to freshmen, a noticeably lower proportion of seniors were in the preconventional stages of Kohlberg's scheme, and proportionally more were in the postconventional stages.

Similar results have been reported by Whitla (1978) with a multi-institutional sample. Using a paper and pencil adaptation of the MJI, Whitla found that seniors at a private college and a state college showed significantly higher levels of moral maturity than did freshmen. At a public junior college sophomores scored significantly higher than freshmen. In all cases the freshman and upperclassman cohorts were matched on entering academic ability (SAT scores) and high school rank, though not on entering MJI scores.

In a longitudinal investigation of changes in moral development with three cohorts of entering freshmen, Loxley and Whiteley (1986) looked at changes on the Moral Judgment Interview as well as on the Defining Issues Test. Freshman-to-senior changes on the MJI were statistically significant for both men and women, but there was also a statistically significant interaction effect between amount of change and gender. This interaction indicated that the freshman-to-senior gain in principled moral reasoning for men was slightly more than twice as large as the gain for women. Since both men and women had similar freshman scores, it is unlikely that these marked differences in gains can be explained away as the result of differential regression artifacts (that is, the initially lower group gaining more than the initially higher group).

In what is probably the most ambitious longitudinal study of moral development to date, Colby, Kohlberg, Gibbs, and Lieberman (1983) followed a sample of men from two suburban Chicago schools (one predominantly upper-middle class and the other predominantly lower-middle and working class) for twenty years. The correlations between stage of moral judgment and level of formal education at four different follow-ups of the sample (ages twenty-four to thirty-six) ranged from .54 to .77, all statistically significant. While such an approach only permits an indirect assessment of gains on the MJI during college, one can reasonably infer from the strong positive correlations that such changes are taking place.

Less convincing evidence of gains in moral maturity during college is presented by Mentkowski and Strait (1983). Following two cohorts of entering freshmen through their senior year, they found an overall small and statistically nonsignificant gain on the MJI. Moreover, from the freshman to sophomore year, the change in moral maturity score was negative, while from the sophomore to the senior year, the change was positive. Such a trend is difficult to explain and may, in fact, be artifactual.

Two additional studies have used a paper and pencil version of the Kohlberg interview known as the Moral Judgment Test (MJT). This instrument attempts to assess both affective and cognitive aspects of moral judgment behavior. A cross-sectional study by Eiferman (1982) found that college seniors age thirty or older in an urban institution had significantly higher MJT scores than did freshmen age thirty or older. This finding tends to be supported by Lind's (1985, 1986) series of longitudinal investigations of German university students from various fields of study. The students were tested with the MJT in their first and third years of college. Over the two-year period there was a modest but statistically significant average gain in the group's capacity to judge social dilemmas by means of moral principles.

Summary of Evidence on Change During College

Clearly, the overwhelming weight of evidence that comes from the Defining Issues Test and the Moral Judgment Interview (and its paper and pencil adaptations) suggests that extent of principled moral reasoning is positively associated with level of formal postsecondary education and that students generally make statistically significant gains in principled moral reasoning during college. The average magnitude of these gains is extremely difficult to determine from the existing studies in that many do not provide the information necessary to make such estimates (for example, standard deviations, percentage of students advancing from one Kohlbergian stage to another). Similarly, since the studies often report different information, it is difficult to compare the size of a statistically significant increase in one sample with that in another. Given these qualifiers, however, we infer from the body of evidence that *a* major (if not *the* major) change that takes place during college is a movement from conventional moral reasoning toward postconventional moral reasoning. It would also appear that the greatest gains in principled moral reasoning occur during the first or the first and second years of college. The latter conclusion is tentative, however, because it is based on a small number of investigations.

Design Issues That Affect Interpretation of Results

As pointed out in previous chapters, simply showing that trends and changes are coincident with college attendance is quite different from demonstrating that they occur as a consequence of college attendance. As with our discussion of gains in learning and cognitive development, a number of factors potentially confound the association between increases in principled moral reasoning and college attendance reported in a large portion of the investigations reviewed.

In cross-sectional designs that simultaneously compare different cohorts of freshmen and seniors, a major confounding factor is age. This is particularly relevant when one considers that the Kohlberg model is based on the concept of life-span developmental stages. Since amount of formal education obviously varies with age, one might question whether the development of principled moral reasoning is due to exposure to college or is simply a function of maturing as one grows older. Interpreting change in moral reasoning during college has the same problem as interpreting change in many of the dimensions of cognitive growth (such as reflective judgment) that are also developmentally based.

Similarly, there may be additional confounding factors such as subject intelligence and social status. Clearly, both of these factors are positively related to college attendance (for example, Wolfle, 1980b, 1983), and there is evidence that both have a modest positive association with level of principled moral judgment (for example, Colby, Kohlberg, Gibbs, & Lieberman, 1983; Coder, 1975). Consequently, the finding that students who complete college tend to have higher levels of principled moral judgment than those whose formal education ends with high school may not represent an effect of college as such. Rather, it may be largely due to the fact that college students represent a more selective population in terms of intelligence and social status than do high school students. In the same way, changes in institutional recruitment standards over time and the natural attrition of less intellectually capable students from freshman to senior year may produce a somewhat more selective population of seniors than the population of freshmen with whom they are compared. Thus, as we have previously seen in the areas of learning and cognitive development, cross-sectional differences in moral judgment between freshmen and seniors could be a consequence of comparing samples from differentially selective populations instead of a result attributable to the collegiate experience.

Although longitudinal designs control for many of these threats to the internal validity of the findings by comparing a cohort with itself over time, the attrition of subjects from the study may yield a less variable sample that is unrepresentative of the population from which the original sample was drawn. Moreover, longitudinal studies without a control group of similar individuals who do not attend college are still potentially confounded by regression and maturation effects. Without such a control group, it is extremely difficult to disaggregate the gains in moral judgment due to the experience of college from those due to regression artifacts or normal cognitive-moral maturation in young adults.

Net Effects of College

Determining whether differential gains in moral judgment are attributable to differences in exposure to postsecondary education is a complex matter. Cross-sectional studies (such as those that compare high school seniors and college seniors) typically attempt to control for the influence of potentially confounding variables such as age and intelligence. Similarly, longitudinal studies generally include a control group of subjects who do not attend college or who have less than four years of exposure to postsecondary education. Because it is nearly impossible to control individual differences by randomly assigning subjects to different levels of exposure to college, these longitudinal studies typically rely on various forms of statistical control (partial correlation, multiple regression, analysis of covariance, and the like) to estimate the net influence of college.

Studies That Use the Defining Issues Test

Cross-sectional studies that employ the Defining Issues Test (DIT) have attempted to determine the extent to which higher levels of principled moral reasoning are attributable to level of formal education by comparing the strength of the association between DIT P-score and education with the corresponding association between P-score and age. In nearly all these studies, level of formal education had a substantially stronger association with P-score than did age. Coder (1975), for example, studied eighty-seven adults (ages twenty-four through fifty) in a religious education program and found a slightly negative ($r = -.10$) correlation between P-score and age. The correlation between P-score and level of formal education achieved by each subject, however, was substantial ($r = .25$) and statistically significant. Crowder (1976), in a study of seventy adults (ages eighteen through fifty-nine), reports findings almost exactly replicating those of Coder. Age correlated $-.05$ with P-score, whereas level of formal education and P-score were correlated .25. Consistently similar results have been reported with American samples (Dortzbach, 1975; Eiferman, 1982; Mentkowski & Strait, 1983), a Chinese sample (Hau, 1983), and an Australian sample (Watson, 1983).

In terms of determining the net effects of college on moral reasoning as measured by the DIT, the most significant longitudinal study is probably that reported by Rest & Thoma (1985). Thirty-nine subjects were tested with the DIT in high school and at two-year intervals over a six-year period following graduation from high school. When subjects were divided into "low-education" (two years or less of college) and "high-education" groups (three or more years of college), the groups showed increasingly divergent developmental pathways in terms of principled moral judgment. The high-education group showed increasing gains after high school, while the low-education group showed a leveling off. At graduation from high school, the low-education group had a P-score of 33, and the high-education group had a slightly higher P-score of 37 (a difference of only 4 points). Six years later, however, the P-score for the low-education group was 34.5, while the high-education group had a much higher P-score of 51 (a difference between groups of 16.5 points). Using analysis of covariance to control for group differences in P-score at high school graduation, Rest and Thoma found that the high-education group still had a significantly higher adjusted P-score after six years than the low-education group. Years of college education accounted for a statistically significant increase in the explained variance in P-scores of 14 percent above and beyond that due to P-score at high school graduation. Such evidence is consistent with Rest's (1979a) contention that principled moral judgment tends to increase with exposure to additional levels of formal education beyond high school. For individuals not exposed to educational environments beyond high school, however, moral judgment development tends to plateau or level off.

Generally confirmatory results are reported in a more limited longitudinal study by Kitchener, King, Davison, Parker, and Wood (1984). Samples of high school juniors, college juniors, and doctoral-level graduate students were matched on gender, hometown size, and Scholastic Aptitude Test scores. They completed the DIT in the fall of 1977 and were followed up two years later. The college undergraduates and graduate students both showed a statistically significant increase in P-score, with the gain for the latter group being somewhat more pronounced. In contrast, the high school students did not show statistically significant P-score increases over the two-year period. Analysis of covariance, controlling for verbal ability (as measured by the Concept Mastery Test), indicated that the group and time effects on P-scores persisted.

Studies That Use the Moral Judgment Interview

Evidence pertaining to the effects of college on moral reasoning as measured by the Moral Judgment Interview is mixed. In a cross-sectional study that used the MJI, Mentkowski & Strait (1983) employed analysis of covariance to statistically remove the confounding influence of student age and found that moral maturity scores between college freshmen and seniors at a single institution were statistically nonsignificant. More positive evidence, however, is reported in Colby, Kohlberg, Gibbs, and Lieberman's (1983) twenty-year longitudinal study of fifty-eight males. The study included an initial testing with the MJI during high school and five follow-ups (using three parallel forms of the MJI) over a twenty-year period. With initial intelligence (based on school records) and socioeconomic status (based on parents' occupation and education) controlled statistically, the partial correlation between level of formal education and the MJI moral maturity score was .26 (statistically significant at $p < .05$). No partial correlations, however, were computed with high school MJI score controlled.

Summary of Evidence on the Net Effects of College

In sum, the confidence with which one can attribute higher levels of moral reasoning to the college experience varies to some extent with the specific instrument used to assess moral reasoning. Studies that used the Defining Issues Test have been quite consistent in indicating that college has a discernible positive effect on the development of principled moral reasoning. Investigations that used the Moral Judgment Interview have been less consistent in their findings. Despite the differences associated with the measurement instrument employed, the weight of evidence in the total body of research is sufficient to suggest that gains in principled moral reasoning are an outcome of the collegiate experience.

This conclusion is consistent with the findings of Hyman and Wright (1979) reviewed in Chapter Five. Recall that in their analysis of thirty-eight national surveys of adults from 1949 to 1975, Hyman and Wright found that attaching importance to civil liberties and due process of law; freedom from the constraints of arbitrary laws in personal, social, economic, and political spheres; and humanitarian conduct toward others represented a profile of values most pronounced among individuals who had gone to college. This profile distinguished college from noncollege respondents even when a number of demographic characteristics (including, age, race, and social class) were taken into account. Thus, it appears that evidence indicating a net effect of college on principled moral judgment is consistent with findings from national surveys suggesting that a general humanization of values and attitudes concerning the rights and welfare of others is associated with college attendance.[1]

Between-College Effects

Evidence pertaining to differential institutional effects on the development of student moral judgment is sparse. Few studies directly address the issue. Consequently, what evidence does exist is only preliminary and suggestive. Rest (1979a) compiled what is probably the most comprehensive data set focusing on the level of college student moral judgment. His data consist of a composite sample of nearly 2,500 students from various colleges and universities across the country. Across all samples, Rest reports an average DIT P-score of 41.6. The lowest P-scores were from colleges in the southeastern United States. The two college samples from Georgia and Virginia had average DIT P-scores of 24.5 and 34.0, respectively. These were the two lowest averages in the combined college sample. Rest speculates that the particularly low scores from these two southern samples could reflect a conservative intellectual milieu that functions to inhibit the development of moral judgment. Such a conclusion is consistent with findings reported by Cady (1982) and Ernsberger (1976) in studies of level of moral judgment among clergy. Alternatively, however, such a finding could simply reflect variations in institutional selection and recruitment procedures rather than the unique effect of different institutional environments.

It is possible, of course, that there is some contextual influence associated with being in an institutional environment dominated by peers with predominantly conventional levels of moral reasoning. This is suggested by evidence reported in Shaver's (1987) comparison of freshman-to-senior DIT P-score changes in a religiously affiliated liberal arts college and a conservative Bible college. Over the four-year period there was a 10.85-point P-score increase for the liberal arts college students (freshman P-score = 41.51, senior P-score = 52.36). This compared with a slight freshman-to-senior decrease of .24 point in the P-score at the conservative Bible college, where the freshman P-score was 33.45 and the senior P-score was 33.21. Thus, not only did the Bible college students enter an institutional environment where freshmen were at less advanced stages of moral reasoning development than in the liberal arts college, but they also had a substantially lower rate of change toward principled or postconventional reasoning than their liberal arts college counterparts.

Although there are problems in comparing change scores (see the Appendix), this trend is just the reverse of what one might expect if the findings were simply the result of regression artifacts (that is, initially lower scores showing greater change toward the mean on a subsequent testing). What the Shaver study suggests instead is that different types of colleges attract or recruit students at different entering levels of moral reasoning. In turn, one impact of distinctive college environments or social contexts appears to be the accentuation of these initial differences. This is quite consistent with the idea of accentuation effects as originally defined by Feldman and Newcomb (1969). The specific mechanism that underlies this impact is difficult to identify from Shaver's study. Nevertheless, one possibility that is consistent both with Shaver's data and with theoretical expectations (Kohlberg, 1969) is the likelihood of interaction with student peers who are themselves reasoning at the postconventional or principled stages.

To further investigate differences among postsecondary institutions in level of student moral reasoning, we conducted a secondary analysis of Rest's (1979a) data on the DIT P-scores of college students. From information on sample characteristics supplied by Rest, we grouped institutions into six basic categories: (1) public research oriented universities (those in the top 100 institutions in federally funded research for fiscal year 1983 as ranked by the National Science Foundation), (2) public comprehensive universities (not in the top 100 research universities), (3) private universities, (4) private liberal arts colleges, (5) church-affiliated liberal arts colleges, and (6) two-year colleges. We then conducted a six-group analysis of covariance with DIT P-scores as the dependent measure and the year of enrollment of each institutional sample (freshman, sophomore, junior, or senior) as the statistically controlled covariate. Each separate institutional sample was considered a single data point.

The results of our analysis indicated that year of student enrollment accounted for a statistically significant portion of the variance in DIT P-scores (22.0 percent, $p < .001$), year in college being positively associated with P-scores. Statistically controlling for differences in year of enrollment across the various samples, institutional type was also associated with a statistically significant increase in the explanation of variance in P-scores (R^2 increase = 31.26 percent, $p < .001$). The adjusted P-scores for institutional type appeared to cluster in three general groups. The lowest-scoring three categories were, in ascending order, public comprehensive universities (P-score = 38.97), private universities (P-score = 40.16), and private liberal arts colleges (P-score = 40.48). Somewhat higher were two-year colleges (P-score = 43.16) and public research universities (P-score = 43.46). Highest of all were church-affiliated liberal arts colleges (P-score = 50.49). Using a subsample of institutions that could be identified, an additional analysis found a significant partial correlation (r = .37) between institutional selectivity (average SAT or ACT composite of the freshman class) and P-score, with sample year in college controlled statistically.

Whether such findings represent national trends is problematic, of course. It is difficult to determine the degree of national representativeness in Rest's data in terms of both individuals and institutions. Moreover, even assuming sample representativeness, our analyses may simply be reflecting differential college recruiting and enrollment trends rather than the net effect of institutional type or institutional selectivity on student moral reasoning. Consequently, firm conclusions about between-institution effects on student moral reasoning from our reconsideration of the Rest data are premature. What is suggested from our analyses, however, is the clear possibility that different institutional environments may have differential impacts on the development of moral reasoning in college students. Whether such impacts are adequately captured by broad institutional classifications or level of student body academic selectivity is questionable. It is likely that there are substantial variations in the press of the intellectual, social, and cultural environments of institutions within the same category or level of selectivity. Thus, identifying the true causal influences of institutional characteristics on the development of moral reasoning may entail analyses that describe how the specific experiences of college differ among institutions.

Within-College Effects

Part of this section draws on an excellent review by Barnett and Volker (1985). Their review, however, focuses on a broader view of life experiences than those that occur during college.

Individual Experiences

A small but growing body of research has investigated the specific types of college experiences systematically associated with moral reasoning or judgment. These investigations have taken several forms. One has been the large longitudinal survey approach as exemplified by the work of Barnett (1982); Biggs, Schomberg, and Brown (1977); Biggs and Barnett (1981); and Schomberg (1978). Since these scholars appear to have been analyzing the same large-sample longitudinal data set, their studies will be reviewed in chronological order.

over a nine-year period for all four subgroups. The negative effect was particularly pronounced for black men.

Similar results are reported by Kocher and Pascarella (1988), who used the same sample but attempted to explain overall educational attainment through the doctoral degree rather than just completion of the bachelor's degree. Controlling for many of the same variables as Pascarella (1985b) plus initial expectations of transfer and academic major, Kocher and Pascarella found that number of institutions attended had a statistically significant negative direct effect on educational attainment for male and female black and white students. In addition, these investigators found that for black men and women the number of institutions attended also had a statistically significant negative indirect effect on educational attainment, mediated through its inhibiting influence on interaction with faculty and social or leadership involvement during college.

There are data limitations in the Pascarella (1985b) and Kocher and Pascarella (1988) analyses. For example, it was impossible to determine the qualitative differences in transfer behavior (for example, from a less to a more selective college, from a public to a private college). Such differences may have a nontrivial impact on attainment. Despite this problem, the findings (along with those of Trent and Medsker, 1968) suggest that institutional continuity during one's undergraduate education has positive implications for one's educational attainment. In turn, this further suggests the potential importance of one's fit with the initial institution of enrollment.

Within-College Effects

As indicated in the preceding section, a number of the structural characteristics of the college attended (selectivity, enrollment, and so on) have statistically significant indirect effects on educational attainment through their shaping of the student's social and academic experience of college. In this section we focus on those specific college experiences or accomplishments that enhance educational attainment independently of where one attends college (even though they may be more likely to occur at some colleges than at others). The volume of literature directly or indirectly addressing this area of inquiry during the last twenty years is extensive to the point of being unmanageable. Consequently, we have been forced to be selective in our synthesis and have turned for focus to a number of relatively recent theoretical statements pertaining to student persistence and degree attainment (for example, Bean, 1980, 1985; Cope & Hannah, 1975; Pascarella, 1980; Spady, 1970, 1971; Tinto, 1975, 1982, 1987). Although these models differ in specific structural elements and nomenclature, they appear to have as a common thread the notion that persistence and thereby educational attainment are largely a function of the student's fit or match with the college environment.

Various terms have been used to represent degree of person-environment fit, including integration, involvement, congruence, and satisfaction. Operationally, however, most definitions of fit are manifest in terms of the student's interactions with the academic and social systems of the college or, indirectly, those factors that shape the nature of such interactions. Our reading of the literature suggests that these may be reasonably grouped in the following categories: academic achievement (grades), peer relationships and extracurricular involvement, interactions with faculty, academic major, residence, orientation and advising, and financial aid and work.[1]

Academic Achievement

A student's grades are probably the single most revealing indicator of his or her successful adjustment to the intellectual demands of a particular college's course of study. Without satisfactory grades, a student will not graduate from college, nor will he or she be admitted to graduate or professional school. Although heavily influenced by academic ability and intelligence, grades in college are not merely a function of those factors. Even with academic ability or intelligence taken into account, grades at the individual level are significantly influenced by such factors as personal motivation, organization, study habits, and quality of effort (for example, Astin, 1971b, 1975b; Cappella, Wagner, & Kusmierz, 1982; Corlett, 1974; Culler & Holahan, 1980; Demitroff, 1974; Hinrichsen, 1972; Lenning, Munday, Johnson, Vander Well, & Brue, 1974a, 1974b; Thompson, 1976). Thus, as a measure of successful adaptation to an academic environment, grades tend to reflect not only requisite intellectual skills but also desirable personal work habits and attitudes.

Given this, it is not particularly surprising that undergraduate grades are perhaps the single best predictor of obtaining a bachelor's degree and also of attending graduate or professional school and obtaining an advanced degree. This effect has been replicated across a number of national samples and holds even when important student precollege characteristics (such as academic ability, aspirations, secondary school achievement), the characteristics of the institution attended (such as selectivity, control), and other collegiate experiences (such as major, social involvement) are taken into account (Anderson, 1986; Ethington & Smart, 1986; Sharp, 1970; Spaeth & Greeley, 1970; Stoecker, Pascarella, & Wolfle, 1988; Tinto, 1981). Moreover, even with such factors as gender, social class, race, and undergraduate major taken into account, grades remain an important determinant of the "prestige" or ranking of the graduate school attended (Lang, 1984).

Factors Influencing Academic Achievement. Although as a measure of academic adjustment, grades are largely an amalgam of individual academic ability and other personal traits (motivation, perseverance, study skills, and the like), they are not beyond the influence of institutional interventions. Kulik, Kulik, and Shwalb (1983), for example, conducted a meta-analysis of sixty published and unpublished studies evaluating the experimental effectiveness of special college programs designed to facilitate the academic adjustment of poorly prepared students. The effects of four types of programs were reviewed: instruction in academic skills, advising and counseling programs, comprehensive support services, and remedial or developmental studies. Kulik, Kulik, and Schwalb report a statistically significant overall effect size in grades favoring the college interventions. On the average, those exposed to the interventions had a grade point average .27 of a standard deviation higher than similar students not so exposed (an advantage of 10.6 percentile points). The overall effect was greatest during the freshman year with remedial or developmental programs being significantly less effective than the other interventions. Kulik, Kulik, and Shwalb also estimated the effect of these programs on college persistence rates and found that on average those exposed to the various interventions had a statistically significant 8 percent advantage in persistence rate over similar students not exposed to the interventions. As with grades, the effect was stronger during the freshman year than thereafter. More recent research not included in the Kulik, Kulik, and Schwalb synthesis is nevertheless consistent with their conclusions concerning effects of academic adjustment interventions on both grades and persistence (for example, Abrams & Jernigan, 1984; Behrman, Dark, & Paul, 1984; Blanc, DeBuhr, & Martin, 1983; Bron & Gordon, 1986; Dubois, Kiewra, & Fraley, 1988; Kenney, 1989; Kirschenbaum & Perri, 1982; Lipsky & Ender, 1990; Martin, Blanc, & De-Buhr, 1983; Nist, Simpson, & Hogrebe, 1985; Walsh, 1985; Wilkie & Kuckuck, 1989).[2]

With a few exceptions (May, 1974; Moos & Lee, 1979), there is little evidence to suggest that when academic ability or prior achievement is held constant, different naturally occurring residence groups (those in dormitories, fraternities or sororities, or off-campus apartments) have a consistently differential influence on academic achievement (for example, Baird, 1969b; Ballou, 1985; Beal & Williams, 1968; Grosz & Brandt, 1969; Longino & Kart, 1973; Phillips, 1976; Pugh & Chamberlain, 1976). Nevertheless, residence groupings provide a readily available laboratory for enhancing the academic and interpersonal quality of student life. It is not surprising, therefore, that a second area where colleges have made a concerted effort to intervene in ways that promote student academic adjustment is the purposeful structuring of residence facilities. Here the body of evidence is extensive, but the interventions are sufficiently diverse in their approach to resist straightforward categorization and therefore simple conclusions. What can be reasonably concluded from this evidence is that when the formal and informal group norms of a residence unit function to reinforce a serious and focused study environment, academic achievement is positively in-fluenced. This influence, however, is not particularly pervasive or dramatic in magnitude. Examples of experimental interventions that have yielded at least modest success in creating such environmental norms include special study floors with enforced quiet hours (Blimling & Hample, 1979), the use of skilled academic tutors on designated residence floors (Taylor, Roth, & Hanson, 1971), and living-learning centers designed to integrate the stu-dent's residential and intellectual life and enhance student-faculty informal interaction (Blimling & Paulsen, 1979; Pascarella & Terenzini, 1981).

There is also evidence that experimentally grouping students in res-idential units by academic aptitude or academic major may positively influ-ence achievement. In the instance of ability grouping, however, it is unclear whether the achievement benefits accrue to the higher-ability students (DeCoster, 1968; Duncan & Stoner, 1977) or lower-ability students (Blai, 1971). Similarly, it is not totally clear whether all students benefit the same from homogeneous grouping by major (Schroeder & Belmonte, 1979; Schroeder & Freesh, 1977), whether men benefit more than women (Snead & Caple, 1971), whether average-ability students benefit more than high-ability students (Taylor & Hanson, 1971), or whether the effect is largely trivial when ability and personality traits are taken into account (Elton & Bate, 1966). An independent review of this literature by Buffington (1984) concludes that there is no consensus as to the benefits of homogeneous grouping in residence halls.[3]

Peer Relationships and Extracurricular Involvement

Extensive theoretical justification exists for the role of social partici-pation in the educational attainment process. On one level this comes from the notion in theoretical models of student persistence that social partici-pation enhances one's social integration and interpersonal bonds with the institution. Other things being equal, this increases one's commitment to and likelihood of persisting at the institution and completing one's degree (for example, Bean, 1980; Spady, 1970; Tinto, 1975, 1987). Similarly, the social-psychological life-cycle models of status attainment briefly introduced earlier in the chapter (for example, Sewell & Hauser, 1975) posit the im-portance of interactions with significant others as an influence on the at-tainment process. From this perspective participation in such things as col-lege extracurricular activities might serve two important functions suggested by Hanks and Eckland (1976). First, it may expose students to a social net-work of other achievement-oriented peers, thereby generating and rein-forcing higher aspirations and goals. Second, it may facilitate the realization of such aspirations and goals by allowing students to acquire the personal resources (interpersonal skills, self-confidence, specialized knowledge, and the like) that better permit such aspirations and goals to be realized.

Given this strong theoretical justification, it is not surprising that substantial research has addressed the relationship between social involvement and both persistence and educational attainment. The weight of evidence is quite clear that both the frequency and quality of students' interactions with peers and their participation in extracurricular activities are positively associated with persistence (for example, Carroll, 1988; Dukes & Gaither, 1984; Faughn, 1982; Husband, 1976; Johnson & Chapman, 1980; Kramer et al., 1985; Mallinckrodt, 1988; Mallinckrodt & Sedlacek, 1987; Nelson, Scott, & Bryan, 1984; Neuman, 1985; Seabrook, 1985; Simpson, Baker, & Mellinger, 1980; Vaughan, 1968; Waldo, 1986). It is less clear, however, that peer relationships and extracurricular involvement have a net influence on persistence when student precollege characteristics or other measures of the college experience are taken into account. For example, Endo and Bittner (1985), Munro (1981), and Pascarella and Chapman (1983a, 1983b) provide evidence to suggest a net positive effect of peer relationships and extracurricular involvement on persistence. Yet the results reported by Bean (1985); Pascarella and Terenzini (1980a); Stinson, Scherer, and Walker (1987); Terenzini and Pascarella (1977, 1978); and Thomas and Andes (1987) are less supportive.

Evidence concerning the net effect of peer relationships or extracurricular involvement on educational attainment, bachelor's degree completion, or entrance into graduate or professional school is reasonably clear. Hanks and Eckland (1976), for example, attempted to estimate the influences on educational attainment (some college to advanced degree) with a national sample of college students who were followed up fifteen years after their sophomore year in high school. Controlling for family socioeconomic status, academic aptitude, high school athletic and social participation, high school grades, and college grades, Hanks and Eckland found that a measure of collegiate social participation had a statistically significant positive effect on educational attainment for both men and women. (The measure of social participation in both high school and college included publications or creative writing, dramatics or music, debate or political groups, student government, social science or religious groups, and science or academic groups.)

More recent studies that controlled for many of the same variables but also for precollege educational aspirations report generally similar findings for bachelor's degree completion (Stoecker, Pascarella, & Wolfle, 1988), entrance into graduate or professional school (Ethington & Smart, 1986), and educational attainment through the doctoral degree (Pascarella, Ethington, & Smart, 1988). The measure of social involvement in these studies typically included items such as serving on a university or departmental committee, being president of a student organization, having a part in a play, and being editor of a student publication. As such, it has somewhat stronger loadings for leadership than does the social participation measure used by Hanks and Eckland (1976). Moreover, the scale used by Ethington and Smart (1986) also included a measure of interaction with faculty. Consequently, their findings may be somewhat ambiguous with respect to the unique influence of social involvement with peers.

It is likely, of course, that the extent to which social involvement with peers influences educational attainment depends to some extent on the characteristics of the peers with whom one interacts. Studies that provide sufficient statistical detail (for example, correlation matrices or full regression equations) to determine this, however, are rare. Nevertheless, using the statistics provided in an analysis of two separate national samples (Pascarella, 1985c; Kocher & Pascarella, 1988), we found positive correlations in the .12 to .20 range between student precollege educational aspirations and subsequent social involvement with peers during college. This suggests that those students engaging in such activities tend to have higher educational aspirations to begin with than their less involved counterparts. As such, they may constitute a viable college subculture whose group norms have a salutary influence on the aspirations of participating individuals.

Indeed, there is modest, though mixed, evidence that extracurricular involvement with peers positively influences educational aspirations. Using a national sample of white students from seventy-four four-year colleges, Pascarella (1985c) sought to determine the influences on educational aspirations at the end of the sophomore year. Controlling for such factors as academic aptitude, precollege educational aspirations, parental education, institutional selectivity and size, college grades, and social interaction with faculty, he found that an eleven-item measure of social involvement with peers had a small but statistically significant and positive direct effect on sophomore educational aspirations. Moreover, when the data were aggregated across the seventy-four institutions and all other variables were controlled, colleges with high levels of student social interaction also had high levels of sophomore student educational aspirations.

Less supportive documentation is provided by Gurin & Epps (1975), who used a sample of black students from nine black institutions. They found no significant association between the percentage of students on each campus who participated in extracurricular activities and educational aspirations at the end of the freshman year when institutional selectivity and initial aspirations were held constant. They did find, however, that net of college selectivity and initial aspirations, the diversity of extracurricular activities offered by an institution was positively and significantly linked to men's aspirations at the end of the freshman year.

While there may be several reasons for the lack of clear correspondence between these findings and those of Pascarella (1985c) (different sample, less diverse institutions, and the like), one possibility is that Gurin and Epps used a measure of extracurricular involvement aggregated at the

campus level. They did not really attempt to link individual social participation with individual aspirations.

Another type of student extracurricular involvement is athletic participation. However, evidence that compares the educational attainment of
athletes with other students who have similar precollege characteristics is
nearly nonexistent. Analyzing a national sample of college students followed over a nine-year period, Pascarella and Smart (1990) sought to determine whether participation in intercollegiate athletics in general influenced bachelor's degree attainment. Net of such factors as family
socioeconomic status, secondary school achievement, educational aspirations, college selectivity, and college grades, male intercollegiate athletes had
a small but significantly greater likelihood of finishing a bachelor's degree
within nine years than their nonathlete counterparts. Unfortunately, the
Pascarella and Smart study could not disaggregate the impact on educational attainment of different kinds of athletic participation (for example,
participation in revenue-producing sports such as football and basketball
versus other sports). Furthermore, we uncovered no additional study that
controlled for important precollege differences between athletes and non-
athletes and replicated their findings. Consequently, we hesitate to offer a
conclusion on the net effects of athletic participation on educational attainment.

Interactions with Faculty

A considerable body of evidence suggests that with the general
exception of small and often selective liberal arts colleges, student-faculty
contact in most institutions is largely restricted to formalized, somewhat
structured situations such as the lecture, laboratory, or discussion section
(Boyer, 1987; Chickering, 1969; Wood & Wilson, 1972). There may be several reasons for this. A substantial number of students may simply desire,
within the limitations of academic requirements, to exclude faculty influence from their nonclassroom lives (Feldman & Newcomb, 1969). Others
may have little nonclassroom contact with faculty because of the constraints
of work and/or commuting to college (Chickering, 1974a). Moreover, generational and organizational status differences separate students and faculty. Such differences, when combined with the sanctions of professional
norms, may lead faculty to designate substantial portions of their nonclassroom time as off-limits to undergraduates (Boyer, 1987; Malkemes, 1972;
Wallace, 1967a).

Despite these impediments, there is considerable evidence that the
impact on students of faculty norms, values, and attitudes, as well as faculty
members' impact as role models, is enhanced when student-faculty interactions extend beyond the formal classroom setting (Pascarella, 1980). This

evidence is consistent with the notion that effective social learning of normative values and attitudes often occurs in informal as well as formal settings. (Indeed, we have already seen evidence of this impact in previous chapters.) Thus, if faculty can be generally assumed to place a high value on educational attainment, one might posit that the more students interact with faculty in informal as well as formal settings, the more likely they are to be influenced by this value. Moreover, as with social interaction with peers, increased interaction between faculty and students may also serve to strengthen the personal bonds between the student and the institution, thereby increasing the likelihood of social integration and persistence.

A substantial body of research addresses these assertions. Evidence concerning the link between student-faculty interaction and institutional persistence is not totally consistent. Pascarella and Terenzini conducted a series of studies on three independent samples of freshmen as they entered the same university in three consecutive years to determine the factors that influence voluntary freshman-year persistence or withdrawal decisions (Pascarella & Terenzini, 1976, 1977, 1979a, 1979b; Terenzini & Pascarella, 1978, 1980b). Controlling for salient student precollege characteristics, such as academic aptitude, educational aspirations, initial commitment to the institution, and personality traits, as well as for freshman-year grades and extracurricular involvement, the investigators found that freshman-to-sophomore persistence was positively and significantly related to total amount of student-faculty nonclassroom contact with faculty and particularly to frequency of interactions with faculty to discuss intellectual matters. The latter finding, they concluded, suggests that the nonclassroom interactions with faculty that are most important to persistence are those that integrate the student's classroom and nonclassroom experiences. Such a conclusion is perhaps further supported by Astin's (1977a) finding that net of student precollege aptitudes and aspirations, involvement with faculty in independent research is positively associated with undergraduate persistence.

Although the potential positive influence of student-faculty informal interaction on persistence has been supported in subsequent research on independent samples (for example, Endo & Bittner, 1985; Endo & Harpel, 1979), there is also a considerable amount of evidence to suggest that the net effect of student-faculty contact on persistence is at best trivial (for example, Bean, 1980, 1985; Bean & Plascak, 1987; Kowalski, 1977; Rossmann, 1968; Voorhees, 1987). Since most of the studies were based on single-institution samples, a possible explanation for the inconsistency of the findings may be variations in measurement error or sampling characteristics across different institutional samples. Conversely, the lack of consistent findings may simply reflect the fact that interaction with faculty has differential impacts on persistence at different kinds of institutions (Pascarella, 1986a).

The weight of evidence from studies that focused on the influence of student-faculty interaction on educational aspirations and educational attainment is less equivocal. Hearn (1987), Gurin and Epps (1975), Gurin and Gaylord (1976), Pascarella (1985c), and Thistlethwaite and Wheeler (1966) report evidence to indicate that even with relevant student background characteristics and other collegiate experiences held constant, the extent of social interaction between students and faculty is significantly and positively related to educational aspirations at either the end of the freshman year, end of the sophomore year, or end of the senior year. Similarly, evidence from analyses of two independent national samples reported by Astin and Panos (1969); Kocher and Pascarella (1988); Pascarella, Smart, and Ethington (1986); and Stoecker, Pascarella, and Wolfle (1988) suggests that degree of student-faculty social contact has a significant positive association with bachelor's degree completion and educational attainment through the doctoral degree. Further, this association remains statistically significant even when controls are made for secondary school achievement, the selectivity and size of the college attended, and other measures of the college experience, such as major, grades, and extracurricular involvement.

Despite the consistency of the evidence, there is some ambiguity in interpreting the causal direction of the link between student-faculty social interaction and educational aspirations and attainment. In the studies reviewed, measures of student-faculty interaction and either educational aspirations or attainment were collected at the same time. Consequently, it is not necessarily clear that student-faculty interaction leads to higher educational aspirations and, subsequently, higher educational attainment. Rather, students with aspirations for graduate or professional school may simply be more likely to share faculty values and enjoy social interaction with them. Indeed, a study of freshman-year educational aspirations by Iverson, Pascarella, and Terenzini (1984) would tend to support the second hypothesis. They used a statistical procedure that permits one to estimate reciprocal causality, and their results suggested that educational aspirations are more likely to influence contact with faculty than contact with faculty is to influence educational aspirations.

Other evidence, however, strongly suggests that faculty have an influential causal role in students' educational aspirations, particularly their decision to attend graduate school. In what is perhaps the most comprehensive study on this topic, Baird and colleagues (Baird, 1976b; Baird, Clark, & Hartnett, 1973) surveyed a national sample of graduate students on the importance of a range of factors concerning their senior-year decisions to attend graduate or professional school. Sixty-five percent of the graduate students in arts and humanities, 62 percent in the biological or physical sciences, and 56 percent in the social sciences said that the personal encouragement of faculty was an "important" or "very important" factor. The positive influence of faculty encouragement on plans for graduate work in these disciplines held net of academic major, initial vocational choice, grades, and academic self-ratings. Faculty influence was less pronounced in decisions to attend law or medical school, yet nearly a third of these students also indicated that faculty encouragement had been "important" or "very important." Similar results have been reported for the postbaccalaureate plans of senior women at a single institution by de Wolf (1976). When matched by major and age with seniors not aspiring to graduate study, those intending to enter graduate school the next year more often indicated having been influenced by a faculty member.

It is also possible, of course, that the link between student-faculty social interaction and educational aspirations and attainment is a proxy for the extent to which specific faculty members serve as influential role models for students. (The assumption here is that students may be more likely to interact socially with such role models.) This is most clearly the case in graduate education, where personal relationships with faculty members and being treated as a junior colleague by a faculty member who acts as a mentor are significant predictors of completing the doctorate (for example, Berg & Ferber, 1983). It may also hold for the educational aspirations of undergraduates, particularly if the role model one seeks to emulate is the same gender as the student. Stake and Noonan (1985), for example, found that when they controlled for initial educational aspirations, the greatest gains in educational aspirations during the freshman year occurred for those students who chose a same-gender faculty role model they wished to emulate.

Related research has suggested that female faculty role models may be a particularly important influence on the educational aspirations of undergraduate women (Esposito, Hackett, & O'Halloran, 1987; Ridgeway, 1978; Stake, 1981). Indeed, Tidball (Tidball & Kistiakowsky, 1976; Tidball, 1986) posits the presence of female faculty role models as a potential causal mechanism that underlies the link found between the number of women faculty members in an institution and the percentage of women graduates of an institution who obtain graduate degrees. In this regard it is worth noting that women in single-sex institutions, in which female faculty are typically in the majority, report more informal interaction and higher levels of supportive interaction with faculty than do women in coeducational institutions (Monteiro, 1980).

A final interpretative point needs to be made concerning the influence of student-faculty relationships on student educational aspiration and attainment. If student-faculty interaction influences students' aspirations and thereby their educational attainment, it is likely that the nature of this influence is to accentuate or affirm rather than to fundamentally change existing aspirations. Consider the evidence reported by Pascarella (1985c) with a sample of students from seventy-four four-year institutions. He found that net of student precollege characteristics and the characteristics of the institution attended, students who developed close personal relationships with faculty during the first two years of college tended to have significantly higher precollege educational aspirations than those who did not. In turn, social interaction with faculty had a statistically significant positive influence on sophomore-year educational aspirations over and above precollege and institutional characteristics, initial educational aspirations, college grades, and social involvement with peers. This set of findings suggests that students with initially high educational aspirations are most likely to interact socially with faculty and that such interaction serves to enhance even further initial aspirations.

Academic Major

In considering the vast majority of colleges and universities, it probably makes little sense to talk about educational aspirations and attainment of students as being influenced by their experience of a single academic or social environment. Rather, as suggested by Feldman and Newcomb (1969); Hackman and Taber (1979); Simpson, Baker, and Mellinger (1980); and Weidman (1979, 1984), the individual student is more likely to identify with and interact with a number of salient subenvironments, each of which may have a unique influence on aspirations and attainment. One of these salient subenvironments is the student's academic major.

Interestingly, evidence on the net influence of academic major on educational attainment is mixed. Using a sample from the NLS-72, Thomas and Gordon (1983), for example, found that for students in four-year institutions, majoring in the hard or technical sciences (versus education and the social sciences) had a statistically significant positive effect on educational attainment even when controls were made for such factors as academic aptitude, high school achievement, precollege educational aspirations, and college grades. (The measure of educational attainment ranged from "less than two years of college" to "graduate or professional degree.") The same effect did not hold for students at two-year colleges. Similar findings for four-year college students have been reported by Sharp (1970) in a national sample of students followed up five years after they attained the bachelor's degree. In the Sharp study humanities and science majors were more likely to attend graduate or professional school than their counterparts who majored in such fields as business, education, and health.

Evidence from two other national samples has failed to support the findings of either Thomas and Gordon (1983) or Sharp (1970). Alexander and Eckland (1977) conducted their analyses on a national sample of high school sophomores who were followed up fifteen years later. Pascarella, Smart, Ethington, and Nettles (1987) analyzed a national sample of students in four-year colleges who were followed up nine years after initial enrollment. Controlling for such factors as family social status, academic ability, precollege educational aspirations, the selectivity of the institution attended, and college grades, neither study found that academic major was

mitment to the institution or the goal of graduation from college. Studies replicating these compensatory effects have been limited largely to residential institutions. It would be of interest to know whether future studies also find these effects to be present in nonresidential colleges.

Long-Term Effects of College

In terms of impact on educational attainment, the evidence is quite clear that the benefits of obtaining a college degree are passed on from one generation to the next. Having a bachelor's degree or above appears to have a positive influence on the educational attainment of sons and daughters even when controls are made for such factors as income, family size, and offspring's intelligence. The most comprehensive analysis suggests that much of this long-term impact is indirect, mediated through the influence of parental education on family financial resources, sons' and daughters' educational aspirations, and the selectivity of the undergraduate institution they attend.

Notes

1. To be sure, there is evidence to suggest that degree of overall person-college fit is positively linked with persistence (for example, Braddock, 1981a; Pervin & Rubin, 1967; Rootman, 1972). Similarly, student use of college facilities is positively associated with persistence (for example, Churchill & Iwai, 1981; Kramer & Kramer, 1968). In both cases, however, this evidence pertains almost exclusively to institutional persistence rather than educational attainment, and it is not nearly as extensive as the evidence produced by studies that focus on specific interactions and/or experiences within the academic and social systems of the institution.

2. A somewhat different type of remedial intervention, known as "attributional retraining," has also shown promise for improving student achievement. The purpose of attributional retraining is to restore a student's perceived control and self-efficacy in an academic situation, that is, to show that academic success or failure is linked to individual effort and not circumstances beyond the individual's control (Forsterling, 1985; Perry & Penner, 1989). Attributional retraining has been shown to enhance academic achievement (for example, Wilson & Linville, 1982, 1985, as reviewed by Perry & Penner, 1989), but the greatest impact may be for those who initially attribute success or failure to external rather than internal causes (Perry & Penner, 1989).

3. Clearly, there are other factors that appear to be significantly related to grades in college. These include the nature of the dominant peer culture with which the student interacts (for example, Gerst & Moos,

1972; Misner & Wellner, 1970; Moos, 1979; Schrager, 1986; Winston, Hutson, & McCaffery, 1980), the student's academic major (Astin, 1982; Stoecker, Pascarella, & Wolfle, 1988), congruence between personality characteristics and choice of major (Aderinto, 1975; Bruch & Krieshok, 1981; Reuterfors, Schneidner, & Overton, 1979; Spokane, 1985; Walsh, Spokane, & Mitchell, 1976), and the congruence between the college environment and student personality characteristics (Hayes, 1974). Grades are also related to congruence in student-faculty interests (Posthuma & Navran (1970), participation in honors programs (for example, Astin, 1977a; Pflaum, Pascarella, & Duby, 1985), the consistency between part-time work and the student's academic program (Hay, Evans, & Lindsay, 1970), and, possibly, student informal contact with faculty that focuses on intellectual matters (Pascarella, Terenzini, & Hibel, 1978; Terenzini & Pascarella, 1980a; Volkwein, King, & Terenzini, 1985). Compared to interventions designed to facilitate academic adjustment or enhance the study climate in residences, however, these associations have received little experimental verification.

4. In addition to studies that focus on the influence of academic major on educational aspirations and attainment, there is also a small body of evidence that considers the effects of varying levels of congruence or fit between a student's personality characteristics and his or her academic major. Nearly all of this research is based on Holland's (1973, 1984) theory of person-environment fit. According to this theory, congruence (typified, for example, by a person whose predominant personality type is artistic and whose major is music) should lead to higher levels of persistence and degree attainment than incongruence. The evidence addressing this proposition is somewhat mixed. Some studies find that congruence is significantly and positively related to persistence (Bruch & Krieshok, 1981; Southworth & Morningstar, 1970), while others report no significant relationship (Elton & Rose, 1981; Holcomb & Anderson, 1978).

5. Despite some findings to the contrary (for example, Hountras & Brandt, 1970; Nowack & Hanson, 1985; Trivett, 1974), the most convincing evidence suggests that living on campus or near campus (versus commuting to college) has little net positive influence on academic achievement (Blimling, 1989; Chickering, 1974a; Grosz & Brandt, 1969; Maurais, 1968; Pascarella, 1985d; Ryan, 1970; Simono, Wachowiak, & Furr, 1984; Weislogel, 1977). The latter conclusion seems to hold even when the characteristics of the institution attended are taken into account (Pascarella, 1985d). There is also single-institution evidence, as yet unreplicated, that living on campus can have a negative impact on various dimensions of general cognitive development (Pike, 1989).

6. See Bean and Metzner (1985) for a cogent and comprehensive review of the factors that influence the persistence or withdrawal behavior of

nontraditional, commuting students. Part of this section draws from that review.

7. Strictly speaking, anticipatory socialization takes place in groups not connected to the college that one will be attending (for example, high school friends). Since orientation programs are obviously tied to the college to be attended, we consider them to be institutionally sponsored attempts at early socialization that are functionally analogous to anticipatory socialization.

8. Evidence from three independent samples (Pascarella & Chapman, 1983b; Pascarella & Terenzini, 1983; Terenzini, Pascarella, Theophilides, & Lorang, 1985) has suggested a mutually compensatory interaction between commitment to the institution attended and commitment to the goal of graduation. In terms of positive influence on persistence, commitment to graduation from college is most important for individuals low in institutional commitment. Conversely, institutional commitment is most important for individuals low in commitment to graduation.

10

Career Choice
and Development

In this chapter we summarize the accumulated evidence on the influence
of college on the noneconomic aspects of career. (Chapter Eleven addresses
the economic returns to a college education.) Not surprisingly, this evidence indicates that college has an important impact on the type of occupation one enters. Indeed, the lack of a bachelor's degree may effectively
exclude an individual from entry into a large number of jobs; and this
effect is likely to increase as American society becomes more technologically
complex (Boudon, 1973; Perella, 1973; Rosen, 1975). In addition to college's undeniably important implications for occupational attainment, college also shapes other dimensions of one's career. These include career
choice, career progression and success, and the transfer of occupational
status advantages from one generation to the next.

By definition, of course, a large portion of the evidence on the impact of college on career concerns long-term effects. Consequently, we de-
cided not to include a separate section on long-term effects in this chapter
but rather to synthesize the evidence on such effects within our other five
sections. In the final section of the chapter we synthesize evidence pertaining to the intergenerational transfer of college effects from parents to children.

Change During College

Astin (1977a) has suggested that for a substantial number of students, career development during college is more a process of implement-
ing a career than of choosing one. There is substantial evidence to support
this claim in that initial career choice at the beginning of college tends to
be the single best predictor of career choice at the end of college and the
career or occupation actually entered (Astin, 1977a; Astin & Myint, 1971;
Braxton, Brier, Herzog, & Pascarella, 1988; Ethington, Smart, & Pascarella,
1987; Pascarella, Brier, Smart, & Herzog, 1987; Tusin & Pascarella, 1985).

Despite this tendency, it is clear that students frequently change their
occupational plans during college (Astin & Panos, 1969; Davis, 1965; Fenske

& Scott, 1973; Hind & Wirth, 1969; Theophilides, Terenzini, & Lorang, 1984a). Feldman and Newcomb (1969) estimated that between one-third and two-thirds of all students change their career choice during college, and this is consistent with more recent national evidence presented by Astin (1977a). A large portion of such changes may be attributable to mobility across related fields or to shifts out of extremely competitive fields such as medicine and engineering (Astin, 1977a; Freiden & Staaf, 1973). Similarly, another portion of these changes may be due to the fact that students become cognizant of national or regional shifts in the employment opportunities and economic returns to different occupations (Cebula & Lopes, 1982; Florito & Dauffenbach, 1982; Freeman, 1971; Koch, 1972). In any case, a considerable amount of useful refocusing or refinement of career thinking is still occurring during college. A number of scholars have in fact addressed the issue of whether college students become more mature in their thinking about and planning for a career with increased exposure to postsecondary education.

Although assessed by several different methods and instruments, *career maturity* as it is operationally defined typically involves reference to the extent to which the individual has accomplished career developmental tasks, the ability to formulate career plans, the accuracy of knowledge about one's preferred occupation (opportunities, financial returns, training requirements, and the like), and the degree of certainty about and planning for one's career choice. A small but reasonably consistent body of evidence indicates that sophomores or upperclassmen tend to exhibit significantly higher levels of mature thinking about or planning for a career than do freshmen (Blann, 1985; Graves, 1975; Healy, Mitchell, & Mourton, 1987; Kennedy & Dimick, 1987; McCaffrey, Miller, & Winston, 1984; Ware & Apprich, 1980). The exceptions to this are studies by Loesch, Shub, and Rucker (1979) and Tilden (1976), who report that differences in level of career maturity noted between freshmen and upperclassmen were statistically nonsignificant. Somewhat mixed results are reported by Nevill and Super (1988), who found that although juniors and seniors did not differ from freshmen or sophomores on all dimensions of career maturity, they did engage in significantly more career planning.

Unfortunately, nearly all the research on the relationship between year in college and maturity of career thinking and planning is cross-sectional. Consequently, it is hazardous to attribute the more mature career thinking of upperclassmen to some internal socialization process that happens during college. Some evidence suggests that maturity in career thinking increases with age (Healy, Mitchell, & Mourton, 1987). This in itself might account for the freshman-upperclassman differences observed. Another alternative hypothesis is based on differential attrition from college. Students less advanced in their career planning may be more likely to withdraw from college than those with more advanced levels of career development. Indirect evidence for this hypothesis is perhaps suggested by the fact that degree of uncertainty about one's academic major tends to be positively linked to withdrawal from college (for example, Bucklin & Bucklin, 1970; Demitroff, 1974; Newton & Gaither, 1980).[1]

Net Effects of College

Occupational Status

As indicated in Chapter Nine, the most influential models of the socioeconomic attainment process in modern American society view formal education as playing a central role in the determination of occupational status. Not only is education seen as mediating the indirect influence of socioeconomic background; it is also considered to have an important direct effect on occupational status, irrespective of social origins.

Occupational status itself can be generally regarded as a hierarchy of occupations that reflects their perceived prestige or desirability (Duncan, 1961; Hauser & Featherman, 1977; Pineo & Porter, 1967; Siegel, 1971). The evidence is quite clear, however, that perceived occupational prestige or desirability has an overwhelming socioeconomic basis consisting largely of education and income. Duncan (1961), for example, found that about 83 percent of the variance in the perceived "prestige" of ninety U.S. occupational titles was accounted for by the typical education and income of individuals in those occupations. Almost exactly the same results have been reported in an independent analysis by Siegel (1971).

The different arrays of occupational prestige or status are themselves highly intercorrelated. Duncan, Featherman, and Duncan (1972), for example, report correlations among different ways of assessing occupational prestige in the .86 to .91 range. This suggests that the different approaches are essentially measuring the same trait and that there is a consistency or invariance in the occupational status hierarchy in the United States (Hauser & Featherman, 1977). Evidence also suggests that there is probably a single occupational prestige hierarchy for men and women (Bose, 1973; Parnes, Shea, Spitz, & Zeller, 1970).

Perhaps the most widely used measure of occupational status or prestige is the Socio-Economic Index (SEI) developed by Duncan (1961). An occupation's SEI score depends on the percentage of individuals working in that occupation who have completed a certain level of formal education or higher and the percentage with incomes at a certain level or higher. An update of the SEI, adjusted to the 1970 Census occupational codes, was completed by Hauser and Featherman (1977). It is obvious that since an occupation's SEI score is a function of its educational requirements, level of education will strongly influence an individual's score. Thus, on first consideration it would seem that any association between formal education and occupational prestige is largely tautological. This overstates the case, however, since as Jencks et al. (1979, p. 8) point out, the link between formal education and occupational status reflects a real social phenomenon. "The average education of men in a given line of work is closely related to the cognitive complexity and desirability of the work. It affects not only the social position of those who engage in the work (Duncan, 1961), but their children's life chances (Klatsky & Hodge, 1971), independent of both the individual's own education and his earnings from his work (Sewell & Hauser, 1975; Bielby, Hauser & Featherman, 1977)."

An extensive body of unequivocal evidence indicates that even when individual background characteristics (such as family social status) and abilities (for example, intelligence) are held constant, level of formal education has a strong positive impact on occupational status throughout the life span. Moreover, the clear weight of this evidence also suggests that among all measurable influences (family status, ability, aspirations, significant others, and so on), education is far and away the strongest (for example, Alexander & Eckland, 1975a; Alexander, Eckland, & Griffin, 1975; Duncan, 1968; Featherman & Carter, 1976; Fligstein & Wolf, 1978; Griffin & Kalleberg, 1981; Jencks, Crouse, & Mueser, 1983; McClendon, 1976; Porter, 1974, 1976; Sewell, Haller, & Ohlendorf, 1970; Sewell, Haller, & Portes, 1969; Sewell & Hauser, 1975, 1980; Treiman & Terrell, 1975).

The influence of educational attainment on occupational status, however, is not simply linear. Individuals appear to receive greater relative occupational status returns from some levels of formal education than from others. Evidence suggests that completing a bachelor's degree provides the single largest incremental return in terms of occupational status. Jencks et al. (1979) provide the most comprehensive evidence to support this assertion. They analyzed data from five national and six special-purpose samples to identify the determinants of occupational and economic success among men twenty-five to sixty-four years old in America. A number of the samples, though by no means all, permitted statistical control of important background variables and individual abilities such as family social status and intelligence. When these controls were made, Jencks et al. found that twelve rather than eight years of secondary school were worth a net average increase of about one-half of a standard deviation in occupational status as measured by the Duncan (1961) SEI. This converts to a 19 percent advantage in occupational status attributable to a high school over an elementary school education. In comparison, four years of college were worth a net average increase of slightly more than one standard deviation in occupational status. This converts to a 34 percentile point advantage in occupational status for completing college versus completing high school. In short, completing college appears to confer an occupational status advantage that is nearly twice as large as that obtained from completing high school.

More recent evidence, though less comprehensive than that of Jencks et al. (1979), also suggests that completing college provides relatively greater occupational status returns than earning an advanced degree. Knox, Lindsay, and Kolb (1988) analyzed the 1986 follow-up data of the National Longitudinal Study of the High School Class of 1972 to determine, among other things, the influence of educational attainment on occupational status as measured by the SEI. Controlling for race, gender, family socioeconomic status, and academic ability, they found that obtaining a bachelor's degree provided a 17.61-point increase in occupational status over and above a high school diploma. In comparison, obtaining an advanced degree was responsible for a 12.05-point increase in occupational status beyond the bachelor's degree. Thus, on average, obtaining an advanced degree returned occupational status advantages beyond the bachelor's degree that were about two-thirds of what a bachelor's degree returned in comparison with a high school diploma.

Obviously, the Knox, Lindsay, and Kolb (1988) study may have masked some differential effects by pooling all advanced degrees into a single category. Certain types of advanced degrees, M.D.s and J.D.s, for instance, may return greater occupational status advantages than others. Despite this limitation, the evidence presented by Knox, Lindsay, and Kolb, when combined with that of Jencks et al. (1979), underscores the central role of completing college in the status attainment process. The contention that a bachelor's degree is a passport to the American middle class has a strong foundation in the power of that degree to provide entry into relatively high paying professional, technical, and managerial occupations.

Moreover, although the net occupational prestige advantage of completing a college degree was stronger for younger men in the samples analyzed by Jencks et al. (1979), occupational differences among mature men with different educational levels was not just a function of college graduates obtaining higher-status jobs when they first entered the labor force. Even after controls were made for initial occupational status, family background, and intelligence, the net difference between the current occupational status of college and high school graduates was about two-thirds of the observed difference.

That college has significant short- and long-term implications for occupational and career placement is not lost on the American public and indeed may even be perceived as increasing in importance. For example, in 1978 the National Gallup Polls found that 36 percent of Americans felt college was extremely important for success; in 1982 the number increased to 58 percent (Elam, 1983).

Causal Mechanisms. The causal mechanism that underlies the power of the bachelor's degree to confer high occupational status has been the subject of considerable debate. On one side are those who believe that college, by means of a series of curricular and extracurricular experiences, imparts cognitive skills, values, personality characteristics, attitudes, and behavior patterns that are valued by employers in high-status occupations. Economists have referred to this as a "human capital" explanation for the effects of college, particularly as it influences requisite cognitive skills (for example, G. Becker, 1964; Hansen, 1970; Schultz, 1961, 1963). Sociologists, understandably, have used the term *socialization* to refer to essentially the same mechanism (Kerckhoff, 1976). The fundamental assumption underlying this explanation is that the college experience itself actually develops the cognitive and noncognitive skills, attitudes, and values necessary to succeed in complex technical, professional, and managerial occupations. There is a certain logical appeal to this argument. Clearly, college does teach some specific skills that may enable one to enter and remain in a high-status occupation. For example, a person entering the engineering profession is expected to have engineering skills that, at least in part, are probably learned in an engineering curriculum. Moreover, as we saw in Chapter Four, college also enhances the development of a number of more general cognitive skills and capabilities. Whether the particular general cognitive skills enhanced by college make the individual more likely to be successful or productive in high-status occupations, however, is less clear (Berg, 1970; Jencks et al., 1979).

Of course, college does more than impart cognitive skills; and it may well be that the important, occupationally relevant socialization that occurs in college is the development of favorable personality styles, attitudes and values, interpersonal and organizational skills, and levels of ambition, motivation, and self-confidence. These may have even greater appeal to employers than cognitive or technical skills in signifying the long-term success and productivity of the individual (H. Becker, 1964; Collins, 1974; Gordon & Howell, 1959; Hoyt & Muchinsky, 1973; Hicks, Koller, & Tellett-Royce, 1984; Useem & Miller, 1975, 1977; Rawlins & Ulman, 1974; Walberg & Sigler, 1975).[2]

Another side of this debate views college less as functioning to develop cognitive and noncognitive skills than as a screening, credentialing, or certifying institution that allocates occupational status to those with the requisite intellectual and personal traits to complete the prescribed course of study. Economists tend to refer to this explanation as "screening" (Taubman & Wales, 1974), while sociologists tend to refer to it as "certification" or "allocation" (Kerckhoff, 1976; Meyer, 1972). The essence of this explanation is that college has been granted a "charter" or "commission" by the larger society to select, sort, and confer adult status on the individual graduate quite apart from whatever he or she may have learned during college (Collins, 1979; J. Meyer, 1972, 1977). From this perspective, the high occupational status of college graduates derives not so much from the actual effects of college on the development of occupationally relevant cognitive and noncognitive skills as from what members of society (including employers) presume those effects to be. Such effects may not occur; yet the perception of society is such that a bachelor's degree generally certifies the holder as acceptable material for a middle-class occupation or position (Jencks & Riesman, 1968).

A variant of certification or screening theory posits that postsecondary education tends to recruit the most ambitious, resourceful, creative, and intellectually competent individuals in society to begin with. Graduation from college further certifies these individuals in terms of such factors as perseverance, drive, and ability to meet organizational demands. As a result, employers can use a bachelor's degree as a convenient screening device to select those employees whose intellectual capacities, ambition, and work patterns make them likely to be productive in complex high-status occupations. In this sense a college degree may simply serve to screen individuals on the basis of preexisting traits such as ability, ambition, and perseverance that are valuable employee traits in many managerial, professional, and technical jobs (Withey, 1971).

Considerable evidence exists to support the notion of the screening or certification effects of college on occupational status. Jencks et al. (1979) found that obtaining a bachelor's degree conferred a "bonus" of about five SEI points over and above the composite SEI increase one would get for four years of college without completing one's degree. Similarly, in their analysis of the NLS-72 data Knox, Lindsay, & Kolb (1988) found that with gender, race, family socioeconomic status, and academic ability held constant, obtaining a bachelor's degree was worth an SEI score more than two and a quarter times that attributable to having two or more years of college. Taken together, these findings suggest that one gains an additional occupational status advantage from college if one is certified as having completed the prescribed course of study. Put another way, the occupational status return for each year invested in college is reduced if the bachelor's degree is not earned.

Whereas evidence for some screening or certification effect of college on occupational status is reasonably clear, it is also the case that each additional year of college has an incremental, positive impact on occupational status irrespective of whether or not the bachelor's degree is completed (Jencks et al., 1979; Knox, Lindsay, & Kolb, 1988). One could obviously argue that each year of college completed is itself a certification that employers use to screen prospective employees. At the same time, however, the fact that extent of exposure to college increases occupational status regardless of degree completion suggests the possibility that college may in fact enhance cognitive and noncognitive skills that increase the likelihood of success in complex jobs. Thus, although there is ample evidence of a certification mechanism in accounting for the impact of college on occupational status, it is not clear that this impact is totally attributable to certification. Some elements of human capital or socialization are probably also at work.

Work Force Participation

In Bowen's (1977) extensive synthesis of the benefits associated with postsecondary education, he concludes that a major effect of a college education on one's career is that it enhances work force participation and stability of employment. Our review of Bowen's evidence and a synthesis of the evidence reported since Bowen's review lead us to agree with his conclusions. The weight of evidence is unequivocal in that of those seeking employment, both men and women who attend or graduate from college are more likely to participate in the work force and less likely to be unemployed than their counterparts whose formal education ends with secondary school. Moreover, those with a bachelor's degree are less likely to experience unemployment than those who attend college but do not complete their degree (for example, Calvert, 1969; Cobern, Salem, & Mushkin, 1973; Dearman & Plisko, 1981; McEaddy, 1975; Melchiori & Nash, 1983; Trent & Medsker, 1968; Wishart & Rossmann, 1977; Young, 1975, 1985; Young & Hayghe, 1984).

The differences in unemployment rates between high school and college graduates do not appear to have decreased substantially from 1960 onward despite the fact that an increasing percentage of those in the work force are college graduates. For example, in 1966 Morgan, Sirageldin, and Baerwaldt (1966), in a national study of "productive Americans," reported that bachelor's degree recipients were slightly less than half as likely to be unemployed as those having only a high school diploma. Nearly twenty years later Young (1985), using the 1984 Current Population Survey, reported that college graduates were only 33 percent as likely as high school graduates to be unemployed.

The nature of this literature makes it difficult to isolate the net effects of college on occupational stability. With few exceptions (for example, Trent & Medsker, 1968), little or no attempt has been made to control for important confounding variables such as ability, ambition, or socioeconomic origins. Nevertheless, one could make a reasonably strong argument that college indirectly contributes to occupational stability in at least two ways. First, as the evidence on occupational status clearly indicates, a college degree significantly increases one's likelihood of entering relatively high status managerial, technical, and professional occupations. This in itself has important implications for occupational stability. As suggested by Bowen (1977), managerial, technical, and professional occupations may be less sensitive than lower-status jobs to employment fluctuations that occur with changing economic conditions.[3] Moreover, since fewer of these occupations are unionized or involve physical labor, there may be less likelihood of experiencing periods of unemployment due to strikes or injury (Lando, 1975).

A second consideration is the notion that college increases the indi-

vidual's "allocative ability." As defined by Schultz (1975), this is the capacity
of the individual to adjust to changing economic or occupational conditions. Given an occupational disequilibrium, how effectively does the individual reallocate resources to deal with it? Schultz hypothesizes that formal
education increases one's ability to deal with occupational disequilibriums
largely because those with more education can bring greater intellectual
and other resources to bear in the process of finding a job. Indeed, there
is considerable evidence to suggest that accuracy in occupational information and efficiency in job search, as well as regional mobility to take advantage of employment opportunities, are associated with college attendance
(for example, Da Vanzo, 1983; Freeman, 1973; Greenwood, 1975; Haveman & Wolfe, 1984; Lansing & Mueller, 1967; Metcalf, 1973; Mincer, 1978;
Parnes & Kohen, 1975; Schwartz, 1971, 1976).

Furthermore, the college-educated individual may have an additional
advantage in dealing with occupational disequilibriums in the form of ac-
quaintanceship networks with college classmates. Evidence suggesting the
importance of such networks or contacts is presented in Granovetter's (1974)
study of managerial individuals who changed jobs in a major metropolitan
area. Not only did the managers locate their new positions more often
through personal contacts than through any other method, but a substantial number of the contacts dated back to college friendships. In this way
college contacts were of continuing significance for the circulation of information and opportunities about high-status occupational positions. Consequently, such contacts may be an efficient resource not only for addressing
occupational disequilibriums but also for taking advantage of opportunities
to enhance one's occupational position (Useem & Miller, 1975).

Related to the notion that college enhances one's allocative ability is
the idea that it provides the basic intellectual, analytical, and interpersonal
competencies that permit one to effectively learn new occupationally relevant skills on the job. This intellectual and interpersonal framework for
learning new skills and adapting to new responsibilities has been frequently
mentioned by graduates as an important work-related benefit of college
(for example, Bisconti, 1987; Bisconti & Kessler, 1980; Bisconti & Solmon,
1976; Mentkowski, 1988). Although specific skills learned in a major field,
such as engineering, may be useful in a person's initial work experience,
the more general intellectual and interpersonal skills learned in college may
be a greater hedge against unemployment in that they permit flexibility and
adaptability in a time when knowledge and jobs can rapidly become obso-
lescent.

Occupational Productivity and Success

In this section we review the evidence pertaining to the impact of
college on occupational productivity and success, exclusive of salary or

earnings. (The latter is addressed at length in Chapter Eleven.) Apart from financial returns, the two primary indicators of productivity and success employed in the literature are, typically, supervisors' ratings of productivity or effectiveness and level of advancement or rate of promotion.

Productivity. A considerable amount of research has addressed the link between formal education and occupational productivity. The findings of this research, however, tend to be inconsistent and in some cases even contradictory. For example, both Berg (1970) and Fuller (1970) found that within fairly narrowly defined blue-collar occupational categories, level of formal education had little systematic association with worker productivity. Similar results have been reported by Little (1980) for clerical workers, even with amount of occupational experience held constant. Conversely, Booth, McNally, and Berry (1978) and Hoiberg and Pugh (1978) report that for-mal education had a statistically significant, positive association with pro-ductivity or performance in various military occupational specialties (for example, medical corpsman, dental technician, noncommissioned officer), even when background characteristics such as age and intelligence were held constant.

Even if this evidence were less equivocal, it would still be difficult to determine the association between a college education and job productivity. Educational attainment in these studies is typically defined as years of formal education completed with no categorical breakdown into college and noncollege groups. Additionally, the occupational levels considered are those that characteristically employ only a limited number of college grad-uates.

The majority of studies that consider productivity differences be-tween college and noncollege individuals in managerial, technical, or re-lated professions yield statistically nonsignificant findings. Berliner (1971), Medoff (1977), and Medoff and Abraham (1980, 1981) report that when college and noncollege individuals hold the same jobs in a managerial field, there is little substantive difference in their productivity or effectiveness as rated by supervisors. Similar results have been reported by Greenberg and Greenberg (1976) for sales effectiveness in twelve industries.

Those investigations that do find statistically significant job produc-tivity differences among those who attended college and those who did not tend to be contradictory. In an extensive longitudinal study of male mana-gerial performance in a single large corporation, Howard (1986) found that college graduates, as compared to those who did not attend college, were judged by supervisors to have significantly greater general managerial ef-fectiveness on a composite scale that included such factors as organizing and planning, leadership, decision making, energy, mental ability, personal impact, and oral communication skills. The college group was not only judged to have significantly greater potential for managerial effectiveness when first employed, but they also showed greater improvement in managerial effectiveness over time. Generally consistent results are reported by DeBack and Mentkowski (1986) in a cross-sectional study of the competencies of baccalaureate and nonbaccalaureate nurses. Conversely, in a longitudinal study of managerial effectiveness in another large corporation, Woo (1986) controlled for job grade level, tenure and experience in the firm, and geographical location and found that having a bachelor's degree actually had a statistically significant negative association with ratings of overall managerial effectiveness.

Our judgment is that the weight of evidence suggests little or no advantage in overall job productivity that can be attributed to college. Even if we give greatest weight to the longitudinal study that showed that bachelor's degree recipients were significantly more effective managers than those with less formal education (Howard, 1986), it is difficult to attribute this outcome to the influence of college rather than to differential recruitment. As compared to their counterparts with less formal education, those who attend and graduate from college may simply possess more of the personal characteristics that contribute to managerial effectiveness to begin with. A similar problem exists in interpreting the findings of DeBack and Mentkowski (1986).

Success. Evidence pertaining to the influence of college on occupational success is decidedly more consistent but by no means totally so. Howard (1986), Rosenbaum (1984), and Medoff and Abraham (1981) all present evidence indicating that bachelor's degree recipients within a large corporation have higher levels of career mobility than those with less formal education. Howard's twenty-year longitudinal analysis of a single firm (AT&T) traced the professional success of two groups of male employees: college graduates who were initially hired into first-level managerial positions and men without college degrees who were initially hired into nonmanagement positions but advanced into management positions by the age of thirty-two. The median age at the time of hiring was twenty-four for the college sample and thirty for the noncollege sample. At the end of the twenty-year period there were marked differences in the management levels attained favoring the college group. Of six management levels, the highest being vice president, the average level of the college group (3.18) was a full level above that of the noncollege group (2.14). Only 3 percent of the noncollege sample had advanced beyond the third level of management compared to 31 percent of the college men, the latter including three vice presidents. A few members of the noncollege group earned college degrees during the twenty-year period. These men attained a typical managerial level (2.56) that was higher than the noncollege sample but lower than the college group. This suggests that promotion advantages that accrue to college graduates are most pronounced when the individual enters the company with a degree.

Although it is clear from Howard's (1986) data that a bachelor's degree allocates substantial advantages in terms of corporate advancement (at least in the particular firm where her study was conducted), it is not necessarily obvious why this is so. In Howard's analyses the college group demonstrated greater managerial skill than the noncollege group, which might account for part of their advantage in promotion rate. Such a conclusion, however, may be confounded by at least two factors. First, some form of credentialing or certification may be at work in the promotion process. As a result college graduates may be regarded more favorably by their supervisors simply because of the normative expectation that those with college degrees *should* advance farther. Some evidence to support this notion is presented in Bills's (1988) analysis of the factors that influenced managers' hiring and promotion decisions in six companies. Although educational credentials were clearly more important in hiring than in advancement in the organization, 54.5 percent of the managers surveyed indicated that amount of formal education still played a "very" or "somewhat" important role in their promotion decisions.

A second and perhaps even more important confounding influence in Howard's (1986) findings is the fact that the college group had the additional advantage of being initially hired into the lower levels of a *managerial* career ladder. This in itself may have placed them on a career path characterized by opportunity for greater occupational mobility than the career path of the noncollege group. A substantial part of the greater occupational advancement enjoyed by college graduates may be attributable to initial job positioning effects rather than to their being decidedly more productive employees (Thurow, 1972). Consistent with this notion is evidence that suggests that net of tenure and race or gender composition, the percentage of bachelor's degree recipients in a job has a strong positive impact on the promotion chances associated with the job (Rosenbaum, 1984).

Rosenbaum (1984) conducted a thirteen-year longitudinal study of career mobility in another large corporation similar to the one studied by Howard (1986). Like Howard (1986), he found that having a bachelor's degree significantly enhanced career mobility and success, particularly if it was earned prior to entering the corporation. Controlling for initial job level (nonmanagement through upper-middle management), age, and tenure, Rosenbaum found that having a bachelor's degree had a statistically significant positive direct effect on subsequent job level for the first seven years of tenure in the firm, though not subsequently. An analysis was also made of a measure of job status within job level. While job level broadly defined job authority, job status defined such dimensions as salary range, benefit package, office size, and degree of autonomy in work tasks. Net of initial job status, age, race, gender, and company tenure, having a bachelor's degree had a statistically significant positive direct effect on job status thirteen years later.

Medoff and Abraham (1981) considered actual promotions of male managerial and professional personnel in a single large manufacturing firm. Controlling for years of company and noncompany experience, supervisors' performance ratings, region of the country, and job level, they found that having a bachelor's degree (versus a high school diploma only) had a statistically significant positive influence on the likelihood of promotion during a three-year period. Given this evidence, it is difficult, at first glance at least, to explain Woo's (1986) conflicting findings on a subsample of what appear to be the same data. Using essentially the same controls, Woo reports a statistically significant negative effect of a bachelor's degree on year-to-year promotion probabilities. One possible explanation for these conflicting results is that those who are hired without a bachelor's degree start at a lower job level than college graduates, and in order to work their way up to the same job level, they may receive more frequent promotions. Conversely, because college graduates are hired at initially higher job levels, promotions for them may be less frequent but more meaningful in terms of long-range consequences for eventual managerial level in the company. It may also be the case that rate of promotion in the company studied is not uniform across job grades but instead is less frequent at higher managerial levels than at lower ones. This might explain the difference noted by Woo (1986) in yearly promotion probabilities between bachelor's degree recipients and those with less formal education. As suggested by Rosenbaum's (1984) analyses, however, when those with and those without a college degree start at the same job level, the overall advancement rates of the former are clearly higher than those of the latter, at least until age thirty-five.

It is also important to note that *frequency* of yearly promotion (even if biased toward those who start at lower-level jobs in a particular company, typically those without a bachelor's degree) is by no means an unequivocal determinant of the managerial level to which one rises in a company. We found no evidence in any of the studies reviewed to suggest that those without a bachelor's degree typically rise to as high a level in a corporate management hierarchy as do college graduates.

In summary, the evidence on job productivity and career mobility reveals few substantive differences between college and noncollege employees in productivity or effectiveness within the same job level. It is undeniably the case, however, that college graduates enjoy significantly higher levels of career mobility. Initial job positioning effects, which place college graduates and those with less education on different career paths, probably account for part of these differences. Similarly, while college graduates may not demonstrate greater productivity at lower-level jobs than their noncollege counterparts, graduates may enjoy greater upward mobility in a particular company because it is expected that their cognitive and noncognitive skills will better equip them for successful adaptation to the demands of more complex, high-level managerial positions (Griliches, 1969).

This suggests one of the significant latent influences of college on career mobility. Bachelor's degree recipients end up advancing farther because college is believed to provide the general cognitive skills and personal dispositions that make such individuals more efficient learners of new occupational competencies (Bisconti, 1987; Bisconti & Kessler, 1980; Bisconti & Solmon, 1976; Mentkowski & Doherty, 1983; Pace, 1974; Wilensky & Lawrence, 1979). In short, college graduates are more promotable to higher-level positions because college has equipped them to be better on-the-job learners.[4] Of course, the effect might be basically the same if college merely "certified" the most efficient learners rather than providing a series of socializing experiences that actually enhance their learning efficiency and interpersonal skills.

Job Satisfaction

As we have seen so far in this chapter, a bachelor's degree typically confers a number of distinct occupational advantages on its owner. These include higher levels of occupational prestige (and a concomitant higher income), job stability, and career mobility. Moreover, as suggested by Lindsay and Knox (1984) and Rosenbaum (1984) college graduates seem better able to compete for jobs within occupational levels that are characterized by autonomy, individual discretion, and relatively challenging levels of complexity and ideational content. In short, within the American occupational structure, the jobs college graduates typically obtain should provide relatively high extrinsic and intrinsic rewards. Thus, we might expect a positive link between college and job satisfaction.

There is reasonably consistent evidence to support this contention, although the link is not particularly strong. In a series of studies, Quinn and associates analyzed data from eleven national surveys of male and female members of the American work force conducted between 1962 and 1977 (Quinn & Baldi de Mandilovitch, 1975, 1980; Quinn & Staines, 1979; Quinn, Staines, & McCullough, 1974). Their analyses indicated a statistically significant positive relationship between level of formal education and overall job satisfaction. The relationship, however, was modest (never accounting for more than 13 percent of the variance in job satisfaction) and not the same across all levels of education. Of the five levels of education completed (grade school or less, some high school, completed high school, some college, and completed college), there was little variance in job satisfaction among the lowest four levels. Only college graduates were consistently and substantially more satisfied with their jobs than individuals at other educational levels. Moreover, in analyses that held age constant, completion of college was probably the only increment of education that contributed appreciably to job satisfaction. Getting a college degree had a statistically significant positive association with two of six specific aspects of job satisfaction: "financial rewards" and "challenge" (the extent to which the individual was stimulated and challenged by the job and had the opportunity to exercise acquired skills at work). There was no statistically significant association between college graduation and satisfaction with resource adequacy, comfort, relationships with co-workers, or promotion, although the last was clearly in the expected direction.

Such evidence is consistent with trends in the occupational status research that suggest a credentialing bonus in job prestige attributable to obtaining the bachelor's degree. That college graduates appear to receive a similar bonus in job satisfaction may reflect the fact that obtaining the degree is a key educational credential for allocating individuals to jobs characterized by intellectual stimulation and challenge and by relatively high financial rewards.

Results generally consistent with those of Quinn and associates have also been reported by Klein and Maher (1968), Mueller (1969), and Glenn and Weaver (1982). The Klein and Maher study was based on a single-company sample of first-level managers, while the Mueller and the Glenn and Weaver studies were based on less extensive national samples of the work force than those analyzed by Quinn and associates. In all three studies the positive association between postsecondary education and overall job satisfaction was small but statistically significant.

The Glenn and Weaver (1982) analyses are interesting in that they also support the notion that education enhances job satisfaction largely by means of the characteristics of the jobs in which the more highly educated are placed. Statistically controlling for age and religious preference, Glenn and Weaver found that much of the total positive influence of education on job satisfaction was indirect, being mediated by education's direct positive effects on intrinsic and extrinsic work characteristics such as autonomy, authority, occupational prestige, and earnings.[5]

It is clear from the studies reviewed above that the overall positive influence of college on job satisfaction is modest. There are two possible explanations for this. The first is that college tends to produce conflicting influences on satisfaction with one's work. On the one hand, college tends to contribute to job satisfaction by increasing the intrinsic (autonomy, challenge, interest) and extrinsic (income) rewards of work. On the other hand, as we have seen in earlier chapters, college tends to develop the capacity for more sophisticated, complex, and critical judgments in students. Consequently, as compared to those with less formal education, college graduates may be more aware of the possible range of work options and more sensitive to unattained possibilities in their jobs and careers (Campbell, 1981).[6]

Some evidence in support of this explanation is presented by Campbell (1981) and Gordon and Arvey (1975). Campbell's analysis of overall job satisfaction among men in a series of national samples yielded a nonlinear association between education and level of job satisfaction. The group who did not go to high school had the highest level of job satisfaction, and the group with some college had the lowest level. College graduates were more satisfied than those who did not finish college but were more critical of their jobs than those with the least education. Gordon and Arvey conducted their analyses on a single-company sample and found no significant association between level of education and satisfaction with the work one actually did. They did, however, find that the more highly educated were significantly more critical of the way the company was being managed than were the less educated.

A second explanation for the modest relationship between college and job satisfaction is that the payoffs in job satisfaction that accompany increasing education can be offset when job demands do not match educational attainment. From this perspective, amount of education relative to job demands may be a more important indicator of job satisfaction than just amount of education. This has become the basis for an "overeducation" hypothesis that argues that because postsecondary education raises occupational expectations, college graduates who find themselves in jobs that do not require a college education will have a particularly high level of occupational dissatisfaction (for example, Berg, 1970; Blumberg & Murtha, 1977; Bowles & Gintis, 1976). Although there are some exceptions (for example, Sheppard & Herrick, 1972; Wright & Hamilton, 1979), the weight of evidence tends to support the presence of a statistically significant link between overeducation and job dissatisfaction (Burris, 1983; Kalleberg & Sorensen, 1973; Quinn & Baldi de Mandilovitch, 1980; Richards, 1984a; Rumberger, 1981). Not all the evidence suggests that the magnitude of the overeducation effect on job satisfaction of college graduates is particularly large or that it has extensive societal consequences (Burris, 1983; Smith, 1986). Moreover, it may not become manifest until the mismatch between educational level and job demands is substantial (for example, college graduates in jobs that typically require a secondary school diploma or less). Nevertheless, overeducation may be a factor in explaining why increased levels of postsecondary education do not always lead to increased job satisfaction.

Between-College Effects

In Chapter Nine on educational attainment we saw that a substantial body of evidence indicates that where a student attends college has a significant net impact on educational attainment. In this section we review the evidence bearing on an analogous question. Do the characteristics of the college or university attended have a nontrivial influence on the various dimensions of an individual's career independent of his or her background and precollege traits? It seems almost self-evident that the answer to this question is yes. In addition to the public folklore about different colleges and universities, there is abundant evidence to suggest that the graduates of certain kinds of institutions or even a small number of specific colleges are simply more successful or eminent than graduates of other institutions (for example, Collins, 1971; Domhoff, 1967; Hardy, 1974; Mortimer, Lorence, & Kumka, 1986; Pierson, 1969; Scientific American, 1965; Useem & Karabel, 1986; Useem & Miller, 1975, 1977). The problem, of course, is that such evidence may simply reflect the kinds of students recruited by certain types of institutions rather than being the actual result of attendance at those institutions. As has been our practice throughout this book, our concern in this section is with the net influence of different college characteristics on career.

Two-Year Versus Four-Year Institutions

In Chapter Nine we saw reasonably clear evidence that net of socioeconomic background, academic ability, and precollege aspirations, students who initially attend a two-year institution are significantly less likely to complete a bachelor's degree and have significantly lower levels of educational attainment generally than their counterparts who initially attend four-year institutions. Since educational attainment plays such a critical role in the achievement of occupational status, one might anticipate that initially attending a two-year college would have deleterious consequences for occupational status.

What little evidence there is on this matter is consistent in supporting this expectation. Breneman and Nelson (1981), analyzing the 1976 follow-up of the NLS-72 data, statistically controlled for a large battery of student characteristics, including race, language spoken at home, high school grades, precollege educational aspirations, and marital status. With these factors held constant, individuals who began postsecondary education in a two-year college held jobs four years later that were significantly lower in prestige (on the Duncan SEI) than those of their counterparts who began in four-year institutions.

Anderson (1984) also analyzed the NLS-72 data but examined occupational status three years later (1979 follow-up) than did the Breneman and Nelson (1981) analyses (1976 follow-up). Controlling for many of the same variables and also for gender, family socioeconomic status, precollege occupational status aspirations, college program, and academic ability, she too found that students who initially attended two-year colleges had jobs significantly lower on the Duncan SEI than did those individuals who started in four-year colleges.

It is likely that much, if not most, of the negative influence of attending a two-year college on occupational status is attributable to the fact that students who initially attend such institutions have lower levels of educational attainment than their counterparts who initially enroll in four-year colleges. It is less clear that attendance at a two-year (versus a four-year) college seriously inhibits occupational status attainment when individuals of equal educational attainment are compared. Monk-Turner (1982, 1983) used the National Longitudinal Survey of Labor Market Experience to compare the occupational attainment of community college and four-year college entrants ten years after they graduated from high school. With controls made for such variables as gender, race, family socioeconomic status, precollege educational aspirations, academic ability, and actual educational attainment, initially attending a two-year institution had a statistically significant but small negative effect on the Duncan SEI score of the job held.

Somewhat different findings, however, have been reported by Thomas and Gordon (1983) and Smart and Ethington (1985), each of whom analyzed the 1979 follow-up of the NLS-72 data. Thomas and Gordon statistically controlled for family socioeconomic status, academic ability, precollege educational and occupational aspirations, college grades, college major, and actual educational attainment. With these factors held constant, they found that attending a two-year versus a four-year college had no statistically significant effect on occupational status for any gender or racial (white, black, Hispanic) subgroups. (Attending a two-year college had a small negative effect when the samples were combined, a result that may have been due to having a much larger sample.)

Similarly, Smart and Ethington (1985) took a subsample of 1976 baccalaureate recipients from the NLS-72 data to determine differences in the job status (and other job characteristics) of those who began in four-year versus two-year institutions. With controls made for academic ability, family socioeconomic status, precollege occupational aspirations, and number of years employed, no statistically significant differences were found in the occupational status (Duncan SEI) of the job held in 1979. This finding held regardless of gender.

Taken as a body of evidence, the studies reviewed above suggest that the "cooling out" function of two-year colleges may have negative implications for occupational status *largely* because initial attendance at these institutions tends to inhibit educational attainment. Such a disadvantage is not immutable, however. Those two-year college students motivated to complete and capable of completing the bachelor's degree in the same period of time as their peers from four-year institutions do not appear to be seriously disadvantaged in competing for jobs of equal occupational status. In short, when educational attainment is held constant, any residual occupational status disadvantages attributable to initial attendance at a two-year college become quite small and perhaps trivial.

Similarly, there is little evidence to suggest that initial attendance at two- or four-year colleges has any important effects on other noneconomic measures of occupational success or satisfaction, either when educational attainment is held constant or when it is not. Smart and Ethington (1985) have provided the most extensive documentation for this claim. In their analyses of bachelor's degree recipients, they found that initially attending a two-year rather than a four-year institution had no statistically significant effect on various measures of job stability, intrinsic job satisfaction, or extrinsic job satisfaction for either sex when academic ability, family socioeconomic status, precollege occupational aspirations, and years employed were held constant. Consistent findings are reported by Breneman and Nelson (1981) for unemployment rate, even though no controls were made for educational attainment between those starting at community college versus those starting at four-year institutions.

Evidence concerning the occupational implications of attending a two-year college for those not aspiring to a bachelor's degree is practically nonexistent. We uncovered only one study that addressed this issue. Somers, Sharpe, and Myint (1971) compared the occupational status and unemployment rate of jobs secured by 1966 vocational program graduates of community colleges and graduates of postsecondary vocational or technical schools three years after program completion. Although the community college vocational students held more prestigious jobs and had a lower rate of unemployment than did their vocational or technical school counterparts, these differences became statistically nonsignificant when controls were made for student background characteristics and educational attainment.

Institutional Quality

The influence of college "quality" on career is an area of substantial research interest. This attention perhaps reflects the extent of a common cultural belief that attendance at certain colleges and universities confers distinctive advantages to an individual in the many dimensions of a career. A broad range of American society seems to believe that men and women enjoy a certain measure of career success precisely because they attend and graduate from these institutions and not others (for example, Mortimer, Lorence, & Kumka, 1986; Rynes & Boudreau, 1986).

According to human capital or socialization theory, graduates of "better" colleges attain greater occupational success because those colleges provide a more rigorous or better education. This view contends that the career success of the graduates of elite institutions is attributable to what they learn or how they are socialized in college. Conversely, those who hold to a screening or certification explanation for the effects of college argue that "high-quality" institutions produce more successful graduates because they confer greater status on their graduates and these status properties enhance the chances for occupational success (Rosenbaum, 1984). Implicit in this view is the notion that the occupational advantages conferred by a quality institution are largely a function of how that institution and its graduates are viewed by important segments of the external society (graduate and professional schools, corporate employers, and so forth). Thus, simply being admitted to a prestigious college affords the individual a considerable status attainment advantage quite apart from the quality of the educational experience provided or the actual change in the individual.

Kamens (1971, 1977) and J. Meyer (1972, 1977) have elaborated on the idea of screening or certification to propose that specific, influential segments of the external society have actually granted implicit "social charters" to colleges. These social charters often afford highly specific social statuses and career niches to graduates (Collins, 1979; Rosenbaum, 1984). Just as West Point has been granted a social charter to produce military leaders, so too many elite colleges and universities have been granted a social charter to produce highly successful graduates in a range of other careers. Thus, graduates of elite schools may benefit from a "signaling" or "labeling" effect (Spence, 1973; Karabel & McClelland, 1983; Klitgaard, 1985). A degree from such a college may identify the person as talented and capable of high-level performance. Consequently, he or she may be most likely to be hired and assigned the most challenging and rewarding jobs (Colarelli, Dean, & Konstans, 1988).

Of course, it is also likely that a major part of the impact of institutional quality on career is attributable not to influences such as socialization or chartering but instead to the types of individuals that elite colleges and universities tend to recruit and enroll. Prestigious colleges may simply enroll high-level talent and provide little in the way of socialization or chartering influences that uniquely enhance one's career. One should not dismiss this possibility too quickly. As will be seen, our synthesis of the evidence suggests that when differences in career-salient student precollege characteristics are taken into account, the effects of institutional quality on career are often small and inconsistent.

Occupational Choice. A substantial amount of evidence suggests that the dimensions of institutional quality (including selectivity, financial and academic resources, and perceived prestige) or reputation have statistically significant positive associations with a number of student background characteristics that are themselves predictive of career success. These include intelligence, academic achievement, and family financial resources (for example, Alwin, 1974, 1976; Smart, 1986; Smart & Pascarella, 1986b; Tusin & Pascarella, 1985). Furthermore, high-quality institutions also appear to attract students who enter college with significantly higher occupational aspirations than their counterparts at less selective or prestigious institutions and who are more certain of their career choice (for example, Clark, Heist, McConnell, Trow, & Yonge, 1972; Smart, 1986; Spaeth, 1970).

If selective or prestigious institutions tend to recruit ambition (along with ability and wealth), do they, as suggested by Trow (1976a), tend to encourage ambition even further? The weight of evidence from studies that address this question suggests that any net positive impact of institutional quality on the overall occupational status of one's career choice (according to the Duncan SEI or a similar index) is quite small and perhaps trivial. Spaeth (1968a, 1977) and Meyer (1970c) both report evidence to suggest that measures of college quality had no important influence on the occupational prestige level of a student's senior-year career choice when factors such as precollege career choice, family social status, and grades during college were taken into account. In contrast, Brown (1979) and Weidman (1984), controlling for essentially the same variables, found that institutional selectivity had a generally positive influence on the occupational status of senior women's career choice but (in the Weidman study) a mixed influence for the career choice of senior men. The influence was positive and statistically significant for male mathematics and history majors, statistically nonsignificant for male English majors, and significantly negative for male political science majors. Most recently, McClelland (1990) found that both men and women with initially high occupational expectations were somewhat more likely to maintain those expectations over a seven-year period after high school if they attended a selective rather than a nonselective college. Part of this finding, of course, might be due to the positive impact of college selectivity on bachelor's degree completion during the time period covered by the study.

There are at least two possible explanations for the equivocal nature of these findings. One is the presence of some form of "frog-pond" or relative deprivation mechanism. In this case, the positive environmental impact of attending an institution with many other academically gifted and ambitious students would be partially offset by the need to reassess one's academic ability and perhaps realistically lower career aspirations in light of relative performance in a competitive academic arena (Davis, 1966; Drew & Astin, 1972; Reitz, 1975).

A second explanation is that the chartering effects of elite institutions may be linked more strongly to specific occupations and careers than to some general hierarchy of occupational status (such as that measured by the Duncan SEI or similar indexes of job prestige). Kamens (1974, 1979) has provided evidence to support this explanation in studies of the influence of different measures of college quality on direction of career choice. He hypothesized that the special charter given elite or high-quality institutions provides faculty in those institutions with a stronger cultural authority to influence student career choice in a direction sanctioned by the values of the academic culture. Thus, he anticipated that irrespective of freshman career choice, students in elite institutions would be more likely than their counterparts in nonelite institutions to choose academic careers.

as the difference among four-year institutions based on Carnegie type. Using data from Olneck and Crouse (1979) with respect to job status increases attributable to a bachelor's degree, the corresponding ratio may be as high as 5 to 1. Part of this difference between the general effect of college and the effect of where one attends college may be due to differences in sample variability. It is difficult, however, to ignore the more substantive interpretation of this evidence, namely, that earning a bachelor's degree counts far more in terms of job status than where one earns it.

11

Economic Benefits
of College

In this chapter we synthesize the evidence on the economic returns to a college education. Such returns are substantial,[1] and this fact probably underlies the motivation of many students who choose to attend college rather than enter the work force immediately after high school graduation (for example, "Nation Top-Heavy with Wealth," 1986; Elam, 1983; Hossler, undated). The chapter addresses the net effects of college, between-college effects, within-college effects, conditional effects of college, and the intergenerational transmission of the economic advantages of investment in postsecondary education.

Net Effects of College

Earnings

One of the safest generalizations one can make about the structure of nearly all highly developed (as well as less developed) societies is that formal education has a strong positive association with earnings, even when such factors as age, gender, and occupational category are held constant (for example, Blaug, 1970, 1972; Psacharopoulos, 1972a, 1972b, 1973, 1985). This generalization clearly holds in American society, although as suggested by status attainment research, much of the impact of formal education on earnings is transmitted indirectly through education's enhancement of occupational status (for example, Bowles, 1972; Campbell & Laughlin, 1987; Duncan, 1968; Jencks, Crouse, & Mueser, 1983; Sewell & Hauser, 1972, 1975). Whether direct or indirect, the association between education and earnings is not merely a function of the different levels of academic ability and social origin that commonly distinguish people with different levels of formal education. It persists even after such influences are taken into account (for example, Becker, 1975; Duncan, 1968; Griliches & Mason, 1973; Jencks et al., 1979; Sewell & Hauser, 1975; Renshaw, 1972; Suter & Miller, 1973). Consistent with the findings on occupational status, however, the influence of different levels of formal education on earnings is not uni-

500

formly linear. Rather, undergraduate education appears to be generally more important than secondary education and perhaps even graduate education. Furthermore, one appears to receive an additional earnings "bonus" for completing the bachelor's degree over and above the incremental advantage associated with years of college completed.

The most extensive evidence with respect to the influence of different levels of formal education on earnings is provided by Jencks et al. (1979) in an analysis of eight independent samples of men in the work force. Controlling for work experience, measures of intelligence, and socioeconomic background, these investigators estimate that a high school diploma provided a 15 to 25 percent earnings advantage over an eighth grade education. With the same factors held constant, a college graduate enjoyed an estimated earnings advantage of between 18.3 and 46.5 percent over those whose formal education ended with high school. Thus, the lower and upper estimates of the net earnings advantage of a college graduate tend to be consistently higher than the lower and upper estimates of the earnings advantage of a high school graduate over someone with an eighth grade education. Similar results are also reported by Goodman using data from the 1970 U.S. Census, one of the samples analyzed by Jencks et al. With controls for age, region of the country, and occupational status of the job held (though not for intelligence or social origins), a bachelor's degree was about twice as important as a high school diploma in increasing earnings.

Present evidence also suggests that the earnings advantage of a bachelor's degree over a high school diploma may be somewhat greater than the corresponding advantage of graduate degrees in general over the bachelor's degree. This evidence comes from two studies. First, Goodman (1979), controlling for age, job status, and region of the country, found that a bachelor's degree was substantially more important than a graduate degree in increasing earnings. (Relative importance was difficult to estimate because a graduate degree had a slight depressing effect on earnings when other factors were considered.) The second study, by Knox, Lindsay, and Kolb (1988), followed up the NLS-72 sample in 1986, some fourteen years after high school graduation. Controlling for such factors as race, gender, family socioeconomic status, and academic ability, Knox, Lindsay, and Kolb found that the net incremental earnings advantage of a graduate degree over a bachelor's degree was only about two-thirds of the corresponding earnings advantage of a bachelor's degree over a high school diploma.

There are, of course, some problems in grouping all graduate degrees together as these studies do. Certainly the marked earnings potential associated with some advanced degrees (for example, law, medicine) is masked. Nevertheless, though less pronounced, the evidence on earnings is consistent with that on occupational status in suggesting that attainment of the bachelor's degree may be the single most important educational step in the occupational and economic attainment process.

Consistent with this conclusion is the evidence suggesting that one receives an earnings "bonus" for completing the bachelor's degree, a bonus above and beyond the increment received for each year of college completed. Goodman's (1979) analysis of census data indicates that a bachelor's degree provided an earnings advantage that was nearly seven times as large as that for the first three years of college. A somewhat more rigorous analysis by Knox, Lindsay, and Kolb (1988) suggests that the advantage may be smaller but nonetheless pronounced. Net of race, gender, social status, and academic ability, they found that the earnings returns to a bachelor's degree were about 2.3 times as large as the returns to completing two or more years of college. Similarly, Hauser and Daymont (1977), in their follow-up of Wisconsin men eight to fourteen years after high school graduation, have suggested that each year of college provided a greater earnings advantage when one attained the bachelor's degree. Controlling for parental income, mental ability, and work experience, they found that the economic returns to college were approximately 6 percent per year when one did not obtain the bachelor's degree and rose to approximately 10 percent per year when one did obtain the degree (see also Martin & Morgan, 1963).

The fact that completing the bachelor's degree enhances the economic returns of college is not particularly surprising. Entry into many relatively high paying technical and managerial positions often requires the bachelor's degree. Furthermore, completing one's undergraduate degree is nearly a universal prerequisite for acceptance at professional schools typically linked to high earnings (such as business, law, and medical schools).

Private Rate of Return

The evidence establishing that college has a significant and substantial effect on earnings net of intelligence, social origins, and other factors does not necessarily provide a complete picture of the economic returns to a college education. It addresses only the economic *benefits* of postsecondary education without considering the attendant *costs*. Unlike secondary school, college often requires a financial investment on the part of the student in the form of tuition, books, and other educational fees. Moreover, for many students, the time they invest in college is a time during which they forego income that they would have earned had they entered the labor force immediately after high school (such foregone earnings are sometimes referred to as the opportunity costs of attending college). These considerations have spawned a parallel line of inquiry that we shall refer to as private rate of return research.

A simple way to estimate the private rate of return to a college education is to divide the difference between average posttax earnings of college graduates and high school graduates by the sum of the private, unsubsidized costs of education plus foregone earnings (Witmer, 1970; Walberg,

1987). Taking an example from Psacharopoulos (1973), suppose that the average annual posttax earnings of a male college graduate in 1959 were $9,255 and the corresponding earnings of a high school graduate were $6,132. Therefore, a college graduate could expect to earn on the average during his working life $3,123 more per year ($9,255 − $6,135) than he would be earning with only a high school diploma. Let's also suppose that the total private costs of a college education in 1959 plus foregone earnings were $14,768. If college were considered an investment, such an arrangement would be the equivalent of purchasing a promise to receive an average of $3,123 annually during one's working life at a present cost of $14,768. If we divide $3,123 by $14,768, we see that the average annual yield of investing in college is about 21 percent. This 21 percent is considered the private rate of return to a college education.[2,3]

A large body of research has addressed the question of the private rate of return to college graduation (for example, Becker, 1960; Bowen, 1977; Carnoy & Marenbach, 1975; Cohen & Geske, 1985; Freeman, 1975, 1977; Hines, Tweeten, & Redfern, 1970; Leslie & Brinkman, 1986, 1988; McMahon & Wagner, 1982; Mincer, 1974; Raymond & Sesnowitz, 1975; Witmer, 1980).[4] In attempting to synthesize the evidence from this research, we have the advantage of access to two existing reviews of the literature (Cohen & Geske, 1985; Leslie & Brinkman, 1986). The Cohen and Geske (1985) review synthesized evidence from nine studies that covered the time period from 1940 to 1976. Using the data supplied for each study, Cohen and Geske found that the private rate of return to a bachelor's degree ranged from about 10 to 21 percent and averaged about 13.8 percent. The Leslie and Brinkman (1986) synthesis reviewed twenty-two studies covering the time period from 1940 to 1982. The private rate of return to a bachelor's degree ranged from 7 to 18 percent and averaged 11.8 percent.

Although such rates of return compare quite favorably with "conventional benchmark rates for alternative investments" (Leslie & Brinkman, 1986, p. 214; see also McMahon & Wagner, 1982), they may overestimate the returns attributable to a bachelor's degree unless differences in background and ability are taken into account. Intellectual ability appears to be among the more important confounding influences (for example, Hansen, Weisbrod, & Scanlon, 1970). When Leslie and Brinkman synthesized thirteen studies that controlled for this variable, they estimated that about 79 percent of the private return to a bachelor's degree was independent of ability. Applying this correction, which Leslie and Brinkman (1988) caution was conservative, we obtain an estimated ability-adjusted private rate of return of 10.9 percent for the Cohen and Geske (1985) synthesis and 9.3 percent for the Leslie and Brinkman (1986) synthesis.

These are admittedly rough estimates of the economic rates of return to a bachelor's degree.[5] However, they still compare favorably to benchmark rates for alternative investments. This is particularly true if individual costs are adjusted for public and private subsidies to education (Leslie, 1984), foregone earnings are adjusted for the fact that many students work and earn wages while they attend college (Crary & Leslie, 1978; Freiden & Leimer, 1981; Parsons, 1974), and job fringe benefits are included as part of earnings (Kiker & Rhine, 1987).[6]

The syntheses by Cohen and Geske (1985) and Leslie and Brinkman (1986) also suggest that the private economic rates of return to graduate education over and above a bachelor's degree tend to be somewhat smaller than the corresponding returns to a bachelor's degree over and above a high school diploma (see also Bailey & Schotta, 1972; Hanoch, 1967; Tomaske, 1974; McMahon & Wagner, 1982). This suggestion is consistent with the status attainment research reviewed in Chapter Ten, that suggests that the net increase in earnings associated with a bachelor's degree is larger than the general increase due to graduate degrees (Goodman, 1979; Knox, Lindsay, & Kolb, 1988.[7]

Causal Mechanisms

It is one thing to determine that a bachelor's degree provides a sound economic return on one's investment. It is a somewhat different matter to determine why. Simply put, there are two major explanations for this, and they are reminiscent of our discussion of career in Chapter Ten. The first is a human capital or socialization hypothesis that suggests that college graduates earn more than high school graduates because college provides the former with the cognitive skills and/or personal traits that make them more productive employees. The second explanation is a certification or screening one. This explanation argues that college does not so much influence the cognitive and personal traits related to productivity as simply certify (by means of the bachelor's degree) those who are most likely to have such traits to begin with. Employers can then use a college education as an inexpensive screening device to select individuals who they believe possess favorable intellectual and personal traits for the highest-paying positions or career paths. Thus, part of the earnings differential noted between college graduates and those with less education might arise because the lack of education credentials is a barrier to entry into high-paying occupations.

An offshoot of the second explanation is the possibility that employers may not select or reward individuals solely on the rational basis of potential productivity. Rather, factors such as simple snobbery, image, and social class may also enter into the decision. This would mean that college graduates might end up being overly rewarded by employers for reasons unrelated to individual productivity (Jencks et al., 1979).

Consistent with our discussion in Chapter Ten, there is evidence to support both general explanations. A number of studies present evidence in support of the certification or screening explanation. Jencks et al. (1979), for example, reasoned that if the college experience actually enhances productivity potential more than high school (as posited by a human capital or socialization explanation), then the effect on earnings of an average year of college will be larger than the effect of an average year of high school. However, when these researchers controlled educational attainment, they found that the percentage effect of an extra year of college was consistently *smaller* than the percentage effect of an extra year of high school.

The evidence presented by Jencks et al. (1979) supports the certification or screening explanation essentially by failing to support the human capital or socialization explanation. More direct evidence in support of certification or screening is presented by Goodman (1979) and Knox, Lindsay, and Kolb (1988). Their work suggests that obtaining the bachelor's degree provides a substantial earnings bonus beyond the expected incremental increase for each additional year of college completed. It is highly doubtful that the final year of college actually enhances individual productivity at a higher rate than the preceding three years. Thus, the bachelor's degree may function as a certification or screening device through which employers assign those who have it to higher-paying jobs or career paths than those who do not, even though the two groups may be equally competent. Indeed, individuals who are not college graduates are disproportionately underrepresented in high-status, high-paying occupations, even when they are similar to college graduates in intellectual ability and other traits (Arrow, 1972; Taubman & Wales, 1974, 1975a). Furthermore, within the same corporation a bachelor's degree appears to provide an earnings advantage even when such factors as experience, tenure in the firm, grade level of job, and job performance ratings are held constant (Woo, 1986). Rosenbaum (1984) and Wise (1979) also document the earnings advantage of bachelor's degree recipients in a single firm but without the controls for job performance employed by Woo (1986).

Despite this evidence, it seems counterintuitive that college merely screens talent or perpetuates social class distinctions in the work force without providing some skills that make individuals more productive. In fields such as engineering, accounting, and architecture, for example, a bachelor's degree may be required not simply because it signals intellectual competence or desirable personal traits but also because it indicates the completion of a course of study that actually provides skills essential to effective job performance.

Empirical support for the human capital or socialization explanation comes mainly from observations of the magnitude of the education-earnings link over time. If college does not simply function as a screen for assigning individuals to the highest-paying jobs but rather enhances skills related to actual job productivity, then the correlation between education and earnings should not decline with work experience. (The key assumption here is that earnings reflect job productivity.) Analyses of a number of national samples have generally found that level of education does not become less important to earnings over time (Chiswick, 1973; Haller & Spenner, 1977; Haspel, 1978; Layard & Psacharopoulos, 1974; Ornstein, 1971) and may actually increase in importance with greater work experience (Lillard, 1977; Lillard & Willis, 1978; Mincer, 1974; Rosen & Taubman, 1982). Consistent with this is evidence suggesting that level of education has a positive effect on earnings, even for individuals in the same job status level (for example, Goodman, 1979; Griliches & Mason, 1972; Sewell & Hauser, 1972, 1975; Wilson & Smith-Lovin, 1983).

Such findings rest largely on the related assumptions that earnings reflect job productivity and that those with more education earn more because they are more productive. It is possible, however, that education may be related to earnings over the occupational life span for reasons unrelated to productivity (for example, differential treatment by employers based on level of education). Moreover, as we saw in Chapter Ten, there is little evidence to indicate that when they hold the same jobs, college graduates are more productive or efficient employees than those with less education. It is difficult to square this latter body of evidence with a human capital or socialization explanation for the link between education and income.

In the final analysis there is less debate about the substantial positive effect of college on earnings than about why college has this effect. A modicum of evidence exists to support both a screening or certification explanation and a human capital or socialization explanation. It is possible, of course, that both processes contribute to the causal link between higher education and earnings. In our judgment, however, neither hypothesis alone provides a completely satisfactory or unequivocal explanation.

Between-College Effects

As we have stressed throughout this book, studies that fail to control for salient differences among students who enter different types of postsecondary institutions will speciously overestimate between-college effects. The same caution clearly holds for estimation of the differential effect of institutional characteristics on earnings or income. Consequently in this section we will concentrate on those studies that provided controls for student background traits or other differences among students attending different kinds of institutions.

Two-Year Versus Four-Year Institutions

In Chapter Ten we saw that much of the negative influence on job status of beginning one's postsecondary experience at a two-year college as compared to a four-year college is attributable to the fact that two-year college entrants are significantly less likely to complete a bachelor's degree than their four-year college counterparts. For those students who successfully negotiate the not inconsequential hurdles of transfer to a four-year institution and completion of a bachelor's degree, any residual negative impact of starting at a community college is small and perhaps trivial.

Since earnings, like job status, are strongly linked to educational attainment, it seems likely that a similar trend would hold for the impact of two-year versus four-year colleges on economic returns. In fact, the evidence, based on analysis of two independent national samples, is mixed, with no clear advantage in methodological rigor to any study. Monk-Turner (1988) analyzed data from the Longitudinal Survey of Labor Market Experience on men and women followed up ten years after high school graduation (in 1976 and 1977). Net of such factors as intelligence, educational aspirations, socioeconomic background, sex, race, and educational attainment, students starting at four-year institutions had a statistically significant 6 percent wage advantage over those starting at two-year institutions. This finding, however, is not supported by two analyses of the NLS-72 data. Breneman and Nelson (1981) and Anderson (1984), controlling for many of the same factors as Monk-Turner, found no significant income penalties associated with two-year compared with four-year college attendance when the sample was followed up either four years (Breneman and Nelson) or seven years (Anderson) after high school graduation. Indeed, in the Anderson analyses community college entrants actually had slightly (though not significantly) higher net earnings than four-year college entrants.

Perhaps the soundest conclusion to be drawn from this rather sparse evidence is that when individuals of equal background traits and educational attainment are compared, any direct earnings penalties for initially attending a two-year college are quite small, at least in the early stages of one's career. Breneman and Nelson (1981) have argued that such penalties may tend to become more pronounced over the occupational life span. This may partially explain the earnings differences of two-year and four-year college entrants found by Monk-Turner (1988) in a ten-year follow-up compared with the general earnings parity between the two groups found by Breneman and Nelson (1981) and Anderson (1984) in follow-ups of four and seven years. Even if Breneman and Nelson's argument were not true, however, it is possible that there are discernible indirect economic penalties associated with initially attending a community college. These indirect penalties arise largely because initial attendance at a two-year college has substantial deleterious consequences for bachelor's degree completion, which in turn is a major determinant of entry into high-status, high-paying jobs. Such indirect effects, however, are not typically considered in the existing research.[8]

Institutional Quality

A large body of research has addressed the issue of whether or not institutional "quality" has a net impact on earnings. The findings are not totally unequivocal, but we believe the weight of evidence suggests that at least one aspect of institutional "quality," the academic selectivity of the undergraduate student body, has a statistically significant, though generally very small, net impact on earnings. The most methodologically rigorous investigations estimate the impact of institutional quality while controlling for important background factors (for example, socioeconomic origin, intelligence) and other other college and postcollege variables that might confound the link between college quality and earnings (for example, educational attainment, occupational status).

An exemplary study by Trusheim and Crouse (1981) analyzed a sample of men from the longitudinal Panel Study of Income Dynamics who were twenty-five to sixty years old in 1972. Controlling for family socioeconomic status, intelligence, a measure of achievement motivation, educational attainment, occupational status (Duncan SEI), and weeks worked per year, Trusheim and Crouse found that the academic selectivity of the college attended (average composite SAT or ACT score of freshmen) had a small but statistically significant positive direct effect on current income. A more subjective measure of college social prestige did not. Although they typically did not control for the range of confounding variables held constant by Trusheim and Crouse, analyses of fourteen independent samples have produced quite similar results (Akin & Garfinkel, 1974; Bisconti, 1978; Daniere & Mechling, 1970; Ehrenberg & Sherman, 1987; Foster & Rodgers, 1980; Jencks et al, 1979; Karabel & McClelland, 1987; McClelland, 1977; Morgan & Sirageldin, 1968; Mueller, 1988; Perrucci, 1980; Phelan & Phelan, 1983; Reed & Miller, 1970; Smart, 1988a; Solmon, 1975a, 1981; Solmon, Bisconti, & Ochsner, 1977; Wachtel, 1975a, 1976; Wales, 1973; Weisbrod & Karpoff, 1968; Wise, 1979). This body of evidence indicates that other aspects of college quality in addition to selectivity (for example, faculty salary, financial expenditures per student, reputational ranking) may also have statistically significant positive net effects on income. However, it is the academic selectivity of the college attended that demonstrates the most consistent positive impact, perhaps because this relatively objective measure is the most frequently employed index of institutional quality in the studies reviewed.

There is also a trend in this evidence suggesting that the positive effects of college selectivity or academic reputation on earnings are not linear. Analyzing data on a national sample of World War II veterans followed up in 1969 (the NBER-Thorndike data), Wales (1973) found that a college's academic reputation, based on the Gourman (1967) ratings, had a statistically significant positive impact on 1969 earnings only when it was in the top fifth of the reputational distribution. The findings of Solmon (1975a), who used the same data, are similar with respect to the statistically significant positive impact of colleges in the top quartile of the Gourman ratings but also indicate a statistically significant negative impact for colleges in the bottom quartile. Results consistent with those of Solmon are reported by Wise (1979) in an analysis of men in a single company. Net of other factors, rate of salary increase was only positively influenced when one attended a college at the very top of the selectivity distribution. Conversely, salary increase was only negatively affected when one attended a college near the bottom of the selectivity distribution.

To be sure, not all of the studies we reviewed found that college selectivity or other dimensions of quality had a positive net impact on earnings. Analyses of seven independent samples indicated a statistically nonsignificant, negative, or mixed impact of college selectivity, prestige, or resource expenditures on earnings (Angle, Steiber, & Wissman, 1980; Astin, 1977a; Griffin & Alexander, 1978; Heckman, Lazenby, & Moore, 1968; Hunt, 1963; Knox, Lindsay, & Kolb, 1988; Rogers, 1969; Sharp & Weidman, 1987). We found little in the way of methodological rigor to distinguish these studies from those that report a statistically significant positive effect of college quality indexes on earnings. Nevertheless, we believe that the weight of evidence from all studies taken together indicates a small but positive net impact of college quality (and, in particular, selectivity) on earnings. When we combine all those analyses that provide adequate statistical information, our best (and admittedly somewhat rough) estimate is that college quality explains on the average somewhere between one and one and a half percent of the differences in individual earnings above and beyond that attributable to other causes.[9]

This estimate is based essentially on the net *direct* effects of college quality on earnings. If one were to add to this the indirect effect of college quality through intervening variables such as educational attainment, the magnitude of the impact might increase. Recall from Chapter Nine on educational attainment that measures of institutional quality such as selectivity or reputation significantly enhance persistence, bachelor's degree completion, and attendance in graduate or professional school. Since educational attainment is such an important determinant of entry into high-paying jobs, it is likely that at least part of the positive impact of college quality on earnings is manifest through this indirect route (that is, college quality enhancing educational attainment, which in turn enhances earnings). Such indirect effects have not typically been estimated in the existing body of research on college quality and earnings. Recently, however, Smart's (1988a) analysis of college graduates followed up nine years after initial enrollment in college suggests that when indirect effects are considered, the overall positive impact of college quality (a composite measure of selectivity, resources, and cost) on earnings is increased between 15 and 30 percent. Much of this indirect effect is transmitted through receiving a graduate or pro-fessional degree.[10]

Causal Mechanisms. It is interesting to consider the possible causal mechanisms that underlie the small positive net influence of college quality on earnings. A human capital or socialization explanation would account for the effect by arguing that colleges with the most educational resources (academically capable and motivated students, large libraries, well-equipped laboratories, and the like) are able to foster more of the cognitive and non-cognitive skills essential to productivity than educationally less-advantaged colleges. This has an extended payoff in greater job productivity and there-fore greater earnings. Conversely, a certification or screening explanation argues that elite institutions function more to enroll and certify high-level talent than to foster it. A degree from an elite institution therefore acts as an inexpensive selection or screening device. Employers can use this device to dip into a pool of talented and ambitious individuals for the highest-paying jobs or career ladders. Being a graduate of certain elite institutions may also lead to preferential treatment by employers for reasons unrelated to demonstrated job productivity.

The strongest evidence mustered in support of the human capital or socialization explanation comes from studies that demonstrate that the ef-fect of college selectivity on earnings increases over time. (The assumption here is that employers will only increase the financial rewards to graduates of elite colleges if they consistently demonstrate greater job productivity.) Solmon (1975a), using a national sample of World War II veterans, found that net of factors such as intelligence, educational attainment, occupation, and labor force experience, the impact on earnings of aspects of college quality such as selectivity, Gourman rankings, and faculty salary becomes more pronounced later in the individual's career (see also Symonette, 1981). Similar results have also been reported by Rosenbaum (1984) and Wise (1979) in longitudinal studies of careers within two large corporations. In the Wise analysis college selectivity actually had no significant link with starting salary. It did, however, have a significant positive effect on *rate* of salary increase, even when controls were made for the job responsibilities of the position to which a person was initially assigned.

Other studies are somewhat less supportive of the notion that grad-uates of elite colleges are paid more because they are more productive em-ployees. In a single-corporation study of accountants, Ferris (1982) found that a reputational measure of college quality was a statistically significant predictor of starting salary, but that this link became nonsignificant with experience and advancement in the firm. Similarly, in analyses of men from the Panel Study of Income Dynamics, Trusheim and Crouse (1981) found that neither college selectivity nor college social prestige had a statistically significant effect on income growth over a three-year period.

The findings of Ferris (1982) and Trusheim and Crouse (1981) are more consistent with the expectation that the earnings advantage enjoyed by graduates of selective or prestigious colleges is due to factors other than simple job productivity (for example, preferential treatment in the initial job assignment or assignment to career ladders with greater earnings potential). Furthermore, their results are also quite consistent with the evidence on college quality and job effectiveness. Evidence summarized in Chapter Ten on career indicates that college selectivity or prestige has little or no impact on an individual's actual job productivity or performance. When that evidence is combined with the results of Ferris (1982) and Trusheim and Crouse (1981), we find a rather compelling reason to believe that graduates of elite colleges may earn more for reasons not always linked to their job performance. Even if one were to dismiss this evidence totally, however, and assume that graduates of elite colleges earn more over the long term simply because they are more productive employees, it would still be risky to conclude that this is an institutional effect. A degree from an elite college or university might function more to screen and certify the talent and ambition necessary for effective long-term job performance than to foster this talent or ambition in any distinctive way. Thus, although the finding in some studies that the link between college quality and earnings strengthens over time is frequently cited in support of a human capital or socialization explanation, the finding is not necessarily incompatible with a screening or certification explanation.

Institutional Type

A small body of research has sought to determine whether institutional type has a net effect on earnings. All of the studies in this area have defined institutional type in terms of the eight Carnegie categories or some variation on that typology. The weight of evidence from this research points to a statistically significant net earnings differential among individuals attending the different types of institutions, but the pattern is only partially consistent across investigations.

The two major studies on this topic have been conducted by Solmon and Wachtel (1975), with a national sample of World War II veterans followed up in 1969 (the NBER-Thorndike data), and Knox, Lindsay, and Kolb (1988), with the 1986 follow-up of the NLS-72. Solmon and Wachtel controlled for educational attainment, experience in the labor force, intelligence, and type of career. With these variables held constant, attendance at colleges in the different Carnegie types explained an additional 1 percent of the variance in 1969 earnings. The highest net earnings were received by men who had attended major research universities and large doctorate-granting institutions, while the lowest earnings were received by those who had attended small doctorate-granting institutions, comprehensive colleges with a limited selection of programs, and nonselective liberal arts colleges. Knox, Lindsay, and Kolb, in an analysis that combined men and women, controlled for gender, race, family socioeconomic status, and academic abilities. With these factors held constant, the highest net earnings were received by those who had attended major research universities and small doctorate-granting institutions, while the lowest net earnings accrued to those who had attended nonselective liberal arts colleges and large doctorate-granting universities.

Readily apparent from these two analyses of major national data bases are clear points of agreement and contradiction. In both studies individuals from major research universities tended to earn relatively high incomes, while those from nonselective liberal arts colleges tended to earn relatively low incomes. Yet the net earnings received by those who had attended large doctorate-granting institutions ranked quite high in the Solmon and Wachtel (1975) study but quite low in the Knox, Lindsay, and Kolb (1988) investigation. Conversely, individuals who had attended small doctorate-granting institutions had relatively high earnings in the Knox, Lindsay, and Kolb study but relatively low earnings in the Solmon and Wachtel analysis.

Perhaps the major conclusion yielded by this research is that a significant net earnings advantage accrues to individuals who attended major research universities (Carnegie type Research I) and that a correspondingly small disadvantage accrues to those who attended nonselective liberal arts colleges. Although other investigations cluster the Carnegie types in different ways, they tend to support this conclusion, particularly with respect to the small earnings advantage of those who attended major research universities (for example, McMahon & Wagner, 1982; Sharp & Weidman, 1987). Of course, any earnings advantage accruing to graduates of major research universities or disadvantage accruing to graduates of nonselective liberal arts colleges may partially reflect differences in the salient measures of institutional quality linked to earnings (selectivity, academic reputation, financial resources, and so on). Solmon and Wachtel's (1975) analysis, for example, found substantial differences among the eight Carnegie institutional categories on such factors as student body selectivity, academic reputational rankings, and faculty compensation. Major research universities generally ranked highest of all institutional types on these indexes, whereas nonselective liberal arts colleges typically ranked at or near the bottom. We suspect that any net earnings differences among the Carnegie institutional types would be dramatically reduced if measures of institutional quality were taken into account.

Institutional Size

In Chapter Ten we reported evidence supporting the hypothesis that large institutions, because of their wider range of programatic links with occupational groups in the society, enhance the occupational status attainment of their students. A small body of research has addressed the issue of whether institutional size is also linked with earnings. The studies we reviewed that controlled for salient confounding influences were fairly consistent in suggesting that institutional size has a small positive and significant net effect on earnings early in one's career. Gruca (1988) analyzed data from a national sample of individuals who began college in 1971 and were followed up in 1980. With controls for student background characteristics, the selectivity of the institution attended, college major and grades, and educational attainment and occupational status, the enrollment of the institution attended had a statistically significant positive direct effect on 1980 earnings for both white men and women. The corresponding effects for black men and women were similar in magnitude but statistically nonsignificant, probably because of smaller sample sizes. Similar results with a somewhat different sample from the same data base are reported by Smart (1988a).

Knox, Lindsay, and Kolb (1988), using the 1986 follow-up of the NLS-72 sample, regressed 1986 annual earnings on a model that controlled for (among other factors) gender, race, socioeconomic status, academic ability, educational attainment, and the institution's selectivity, control (private versus public), and vocational emphasis. With these influences held constant, student enrollment had a small but positive and statistically significant direct effect on earnings.[11]

It is important to point out that as with college quality, the net impact of institutional size is small, probably accounting for little more than 1 percent of the variance in earnings in either study. At the same time, however, both Gruca (1988) and Knox, Lindsay, and Kolb (1988) controlled for institutional selectivity in their analyses. Thus, it is unlikely that the modest effect of institutional size was a proxy for the effects of college quality on earnings.

Institutional Control (Public Versus Private)

A small body of research has estimated the effect of institutional control on earnings while specifically controlling for salient confounding influences. The results of this research are mixed, and there is little in the way of differences in methodological rigor between studies to assist us in giving more weight to some findings than to others. Solmon (1981) analyzed data from two national samples of college students, one of which entered college in 1961 and was followed up in 1974 and the other of which entered in 1970 and was followed up in 1977. Controlling for such factors as college major and grades, marital status, length of employment, college selectivity, and educational attainment, Solmon found that attending a private institution had a small but statistically significant negative effect on earnings for both men and women.

Just the opposite, however, is reported by Knox, Lindsay, and Kolb (1988) in their analysis of the 1986 follow-up of the NLS-72 data. Net of race, gender, academic ability, socioeconomic status, educational attainment, and the selectivity, size, and vocational emphasis of the college attended, private control had a small but statistically significant positive effect on 1986 earnings.

The waters are muddied even further by the findings of Sharp and Weidman (1987) in their analysis of the 1979 follow-up of humanities graduates in the NLS-72 data and Solmon (1975a) in his analysis of a national sample of World War II veterans followed up in 1955 and 1969. Both studies found that institutional control had no significant impact on earnings net of individual traits and other institutional characteristics.

Institutional Gender and Race Composition

We found little evidence to suggest that attending a women's college rather than a coeducational institution has more than a trivial net impact on a woman's early career earnings when background characteristics, college achievement, educational attainment, and institutional selectivity are taken into account (Stoecker & Pascarella, 1988). Some evidence does suggest that graduates of predominantly black colleges have lower earnings than their counterparts from predominantly white institutions (for example, Baratz & Ficklen, 1983). It is questionable, however, whether such differences would remain if salient confounding influences were controlled. Pascarella, Smart, and Stoecker (1987) found that predominant college race had no statistically significant impact on the early career earnings of black men and women when individual factors such as socioeconomic status, high school achievement and aspirations, and institutional factors such as selectivity, prestige, and size were held constant.

Transfer Between Four-Year Institutions

In Chapter Ten we described how the inhibiting influence on educational attainment of transfer between four-year institutions has negative consequences for early occupational status. It seems reasonable, therefore, to expect that institutional transfer might also have deleterious consequences for income in the early career. Modest support for this expectation can be found in Kocher and Pascarella's (1988) analysis of a national sample of students who began college in 1971 and were followed up in 1980. Net of such influences as socioeconomic status, occupational aspirations, the selectivity of the first college attended, undergraduate major and grades, educational attainment, and occupational status, transferring between four-year institutions had a statistically significant negative direct effect on the 1980 earnings of white men and a statistically significant negative indirect effect on the 1980 earnings of black women. The corresponding effects for white women and black men were also negative but not statistically significant.

Within College Effects

A fairly large body of research addresses the question of whether or not different college experiences influence an individual's earnings. As with Chapter Ten on career, however, we found no common theoretical perspective or unifying thread running through this literature. The evidence, nevertheless, primarily clusters into the following categories: academic major, academic achievement, extracurricular involvement, and work experience.

Academic Major

Academic major in college clearly has an impact on early career earnings that cannot be totally accounted for by differences in the background characteristics of students selecting different fields of study. Two typical studies were conducted by Griffin and Alexander (1978) and Phelan and Phelan (1983). Griffin and Alexander analyzed a national sample of men first surveyed in 1955 as high school sophomores and followed up in 1970. Statistical controls were made for such factors as academic ability, family socioeconomic status, occupational aspirations, college selectivity, college grades, educational attainment, and occupational status. With these factors held constant, men who had majored in engineering or business had significantly higher 1970 earnings than those who had majored in other fields of study.

Phelan and Phelan (1983) analyzed the 1977 follow-up of a national sample of students who began college in 1970. With controls for family socioeconomic status, high school academic achievement, race, gender, college grades, and a college typology that was largely a measure of selectivity, the effects of college major on earnings were quite consistent with those of Griffin and Alexander (1978). Individuals who had majored in business, engineering, and professional fields had the highest net 1970 earnings, while those who had majored in the humanities and social sciences had the lowest. Physical science and other majors had net earnings in the middle.

Although the vast preponderance of investigations on other samples controlled for somewhat different sets of confounding influences, these studies report results remarkably consistent with those of Griffin and Alexander (1978) and Phelan and Phelan (1983) (Angle & Wissmann, 1981; Daymont & Andrisani, 1984; Gardner & Hwang, 1987; Groat, Chilson, &

Neal, 1982; Koch, 1972; Kocher & Pascarella, 1988; McMahon & Wagner, 1982; Raymond & Sesnowitz, 1983; Reed & Miller, 1970; Seeborg, 1975; Smart, 1988a; Solmon, 1981; Weinstein & Srinivasan, 1974; Wise, 1979).[12] This consistency of results holds regardless of whether the analyses were based on independent national samples (of which there were eight), single-institution samples (of which there were six), or single-company samples (of which there was one). Moreover, the findings are also consistent regardless of whether the outcome was actual earnings or the estimated private rate of return to different academic fields of study.

The generalization that appears warranted from this evidence is that certain undergraduate fields of study tend to provide consistently an advantage in earnings or return on educational investment, at least during the early stages of one's career. These particular fields of study are characterized by a relatively well defined body of knowledge and skills, an emphasis on scientific or quantitative methods of inquiry, and, quite often, an applied orientation (for example, Smart, 1988a). To some extent the findings on field of study and earnings may reflect the fact that employers use undergraduate major as a sorting device, either for purposes of hiring or for assigning individuals with equal amounts of education to different-paying positions. From this perspective those in such majors as engineering, business, or the natural sciences may have several advantages. Employers may believe that students selecting those fields are typically brighter than those in other majors, that they have more useful interests and abilities, or that their academic training is more rigorous and more immediately relevant to a range of jobs (Solmon, 1981).

A related explanation is that the earnings differential across undergraduate majors is largely a function of prevailing market conditions, and marketability may be in the minds of those who hire employees. Thus, companies may be more likely to hire engineers and business majors at higher salaries than other college graduates because they believe their company needs engineers and business majors.

From another perspective the findings on field of study and earnings may also reflect the simple fact that individuals choose their major with specific occupational and economic goals in mind (Wilson, 1978). The quite reasonable assumption here is that certain fields of study are expected or known to be linked to jobs with relatively high earnings (Cebula & Lopes, 1982; Florito & Dauffenbach, 1982; Koch, 1972; McMahon & Wagner, 1981; Wilson & Smith-Lovin, 1983). Thus, academic major is a vehicle by which students "target" their college training toward jobs with different economic payoffs (Wilson & Smith-Lovin, 1983).

Wilson and Smith-Lovin (1983) provide documentation for this "targeted education" explanation in an analysis of the 1968 follow-up of a national sample of 1961 college graduates. College majors (fields of study) were placed on a continuum in terms of the extent to which they typically lead to specific occupations with different average wages. (The specific procedures for doing this are described in Chapter Ten.) Majors typically linked to occupations with relatively high average earnings are business, engineering, several of the physical sciences, and preprofessional majors in medicine and dentistry. Majors in the humanities, social sciences, and education are typically linked to jobs with relatively low earnings. When controls were made for such factors as socioeconomic status, sex role attitudes, educational attainment, marital status, number of children, occupational status, and work experience, the continuum of majors had a statistically significant positive effect on the 1968 earnings of both men and women.

The idea that the content of one's undergraduate training is a determinant of earnings has been used to explain gender and race differences in earnings. There is clear evidence that women are substantially less likely than men and that minorities are somewhat less likely than whites to select majors linked to high economic rewards (for example, Angle & Wissmann, 1981; Daymont & Andrisani, 1984; Ferber & McMahon, 1979; Solmon, 1981; Trent, 1984; Wilson & Shin, 1983; Wilson & Smith-Lovin, 1983). In the case of gender, however, controlling for college major typically reduces sex differences in earnings, but it does not eliminate them (Angle & Wissmann, 1981; Daymont & Andrisani, 1984; Wilson & Smith-Lovin, 1983). There is evidence for a similar conclusion with respect to the effect of racial differences in earnings (for example, Reed & Miller, 1970), but the research does not appear to be as extensive as that focusing on gender differences.

A final point should be made about the net impact of field of study on earnings. Nearly all the studies reviewed in this section deal with the impact of major on earnings during the early stages of one's career, typically in the first ten years. As in Chapter Ten, the specific skills learned in one's major seem most important in preparing for one's first job after graduation rather than for subsequent jobs (Bisconti, 1987; Ochsner & Solmon, 1979). Moreover, there is clear evidence that in terms of long-term career mobility within the same technically oriented company, humanities and social science majors do as well as if not better than those with science, business, or engineering degrees (Beck, 1981; Howard, 1986). Consequently, it seems reasonable to expect that the impact of major field may be substantially reduced or perhaps changed when later career earnings is the criterion. The evidence here is sparse. However, a longitudinal study by Harrell and Harrell (1984) provides at least some support for this expectation. They found that after twenty years, engineers had lower salaries than economics, business, and English majors.

Academic Achievement

In Chapter Ten we saw that grades in college have small but significant and positive associations with measures of job productivity and career mobility. It seems reasonable to assume, therefore, that there will also be a significant positive link between college grades and earnings. A large body of evidence, consisting basically of two types of studies, has addressed this issue. One type of study estimates the simple correlation between academic achievement in college and subsequent earnings.[13] Typically, such studies do not address the factors that might confound the link between college grades and earnings (ability, socioeconomic status, aspirations, college selectivity, and so on). As with the evidence on grades and the noneconomic dimensions of career, we are aided in synthesizing this research by the presence of a number of quantitative and nonquantitative reviews of the literature (for example, Adkins, 1975; Baird, 1985; Calhoon & Reddy, 1968; Cohen, 1984; Nelson, 1975; Samson, Graue, Weinstein, & Walberg, 1984). These reviews are quite consistent in concluding that the average correlation between college grades and earnings is statistically significant and positive but quite modest in magnitude. There is some (though perhaps not serious) disagreement across the reviews as to the exact magnitude of the average correlation. From the designs and data presented in the quantitative syntheses, as well as our review of a number of the original investigations, we estimate the average correlation between college grades and earnings to be about .15. (Interestingly, this is somewhere between the estimates provided by the two most comprehensive quantitative syntheses: Cohen, 1984; Samson, Graue, Weinstein, & Walberg, 1984.) This means that only about 2.3 percent (that is, the square of the average correlation) of the differences in income are explainable by differences in college grades, and this itself may represent an inflated estimate because the correlation is not adjusted for potential confounding influences.

The second type of study puts greater emphasis on determining whether or not the positive link between academic achievement and earnings is causal. This is typically accomplished through statistical control of potential confounding influences such as academic ability, socioeconomic status, aspirations, college major, educational attainment, and occupational status. With some exceptions (for example, Griffin & Alexander, 1978), the weight of evidence from analyses of national samples is reasonably consistent in indicating that college grades have a small but statistically significant positive direct effect on early career earnings. In a typical study, Phelan and Phelan (1983) analyzed data on a national sample of men and women who began college in 1970 and were followed up in 1977. Net of such factors as secondary school grades, family socioeconomic status, race, gender, college type and selectivity, and college major, grades during college had a small but statistically significant positive impact on 1977 earnings. Studies on seven other national samples that controlled for similar variables, as well as for such factors as intelligence, educational attainment, occupational status, and region of employment, report findings generally consistent with those of Phelan and Phelan (for example, Astin, 1977a; Ehrenberg & Sherman, 1987; Hunt, 1963; Kinloch & Perrucci, 1969; Kocher

& Pascarella, 1988; Penley, Gould, & de la Vina, 1984; Perrucci, 1980; Sharp & Weidman, 1987; Smart, 1988a; Solmon, 1981; Solmon, Bisconti, & Ochsner, 1977).

Some research has also been conducted on more focused samples. Typically, these studies are based on alumni from a single college or from a few colleges similar in geographical location or institutional type. Again, the weight of evidence suggests that when such factors as family socioeconomic status, gender, race, college major, educational attainment, and work experience are held constant, college grades continue to have a positive effect on earnings (for example, Gardner & Hwang, 1987; Johnson, 1987; Lauman & Rapoport, 1968; Perrucci, 1969; Perrucci & Perrucci, 1970; Seeborg, 1975). This effect, however, is very small. Taking into account nonsupportive findings with business graduate students (for example, Dreher, Dougherty, & Whiteley, 1985; Pfeffer, 1977), the evidence is less consistent than that found with national samples.

There is also some evidence on the impact of college grades on earnings of employees within the same company. The findings, however, are inconsistent. Ferris (1982) studied the careers of staff accountants in a large accounting firm. Controlling for educational attainment and a measure of the prestige and academic strength of the undergraduate college attended, he found that college grades had no statistically significant impact on initial or subsequent salary. In contrast, Wise (1979) found that although college academic achievement had no impact on the starting salary of college graduates working in a large corporation, it did have a statistically significant positive effect on rate of salary increase over a three- to twenty-two-year period. This effect held regardless of high school grades, family socioeconomic status, college selectivity, college major, educational attainment, length of experience with the company, a measure of the individual's leadership and organizational ability, and the job responsibilities of the position to which the individual was initially assigned.

Since the Wise (1979) study focused on employees who worked for the same corporation for three to twenty-two years, it is one of the few investigations to indicate that college grades may have an independent impact on earnings beyond one's early career (for example, after the first ten years). Other evidence, however, is less consistent. For example, Taubman and Wales (1974) examined the factors influencing after-tax income of the top five executives of fifty of the seventy largest manufacturing firms in the country. Controlling for factors similar to those held constant by Wise, they found that outstanding academic performance in college actually had a negative effect on long-term earnings.

Given the entire body of evidence, we are led to conclude that grades in college probably do have a net positive direct effect on early career earnings. Evidence concerning a longer-term net effect is less extensive and also inconsistent. It is likely, however, that any such causal influence is small, probably accounting on the average for no more than 1 percent of the variance in individual income above and beyond other factors. At the same time, it is also possible that the studies reviewed underestimate the total impact of grades on earnings because they tend to ignore possible indirect influences. Studies by Kocher and Pascarella (1988); Pascarella, Smart, and Stoecker (1987); and Smart (1988a) on a national sample of 1971 college entrants followed up in 1980 report that college achievement often had a statistically significant positive indirect effect on early career earnings through its enhancement of educational attainment. When added to the direct effect, this indirect effect may increase the overall positive net impact of grades on earnings by as much as one-third.[14]

Extracurricular Involvement

A small body of research has investigated the link between collegiate extracurricular involvement and earnings. With some exceptions (for example, Havemann & West, 1952), the weight of evidence suggests that there may be a small positive and statistically significant correlation between involvement in extracurricular activities, particularly in a leadership role, and subsequent earnings (Calhoon & Reddy 1968; Jepsen, 1951; Walters & Bray, 1963). The evidence is less consistent, however, when statistical controls are made for potential confounding influences. In an early study, Hunt (1963) analyzed data on national samples of college students collected in 1947 by *Time* magazine. Controlling for such factors as years since graduation, parental education, academic ability, type of work, college grades, and various dimensions of institutional quality, he found that involvement in college extracurricular activities had a statistically significant positive effect on earnings in one sample but not in another.

More recent research on a national sample of individuals who began college in 1971 and were followed up in 1980 (Kocher & Pascarella, 1988) suggests that any direct influence of leadership positions or other indicators of extracurricular success is trivial when salient confounding influences are taken into account. After controls were made for such factors as family socioeconomic status, high school academic and social achievement, occupational aspirations, institutional selectivity, college grades and major, educational attainment, and occupational status, a measure of extracurricular leadership or success had no statistically significant direct impact on 1980 income for black or white men and women. (The measure of extracurricular leadership or success consisted of items such as being president of a student organization, being editor of a school publication, having a major part in a play, or winning a varsity letter.) There was some indication that for white women and black men extracurricular achievement had a statistically significant positive indirect effect on 1980 earnings through its enhancement of educational attainment. This, however, was not replicated for black men in a study that used a slightly different sample and operational definitions of variables (Pascarella, Smart, & Stoecker, 1987).

We uncovered only two studies that estimated the impact of intercollegiate athletic participation on earnings and that also employed reasonably adequate statistical control of confounding influences. In one study—of the early career earnings of men who had attended three public institutions—DuBois (1978) controlled for age, father's occupational prestige, race, college grades, work experience, and educational attainment. Net of these factors, intercollegiate athletic participation had no significant influence on earnings. Similar findings are reported by Pascarella and Smart (1990), who employed similar controls and analyzed data from a national sample of black and white men.

Work Experience During College

Evidence on the influence of work during college on postcollege earnings is inconsistent and prevents the forming of firm conclusions. Stephenson (1982) used the National Longitudinal Study of Young Men to estimate the postcollege wage determinants during the 1966–1971 period for a sample of white male college graduates. Earnings for 1971 were regressed on such factors as academic aptitude, health limits on work, military service, region of the country in which the person resided, and time since graduation. With these factors held constant, full- or part-time employment during college had a small but statistically significant positive effect on postcollege earnings. Forgey (1973) reports similar results for graduates of five junior colleges, though without the controls adopted by Stephenson.

A refinement of Stephenson's (1982) results is suggested by San (1986), who used a subsample of the same data. Controlling for many of the same variables as Stephenson did, San found that the relationship between work during college and earnings during the first five years after college was nonlinear. Work of twenty-seven hours per week or less during college had a positive influence on postcollege earnings, but work in excess of this amount adversely affected earnings. There was little to suggest that this effect was significantly altered by whether one worked on or off campus.

Other studies have shown less support for the link between work during college and postcollege earnings. Hunt's (1963) analysis of the 1947 *Time* magazine surveys found that supporting oneself during college had no statistically significant effect on subsequent earnings net of ability, social origins, college quality, and college grades. Similar results are reported by Ehrenberg and Sherman (1987) in an analysis of men in the NLS-72 sample. With such factors as academic ability, family socioeconomic status, race, college selectivity, college grades, and average regional earnings in the state of employment held constant, weekly hours of work during college had no statistically significant impact on early career earnings.

to address issues and problems for which there are no verifiably correct answers, an increased intellectual flexibility that permits one to see both the strengths and weaknesses in different sides of a complex issue, and an increased capacity for cognitively organizing and manipulating conceptual complexity.

It is likely that gains in college on such dimensions as abstract reasoning, critical thinking, reflective judgment, and intellectual and conceptual complexity also make the student more functionally adaptive. That is, other things being equal, this enhanced repertoire of intellectual resources permits the individual to adapt more rapidly and efficiently to changing cognitive and noncognitive environments. Put another way, the individual becomes a better learner. It is in this area, we believe, that the intellectual development coincident with college has its most important and enduring implications for the student's postcollege life.

Attitudes and Values

Table 13.2 shows our estimates of the typical freshman-to-senior changes during college in the general area of values and attitudes. A number of these changes are quite consistent with the changes noted in the area of learning and cognitive development. Students not only become more cognitively advanced and resourceful, but they also make gains in their aesthetic, cultural, and intellectual sophistication, gains that are complemented by increased interests and activities in such areas as art, classical music, reading, and creative writing; discussion of philosophical and historical issues; and the humanities and performing arts. Similarly, there are clear gains in the importance students attach to liberal education and exposure to new ideas. In short, the enhancement of cognitive skills during college appears to be concurrent with an increased valuing of and interest in art, culture, and ideas.

If one theme underlying changes in values and attitudes during college is that they tend to be supportive of or at least consistent with observed changes in cognitive growth, a second theme is that the changes also coalesce around a general trend toward liberalization. Considering consistent changes in the areas of sociopolitical, religious, and gender role attitudes and values, it would appear that there are unmistakable and sometimes substantial freshman-to-senior shifts toward openness and a tolerance for diversity, a stronger "other-person orientation," and concern for individual rights and human welfare. These shifts are combined with an increase in liberal political and social values and a decline in both doctrinaire religious beliefs and traditional attitudes about gender roles. The clear movement in this liberalization of attitudes and values is away from a personal perspective characterized by constraint, narrowness, exclusiveness, simplicity, and

Table 13.2. Summary of Estimated Freshman-to-Senior *Changes: Attitudes and Values.*

Outcome	Estimated Magnitude of Change		
	Effect Size[a]	*Percentile Point Difference*[b]	*Percentage Point Difference Between Freshmen & Seniors*[c]
Aesthetic, cultural, and intellectual values	.25–.40	10–15	
Value placed on liberal education			+20 to +30%
Value placed on education as vocational preparation			−10 to −30%
Value placed on intrinsic occupational rewards			+12%
Value placed on extrinsic occupational rewards			−10 to −15%
Altruism, social and civic conscience, humanitarianism	.10–.50	4–19	+ 2 to + 8%
Political and social liberalism	.20	8	+15 to +25%
Civil rights and liberties			+ 5 to +25%
Religiosity, religious affiliation	−.49	19 (in religiosity)	Up to −11% in conventional religious preferences
Traditional views of gender roles			−10 to −25%

[a] Effect size = (senior mean minus freshman mean) divided by freshman standard deviation.

[b] Effect size converted to the equivalent percentile point under the normal curve. This is the percentile point difference between the freshman- and senior-year means when the freshman mean is set at the 50th percentile.

[c] Percentage point increase or decrease of seniors (versus freshmen) holding a particular view or position.

intolerance and toward a perspective with an emphasis on greater individual freedom, breadth, inclusiveness, complexity, and tolerance.

A third unifying thread that characterizes attitude and values change during college is a shift away from the instrumental or extrinsic values of education and occupation toward a higher valuing of intrinsic rewards. Compared to freshmen, seniors attach greater importance to the value of a liberal education and less importance to the value of a college education as vocational preparation. Consistently, seniors (as compared to freshmen) also place greater value on the intrinsic characteristics of a job (intellectual challenge, autonomy, and so forth) and less value on extrinsic rewards (salary, job security, and the like).

At first glance such changes may seem inconsistent with what was clearly an increasing trend between 1970 and 1985 toward vocationalism or materialism in the reasons underlying an individual's decision to attend college (Astin, Green, & Korn, 1987). The motivation for attending college and the changes that occur during college, however, may be largely independent of each other. Thus, even if succeeding cohorts of recent freshmen have increasingly chosen to attend college for its instrumental or extrinsic returns, it would still appear that the freshman-to-senior changes that occur during college lead to an increased value being placed on the nonvocational aspects of one's educational experience and the intrinsic rewards of one's prospective work.

Psychosocial Changes

The motif noted earlier of the interrelatedness of student change during the college years is apparent in the several areas of student psychosocial change summarized in Table 13.3. While the changes in these areas are, on the whole, more modest than those relating to learning and cognitive development, they are approximately the same size as the shifts in attitudes and values. Moreover, their general character and direction are clearly

Table 13.3. Summary of Estimated Freshman-to-Senior *Changes: Self and Relational Systems in Psychosocial Development.*

	Estimated Magnitude of Change		
Outcome	Effect Size[a]	Percentile Point Difference[b]	Percentage Point Difference Between Freshmen & Seniors[c]
Self Systems			
Identity status			+15 to +25% (in reaching identity achievement status)
Ego development	.50	19	
Self-concept			
Academic			+4 to +14% (rating self "above avg.")
Social			+7% (rating self "above avg.")
Self-esteem	.60	23	
Relational Systems			
Autonomy, independence, and locus of control	.36	14	
Authoritarianism	−.81	29	
Ethnocentrism	−.45	17	
Intellectual orientation	.30	12	
Interpersonal relations	.16	6	
Personal adjustment and psychological well-being	.40	16	
Maturity and general personal development	Not available		

[a] Effect size = (senior mean minus freshman mean) divided by freshman standard deviation.

[b] Effect size converted to the equivalent percentile point under the normal curve. This is the percentile point difference between the freshman- and senior-year means when the freshman mean is set at the 50th percentile.

[c] Percentage point increase or decrease of seniors (versus freshmen) holding a particular view or position.

consistent with those of the other two areas. Gains in various kinds of substantive knowledge and in cognitive competence may provide both a basis and the intellectual tools for students to examine their own identities, self-concepts, and the nature of their interactions with their external world.

Thus, perhaps as a partial consequence of their cognitive gains, students appear to move toward greater self-understanding, self-definition, and personal commitment, as well as toward more refined ego functioning. Similarly, students' academic and social self-images, as well as their self-esteem, while perhaps somewhat bruised initially, not only recover but become more positive over the college years.

The psychosocial changes experienced during the college years extend beyond the inner world of the self to include the relational aspects of students' lives: the manner in which they engage and respond to other people and to other aspects of their external world. As students become better learners, they also appear to become increasingly independent of parents (but not necessarily of peers), gain in their sense that they are in control of their world and what happens to them, and become somewhat more mature in their interpersonal relations, both in general and in their intimate relations with others, whether of the same or opposite sex. They also show modest gains in their general personal adjustment, sense of psychological well-being, and general personal development and maturity. Moreover, consistent with the observed shifts toward greater openness in attitudes and values, the evidence quite consistently indicates that students gain in their general intellectual disposition or orientation toward their world, their willingness to challenge authority, their tolerance of other people and their views, their openness to new ideas, and their ability to think in nonstereotypic ways about others who are socially, culturally, racially, or ethnically different from them.

Moral Development

As suggested in Table 13.4, there is clear and consistent evidence that students make statistically significant gains during college in the use of principled reasoning to judge moral issues. This finding holds across different measurement instruments and even different cultures. The absence of descriptive statistics in much of the evidence, however, makes it difficult if not impossible to estimate with confidence the magnitude of the freshman-to-senior change in the same way that we have done for other outcomes. As we have stressed in Chapter Eight on moral development, the magnitude of the freshman-to-senior gain may not be as important as the fact that the major shift during college is from conventional to postconventional or principled judgment. (The former is based strongly on morality as obedience to rules and meeting the expectations of those in authority, while the latter is based strongly on a view of morality as a set of universal

Table 13.4. Summary of Estimated Freshman-to-Senior *Changes: Moral Development*.

| | *Estimated Magnitude of Change* | | |
Outcome	*Effect Size* [a]	*Percentile Point Difference* [b]	*Percentage Point Difference Between Freshmen & Seniors* [c]
Use of principled reasoning in judging moral issues	Difficult to estimate magnitude of effect, but major change during college is from the use of "conventional" to "postconventional" or "principled" reasoning		

[a] Effect size = (senior mean minus freshman mean) divided by freshman standard deviation.

[b] Effect size converted to the equivalent percentile point under the normal curve. This is the percentile point difference between the freshman- and senior-year means when the freshman mean is set at the 50th percentile.

[c] Percentage point increase or decrease of seniors (versus freshmen) holding a particular view or position.

principles of social justice existing independently of societal codification.) This shift in and of itself represents a major event in moral development.

The freshman-to-senior changes in moral judgment noted in our synthesis are perhaps another example of how change during college on one dimension is typically consistent with change in other areas. Measures of moral reasoning are themselves positively correlated not only with areas of general cognitive development that increase during college (such as abstract reasoning, critical thinking, and reflective judgment) but also with the general liberalization of personality and value structures coinciding with college attendance (for example, decreases in authoritarianism or dogmatism; increases in autonomy, tolerance, and interpersonal sensitivity; increased concern for the rights and welfare of others). Thus, the enhancement of principled moral judgment during college is embedded within an interconnected and perhaps mutually reinforcing network of cognitive, value, and psychosocial changes that occur at approximately the same time.

Some Final Thoughts on Change During College

Our conclusions about the changes that occur during college differ in only minor ways from those of Feldman and Newcomb (1969) and Bowen (1977). Indeed, taken as a total body of evidence, all three syntheses suggest that a reasonably consistent set of cognitive, attitudinal, value, and psychosocial changes have occurred among college students over the last four or five decades. Students learn to think in more abstract, critical, complex, and reflective ways; there is a general liberalization of values and attitudes combined with an increase in cultural and artistic interests and activities; progress is made toward the development of personal identities and more positive self-concepts; and there is an expansion and extension of interpersonal horizons, intellectual interests, individual autonomy, and general psychological maturity and well-being. Thus, it can be said that the nature and direction of freshman-to-senior changes appear to be reasonably stable and to some extent predictable.

In some instances our estimate of the *magnitude* of freshman-to-senior changes differs from estimates of previous syntheses, particularly Bowen's (1977). Since the differences are quite modest, however, we are inclined to attribute them to chance variations in the bodies of literature reviewed and perhaps even different typologies or operational definitions of outcomes. At any rate, it would seem that the consistency in the nature and direction of changes across syntheses is a much more salient and noteworthy characteristic of the evidence than are small differences in estimates of the magnitude of the changes across the same syntheses.

It may also be the case that the absolute magnitude of freshman-to-senior changes is not as educationally important as either the qualitative nature or the breadth and scope of the changes. One danger in focusing on quantitative estimates of change such as effect size is that one tends to consider change as happening on a continuum where all change is smoothly continuous and equally important. Many developmental theorists would argue that development does not always happen in such even and equivalent fashion (for example, Kitchener & King, 1990; Kohlberg, 1969; Perry, 1970; Rest, 1986b). Moreover, not all changes are equivalent in size or importance: Some shifts are particularly critical to development irrespective of whether or not they are reflected in a large quantitative change on some continuous scale. For example, the qualitative shift during college from a style of reasoning based on beliefs to one relying on evidence in making judgments represents a key prerequisite to rational problem solving. Similarly, the shift from conventional to principled reasoning during college represents a major qualitative advance in moral development. On both of these dimensions of development, the qualitative nature of the change is likely to be of greater consequence than the magnitude of the change.

We would also suggest that the magnitude of change on any particular dimension or set of dimensions during college may not be as significant as the pronounced breadth of interconnected changes we noted in our synthesis. As posited by major models of student development (for example, Chickering, 1969; Heath, 1968), the evidence indicates not only that individuals change on a broad developmental front during college but also that the changes are of a mutually consistent and supporting nature. Although there may be insufficient empirical grounds to speak of changes in one area causing or permitting changes in other areas, it is clear from the body of evidence we reviewed that the changes coincident with college attendance involve the whole person and proceed in a largely integrated manner. Certainly the notion of broad-based integrative change during college is not a new finding, but the evidence we reviewed was sufficiently compelling to warrant its reaffirmation.

There are, of course, at least three nontrivial problems endemic to the study of freshman-to-senior change. The first stems from the fact that the evidence is based largely on studies measuring typical or average change in some sample (longitudinal studies) or typical or average differences between samples (cross-sectional studies). By focusing on average group shifts or differences, the findings of such studies tend to mask individual differences in patterns of change. Some students may change substantially during college, some may change little or not at all, and some may actually shift in a direction counter to the typical movement of the group. Moreover, some students may change in one way on certain variables and in opposite ways on other variables. Thus, although the average change may be our best estimate of the dominant shift or development occurring in a group, it is not without limitations.

A second problem, one that we have emphasized throughout the book, is that freshman-to-senior change during college does not necessarily reflect the impact of college. Many of the dimensions on which change occurs during college may have a developmental base. If so, this means that individuals tend to exhibit more sophisticated levels of development through the process of maturation or simply growing older. Consequently, similar individuals not attending college might well change in essentially the same ways as college students over the same time period. In the absence of a control group of noncollege attenders (a typical weakness in most studies of change during college), it is essentially impossible to separate the changes due to college attendance from those attributable to natural maturation.

The focus on change during college as an indication of college impact can also be misleading in another way. Just as the presence of change does not necessarily indicate the impact of college, so too the absence of change does not necessarily indicate the absence of college impact. One important consequence of college attendance may be to fix development at a certain level and prevent reversion or regression (Feldman & Newcomb, 1969). If such were the case on a specific trait, little or no freshman-to-senior change would be noted. Those not attending college, however, might well regress or change in a negative direction. We will see an example of this as we turn to a summary of the net effects of college.

Finally, it is important to differentiate change from development. Whereas *change* simply means that some fact or condition at Time$_2$ is different from what it was at Time$_1$, *development* implies ordered, predictable, even hierarchical shifts or evolution have taken place in fundamental, intra-individual structures or processes. In many areas of observed change during college, it is tempting simply to conclude that observed change reflects some form of internal growth or development in the individual, that an inner restructuring has taken place, and that the senior is functioning with an advanced set of inner rules or perspectives not present in the typical freshman. This is a particular temptation when the changes that occur are consistent with those posited by developmental models or theories. The danger inherent in this assumption is that what we commonly refer to as development may in large measure be the result of an individual's response to the anticipated norms of new social settings or social roles. Different categories of people may be socialized to think and behave differently in society, and a substantial part of this categorization may have its basis in educational level. Thus, for example, college-educated men and women may have certain psychosocial traits and values and may think about controversial issues in certain ways not necessarily because of some inner developmental restructuring but because they have been socialized to behave and think in ways consistent with dominant cultural norms for educated adults.

This is not to say that the changes that occur during college merely represent the learning of social or cultural norms instead of important developmental steps. Rather, it is to suggest that we need to be wary of the tendency to equate the learning of social or cultural norms with development. It behooves us to bear in mind that change during the college years is produced by multiple influences, some internal (and perhaps ontogenetic) and others external to the individual. Theories can overly restrict as well as focus vision.

Net Effects of College

Because self-selection, as opposed to random assignment, determines who attends and who does not attend college, studies that seek to estimate the unique or net impact of college (as distinct from normal maturation, mere aging, or other noncollege sources of change) employ some rather creative research designs or, more typically, statistical controls. Although the causal inferences one can make from such studies are not of the same order of certitude as those made from randomized experiments, we can nevertheless arrive at a reasonably valid set of tentative conclusions about the changes or outcomes observed that are attributable to college attendance and not to rival explanations. It is worth recalling, however, that change during the college years involves a complex, weblike network. Change in one area may cause or be accompanied by change in other areas as well. Given this interrelatedness, estimates of change and of college's net effect in each discrete area no doubt understate college's overall, cumulative impact.

Tables 13.5 through 13.8 array those dimensions on which the weight of evidence offers support for claims about college's unique or net impact. (When we use the term *unclear* in the column reporting the magnitude of net effects in this and all subsequent tables in the chapter, we are acknowledging that the studies do not allow such estimates or that the evidence, though generally consistent, is still sufficiently complex to make an estimate of effect size hazardous.) As Tables 13.5 through 13.8 show, we judge the evidence on net impact to be more compelling for some outcomes than for others. Specifically, there is more extensive and consistent evidence to support the net impact of college on learning and cognition, moral reasoning, and career and economic returns than in the areas of attitudes, values, and psychosocial characteristics. This does not necessarily mean that college has a stronger impact on the former outcomes than on the latter ones. Indeed, we had a difficult time estimating the magnitude of the net impact of college in nearly all areas of our synthesis. Some of these differences could be more a reflection of variations in the extent and quality of the available evidence across different areas of inquiry than of major differences in the actual impact of college. More likely, they are real. It would probably be unreasonable to expect uniform changes across substantive areas. Students vary considerably in the characteristics they bring with them to college, not only in a wide variety of personal, educational, and family background traits but also in their readiness and capacity for change. Moreover, higher educational institutions do not invest their energies and resources equally across areas of change.

Learning and Cognitive Changes

Table 13.5 shows those learning and cognitive development outcomes that the weight of evidence suggests are significantly influenced by college attendance. Perhaps the clearest generalization to be made from this evidence is that on nearly all of the dimensions on which we find freshman-to-senior change, a statistically significant part of that change is attributable to college attendance, not to rival explanations. College not only appears to enhance general verbal and quantitative skills as well as oral and written communication, but it also has a statistically significant positive net effect on general intellectual and analytical skills, critical thinking, the use of reason and evidence in addressing ill-structured problems, and intellectual flexibility. These effects cannot be explained away by maturation or differences between those who attend and those who do not attend college in intelligence, academic ability, or other precollege characteristics.

These conclusions about the net effects of college on learning and cognitive development are limited by those dimensions that individual scholars have chosen to investigate. It is perhaps useful to think of these dimensions of net college effects as analogous to geological probes designed to define the nature and extent of mineral or oil deposits. They sample and begin to define the boundaries, but they may not capture the fullness of the phenomenon being measured. From this perspective, it is reasonable to conclude that college attendance positively influences a wide range of cognitive skills and intellectual functioning. The existing research, however,

Table 13.5. Summary of Estimated *Net* Effects of College: *Learning and Cognitive Development*.

Outcome	Strength of Evidence	Direction of Effect	Major Rival Explanations Controlled	Magnitude of Net Effect
General verbal skills	Strong	Positive	Precollege verbal skills, race, socioeconomic status	.26 to .32 SD (10 to 13 percentile point advantage)
General quantitative skills	Strong	Positive	Precollege quantitative skills, race, socioeconomic status	.29 to .32 SD (11 to 13 percentile point advantage)
Oral communication skills	Moderate	Positive	Age, academic ability	Unclear[a]
Written communication skills	Moderate	Positive	Age, academic ability	Unclear
General intellectual and analytical skill development	Moderate	Positive	Age, verbal ability, quantitative ability	Community college graduates higher than incoming freshmen; magnitude of effect unclear
Critical thinking	Strong	Positive	Precollege critical thinking, academic aptitude, socioeconomic status, educational aspirations	Freshman-year net effect, .44 SD (17 percentile point advantage); magnitude of net four-year effect unclear
Use of reason and evidence to address ill-structured problems (reflective judgment, informal reasoning)	Moderate to strong	Positive	Age, academic ability	Unclear
Intellectual flexibility	Moderate to strong	Positive	Age, intelligence, academic aptitude	Unclear

[a]"Unclear," as used in this table, means we are acknowledging that the studies do not allow such estimates or that the evidence, though generally consistent, is still sufficiently complex to make an estimate of effect size hazardous.

probably provides only a rough outline of the types of learning and cognitive development enhanced by college without necessarily tapping the full range or richness of effects.

As briefly alluded to in the previous section on change during college, research on college's net effects illustrates the potentially misleading nature of change. The net positive effect of college on general quantitative skills, for example, occurred not because students who attended college made greater gains than those who did not attend. Instead, the effect was largely attributable to the fact that college attendance tended to anchor quantitative skills at precollege levels while those not attending college actually regressed. Thus, an important net effect of college may be to stabilize an individual's development on certain dimensions and to prevent the regressions that might occur in the absence of college attendance.

Attitudes and Values

Evidence concerning the net impact of college on attitudes and values is summarized in Table 13.6. Although the weight of this evidence is not totally consistent and certainly not without rival explanations, it nevertheless suggests that a statistically significant, if modest, part of the broad-based attitudinal and value changes that occur during college can be attributed to the college experience. Perhaps of equal importance, the net effects of college, particularly in the areas of social, political, and sex role values, appear not to be simple reflections of trends in the larger society across the last two decades. Rather, college attendance seems to have an impact on attitudes and values in these areas, an impact that is generally consistent both within and across age cohorts.

This is not to say that what occurs during college happens in total isolation from cultural and social forces. Clearly, student values are significantly affected by those dominant in society, and general societal changes make unambiguous attributions of change to college more difficult. Nevertheless, college attendance would appear to influence political, social, and gender role attitudes and values in consistent ways regardless of cultural and societal trends.

A note of caution needs to be made with respect to this conclusion, because there is some evidence to suggest that recent college effects on social and political values may be less pronounced than earlier studies have indicated. Whether this is a chance fluctuation or the precursor of an important generational effect, however, awaits replication of the findings on future samples.

Psychosocial Changes

Table 13.7 summarizes the evidence relating to college's psychosocial net effects. As can be seen there, virtually nothing can be said with confi-

Table 13.6. Summary of Estimated *Net* Effects of College: *Attitudes and Values.*

Outcome	Strength of Evidence	Direction of Effect	Major Rival Explanations Controlled	Magnitude of Net Effect[a]
Aesthetic, cultural, and intellectual values	Moderate	Positive	Age, gender, religion, socioeconomic status, residential origin	Unclear[a]
Value placed on liberal education	Strong	Positive	Aptitude, race, gender, family socioeconomic status, precollege values	Graduates two to three times more likely to value education than are people with less education
Value placed on education as vocational preparation	Moderate	Negative	Aptitude, occupation, interaction thereof	Unclear
Value placed on intrinsic occupational rewards	Strong	Positive	Gender, race, socioeconomic status, job characteristics	Unclear, probably small
Value placed on extrinsic occupational rewards	Strong	Negative	Gender, race, socioeconomic status, job characteristics	Small
Social liberalism	Weak	Positive	Gender, race, age, religion, socioeconomic status, residential origin, cohort, aging and period effects	Unclear
Political liberalism	Strong	Positive	Gender, race, age, religion, socioeconomic status, residential origin, cohort, aging and period effects	Unclear
Civil rights and liberties	Mixed	Positive	Age, income, socioeconomic status, religion	Unclear, probably small
Secularism	Weak	Positive	Gender, race, initial religious attitudes	Unclear
Gender roles (toward the "modern")	Strong	Positive	Initial gender role values, gender, age, race, income, religion, marital status, work history, number of children, period and cohort effects	Unclear

[a]"Unclear," as used in this table, means we are acknowledging that the studies do not allow such estimates or that the evidence, though generally consistent, is still sufficiently complex to make an estimate of effect size hazardous.

Table 13.7. Summary of Estimated *Net* Effects of College: *Psychosocial Development*.

Outcome	Strength of Evidence	Direction of Effect	Major Rival Explanations Controlled	Magnitude of Net Effect
Identity and ego development	Very weak	Positive	Few	Unknown
Self-concept: Academic	Strong	Positive	Gender, race, prior achievement, socioeconomic status, degree aspirations	Small, indirect
Self-concept: Social	Strong	Positive	Gender, race, prior achievement, socioeconomic status, degree aspirations	Small, indirect
Self-concept: Self-esteem	Strong	Positive	Ability, achievement, socioeconomic status, race, precollege self-esteem	Small
Autonomy, independence, and internal locus of control	Weak to moderate (strong for locus of control)	Positive	Ability, socioeconomic status, precollege locus of control	Unclear[a] (small for locus of control)
Authoritarianism, dogmatism, and ethnocentrism	Moderate	Negative	Gender, ability, socioeconomic status	Unclear
Intellectual orientation	Moderate	Positive	Gender, ability, socioeconomic status	Unclear
Interpersonal relations	Weak	Mixed	None	Unclear
Personal adjustment and psychological well-being	Strong	Positive	Socioeconomic status, family situation, religiosity	Small
Maturity and general personal development	No evidence	Unknown	None	Unclear

[a]"Unclear," as used in this table, means we are acknowledging that the studies do not allow such estimates or that the evidence, though generally consistent, is still sufficiently complex to make an estimate of effect size hazardous.

dence about the net effects of college on changes in students' identity statuses or their stages of ego development. The research literature simply does not deal with the effects of college in these areas in any methodologically rigorous or generalizable way. The vast majority of studies are concerned with structural rather than process questions, with whether hypothesized statuses or stages exist and the characteristics of the individuals at any given stage rather than with the variables (including education) that influence status or stage change. Where change is examined, educational and age or maturational effects remain confounded.

Persuasive evidence exists to indicate that college attendance is reliably and positively related to increases in students' academic and social self-concepts, as well as their self-esteem. After holding constant a variety of relevant precollege characteristics, educational attainment is consistently and positively related to increases in students' perceptions of themselves relative to their peers in both academic areas (for example, writing and mathematical abilities, general academic abilities, intellectual self-confidence) and social areas (leadership abilities, popularity in general and with the opposite sex, general social self-confidence, and the like). Net college effects are also apparent in the increases students experience in their self-esteem: the general regard in which they hold themselves and their abilities, the extent to which they consider themselves to be capable, significant, worthy, or of value. After precollege self-concepts or self-esteem and other background characteristics have been controlled, however, college's effects in each of these areas appear to be small. Moreover, college's influence on students' self-concepts appears to be *indirect* rather than direct, being mediated through certain characteristics students bring with them to college and through the kinds of academic and interpersonal experiences they have once on campus.

The net effects of college on changes in the ways students relate to people, institutions, and conditions in their external world are somewhat less limited. Consistent with the net gains made in cognitive areas, we can attribute to college (with moderate to considerable confidence) declines in authoritarianism and dogmatism and increases in students' internal sense (locus) of control, intellectual orientation, personal adjustment, and general psychological well-being. College's contributions to the declines in authoritarianism and dogmatism appear to be strong, but its effects in the other areas are much more modest, even small. Because of methodological limitations, however, few claims (if any) can be made with confidence about college's net effects on changes in students' levels of autonomy or independence, the maturity of their interpersonal relations, or their overall maturity and personal development.

Moral Development

Table 13.8 reveals that college has a net positive effect on the use of principled reasoning in judging moral issues. This effect holds even when controls are made for maturation and for differences between those who attend and those who do not attend college in level of precollege moral reasoning, intelligence, and socioeconomic status. The net impact of college on actual moral behavior is less clear. On the basis of a synthesis of two separate bodies of research, however, we hypothesize a positive indirect effect. College enhances the use of principled moral reasoning, which in turn is positively linked to a variety of principled actions. These include resistance to cheating, social activism, keeping contractual promises, and helping behavior. The acceptance of this hypothesis is tentative, however, and awaits fuller empirical support.

Long-Term Effects of College

Nearly all of the considerable body of research on the long-term effects of college is concerned with estimating the enduring impact of attending versus not attending college. Consequently, it has much in common, both conceptually and methodologically, with research that attempts to estimate the net effects of college. Indeed, one could reasonably regard evidence on the enduring impact of college attendance essentially as an estimate of the net effects of college extended over time. For this reason we depart from the typical pattern of most chapters and summarize the evidence on the long-term effects of college here rather than near the end of this chapter.

Our synthesis of the evidence suggests that college has a rather broad range of enduring or long-term impacts. These include not only the more obvious impacts on occupation and earnings but also influences on cognitive, moral, and psychosocial characteristics, as well as on values and attitudes and various quality of life indexes (for example, family, marriage, consumer behavior). Moreover, it would also appear that the impacts extend beyond the individuals who attend college to the kinds of lives their sons and daughters can expect.

It is clear that part of the long-term impact of college (for example, on job status and income) can be traced directly back to college attendance or degree attainment. Another part of this impact, however, may be an indirect result of the socioeconomic positioning and kinds of life interests, experiences, and opportunities made more likely by being a college graduate. As suggested by Withey (1971) and Bowen (1977), part of the impact of college arises out of the distinctive kinds of lives led by the people who attend and graduate from college. Such indirect routes of influence are a major consideration in understanding the long-term and full impact of college. In short, our conclusion about the nature of the long-term effects of college is generally consistent with that of Feldman and Newcomb (1969). The distinctive effects of college tend to persist in large measure as a result of living in postcollege environments that support those effects.

Table 13.8. Summary of Estimated *Net* Effects of College: *Moral Development*.

Outcome	Strength of Evidence	Direction of Effect	Major Rival Explanations Controlled	Magnitude of Net Effect[a]
Use of principled reasoning in judging moral issues	Strong	Positive	Age, precollege differences in moral reasoning, intelligence, socioeconomic status	Unclear[a]
Principled behavior or action	Weak	Positive		Hypothesized effect is indirect and probably small

[a]"Unclear," as used in this table, means we are acknowledging that the studies do not allow such estimates or that the evidence, though generally consistent, is still sufficiently complex to make an estimate of effect size hazardous.

Table 13.21. Summary of Estimated *Between-College* Effects: *College Environments*.

Outcome	Strength of Evidence	Direction of Effect	Major Rival Explanations Controlled	Magnitude of Net Effect
Learning (typically on standardized measures such as the Graduate Record Examination)	Moderate	Positive in direction of (1) frequent student-faculty interaction, (2) degree of curricular flexibility, (3) faculty formal education level	Academic aptitude, major field of study	Very small
Cognitive development (such as critical thinking, adult reasoning skills)	Moderate	Positive in direction of general education emphasis in curriculum	College selectivity	Small to moderate
Educational attainment	Moderate	Positive in direction of (1) cohesive peer environment, (2) participation in college activities, (3) perception of personal concern for student, (4) emphasis on supportive student personnel services	Family socioeconomic status, secondary school achievement, educational aspirations, college size and selectivity	Unclear,[a] but probably small
Aesthetic, cultural, and intellectual attitudes and values	Weak	Positive in direction of campuses high in awareness and scholarship; negative on campuses high in propriety and practicality	None	Unclear
Internal locus of control	Moderate	Positive in direction of cohesive peer environment	Gender, race, socioeconomic status, ability, initial level of internality	Unclear

Table 13.21. Summary of Estimated _Between-College_ Effects: _College Environments._ Cont'd

Outcome	Strength of Evidence	Direction of Effect	Major Rival Explanations Controlled	Magnitude of Net Effect
Authoritarianism and dogmatism	Weak	Negative in direction of schools with liberal campus climate, large proportion of non-conformists, student involvement in class activities, emphasis on intrinsic motivations	Gender, ability, socioeconomic status	Unclear
Personal adjustment and psychological well-being	Weak	Positive in direction of campus with high proportion of "expressive" students, classroom participation, emphasis on complex mental activities, intrinsic awards	Gender, socioeconomic status, ability	Unclear
Career choice and career entered	Strong	Positive in direction of "progressive conformity" hypothesis	Initial career choice, major field choice, educational aspirations, academic aptitude, college grades	Small

[a]"Unclear," as used in this table, means we are acknowledging that the studies do not allow such estimates or that the evidence, though generally consistent, is still sufficiently complex to make an estimate of effect size hazardous.

confer an occupational advantage on a graduate is through its geographical and social proximity to a prospective employer. (See Table 13.22.) A college that is geographically close to a company, that has frequent professional and consultative interactions with the company, and whose graduates are represented in the company's management tends to confer on its graduates employed by that company an advantage in initial job level and promotion rate. This advantage, moreover, appears to function independently of the selectivity of the college.

Thus, the occupational impact of where one attends college may not be independent of one's employment context. Indeed, the career mobility of graduates of certain colleges may be at least partially influenced by the dominant managerial culture of an employing organization.

Transfer Between Four-Year Institutions

Educational attainment is not only influenced by the type of institution in which one enrolls; it is also affected by the continuity of one's experience in that institution. An interruption in this continuity in the form of transfer from one four-year institution to another tends to inhibit degree attainment (see Table 13.23). This holds irrespective of race and gender but is particularly pronounced for black men. Not surprisingly, the inhibiting influence of transfer on degree attainment leads to a consistent set of negative indirect effects on occupational status and a less consistent set of negative impacts on earnings. Thus, institutional continuity in one's postsecondary educational experience not only enhances degree attainment but also has additional positive implications for early occupational and economic attainments. This suggests the potential importance of one's fit with the initial college of enrollment.

Within-College Effects

As evidenced in Chapters Three through Twelve, an extensive variety of within-college effects on students have been examined. Although a substantial number of individual studies have proceeded from a theoretical base, the evidence as a whole is not founded on a common set of conceptual or theoretical themes. Consequently, we organize the synthesis of this large body of research around our own understanding of the common threads running through the evidence. First, we offer several conclusions about the evidence as a whole. Second, we offer our conclusions about the major determinants of within-college effects, as organized under the categories of residence, major field of study, the academic experience, interpersonal involvement, extracurricular involvement, and academic achievement.

Table 13.22. Summary of Estimated Between-College Effects: Geographical and Social Proximity.

Outcome	Strength of Evidence	Direction of Effect	Major Rival Explanations Controlled	Magnitude of Net Effect
Initial job level and promotion rate	Weak	Positive in direction of proximity	College selectivity, age, tenure in firm	Unclear,[a] but probably small

[a]"Unclear," as used here, means we are acknowledging that the studies do not allow such estimates or that the evidence, though generally consistent, is still sufficiently complex to make an estimate of effect size hazardous.

Table 13.23. Summary of Estimated _Between-College_ Effects: _Transfer Between Four-Year Institutions._

Outcome	Strength of Evidence	Direction of Effect	Major Rival Explanations Controlled	Magnitude of Net Effect
Educational attainment, occupational status, and earnings	Weak	Negative in direction of transfer	Family socioeconomic status, aspirations, expectations of transfer, selectivity of first college attended, college grades	Moderate negative direct effect on educational attainment; small negative indirect effect on occupational status transmitted through educational attainment; small negative direct and indirect effects on earnings

General Conclusions

The types of within-college experiences that maximize impact are not independent of the kind of college attended. Certain experiences that maximize change are more likely at some institutions than at others. For example, a social context that enhances frequent student-faculty informal interaction is more likely at small, primarily residential colleges than at large universities with a mix of residential and commuter students. Nevertheless, nearly all of the important within-college impacts persist irrespective of the institutional context in which they occur.

Similarly, many of the experiences that maximize impact are not independent of the kinds of students who engage in them. For example, students who are most likely to develop close informal relationships with faculty members are also likely to aspire to graduate or professional school when they enter college. The net impact of their informal interaction with faculty would be to even further strengthen their plans. Thus, consistent with Feldman and Newcomb's (1969) conclusion, we found many within-college effects to be essentially the accentuation of initial student characteristics. Certain experiences tend to attract students with certain traits or dispositions and, in turn, tend to accentuate the traits or dispositions that drew those students to the experiences in the first place.

A third generalization is that within-college effects, like between-college effects, tend to be substantially smaller in magnitude than the overall net effect of college attendance. As with the research on between-college effects, there are several possible methodological reasons for this. Substantive explanations, however, are perhaps more valid. Most theoretical models of development in no way guarantee that any single experience will be an important determinant of change for all students. A majority of important changes that occur during college are probably the cumulative result of a set of interrelated experiences sustained over an extended period of time. Consequently, research that focuses on the impact of a single or isolated experience, a characteristic of most investigations of within-college influences, is unlikely to yield strong effects.

A final generalization concerns empirical support for theoretical models of college impact. In Chapter Two we briefly summarized the major elements of several such theories. On the basis of the extensive body of evidence reviewed, much of which would confirm expectations based on those theories, one of the most inescapable and unequivocal conclusions we can make is that the impact of college is largely determined by the individual's quality of effort and level of involvement in both academic and nonacademic activities. This is not particularly surprising; indeed, the positive effects of both the quality and extent of involvement have been repeatedly stressed by Astin (1984) and Pace (1984, 1987).

Such a conclusion suggests that the impact of college is not simply the result of what a college does for or to a student. Rather, the impact is a result of the extent to which an individual student exploits the people, programs, facilities, opportunities, and experiences that the college makes available. Students are not simply the recipients of institutional effects. They themselves bear a major responsibility for the impact of their own college experience. From this perspective it is the individual student who perhaps most determines the extent to which college makes a difference.

Although this conclusion stresses the salience of individual student involvement, it in no way means that individual campus policies and programs are unimportant. Indeed, we would strongly argue the contrary. If individual effort or involvement is the critical determinant of college impact, then a key question focuses on the ways in which a campus can shape its intellectual and interpersonal environments to invite increased student involvement. In the next sections we summarize salient within-college influences, some of which may provide colleges with programmatic or policy levers by which student involvement can be maximized.

Residence

Living on campus (versus commuting to college) is perhaps the single most consistent within-college determinant of impact (see Table 13.24). This is not particularly surprising because residential living creates a social-psychological context for students that is markedly different from that experienced by those who live at home or elsewhere off campus and commute to college. Simply put, living on campus maximizes opportunities for social, cultural, and extracurricular involvement; and it is this involvement that largely accounts for residential living's impact on student change. To be sure, those who live on campus may, as a group, be psychologically more open to many of the impacts of college to begin with than are their commuting counterparts. Even with this initial difference held constant, however, residential living is positively, if modestly, linked to increases in aesthetic, cultural, and intellectual values; a liberalizing of social, political, and religious values and attitudes; increases in self-concept, intellectual orientation, autonomy, and independence; gains in tolerance, empathy, and ability to relate to others; persistence in college; and bachelor's degree attainment.

Since the facilitation of campus social involvement or participation is the probable causal mechanism underlying the impact of living on campus, it is not surprising that the majority of the demonstrated effects of living on campus are in the areas of student values, attitudes, and psychosocial development. There is little compelling evidence to suggest that the knowledge acquisition or general cognitive effects of college are significantly related to living on campus compared with commuting to college. Indeed, there is at least a modicum of evidence to suggest that a high level of in-

Table 13.24. Summary of Estimated Within-College Effects: Residence.

Outcome	Strength of Evidence	Direction of Effect	Major Rival Explanations Controlled	Magnitude of Net Effect[a]
Aesthetic, cultural, and intelletual values	Moderate	Positive in direction of on-campus residence	Gender, race, socioeconomic status, ability, initial values	Unclear
Sociopolitical attitudes and values	Moderate	Positive in direction of on-campus residence	Gender, race, socioeconomic status, ability	Unclear
Secularism	Moderate	Positive in direction of on-campus residence	Gender, race, socioeconomic status, ability, initial values	Unclear
Self-concepts	Weak to moderate	Positive in direction of on-campus residence	Gender, race, socioeconomic status, ability, initial concepts	Unclear, but probably small and indirect via interpersonal relations
Autonomy, independence, internal locus of control	Weak	Positive in direction of on-campus residence	Gender, ability	Unclear
Intellectual orientation	Moderate	Positive in direction of on-campus residence	Gender, ability, initial levels	Unclear, but probably small and indirect, mediated by interpersonal relations and residence environment
Persistence and degree attainment	Strong	Positive in direction of on-campus residence, especially in living-learning center	Gender, ability, socioeconomic status, educational aspirations, high school achievement	Unclear
Moral development	Weak	Positive in direction of on-campus residence	Initial level of moral development	Unclear

[a] "Unclear," as used in this table, means we are acknowledging that the studies do not allow such estimates or that the evidence, though generally consistent, is still sufficiently complex to make an estimate of effect size hazardous.

volvement in dormitory life and activities can actually function to isolate an individual from the intellectual life of a college and inhibit some aspects of cognitive growth.

It is likely that the impact of living on campus is not monolithic. Considerable evidence suggests discernible differences in the social and intellectual climate of different residences on the same campus. With a few exceptions (such as college grades), unfortunately, there is little consistent evidence linking differences in the climate of residences to various college outcomes. Not surprisingly, what evidence we do have suggests that those residence climates with the strongest impacts on cognitive development and persistence are typically the result of purposeful programmatic efforts to integrate the student's intellectual and social life during college. Moreover, as will be discussed in greater detail below, residential effects may well be indirect ones, mediated through the interpersonal experiences students have with peers and faculty members that are shaped by the residential setting.

It is important to be aware of two limitations if one is to place the impact of living on campus in its proper perspective. First, it is quite clear that over half of all students in American postsecondary education commute to college and if current trends continue that proportion is likely to increase. Similarly, fully a third of the nation's colleges and universities have no residential facilities, and given financial and student demographic exigencies, they are unlikely to ever have them. For this major group of students and institutions the potential educational benefits of living on campus are largely moot. Developing programs and policies that approximate the student involvement facilitated by residential living is a major challenge for those who educate commuter students or who administer commuter campuses.

A second limitation involves the somewhat narrow view many scholars have taken in assessing the impact of place of residence during college. The focus has been largely on outcomes traditionally valued by the academic community (intellectual values, tolerance, liberalization of social attitudes, and the like). Less sensitivity has been shown to the types of learning and maturing that may occur when the individual must successfully attend to work and family as well as to educational responsibilities. A far larger percentage of commuter students than of resident students are confronted with these additional responsibilities. As a result, the challenges that they face but that their resident counterparts are less likely to confront may lead to comparatively greater growth in areas not now explored by studies of traditional residential students.

Major Field of Study

One's major field of study creates a potentially important subenvironment during college. It not only focuses one's intellectual efforts in a particular direction, but it also has an influence on the kinds of students and faculty with whom one interacts. Consequently, it might be expected that in addition to what one learns, academic major would also have a significant impact on such outcomes as values, attitudes, and psychosocial change. The total body of evidence, however, suggests that the impacts of academic major are markedly stronger and more consistent in cognitive areas than in noncognitive ones.

As might be expected, and as indicated in Table 13.25, the cognitive impact of major field of study is selective. Students tend to demonstrate the highest levels of learning on subject matter tests most congruent with their academic major. Similarly, they tend to demonstrate the greatest proficiency on measures of general cognitive development when the content of problems is most consistent with their academic major or the disciplinary emphasis of their course work. Thus, for example, social science majors outperform others on tests of social science content and on measures of abstract reasoning and critical thinking applied to social science tasks and problems. The same tendencies hold for science and humanities majors. Beyond these selective impacts, however, we found little consistent evidence that one's major has more than a trivial net impact on one's general level of intellectual or cognitive outcomes.

In contrast, the impact of major field of study on noncognitive outcomes is substantially less apparent or consistent. The effects of major field on changes in students' identity status or ego development stage remain unexamined. Students majoring in the natural or physical sciences, mathematics, or technical fields appear to enjoy slightly greater gains in developing a positive academic self-concept, but major field is unrelated to changes in social self-concept. Similarly, the weight of evidence consistently indicates that few if any differential changes in any of the facets of students' relational systems or in attitudinal and value areas are attributable to academic major. As with the research on the effects of residence in these areas, however, there is some evidence to suggest that departmental environment, whatever the department, may be more important than the characteristics of the discipline in shaping psychosocial and attitudinal changes among students. The interpersonal climate and value homogeneity and consensus within a department appear to be particularly important. The salience of interpersonal relations is discussed at greater length below.

Major field of study does have a number of statistically significant links to the occupational structure in American society. Consequently, what one majors in during college has potentially important implications for the occupation one enters and the economic rewards one receives from his or her work. For example, majors in such areas as business, engineering, some preprofessional programs, and some natural sciences increase the likelihood that one will enter a job with skill requirements consistent with one's academic training, that women will enter relatively high status, male-domi-

with only a high school diploma. But the evidence also consistently indicates that the advantages are even greater for baccalaureate degree holders when compared with two-year college graduates. So great are the differences that three decades ago Clark (1960) argued that community colleges, despite their many positive and facilitative functions, can also serve to "cool out" high-aspiration but low-achieving and/or low-socioeconomic-status students, discouraging continued enrollment and reducing the likelihood that two-year students would enjoy educational benefits equal to those of four-year college graduates. More recently, Karabel (1972, 1986; Brint & Karabel, 1989) and Astin (1977a) have commented on the paradox of the proliferation of public community colleges and the evidence that because of demonstrably lower persistence and baccalaureate degree attainment rates, community colleges may not really serve well the interests of students aspiring to a bachelor's degree and to the careers that require it. Providing equal access to participation in the postsecondary educational system is only half of the solution to educational inequities. The other half requires equal access to opportunities to enjoy the full benefits of postsecondary participation.

The research published in the last two decades has consistently found—even after holding constant a variety of relevant personal, academic, and family background characteristics and when studying only students in "college transfer" programs—that students entering a four-year institution are substantially more likely than two-year college entrants to persist in their education, to complete a baccalaureate degree, and to attend graduate or professional school. Lower degree attainment rates are compounded in reduced expectations in other areas, including occupational status and income. Although where one enters college makes little difference *once the baccalaureate degree is earned,* the fact remains that students at two-year colleges are substantially less likely than their peers at four-year colleges to complete a bachelor's degree program and to reap the associated benefits. The magnitude of the problem expands, moreover, when we recall the evidence in our review of the intergenerational effects of college attendance. Parents with higher educational attainment levels pass on to their children certain educational, economic, and occupational advantages in terms of precollege backgrounds, schooling, and educationally and occupationally relevant attitudes, values, and expectations. Thus, the children of better-educated parents indirectly derive certain benefits from their parents' education, beginning their own intellectual, economic, and occupational development with advantages that have not been available to children whose parents are not as well educated. It follows, of course, that if there are intergenerational benefits, there are also intergenerational liabilities, which are being compounded in each succeeding generation.

Despite such evidence (about which they are doubtless unaware), significant numbers of high school graduates, their parents, and policymakers continue to believe that attendance at a two-year college followed by transfer to a four-year college for completion of the baccalaureate degree is the low-cost equivalent of the full tour of duty at a four-year institution. This misperception, of course, is particularly damaging among minority and economically disadvantaged groups, for whom the two-year college is the most likely point of entry into the postsecondary educational system. These are the same groups for whom the need for educational and occupational benefits may be greatest and among whom the promise of those benefits may be the most alluring. It is a cruel irony, then, that while the incremental socioeconomic benefits of a bachelor's degree are greatest for these groups (compared to white or higher socioeconomic groups), the likelihood of their obtaining those benefits is lowest. Astin (1977a, p. 247) puts it bluntly: "For the eighteen-year-old going directly to college from high school, the public community college does not represent an 'equal educational opportunity' compared with other types of institutions."

Thus, with respect to both two-year and commuter colleges (but primarily the former), the issue is one of educational and social equity, of deciding whether as a matter of public policy such discrepancies in educational impacts should continue or whether ways can be found to narrow the gaps. As Astin (1977a) has suggested, the presumed economic advantages of two-year (versus four-year) and commuter (versus residential) institutions to state and local governments in terms of cost per student might well be more apparent than real if costs *per degree granted* were used as the yardstick.

The matter goes well beyond capital and operational costs to the public, however. The calculus of the public "economy" of two-year and commuter campuses must also somehow take into account the indirect costs to students and their families in the form of reduced prospects for degree attainment, lower postcollege occupational status and earnings, and fewer opportunities for gains in a variety of widely accepted cognitive and psychosocial outcomes. These personal and family costs, when aggregated, can lead to substantial additional economic, social, and political costs, particularly in light of current projections for substantial growth in minority group populations over the next decade.

Failure on the part of educators and public policymakers to acknowledge that two-year and four-year colleges do *not* lead to the same set of educational and economic outcomes and failure to act on that recognition will mean that unequal educational opportunity will continue, not in the opportunities to participate in higher education but in the opportunities to reap the full benefits of participation. It will mean the perpetuation of the very inequities in educational and social mobility the community college movement was intended to eliminate. It will mean the continued loss of talented individuals and at the least a reduction in their contributions to our educational, cultural, economic, social, and political systems. The burdens of those losses may be compounded by greater demands for welfare and unemployment supports and other social services, the loss of tax revenues, and larger numbers of underemployed individuals living unnecessarily limited lives. Over a long period of time, it could mean the diminishment or loss of a historic national faith in the efficacy of education as a vehicle for improving one's own and one's children's station in life.

As has been suggested elsewhere (for example, Bernstein, 1986; Brint & Karabel, 1989; Donovan, Schaier-Peleg, & Forer, 1987; Palmer, 1986), it appears that the time has come to reconsider the role of two-year colleges' transfer programs. Kinnick & Kempner (1988) suggest at least two alternative courses of action are open. One is to acknowledge the current inequalities and remove the transfer function from the mission of public two-year colleges. Resources and energies could then be redirected and concentrated on the other multiple dimensions of the public two-year college's mission (vocational and technical training, adult literacy, continuing education, community economic development, and the like). Or resources could be redirected to four-year institutions, which would be charged with full responsibility for meeting the demand for education at the baccalaureate degree level. Such a course, however, would in all likelihood even further disadvantage those individuals who, for whatever reasons, would be unable to enroll in a four-year institution or who might initially seek only a two-year degree (or less) but subsequently switch into a transfer program.

A second, more realistic and responsible course of action would be to initiate serious and coordinated efforts at local, state, and federal levels to revitalize the apparently moribund transfer function of two-year colleges. Such regeneration would necessitate revised public-funding formulas and structures. Under most state funding formulas, community colleges are budgeted at lower levels than four-year institutions. Additionally, their missions preclude their access to the additional revenue-generating capacity available to upper-division and graduate-level instruction and research, which also benefit lower-division programs and students. Revitalization would in addition require elimination of some of the obstacles to transferring that contribute to the current inequalities in outcomes. The removal of barriers would require more energetic, systematic, and coordinated efforts at articulation at two points: between the high schools and community colleges and between the community colleges and four-year institutions. Community colleges would have to set and make clear to high schools the nature of the courses and academic skills students entering a college transfer program should have, as well as the curricular and performance standards they would be expected to meet. Four-year institutions would have to do likewise for community colleges (see Commission for Educational Quality, 1985).

At two-year colleges, efforts would also probably involve more intensive remedial programs in reading, writing, mathematical, and general learning skills; more effective academic and personal support programs for

transfer candidates; curricula and course offerings that would unequivo-
cally satisfy four-year institutions' admissions and academic major requirements; and increased rigor in instruction and grading. At four-year colleges, easing the transition from two-year to four-year institutions and
increasing the likelihood of degree completion would require simpler and
more flexible admissions procedures, admissions criteria not limited to standardized test scores and prior academic performance records, greater flexibility in transfer credit policies and criteria (not standards), easier access to
larger amounts and more varied forms of financial aid, more equitable opportunities for on-campus housing, and more sustained and aggressive academic and personal support programs, including remedial programs in
basic academic skills. More detailed discussions and recommendations for
revitalizing the transfer function of two-year colleges are given by Bernstein
(1986); Cohen and Brawer (1987, 1989); Donovan, Schaier-Peleg, and Forer
(1987); Kintzer and Wattenbarger (1985); Palmer (1986); Pincus and Archer
(1989); Richardson and Bender (1985); and Wechsler (1989). Levine and
Associates (1989) discuss changes in current practices that will be needed to
accommodate higher education's increasingly diverse clientele. (See Palmer,
1986, for a review of related literature.)

White Campuses and Nonwhite Students. The notion of educational
inequality has another set of policy implications, primarily at the institutional level, relating to the sociopsychological climate of many predominantly white institutions as it is experienced by nonwhite students. It is clear
that many of the most important effects of college occur through students'
interpersonal experiences with faculty members and other students. It is
equally clear that the academic, social, and psychological worlds inhabited
by most nonwhite students on predominantly white campuses are substantially different in almost every respect from those of their white peers. On
some (perhaps many) campuses, minority students feel a powerful need to
band together for psychological and social support of one another, sometimes in defense against the tacit and not-so-tacit condescension and hostility some feel from white faculty, students, and staff alike. While confirming
evidence may be scarce, it does not seem unreasonable to suggest that under such conditions the educational experiences and outcomes of college
for nonwhite students are probably also very different from those for white
students, perhaps significantly so. Certainly, more research is needed to
clarify the nature of the college experience and its effects on cognitive and
psychosocial change among nonwhite students.

If this speculation is anywhere near accurate, it is not too soon to
begin reviewing and changing institutional policies and programs that create or tolerate activities or conditions that are academically and socially un-

congenial, if not downright hostile, to nonwhite students. These would include (but not be limited to) policies and programs relating to increased minority faculty and staff recruitment and retention, institution-wide faculty and staff recruitment and rewards, student housing and financial aid, social organizations, instructors' classroom attitudes and behaviors, and any other conditions that sustain or permit educational inequalities for minority students on predominantly white campuses. But it is not enough, of course, simply to identify and eliminate aversive policies, programs, and conditions. Good educational practice, as well as fundamental fairness, also calls for the development of new policies, programs, and conditions that will create campuswide and specific learning environments and an institutional "tone" that is congenial to *all* students (this includes remedial or developmental studies students as well) (see Allen, 1987).

Organizational Tolerance for Individual Differences

Students manifestly differ in their educational and career goals, motivational levels, readiness to learn, prior preparation, and developmental status in both cognitive and noncognitive areas and in a range of other ways. This heterogeneity exists across institutions (even among those in presumably homogeneous categories) and, indeed, within any given institution. How, then, does one reconcile such student heterogeneity with the homogeneity of most institutions in their academic and administrative organizational structures, curricular content and structures, course content and sequences, instructional methods, housing designs and programming, nonclassroom activities, and campus life generally?

While much has been made of the importance of recognizing and adapting educational programs and experiences so that they are more responsive to individual differences among students, there is little evidence to suggest that the challenge has been taken seriously on more than a handful of campuses. Part of the fault for this may lie with researchers, who with a few exceptions have given little attention to the ways in which college's effects might vary for different kinds of students. With respect to learning and cognitive development, however, the evidence is convincing that certain kinds of students benefit more from certain kinds of instructional approaches than they do from others. These differential effects appear to be related to students' personality or psychosocial orientations. For example, compared to their peers, students with a higher need for independent achievement and students with a stronger internal locus of control appear to learn more in instructional settings that give them the freedom to guide their own course of study and learning and that involve them more directly in the design and implementation of their learning experiences. On the other hand, students high in dependence and in the need for structure and guidance from external authorities appear to learn better in more structured, instructor-centered learning settings. In short, there is good reason to believe that not all students respond in the same fashion to the same instructional format.

Similarly, our review indicates that individualized instructional approaches that accommodate variations in students' learning styles and rates consistently appear to produce greater subject matter learning than do more conventional approaches, such as lecturing. These advantages are especially apparent with instructional approaches that rely on small, modularized content units, require a student to master one instructional unit before proceeding to the next, and elicit active student involvement in the learning process. Perhaps even more promising is the evidence suggesting that these learning advantages are the same for students of different aptitudes and different levels of subject area competence. Probably in no other realm is the evidence so clear and consistent.

Nonetheless, whether out of ignorance of the evidence or for other (most likely financial) reasons, the largest proportion of instruction on most campuses, particularly at the lower-division level, continues to be delivered in conventional lecture and recitation formats. Course content continues to be presented in ways that make students passive participants in their learning, in content units tailored across disciplines to the same number of class periods of the same duration, meeting the same prespecified number of times during a semester or a quarter, betraying a reliance on academic content packaging bereft of variety and flexibility. Considerations other than course objectives, content, and student learning dictate the character of most college instructional settings. One can and must acknowledge that other factors impinge on course and curriculum design: Individualized instruction is more expensive in terms of credit-hour costs, as well as more demanding of faculty time and energy. While these considerations cannot be ignored, it seems clear that current course and curriculum planning are not heavily influenced by individual variations in students' learning styles or readiness to learn. Quite the contrary: Modern colleges and especially universities seem far better structured to process large numbers of students efficiently than to maximize student learning.

Change in these circumstances can be induced in several ways: for example, through state-level program initiation and review processes, through increased funding for individualized instruction programs, and through incremental budgetary support for other programmatic initiatives that reflect institutional efforts to respect individual differences in the learning process more fully. Some of these possibilities are discussed below. Others are given in the several reports on improving undergraduate education that have been published in recent years (see, for example, Association of American Colleges, 1985; Astin, 1985a; Bennett, 1984; Boyer, 1987; Study Group on the Conditions of Excellence in American Higher Education, 1984).

Economy, Efficiency, and Effectiveness

More than a decade ago, Astin (1977a, chap. 9) identified seven policy trends that ran counter to what his extensive analyses suggested would be sound educational policy: (1) expansion of the public sector, (2) the trend toward larger institutions, (3) the disappearance of single-sex colleges, (4) the proliferation of public community colleges, (5) the deemphasis of the residential experience, (6) open admissions, and (7) the denigration of the grade point average. The preceding discussion makes clear that some of these conflicts remain between current policies and what is now known about sound educational practice, particularly those relating to two-year and residential colleges.

The underlying determinant in these policy-research paradoxes is, of course, economic. Larger schools generate economies of scale. Two-year and commuter campuses are less expensive to construct and maintain than residential campuses of comparable size. Single-sex institutions can no longer compete for enrollments with coeducational institutions. As we have seen, these public policies have resulted in fundamental educational inequalities in both the experiences and outcomes of college for significant numbers of students.

We are not confident that state and federal policymakers can or will soon abandon costs as a basis for policy-making. It is entirely possible, however, to shift the emphasis of public policy at least somewhat more toward educational effectiveness. Indeed, that shift is already under way in increased state interest in colleges' and universities' "assessment" activities. Many states now have some agency or legislative requirement (or milder prod) for the examination of institutional influences on student cognitive and noncognitive outcomes. States' efforts span a considerable range, from Tennessee's budgetary performance incentives to the more common, gentle, and flexible requirement that annual reports or other reporting mechanisms discuss what an institution knows about its impact on its students. We believe that the potential of such institutional assessment efforts for increasing the impact of college on students is substantial and should be encouraged.

We also believe, however, that state-level policies and incentives are limited in what they can accomplish. To be effective, specific institutional changes must be determined internally if the hoped for alterations are to receive the support they will need to be successful. Thus, we believe a more immediately promising course of action lies in the concerted efforts of individual institutions, with state encouragement and support, to restructure themselves philosophically and programmatically in order to ameliorate some of the inequalities identified above and to increase their present educationally positive impact on students. We now turn to some of the ways that might be accomplished.

Implications for Institutional Practice

Our review indicates two persistent themes in the research literature on college effects. The first is the central role of other people in a student's life, whether students or faculty, and the character of the learning environments they create and the nature and strength of the stimulation their interactions provide for learning and change of all kinds. The second theme is the potency of students' effort and involvement in the academic and non-academic systems of the institutions they attend. The greater the effort and personal investment a student makes, the greater the likelihood of educational and personal returns on that investment across the spectrum of college outcomes.

Thus, the major implication of our review for individual campuses and their faculty and administrators is to shape the educational and interpersonal experiences and settings of their campus in ways that will promote learning and achievement of the institution's educational goals and to induce students to become involved in those activities, to exploit those settings and opportunities to their fullest.

Kuh and colleagues (Kuh et al., in press), on the basis of their case studies of fourteen institutions reputed to be particularly effective in promoting student involvement in the life of the campus and in their own learning and personal development, identify five characteristics common to those "involving" institutions: "clear institutional missions and educational purposes; campus environments that are compatible with the institution's mission and philosophy; opportunities for meaningful student involvement in learning and personal development activities; an institutional culture (history, tradition, rituals, language) that reinforces the importance of student involvement; and policies and practices consistent with institutional aspirations, mission, and culture." The authors provide detailed descriptions of these characteristics and give examples drawn from the institutions they studied. Chickering (1969, chaps. 8–13) identifies similar "conditions for impact" on students, including clear and consistent educational and institutional objectives; an institutional size that affords students opportunities to participate in a variety of activities; curriculum, teaching, and evaluation practices that strive for variety and active student involvement; residence hall arrangements that promote intellectual diversity and meaningful interchange among students; student and faculty interactions; and a student culture that reinforces rather than counterbalances institutional efforts to educate undergraduates. Discussion of the role of these conditions in any detail is beyond the scope of this volume, but readers are encouraged to refer to the original sources, as well as to Baird (1976c), who provides useful guidance for purposefully shaping environments in order to improve educational outcomes. The following sections offer suggestions based on our review that might be helpful in increasing students' involvement in their own learning.

Admissions and Faculty Recruitment and Rewards

Student admissions and faculty hiring decisions can be powerful tools in shaping an institution's intellectual and interpersonal climate and the nature of the influence it exerts on students. Taking full advantage of that power, however, may mean a thorough review and redefinition of the processes, criteria, and standards for both student and faculty recruitment and decision making. If admissions decisions are based solely on applicants' academic credentials and their promise for successful grade performance, important opportunities to enroll students with special talents or gifts that would enrich the academic or interpersonal climate of the school may be lost. Moreover, there is mounting evidence that traditional admissions criteria (test scores and grades) are not the best predictors of college performance and retention for all students. For example, certain student personal, attitudinal, and behavioral characteristics are better predictors of minority student performance than are standardized test scores (see, for example, Nettles, Thoeny, & Gosman, 1986). The ease with which admissions criteria can be redefined and with which nonmachine-processable information can be incorporated into the admissions decision-making process will, of course, be inversely related to the number of applications. The nature of the community of students, faculty, and staff and the homogeneity of the interests, abilities, attitudes, and values they share are, however, powerful instruments of education and socialization. The influences on the character of that community that are exerted by each new class of students should not be left to chance.

Institutional climate is also heavily influenced, of course, by faculty members and by their activities that are rewarded, such as the relative weight given to teaching and research in the faculty reward system. Significant involvement in students' out-of-class lives cannot be expected from faculty members who are recruited because of their research potential and whose research is more quickly, visibly, and amply rewarded than their involvement with undergraduate students. Faculty recruitment and reward processes may have to be redesigned to reflect an institution's serious interest in student learning in all areas. For example, when new faculty members are recruited, they might be asked to submit evidence of their teaching abilities and other student-oriented activities, as well as their research bibliographies. Candidates might be required to meet with and to make presentations to students as well as faculty members. Such attention to teaching ability and interest in students in the selection process would send new faculty members a clear message about the importance the institution attaches to instruction. The presumption, of course, is that such values would also be reflected subsequently in promotion, tenure, and compensation decisions. Clearly, in many colleges and universities good teaching is its own reward, but even here there may be more tangible ways for institutions to acknowledge professorial excellence and effort in the classroom. Whatever steps are taken, ways must be found to give faculty members more incentives to become involved in student learning, both in and out of the classroom.

Orientation

One of the major transitions from high school to college involves the unlearning of past attitudes, values, and behaviors and the learning of new ones (Feldman & Newcomb, 1969). For students going away to college, it also means cutting loose from past social networks and established identities. In their place, new identities and interpersonal networks must be constructed, and new academic and social structures, attitudes, values, and behaviors must be learned. This represents a major social and psychological transition and a time when students may be more ready to change than at any other point in their college career.

Orientation programs serve an important early socialization function. These programs involve a series of experiences by means of which individuals come to anticipate and understand the value and behavioral norms that characterize their new social setting and that will be expected of them as members of that community. If successful, the orientation process can lead to earlier and more enduring involvement in the academic and social systems of an institution. It is also reasonable to expect that student involvement will be greatest if new students can be immediately linked with people who are already invested in the institution, whether faculty members or other students. New students' initial encounters with the institution may have profound effects on subsequent levels of involvement, and these encounters should be carefully designed to socialize students to the institution's highest educational values and goals. Introducing students to available support services, key administrators, student social life, and major and degree requirements, as well as their early course registration, is important for students and institutions. If these introductions define an orientation program, however, then once-in-a-lifetime opportunities to orient students to the institution's intellectual and cultural life and values may be lost. Intentionally or not, institutional values are on display during orientation, and the program's activities send subtle but powerful messages to new students about what and who is valued (and not valued) on a campus.

Scholars and administrators are increasingly coming to realize that the most effective orientation programs are not limited to the first few days or weeks of the first semester. Rather, orientation activities are being ex-

pretative conclusion. In an important discussion of the meaning of regression coefficients, however, Pedhazur (1975, 1982) makes an important distinction between the causal meaning of regression coefficients derived from experimental data and those yielded by correlational data.

The easiest way to illustrate this distinction is through an admittedly contrived example. Suppose we randomly provide half the entering freshmen in a particular college with a dictionary-thesaurus combination and withhold it from the remaining half. At the end of the freshman year we give the entire class a test of vocabulary and find that those who received the dictionary thesaurus scored significantly and substantially higher than the nonrecipients. The unstandardized regression equation would tell us the average advantage in vocabulary test achievement accruing to those freshmen provided with the dictionary thesaurus (group coded 1) versus those not provided with it (group coded 0). Given this randomized, true experiment, we could estimate (by means of the *b* weight) the typical improvement in vocabulary achievement we might get by routinely providing all incoming freshmen with a dictionary thesaurus.

Conversely, suppose in a correlational, panel study we find that net of precollege level of vocabulary achievement, having a dictionary thesaurus has a net positive association with vocabulary achievement at the end of the freshman year. In this situation we have not been able to manipulate and control the conditions under which the relationship between having a dictionary thesaurus and outcome vocabulary achievement is observed. Consequently, the regression coefficient allows us *only* to estimate the average difference in vocabulary achievement between freshmen who own a dictionary thesaurus and those who do not, net of precollege vocabulary achievement. We cannot tell from the regression coefficient whether purposefully providing freshmen with a dictionary thesaurus would produce the same effect (Pedhazur, 1975).

In short, we cannot interpret regression coefficients from naturally occurring correlational data as though the variables they are associated with had been purposefully manipulated under experimental conditions. It would be misleading, therefore, to interpret them as the change in the dependent variable that we can *expect* from a purposeful unit increase in the independent variable, net of other independent variables. Regression coefficients from correlational data can be quite useful in identifying *possibly* causal associations among variables. In the vast majority of investigations on the influence of college, however, the regression coefficients are, in and of themselves, insufficient evidence for causality.

Hierarchical and Stepwise Regression Analysis

In the approach to regression or commonality analysis discussed above, all independent variables in the model are entered into the equation at the same time. It is worth briefly mentioning two other approaches to regression analysis that are concerned with the order in which independent variables enter a regression equation. The first is termed hierarchical regression, and it is often used when the researcher can posit an explicit causal or temporal ordering or hierarchy to the independent variables (for example, Chapman & Pascarella, 1983; Pascarella & Terenzini, 1980a; Terenzini & Pascarella, 1978).

For example, suppose in our fictitious data we are interested only in whether measures of the college environment and experience (for example, institutional size and informal contact with faculty) account for a substantive increase in the explained variance in freshman-year intellectual orientation over and above the individual's level of precollege intellectual orientation. Consistent with our question, we would solve the regression analyses in two steps. In the first step, IO_2 would be regressed on IO_1, and in the second step, $SIZE$ and IWF would be added to the equation. The increase in R^2 from step 1 to step 2 would represent the unique contribution of college environment and experience variables ($SIZE$ and IWF) over and above that due to input (IO_1). (In the actual data, the R^2 in IO_2 increases from .360 with only IO_1 in the equation to .426 with $SIZE$ and IWF added, or an R^2 increase due to $SIZE$ and IWF of .066 or 6.6 percent.) Hierarchical analysis makes no attempt to find the joint or common variance due to input (IO_1) and college environment and experience ($SIZE$ and IWF). Rather, it attributes any joint influence to input alone. As such, hierarchical approaches provide a conservative or lower-bounds estimate of the output variance associated with college environment or experience. This, however, may accurately reflect the analyst's conceptualization of the process.

Although hierarchical analysis enters variables or sets of variables in steps, it does so in accordance with a conceptual or causal hierarchy specified by the researcher. Thus, it must be distinguished from another type of analysis, termed stepwise regression, with which it is sometimes confused. In stepwise analyses, variables are entered (or removed) in steps, but the criteria and order of entry (or removal) are empirically rather than conceptually determined. In one type of stepwise analysis, for example, the computer searches first for the independent variable with the largest simple or zero-order correlation with the dependent measure and enters it into the regression equation in step 1. In step 2, the computer searches the *remaining* independent variables and selects the one with the largest partial correlation with the dependent variable (net of the variable already in the equation) and adds it to the equation. This step-by-step, empirically driven procedure continues until a specified criterion for entry is no longer met (for example, the R^2 increase is no longer statistically significant or is less than 1 percent, and so on).

The basic purpose of stepwise analysis is to develop a parsimonious accounting of variance in the dependent variable (that is, an optimal accounting with the fewest and most important predictors). This has a lot of intuitive appeal, but stepwise analysis has some serious limitations. The most important of these is that it capitalizes on chance covariation in a sample. The easiest way to show this is through an example. Suppose in sample 1 we have ten independent variables, but the two variables with the highest simple correlations with the dependent measure are A ($r = .31$) and B ($r = .30$). In sample 2, with the same set of independent variables, the two respective highest correlations are $A = .30$ and $B = .31$ (just the reverse). In a stepwise analysis conducted with sample 1, variable A would enter the equation first and, if A and B are highly correlated, B might never enter the equation. In sample 2, variable B would enter first, and if B and A are correlated sufficiently, A might never be selected for inclusion. Moreover, in sample 1 the variables entering the equation would be strongly determined not only by their correlation with the dependent variable but also by how much they covary with A. In sample 2, however, an important factor determining the final equation would be correlations between the remaining independent variables and variable B. If these respective correlation patterns differ, the result could be quite different equations in sample 1 and sample 2 even when the same independent variables are being considered.

What this comes down to is that regression equations determined by stepwise analysis can be unstable across independent samples. Indeed, as a rule of thumb, it is probably wise to trust stepwise-determined equations only when the results have been validated on another independent sample (Kerlinger & Pedhazur, 1973).

Causal Modeling

Regression analysis provides the same level of statistical control as the use of residual scores and partial correlations. In addition, it permits partitioning of the total variance in the dependent measure and provides (through regression coefficients) ways of estimating the net magnitude of the influence of each independent variable on the dependent measure. Due in large part to these and related advantages, regression analysis has generally replaced the use of residual scores and partial correlations in studies concerned with the influence of college.

Despite its utility as a general data analytical system, however, regression analysis in the forms discussed above is largely predictive rather than explanatory in nature. For example, when we regress IO_2 on IO_1, $SIZE$, and IWF in our fictitious data set, the resultant regression equation allows us to determine the unique and joint variance increments in IO_2 associated with the three predictors. It also allows us to estimate the net change in IO_2 associated with unit changes in each of the three predictors. It does not, however, provide much information in terms of explaining the interactive process through which student precollege traits (for example, IO_1), institutional characteristics (for example, *SIZE*), and individual collegiate experiences (for example, *IWF*) influence one another as well as freshman-year outcomes (for example, IO_2). Moreover, simple regression analysis does not really help us understand the various mechanisms through which the joint or common influences among independent variables may have an effect on the dependent measure.

Causal modeling is a use of regression analysis that focuses on explanation rather than prediction and provides an efficient method for determining the indirect as well as the direct influences of each independent variable in a theoretically guided causal system (Anderson & Evans, 1974; Duncan, 1966, 1975; Feldman, 1971a; Heise, 1969; Werts & Linn, 1970; Wolfle, 1977, 1980a; Wright, 1934, 1954). As argued by Wright (1934) and discussed by Wolfle (1985a), the purpose of causal modeling is not to accomplish the impossible (that is, to attribute experimental causality from correlational data). Rather, its purpose is to determine the extent to which an *a priori* system of hypothesized causal effects is supported by actual data. Thus, causal relationships exist in models not because they are "proven" by regression coefficients but because theories posit them. From this perspective, if regression coefficients tend to support the presence of a hypothesized causal relationship, this suggests only the *possibility* that the observed relationship may be causal. One does not confirm a causal relationship with regression coefficients in causal modeling; one only "fails to disconfirm it" (for example, Cliff, 1983; Kenny, 1979; Wolfle, 1985a).

As suggested in a comprehensive and readable discussion of causal modeling by Wolfle (1985a), the use of causal models in research on the influence of college may have two important advantages. First, causal modeling requires that the researcher give considerable thought to the theoretical structure of the problem. This means that he or she must not only specify the relevant independent and dependent variables but must also be explicit about the presumed causal ordering and patterns of cause and effect in the model. Often this is accomplished by drawing a path diagram of the causal model in which causal arrows reflect relationships among variables suggested by theory or relevant literature. The explicitness of causal modeling can be important in preventing the misinterpretation of results. As Wolfle (1985a, p. 383) puts it, the "researcher may, of course, be wrong but he won't be misunderstood."

The second advantage of causal modeling is that it moves beyond typical regression analysis and allows the researcher to investigate not only the direct unmediated causal effects of each independent variable but also their indirect effects through intervening variables in the model (Finney, 1972; Wolfle, 1985a). It is in the investigation of indirect effects that causal modeling provides substantively more information than do typical regression analyses. The estimation of direct effects in a causal model can be achieved through the simple regression of the dependent variable on all independent variables in the model. Thus, direct effects in causal models are the same as standardized regression weights in regression analysis, and both are analogous to the unique variance estimates in commonality analysis. The indirect effects in causal modeling, however, can be thought of as a way to further understand and disaggregate the joint or common variance among independent variables (Alwin & Hauser, 1975; Feldman, 1971a).

Decomposition of Effects in Causal Modeling. There are three types of effects in causal modeling. (Note that the terms *path analysis* and *structural equations modeling* are often used interchangeably with *causal modeling*.) These types are direct effects, indirect effects, and total effects. The direct effects have been defined above, the indirect effects are the sum of the products of direct effects through intervening variables, and the total effects are the sum of the direct and indirect effects. The difference between the simple or zero-order correlation between an independent and a dependent variable and the total effect of that independent variable can be considered the spurious or noncausal part of the relationship.

A simple way to understand indirect effects is to visualize three billiard balls: *A, B,* and *C.* If ball *A* strikes ball *B*, which in turn strikes ball *C*, then ball *A* can be thought of as having an indirect effect on ball *C* through ball *B*. Thus ball *A* has an effect on ball *C* even though it may never strike it directly. Similarly, college grades may not directly influence income. Nevertheless, they clearly have a strong positive influence on degree attainment, which in turn is a key determinant of income. Consequently, grades in college may have an important indirect effect on income through educational attainment.

The easiest way to demonstrate the decomposition of effects in a causal model is through the use of an example. Again, we will use the fictitious correlation matrix found in Table A.1. The difference, however, is that this time we will posit a hypothetical causal structure to the variables. Let's suppose that on the basis of some theory, we hypothesize that the enrollment of the institution attended *(SIZE)* is a function of precollege level of intellectual orientation, with students initially high in intellectual orientation tending to select and attend smaller schools. In turn, informal contact with faculty *(IWF)* is hypothesized as being a function of both precollege intellectual orientation and institutional size. The former is hypothesized as positively influencing informal contact with faculty, while institutional size is hypothesized to inhibit faculty contact. Finally, end-of-freshman-year intellectual orientation *(IO$_2$)* is posited as being positively influenced by IO_1 and *IWF* and negatively influenced by *SIZE*. A visual portrayal of the model is shown in Figure A.5. In the model, IO_1 is considered an exogenous variable because it is determined by effects outside the model. *SIZE, IWF,* and *IO$_2$* are considered endogenous variables and are determined by exogenous variables and all other causally antecedent endogenous variables in the model.

Figure A.5. Proposed Causal Model.

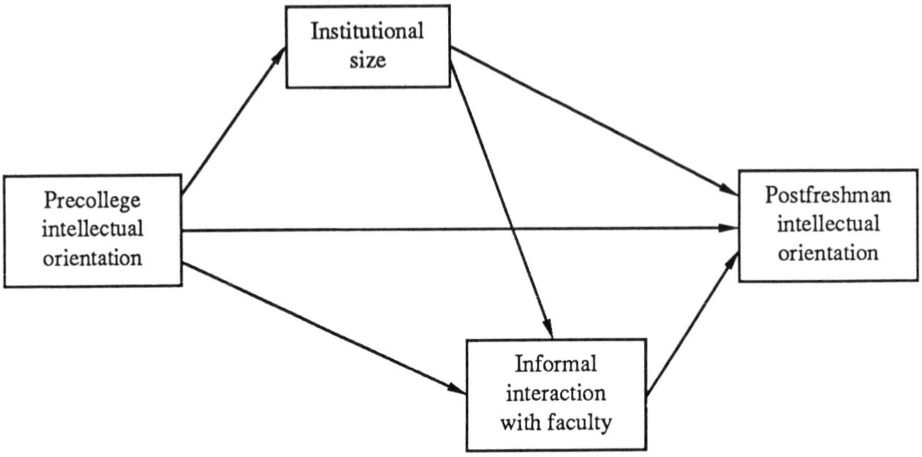

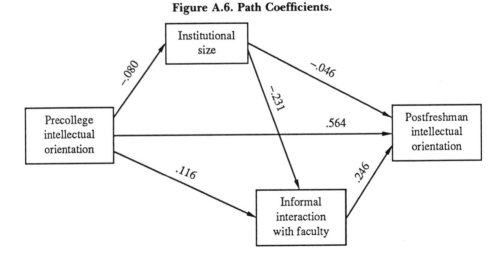

In order to estimate the direct and indirect effects specified by the model, it is necessary to solve a series of regression equations that define the structure of effects in the model. These "structural equations" for the model shown in Figure A.5 are as follows:

$$SIZE = a + B_1(IO_1) + \text{error}$$
$$IWF = a + B_1(IO_1) + B_2(SIZE) + \text{error}$$
$$IO_2 = a + B_1(IO_1) + B_2(SIZE) + B_3(IWF) + \text{error},$$

where B equals the standardized regression or path coefficient and a is a constant. Thus, the structural equations provide all the direct effects, which in turn can be used to compute indirect effects. Figure A.6 shows the ap-

Figure A.6. Path Coefficients.

propriate direct effects (beta weights) for each causal path computed for our fictitious correlation matrix. The decomposition of causal effects on IO_2 is summarized in Table A.3. As this table shows, the direct or unmediated effects of IO_1 (.564) and IWF (.246) on IO_2 were positive and substantial; both were also statistically significant. The direct effect of $SIZE$ (-.046), however, was small and nonsignificant.

Had we ended our analysis here, essentially the results of a simple multiple regression, we would have concluded that both precollege intellectual orientation and informal contact with faculty may causally influence freshman-year intellectual orientation but that the size of the institution attended is essentially unimportant. This would have been misleading, however, since as we can see from Figure A.6, $SIZE$ has a substantial (-.231) negative effect on IWF, which in turn positively influences IO_2 (.246). Based on our computational definition of indirect effects (the sum of the products of direct effects through intervening variables), the indirect effect of $SIZE$ on IO_2 through $IWF = (-.231) \times (.246) = -.057$. Though modest, this indirect effect is larger than the direct effect and is statistically significant, while the latter is not. (The statistical significance of indirect effects can now be computed quite simply via a computer program developed by Wolfle and Ethington, 1985, based on the work of Sobel, 1982.)

This example demonstrates an important analytical advantage of causal modeling over simple regression analysis. By permitting one to estimate indirect (mediated) as well as the direct (unmediated) effects, it provides a more complete estimate of a variable's total influence on the criterion. In this sense it addresses and helps illuminate the nature of a variable's influence through its joint covariation with other independent variables (that is, the joint or common variance from a commonality analysis). In doing so, it may alter one's conclusions about the importance of a variable's impact versus the estimate one would get from an examination of direct effects only. In the present case, the total effect of $SIZE$ on IO_2 —that is, the sum of the direct (-.046) and indirect (-.057) effects—is -.103, which is also statistically significant. This suggests that in our hypothetical example, the enrollment of the institution attended has a modest negative influence on the development of intellectual orientation, primarily by inhibiting student informal contact with faculty. Our conclusion based on direct effects only

Table A.3. Direct, Indirect, and Total Effects.

Variable	Direct Effect	Indirect Effect	Total Effect
IO_1	.564[a]	.036	.600[a]
$SIZE$	-.046	-.057[a]	-.103[a]
IWF	.246[a]		.246[a]

[a] $p < .01$.

would have essentially dismissed any influence of *SIZE* on IO_2 as trivial and statistically nonsignificant.

It is worth noting that there are different ways of computing indirect and total effects in a causal model. Indirect effects can be computed as shown above. In complex models, however, the summing of the products of direct effects through the various paths leading to the dependent measure can be tedious and fraught with computational errors. A simpler way is to compute direct effects and total effects and then subtract the former from the latter to get indirect effects. Direct effects, of course, can be obtained from the simple regression of the dependent measure on all relevant independent measures. Total effects and their statistical significance can be obtained by using "reduced form" regression equations (Alwin & Hauser, 1975). These are simply the regression of the dependent measure on the variable of interest and all causally concurrent or antecedent variables in the model. Intervening variables between the variable of interest and the dependent measure are not in the equation—thus the term *reduced form*. For example, the total effect of IO_1 on IO_2 is simply the regression of IO_2 on IO_1. The independent variable here is exogenous, so it has no causal antecedents defined by the model. The total effect of *SIZE* is obtained from the regression of IO_2 on IO_1 and *SIZE*. Finally, since *IWF* has no indirect effect on IO_2 through intervening variables in the model, its direct effect is also its total effect.

Problems in the Use of Causal Modeling. While causal models have great potential for increasing the information gained about the process of collegiate influence on student development, a number of problems are inherent in their use. The first of these focuses on the issue of adequate model specification. This means that in constructing causal models the researcher must give considerable thought both to including all important relevant variables in the model and to specifying their appropriate causal ordering. If important causal influences are excluded, the result is often seriously biased or inflated path coefficients. For example, with IO_1 and *SIZE* also in the equation, the direct effect of *IWF* on IO_2 is .246. However, if IO_1 is left out, the direct effect of *IWF* on IO_2 jumps spuriously to .312. On the other hand, if the model specifies an inappropriate or implausible causal ordering in the variables, the indirect effects can be misleading and perhaps even meaningless.

What determines an adequately specified model, of course, is the soundness of its theoretical structure. Indeed, as noted by Duncan (1975, p. 149), quoted in Wolfle (1985a), "The study of structural equation [causal] models can be divided into two parts: the easy part and the hard part." The easy part is the solution of structural equations and the computation of direct, indirect, and total effects. The hard part is the construction of causal models that reflect sound social theory.

In addition to adequate model specification, a second assumption of causal modeling, and indeed of ordinary least-squares multiple regression generally, is recursiveness. *Recursiveness* refers to the assumption of unidirectional causal influence (for example, *A* influences *B* but not vice versa) in the model and the absence of causal feedback loops. Thus, in the example data, informal contact with faculty is presumed to influence freshman-year intellectual orientation, but the reverse is not hypothesized. The only way to ensure that causal feedback loops (or correlated errors) are not present is to collect longitudinal data in a manner that reflects the causal ordering of variables in the model. For example, in our fictitious study, measures of IO_1 were collected prior to measures of *IWF*, which in turn preceded the collection of data relevant to IO_2. This means that while *IWF* may causally influence IO_2, the reverse is not possible (for example, Kenny, 1979). If, however, independent measures such as *IWF* and dependent measures such as IO_2 had been collected simultaneously on the same instrument (a practice quite common in educational research), the direction of causal effects could be ambiguous. Does informal interaction with faculty influence intellectual orientation, or do increases in intellectual orientation lead students to seek out more frequent nonclassroom interaction with faculty?

Consistent with what we know about the developmental nature of student growth and maturation during college (for example, Chickering, 1969; Feldman, 1972; Heath, 1968), causal models assume longitudinality in the data being analyzed. In the absence of carefully collected *longitudinal* data, it is extremely hazardous to assume the presence of unidirectional causal effects. Moreover, when there is simultaneous assessment of the dependent variable and independent causal variables on the same instrument (that is, cross-sectional data), the frequent result is a correlation between those independent causes and errors of measurement on the dependent variable. This violates one of the assumptions of any ordinary least-squares regression analysis and can lead to biased regression coefficients (Pedhazur, 1982).

This problem has led to the development of nonrecursive causal models in which the researcher actually hypothesizes the presence of causal loops or two-way causality (Anderson, 1978). Estimating nonrecursive causal models requires the use of a procedure termed two-stage least-squares regression analysis. One of the assumptions of two-stage least squares is the presence of "instrumental" exogenous variables. By definition, an instrumental exogenous variable is one that causally influences one of the dependent (endogenous) variables in the causal loop but has zero effect on the other (Anderson, 1978; Wolfle, 1985a). Once these instrumental exogenous variables are identified and the causal model is specified, existing two-stage least-squares regression programs, such as those available in the Statistical Analysis System (SAS), can be used to estimate the direction and strength of causal influences. Unfortunately, given the considerable correlations among student precollege traits, institutional characteristics, and measures of the collegiate experience in research on college influence, it is extremely difficult to find exogenous variables that meet the assumption of also being instrumental variables. Wolfle (1985a, p. 395) has suggested that this problem may make "most nonrecursive models implausible for social science applications." Nevertheless, there are a few uses of nonrecursive models and two-stage least-squares regression in research on the college student (for example, Bean & Bradley, 1986; Bean & Kuh, 1984; Iverson, Pascarella, & Terenzini, 1984).

A third important issue in the use of causal models is measurement error. One of the assumptions of any regression analysis is that both the independent and dependent variables are measured without error; however, this is almost never the case. In the presence of measurement error, regression or path coefficients will be biased, and it is extremely difficult to determine both the magnitude and the direction of the biases (Maruyama & Walberg, 1982; Stage, 1989, 1990). Recently, however, there have been a number of advances with maximum likelihood estimation procedures such as linear structural relations (LISREL) (Joreskog, 1973; Joreskog & Sorbom, 1979, 1983). These procedures permit correction for differential measurement errors and thus yield less biased regression coefficients than do ordinary least-squares regression approaches. As such, they represent an important refinement in the application of causal modeling to questions of the influence of college on student development.

The Unit of Analysis

An important question in investigations of the influence of college on student development is the appropriate unit of analysis. This is most apparent when one is analyzing multi-institutional samples where data are collected at the individual level but where it is also possible to obtain average scores at the institutional or other level of aggregation (for example, the Cooperative Institutional Research Program data, the National Longitudinal Study of the High School Class of 1972, High School and Beyond). It is also possible, however, that one needs to consider the appropriate unit of analysis even when the data come from single-institution samples. What, for example, are the effects of classroom climate or residential unit composition on student learning (for example, Pascarella & Terenzini, 1982; D. Smith, 1977; Terenzini & Pascarella, 1984)?

The unit of analysis issue has been a complex and somewhat controversial one in research on the influence of college. It is often the case that scholars interested in essentially the same question have in various studies used institutions, departments, or individuals as the unit of analysis. Consider, for example, studies of the influence of different college characteristics on student learning (for example, Astin, 1968c; Ayres, 1983; Ayres & Bennett, 1983; Centra & Rock, 1971; Hartnett & Centra, 1977). Variation in the unit of analysis has perhaps contributed to the lack of consistent findings in several areas of inquiry (for example, Pascarella, 1985a). As suggested in a sophisticated and cogent discussion by Burstein (1980a), the issue is not so much that one unit of aggregation is more appropriate than another. Rather, the issue needs to be understood in light of the fact that different units of aggregation or analysis are asking different questions of the data. When the institution is the unit of analysis, for example, one is essentially asking what the average influence of certain college characteristics (student body selectivity, average faculty salary, and so on) is on average student development. Thus, one is primarily concerned with average effects among or between institutions. When individuals are the unit of analysis, however, the question is typically whether differences in individual students' collegiate experiences (for instance, academic major, extracurricular involvement, interaction with faculty) lead to differences in specified outcomes. Here the focus is on the effects of different experiences or exposures among or between individual students, even if the data are multi-institutional in form.

By focusing on one question, both institutional and individual levels of aggregation tend to ignore other questions. Aggregating at the level of the institution tends to mask possibly substantial variations between individual students' experiences within the same institution (Cronbach, 1976). Assuming, for example, that an aggregate or global measure of the college environment accurately portrays a homogeneous stimulus experienced by all students in the institution ignores substantial evidence of influential subenvironments in an institution, subenvironments that are more proximal to the student's daily experience (for example, Baird, 1974; Berdie, 1967; Lacy, 1978; Newcomb & Wilson, 1966; Pascarella, 1976; Phelan, 1979; Weidman, 1979). Conversely, using individuals as the unit of analysis tends to ignore the dependencies (or correlations) of individual subject experiences within institutions; that is, the shared educational experience among individual students within the same college leads to the nonindependence of individual behaviors within the college (Burstein, 1980a). Thus, for example, institutional enrollment (size) may facilitate certain types of student-faculty relationships in a small liberal arts college that are quite different from the nature of the student-faculty relationships typically found in large research universities. These types of relationships may differentiate small and large institutions even when individual differences in student characteristics are taken into account. Moreover, as suggested by Burstein (1980a), standard statistical estimation techniques such as ordinary least-squares regression analysis can yield flawed or biased estimates in the presence of within-group dependencies.

Because of the dilemmas inherent in choosing one level of aggregation or unit of analysis over another, a number of scholars have suggested the appropriateness of using multilevels of analysis guided by appropriate theory (for example, Astin, 1970b; Burstein, 1980a, 1980b; Cooley, Bond, & Mao, 1981; Cronbach, 1976; Cronbach & Webb, 1975; Terenzini & Pascarella, 1984; Rogosa, 1978). In such analyses, both between-student and between-aggregation effects could be estimated when one has multi-institutional (or even multimajor, multiclassroom, or multiresidential arrangement) data. (The appropriate level of aggregation, of course, depends on the substantive question being asked.) Routine use of a multilevel approach such as this might be one way to permit a more valid and informative comparison of results across studies. It would also permit one to compare differences in the aggregate effects of college (or some other unit of aggregation) with the effects of individual student characteristics and experiences. As suggested by Burstein (1980a), variables can have different meanings at different levels of analysis. Studies that choose colleges as the unit of analysis are asking different questions than studies that use the individual as the unit of analysis; consequently, we should expect different results.

Contextual Analysis

One way of combining aggregate and individual levels of analysis simultaneously is through a procedure known as contextual analysis. Contextual analysis is essentially the study of the influence of group- or aggregate-level variables on individual-level outcomes (Erbring & Young, 1980; Firebaugh, 1978, 1980; Lazarsfeld & Menzel, 1961). In this procedure the individual is the true unit of analysis, but instead of focusing only on the developmental effects of individual college experiences, one also attempts to estimate the effect of being a member of a particular group or aggregation (for example, college academic major, residential unit, classroom).

In its simplest form, contextual analysis can be defined by the following regression equation:

$$Y_{ij} = a + b_1 X_{ij} + b_2 \overline{X}_j + \text{error},$$

where Y_{ij} might represent the academic achievement (for instance, Graduate Record Examination Scores) of the ith student in college j, X_{ij} might be a measure of academic aptitude for the same student, and $\overline{X}_j$ would be the average (mean) value of student academic aptitude in college j. In short, X_{ij} might be thought of as a measure of student input or background, while $\overline{X}_j$ could be considered an estimate of college context or environment. The error or random disturbance term represents errors of measurement plus all causes of Y_{ij} (achievement) unspecified by the equation, such as student motivation and efficiency of study habits (Hanushek, Jackson, & Kain, 1974). The coefficients a (constant) and b_1 and b_2 (regression coefficients) can be estimated by ordinary least-squares regression procedures. A contextual or environmental effect is said to occur in this equation if the aggregate measure of student body aptitude has a significant regression coefficient with individual GRE achievement net of individual aptitude. If the coefficient for the contextual effect is positive, it would suggest that attending a college with a student body composed of "bright" students tends positively to influence a student's standardized academic achievement above and beyond his or her own academic aptitude.

One might posit the causal mechanism underlying the above example as due to the tendency for college faculty to gear the cognitive and conceptual level of instruction to the academic capacities of the students being taught or to the generally "higher" intellectual level of student discourse inside or outside the classroom. Hypothetically, then, students in more selective colleges might benefit from instruction (or an overall environment) geared to higher-level cognitive processes such as analysis, synthesis, and evaluation (Bloom, 1956), the results of which are manifest in higher GRE scores. In positing such a causal mechanism, however, we are again confronted by the disconcerting likelihood that selection (input) and aggregation (environmental) effects are substantially correlated. As such, it is extremely difficult, if not impossible, to accurately estimate and separate the effects of the latter from those of the former (Cronbach, Rogosa, Floden, & Price, 1977; Werts & Linn, 1971). In the above specification of the model, the unique effects of context or environment (as indicated by b_2) are likely to be quite conservative. Thus, a significant regression coefficient for average student body aptitude is reasonably convincing evidence of a unique contextual or environmental influence (Burstein, 1980a).

Frog-Pond Effects

Another approach to the combining of individual and aggregate level data is the "frog-pond" or relative deprivation effect as suggested by the work of Davis (1966), Alexander and Eckland (1975b), and Bassis (1977). This approach suggests that in order to understand individual behavior, one needs to be cognizant not only of individual attributes but also of how individual attributes position one in relationship to an important reference or peer group. In the above example of aptitude and achievement, the regression equation might be specified as follows:

$$Y_{ij} = a + b_1 X_{ij} + b_2(\overline{X}_j - X_{ij}) + \text{error}$$

In this specification, hypothetical GRE achievement for an individual student (Y_{ij}) is posited as a function of individual academic aptitude (X_{ij}) and the difference between individual aptitude and the average college aptitude ($\overline{X}_j - X_{ij}$). A significant regression coefficient would indicate that a student's academic ability relative to the student average at the college attended has an influence on GRE achievement above and beyond individual aptitude alone. The sign of the regression coefficient would indicate whether the effect is generally beneficial to students below $(+)$ or above $(-)$ the college average.

As demonstrated by Burstein (1980a, 1980b), a regression equation including individual, contextual, and frog-pond effects is not estimable by standard means because the variables representing the three effects have a linear dependency. (The coefficients in an equation with any combination of two of the three effects represented, however, can be estimated.) Burstein (1980a) has suggested a way to deal with this problem. Specifically, he suggests that the investigator obtain more direct measures of the contextual or frog-pond effects. This means giving considerable thought to the specific and underlying causal mechanisms at work. For example, research conducted by Terenzini and Pascarella (1984) found that net of individual levels of institutional commitment, freshman-year persistence was independently and positively influenced by the average level of institutional commitment in the student's residence unit (contextual).

It is also possible that the student's level of institutional commitment relative to that of his or her residential unit peers (frog pond) would add significantly to an understanding of individual persistence or withdrawal behavior (an influence not estimated by Terenzini & Pascarella, 1982). That this effect operates through the influence of social involvement or integration is suggested by the theoretical work of Tinto (1975, 1982, 1987). Thus, instead of entering an unestimable frog-pond term operationalizing the student's standing relative to the average institutional commitment of the residence unit, one could substitute relative standing on level of social involvement. The equation then might be specified as follows:

$$P_{ij} = a + b_1 (IC_{ij}) + b_2 (\overline{IC}_j) + b_3 (\overline{SI}_j - SI_{ij}),$$

where

P_{ij} = an individual student's persistence or withdrawal behavior,
IC_{ij} = an individual student's level of institutional commitment,
$\overline{IC}_j$ = average level of institutional commitment in a particular student's residence unit,
$(\overline{SI}_j - SI_{ij})$ = an individual student's level of social integration relative to the average in his or her residence unit.

Burstein's (1980a) argument for focusing on direct measures of aggregate and/or frog-pond effects underscores a major conceptual problem in multilevel analysis. This problem, which has been forcefully articulated by analysts such as Hauser (1970, 1974) and Firebaugh (1978), is that contextual or frog-pond effects estimated atheoretically are often mechanistic and distally related to the underlying social-psychological processes they were designed to represent (Burstein, 1980a). For example, contextual or frog-pond effects estimated at the institutional level may have little relevance to and therefore little impact on individual cognitive development during college. Greater understanding may come from estimating contextual and relative standing effects at levels of aggregation that are not only theoretically justifiable but also more proximal and directly related to student learning (for example, classrooms, peer groups, roommates). In short, the most informative multilevel analyses are likely to be those "based on theories in which the source and form of group effects are measured directly" (Burstein, 1980a, p. 207).

It may be, of course, that aggregate effects at almost any level are simply too psychologically remote (or too globally measured) to have important direct effects on student development. Instead, the major aggregate-level influences on student development in college may be indirect, transmitted through their shaping of the individual student's interaction with important agents of socialization on campus, such as peers and faculty.

Change Scores

A substantial amount of the more recent research on the influence of college has a developmental focus and attempts to estimate how exposure to different collegiate experiences or environments leads to differential change on some trait over time. For example, do students who reside on campus tend to change more in critical thinking than students who commute to campus? One way in which this type of question has traditionally been approached is to compare pre- to postdifferences (such as freshman-to-senior scores) on an appropriate measure between groups of interest. If, for example, students residing on campus tend to change more in critical thinking than do those commuting to campus, one might conclude that the residential experience increases the impact of college, at least on critical thinking.

This is an intuitively appealing approach. There are, however, two problems with the use of change scores: reliability and the fact that the magnitude of the change or gain is typically correlated with the initial score (Linn, 1986). Reliability is an issue because change scores incorporate the unreliability of both the pre- and posttest measures (Thorndike & Hagen, 1977). This can be a major problem when difference scores are used to make decisions about individuals, but it may not be a major issue when group comparisons are being made (Cronbach, 1970; Linn, 1986). The second problem with change scores, their correlation with the initial score, however, can confound attempts to attribute differential change to exposure to a particular group or educational experience. If one simply compared changes in critical thinking between residents and commuters, it would be extremely difficult, if not impossible, to determine whether the differential changes were due to differences in actual residence status or simply to differences in initial critical thinking status between the two groups.

Comparing simple change or gain scores cannot correct for the lack of random assignment to different groups or collegiate experiences. A better (though not totally adequate) approach would be to employ change or gain in critical thinking as a dependent measure in a regression model that includes both a measure of group membership (for example, 1 = residents, 0 = commuters) and initial level of critical thinking. This would indicate whether or not residence arrangement is significantly associated with critical thinking gains when the influence of initial critical thinking status is partialed out. It is of interest to note, however, that one need not use change scores to obtain essentially the same information. Exactly the same results in terms of the statistical significance of residence status would be obtained if senior-year critical thinking were regressed on a model containing both residence status and initial freshman-year critical thinking (Linn, 1986; Linn & Slinde, 1977). Similarly, in the fictitious example we have been using throughout this appendix, essentially the same *net associations* for *SIZE* and *IWF* would be obtained in either of the following regression equations:

$$IO_2 - IO_1 = IO_1 + SIZE + IWF + \text{error}$$
$$IO_2 = IO_1 + SIZE + IWF + \text{error}$$

In what has come to be regarded as a classic paper, Cronbach and Furby (1970, p. 80) have suggested that "investigators who ask questions regarding gain scores would ordinarily be better advised to frame their questions in other ways." In fact, as suggested above, questions about gain or change can typically be reformulated without sacrificing information. Regression analyses that treat the pretest (precollege) scores no differently from other independent variables in the model and use the posttest (senior-year) scores as the dependent variable provide essentially the same information while avoiding many of the problems associated with change scores (Linn & Slinde, 1977).

This is not to suggest that change should not be studied. Recent work by Bryk and Raudenbush (1987) and Willett (1988), as reviewed by Light, Singer, and Willett (1990), has suggested that the study of change becomes more valid and less ambiguous when it is measured over more than two time points. Light, Singer, and Willett (1990, p. 147) argue that assessing change over three, four, or even more time points permits one to trace the "shape of each student's growth trajectory" rather than just the difference between the beginning and end points. The use of multiple estimates of student status over time is a promising new methodological approach to the assessment of change or growth.

Conditional Versus General Effects

The analytical procedures we have discussed in the preceding sections have all assumed that the net effects of each independent variable on the dependent variable are general. That is, the effect is the same for all students irrespective of their status on other independent variables (Kerlinger & Pedhazur, 1973). Thus, in our fictitious example we are assuming that the net direct effect of IWF on IO_2 is the same regardless of the student's level on IO_1 or the size of the institution attended. This assumption certainly has the appeal of parsimony (that is, other things being equal, the simplest explanation is often the optimal one). On the other hand, it can be argued that assuming only general effects in one's analytical approach ignores individual differences among students attending the same institution or exposed to the same educational or instructional experience. These individual differences among students may interact with different institutional, instructional, curricular, or other educational experiences to produce "conditional" rather than general effects. In a conditional effect, the magnitude of the influence of certain educational experiences on the dependent measure may vary for students with different individual characteristics. Thus, for example, the magnitude of the direct effect of IWF on IO_2 may vary, depending upon the student's precollege level of intellectual orientation (IO_1) or on other individual traits such as gender or race.

It is also possible that there may be patterns of conditional relationships or interactions that involve different levels of aggregation (Bryk & Thum, 1989; Raudenbush & Bryk, 1988). In a contextual analysis, for example, individual aptitude may influence achievement differently depending upon the aggregate level of institutional, departmental, or residence unit aptitude. Similarly, there may be interactions among college experience variables that do not directly involve individual differences among student precollege characteristics. The influence of informal contact with faculty on intellectual orientation, for example, may vary in magnitude in institutions of different size enrollment. Conditional effects of the various types described above may be masked by analyses that consider general effects only. Under certain circumstances this may lead the researcher to conclude that the effects of specific educational experiences are trivial or nonsignificant when, in fact, they may have statistically significant and nontrivial influences for certain subgroups in the sample. Thus, a narrow focus on aggregate means or tendencies as an index of college impact may mask important changes in individuals or student subgroups. (See Clark, Heist, McConnell, Trow, & Yonge [1972] or Feldman & Newcomb [1969, pp. 53–58] for a more extensive discussion of this point.)

The concept of conditional effects determined by the interaction of individual differences among students with different methods of teaching or the presentation of course content has a respected tradition in instructional research. Here it is typically referred to as aptitude (or trait) × treatment interaction (Berliner & Cahen, 1973; Cronbach & Snow, 1977). Underlying its application in instructional research is the more general perspective, stemming from the psychology of individual differences, that not all individuals will benefit equally from the same educational experience. Applications of the investigation of conditional effects with postsecondary samples are provided by Romine, Davis, and Gehman (1970) for college environments and achievement; by Holland (1963) for career choice and academic achievement; by Pfeifer (1976) for race and grades; by Andrews (1981), Born, Gledhill, and Davis (1972), Buenz and Merrill (1968), Domino (1968), Daniels and Stevens (1976), Gay (1986), Horak and Horak (1982), Parent, Forward, Canter, and Mohling (1975), Pascarella (1978), Peterson (1979), Ross and Rakow (1981), and Stinard and Dolphin (1981) for different instructional approaches; by Cosgrove (1986) for the effects of programmatic interventions; by Bean (1985), Pascarella and Terenzini (1979a), and Terenzini, Pascarella, Theophilides, and Lorang (1985) in research on student persistence and withdrawal behavior in college; and by Chapman and Pascarella (1983) on students' levels of social and academic integration in college.

The computational procedure for estimating conditional effects involves the addition of a cross-product term to a general effects equation. Thus, if one is interested in the interaction of IO_1 and IWF, the required regression would be the following:

$$IO_2 = IO_1 + SIZE + IWF + (IO_1 \times IWF) + \text{error}$$

Because the cross-product of $IO_1 \times IWF$ is composed of variables already in the equation, its introduction produces a high level of multicolinearity or intercorrelation among the independent variables. Since this can lead to biased and unstable regression coefficients, the estimation of conditional effects is usually conducted via a hierarchical regression approach (Overall & Spiegel, 1969). In this approach, the general effects IO_1, $SIZE$, and IWF (sometimes called main effects) would be entered in the first step. This would be followed by the addition of the cross-product or interaction term in the second step. If the cross-product of $IO_1 \times IWF$ is not associated with a significant increase in R^2, one can then eliminate the cross-product term from the equation and interpret the equation in terms of its general effects results. If, however, the cross-product is associated with a significant increase in R^2, it suggests the presence of a significant conditional effect (that is, the magnitude of the influence of IWF on IO_2 varies with the student's precollege status on IO_1).

This being the case, the results yielded by the general effects equation would be misleading. Rather, one would interpret the nature of the $IO_1 \times IWF$ interaction to determine variations in the effects (unstandardized regression coefficient) of *IWF* on IO_2 at different levels of IO_1. Cohen and Cohen (1975) provide a simple computational formula for interpreting the nature of a conditional effect when the two interacting variables are continuous in nature. This formula can also be applied when one variable is categorical (for example, treatment versus control) and one is a continuous covariate (for example, aptitude). In the latter case an additional analysis can be conducted to determine the range of the continuous variable (aptitude) for which significant differences in the dependent variable exist between treatment and control groups (Johnson & Fay, 1950; Serlin & Levin, 1980).

A final point needs to be made about the estimation of conditional effects. The presence of replicable aptitude × treatment interaction effects has not been particularly common in experimental instructional research. Thus, in correlational data where one needs to rely on less effective statistical controls, the presence of conditional effects can often be artifacts idiosyncratic to the particular sample being analyzed. Considerable caution is therefore recommended in substantively interpreting conditional effects in correlational data. The most trustworthy are those suggested by theory and replicable across independent samples.

Final Note

At about the time this volume went into production, two potentially important books on the methodology of research and assessment in higher education were published. The first, by Light, Singer, and Willett (1990), uses case studies of actual investigations in postsecondary settings to introduce and explicate in greater detail many of the issues in research methodology touched upon in this appendix. The second, by Astin (1990), is a detailed treatment of many of the important conceptual, methodological, and analytical issues involved in assessing the impact of college and the impact of different experiences in college. Of particular relevance to the present discussion is Astin's own technical appendix on the statistical analysis of longitudinal data. Therein, he deals with many of the statistical and analytical issues we have just discussed, though from a somewhat different perspective. He also demonstrates how elements of regression analysis and causal modeling are combined to assess college effects within his input-environment-output model. Both books provide important conceptual, methodological, and analytical tools for scholars interested in the impact of college on students.

Davis, H. (1977). A comparison of academic achievement of black PE majors at predominantly black and predominantly white institutions. *Journal of Physical Education and Recreation, 48,* 24–25.

Davis, J. (1965). *Undergraduate career decisions: Correlates of occupational choice.* Chicago: Aldine.

Davis, J. (1966). The campus as frog pond: An application of the theory of relative deprivation to career decisions of college men. *American Journal of Sociology, 72,* 17–31.

Davis, J. (1975). Communism, conformity, cohorts, and categories: American tolerance in 1954 and 1972–73. *American Journal of Sociology, 81,* 491–513.

Davis, J. (1980). Conservative weather in a liberalizing climate: Change in selected NORC General Social Survey items. *Social Forces, 58,* 1129–1156.

Davis, J., & Borders-Patterson, A. (1973). *Black students in predominantly white North Carolina colleges and universities.* (Research Rep. No. 2). New York: College Entrance Examination Board.

Davis, R. (1986). *Social support networks and undergraduate student academic-success related outcomes: A comparison of black students on black and white campuses.* Paper presented at the meeting of the American Educational Research Association, San Francisco.

Daymont, T., & Andrisani, P. (1984). Job preferences, college major, and the gender gap in earnings. *Journal of Human Resources, 19,* 408–428.

Dearman, N., & Plisko, V. (1981). *The condition of education, 1981 edition.* Washington, DC: National Center for Education Statistics.

DeBack, V., & Mentkowski, M. (1986). Does the baccalaureate make a difference? Differentiating nurse performance by education and experience. *Journal of Nursing Education, 25,* 275–285.

DeCoster, D. (1968). Effects of homogeneous housing assignments for high ability students. *Journal of College Student Personnel, 8,* 75–78.

DeCoster, D. (1979). The effects of residence hall room visitation upon academic achievement for college students. *Journal of College Student Personnel, 20,* 520–525.

Deemer, D. (1985). *Research in moral development.* Paper presented at the meeting of the American Educational Research Association, Chicago.

DeFleur, L., Gillman, D., & Marshak, W. (1978). Sex integration of the U.S. Air Force Academy. *Armed Forces and Society, 4,* 607–622.

DeLisi, R., & Staudt, J. (1980). Individual differences in college students' performance on formal operations tasks. *Journal of Applied Developmental Psychology, 16,* 121–131.

Demitroff, J. (1974). Student persistence. *College and University, 49,* 553–565.

Denham, M., & Land, M. (1981). Research brief-effect of teacher verbal fluency and clarity on student achievement. *Technical Teachers Journal of Education, 8,* 227–229.

Dent, P., & Lewis, D. (1976). The relationship between teaching effectiveness and measures of research quality. *Educational Research Quarterly, 1,* 3–16.

Deppe, M. (1989). *The impact of racial diversity and involvement on college students' social concern values.* Paper presented at the meeting of the Association for the Study of Higher Education, Atlanta.

Deppe, M. (1990). The impact of racial diversity and involvement on college students' social concern values (Doctoral dissertation, Claremont Graduate School, 1989). *Dissertation Abstracts International, 50,* 2397A.

Dettloff, J. (1982). *Predicting achievement in community college science students.* Unpublished doctoral dissertation, University of Michigan, Ann Arbor.

de Vries, B., & Walker, L. (1986). Moral reasoning and attitudes toward capital punishment. *Developmental Psychology, 22,* 509–513.

de Wolf, V. (1976). *Factors related to postgraduate educational aspirations of women college graduates.* Paper presented at the meeting of the American Psychological Association, Washington, DC.

Dey, E. (1989). *College impact and student liberalism revisited: The effect of student peers.* Unpublished manuscript, University of California, Graduate School of Education, Higher Education Research Institute, Los Angeles.

Diamond, M., & Shapiro, J. (1973). Changes in locus of control as a function of encounter group experiences. *Journal of Abnormal Psychology, 82,* 514–518.

Dickstein, E. (1977). Self and self-esteem: Theoretical foundations and their implications for research. *Human Development, 20,* 129–140.

Diener, E. (1984). Subjective well-being. *Psychological Bulletin, 95,* 542–575.

Digest of educational statistics 1985–1986. (1986). Washington, DC: U.S. Department of Education.

Dignan, M., & Adams, D. (1979). Locus of control and human sexuality education. *Perceptual and Motor Skills, 49,* 778.

DiMaggio, P., & Mohr, J. (1985). Cultural capital, educational attainment, and marital selection. *American Journal of Sociology, 90,* 1231–1261.

DiNuzzo, T., & Tolbert, E. (1981). Promoting the personal growth and vocational maturity of the re-entry woman: A group approach. *Journal of the National Association of Women Deans, Administrators, and Counselors, 45,* 26–31.

Dispoto, R. (1974). *Socio-moral reasoning and environmental activity, emotionality and knowledge.* Unpublished doctoral dissertation, Rutgers University, New Brunswick, NJ.

Dispoto, R. (1977). Moral valuing and environmental variables. *Journal of Research in Science Teaching, 14,* 273–280.

Disque, C. (1983). The relationship of student characteristics and academic integration to college freshman attrition. *Dissertation Abstracts International, 43,* 3820A–3821A.

Doherty, W., & Corsini, D. (1976). Creativity, intelligence, and moral development in college women. *Journal of Creative Behavior, 10,* 276–284.

Domhoff, G. (1967). *Who rules America?* Englewood Cliffs, NJ: Prentice-Hall.

Domino, G. (1968). Differential prediction of academic achievement in conforming and independent settings. *Journal of Educational Psychology, 59,* 256–260.

Domino, G. (1971). Interactive effects of achievement orientation and teaching style on academic achievement. *Journal of Educational Psychology, 62,* 427–431.

Donald, J., & Bateman, D. (1989). *Developing students' ability to think critically.* Paper presented at the meeting of the American Educational Research Association, San Francisco.

Donovan, J. (1970). A study of ego identity formation. *Dissertation Abstracts International, 31,* 4986B.

Donovan, R. (1984). Path analysis of a theoretical model of persistence in higher education among low-income black youth. *Research in Higher Education, 21,* 243–252.

Donovan, R., Schaier-Peleg, B., & Forer, B. (1987). *Transfer: Making it work.* Washington, DC: American Association of Community and Junior Colleges.

Dortzbach, J. (1975). *Moral judgment and perceived locus of control: A cross-sectional developmental study of adults, aged 25–74.* Unpublished doctoral dissertation, University of Oregon, Eugene.

Dougherty, K. (1987). The effects of community colleges: Aid or hinderance to socioeconomic attainment? *Sociology of Education, 60,* 86–103.

Douvan, E., & Adelson, J. (1966). *The adolescent experience.* New York: John Wiley & Sons.

Doyle, K. (1975). *Student evaluation of instruction.* Lexington, MA: D. C. Heath.

Draper, N., & Smith, H. (1966). *Applied regression analysis.* New York: John Wiley & Sons.

Dreher, G., Dougherty, T., & Whiteley, B. (1985). Generalizability of MBA degree and socioeconomic effects on business school graduates' salaries. *Journal of Applied Psychology, 70,* 769–773.

Dressel, P., & DeLisle, F. (1969). *Undergraduate curriculum trends.* Washington, DC: American Council on Education.

Dressel, P., & Mayhew, L. (1954). *General education: Explorations in evaluation.* Westport, CT: Greenwood Press.

Drew, D., & Astin, A. (1972). Undergraduate aspirations: A test of several theories. *American Journal of Sociology, 77,* 1151–1164.

Dreyer, N., Woods, N., & James, S. (1981). ISRO: A scale to measure sex-role orientation. *Sex Roles, 7,* 173–182.

Drum, D. (1980). Understanding student development. In W. Morrill & J. Hurst (Eds.), *Dimensions of intervention for student development.* New York: John Wiley & Sons.

Dubin, R., & Taveggia, T. (1968). *The teaching-learning paradox.* Eugene: University of Oregon, Center for the Advanced Study of Educational Administration.

Dubois, N., Kiewra, K., & Fraley, J. (1988). *Differential effects of a learning strategy course with a cognitive orientation.* Paper presented at the meeting of the American Educational Research Association, New Orleans.

DuBois, P. (1978). Participation in sports and occupational attainment: A comparative study. *Research Quarterly, 49,* 28–37.

Duby, P. (1981). *Attributions and attributional change: Effects of a mastery learning instructional approach.* Paper presented at the meeting of the American Educational Research Association, Los Angeles.

Dukes, F., & Gaither, G. (1984). A campus cluster program: Effects on persistence and academic performance. *College and University, 59,* 150–166.

Dumont, R., & Troelstrup, R. (1980). Exploring relationships between objective and subjective measures of instructional outcomes. *Research in Higher Education, 12,* 37–51.

Dumont, R., & Troelstrup, R. (1981). Measures and predictors of educational growth with four years of college. *Research in Higher Education, 14,* 31–47.

Duncan, B. (1976). Minority students. In J. Katz & R. Hartnett (Eds.), *Scholars in the making: The development of graduate and professional students.* Cambridge, MA: Ballinger.

Duncan, C., & Stoner, K. (1977). The academic achievement of residents living in a scholar residence hall. *Journal of College and University Student Housing, 6,* 7–9.

Duncan, O. (1961). A socioeconomic index for all occupations. In A. Reiss (Ed.), *Occupations and social status.* New York: Free Press.

Duncan, O. (1966). Path analysis: Sociological examples. *American Journal of Sociology, 72,* 1–16.

Duncan, O. (1968). Ability and achievement. *Eugenics Quarterly, 15,* 1–11.

Duncan, O. (1975). *Introduction to structural equation models.* Orlando, FL: Academic Press.

Duncan, O., Featherman, D., & Duncan, B. (1972). *Socioeconomic background and achievement.* New York: Seminar Press.

Dunivant, N. (1975). *Moral judgment, psychological development, situational characteristics and moral behavior: A mediational interactionist model.* Unpublished doctoral dissertation, University of Texas, Austin.

Dunkin, M., & Barnes, J. (1985). Research on teaching in higher education. In M. Wittrock (Ed.), *Handbook of research on teaching* (3rd ed.). New York: Macmillan.

Dunlop, D., & Fazio, F. (1976). Piagetian theory and abstract preferences of college science students. *Journal of College Science Teaching, 5,* 297–300.

Dunphy, L., Miller, T., Woodruff, T., & Nelson, J. (1987). Exemplary retention strategies for the freshman year. In M. Stodt & W. Klepper (Eds.), *Increasing retention: Academic and student affairs administrators in partnership.* (New Directions in Higher Education No. 60). San Francisco: Jossey-Bass.

Easterlin, R. (1968). *Population, labor force and long swings in economic growth: The American experience.* New York: National Bureau of Economic Research.

Easterlin, R. (1975). Relative economic status and the American fertility swing. In E. Sheldon (Ed.), *Family economic behavior.* Philadelphia: Lippincott.

Eckland, B., & Henderson, L. (1981). *College attainment four years after high school.* National Longitudinal Study Sponsored Reports Series. Washington, DC: National Center for Education Statistics.

Eddins, D. (1982). *A causal model of the attrition of specially admitted black students in higher education.* Paper presented at the meeting of the American Educational Research Association, New York.

Eddy, E. (1959). *The college influence on student character.* Washington, DC: American Council on Education.

Edmonds, G. (1984). Needs assessment strategy for black students: An examination of stressors and program implications. *Journal of Non-White Concerns, 12,* 48–56.

Edmonson, J., & Mulder, F. (1924). Size of class as a factor in university instruction. *Journal of Educational Research, 9,* 1–12.

Education has little impact on minority unemployment, study finds. (1982, November 29). *Higher Education Daily,* p. 2.

Educational Testing Service. (1954). *Institutional testing program: Summary statistics 1953–1954* (ETS Archives Microfiche No. 40). Princeton, NJ: Author.

Educational Testing Service. (1976). *Undergraduate assessment program guide.* Princeton, NJ: Author.

Educational Testing Service. (1978). *Undergraduate assessment program guide.* Princeton, NJ: Author.

Edwards, H. (1970). *Black students.* New York: Free Press.

Edwards, K., & Tuckman, B. (1972). Effect of differential college experiences in developing the students' self- and occupational concepts. *Journal of Educational Psychology, 63,* 563–571.

Edwards, L., & Grossman, L. (1979). The relationship between children's health and intellectual development. In S. Mushkin (Ed.), *Health: What is it worth?* Elmsford, NY: Pergamon Press.

Ehrenberg, R., & Sherman, D. (1987). Employment while in college, academic achievement, and postcollege outcomes: A summary of results. *Journal of Human Resources, 22,* 1–23.

Eiferman, D. (1982). *Moral judgment in adult urban college students.* Paper presented at the East Coast Forum on Urban Higher Education Research, New York.

Eisert, D., & Tomlinson-Keasey, C. (1978). Cognitive and interpersonal growth during the college freshman year: A structural analysis. *Perceptual and Motor Skills, 46,* 995–1005.

Eitzen, D., & Brouillette, J. (1979). The politicization of college students. *Adolescence, 14,* 123–134.

Elam, S. (1983). The Gallup education surveys: Impressions of a poll watcher. *Phi Delta Kappan, 64,* 14–22.

Elashoff, J. (1969). Analysis of covariance: A delicate instrument. *American Educational Research Journal, 6,* 383–401.

Elfner, E., McLaughlin, R., Williamsen, J., & Hardy, R. (1985). *Assessing goal related student outcomes.* Paper presented at the annual meeting of the Association for Institutional Research, Portland, OR.

El-Khawas, E. (1980). Differences in academic development during college. In *Men and women learning together: A study of college students in the late 70s.* Report of the Brown Project. Providence, RI: Brown University.

Ellis, V. (1968). Students who seek psychiatric help. In J. Katz & Associates, *No time for youth: Growth and constraint in college students.* San Francisco: Jossey-Bass.

Ellison, A., & Simon, B. (1973). Does college make a person healthy and wise? In L. Solmon & P. Taubman (Eds.), *Does college matter?* New York: Academic Press.

Elton, C. (1969). Patterns of change in personality test scores. *Journal of Counseling Psychology, 16,* 95–99.

Elton, C. (1971). Interaction of environment and personality: A test of Holland's theory. *Journal of Applied Psychology, 55,* 114–118.

Elton, C., & Bate, W. (1966). The effect of housing policy on grade-point average. *Journal of College Student Personnel, 7,* 73–77.

Elton, C., & Rose, H. (1969). Differential change in male personality test scores. *Journal of College Student Personnel, 10,* 373–377.

Elton, C., & Rose, H. (1981). *Retention revisited: With congruence, differentiation, and consistency.* Unpublished manuscript, University of Kentucky, Lexington.

Endo, J., & Bittner, T. (1985). *Using an integrated marketing and attrition model from a student information system to examine attrition after one year.* Unpublished manuscript, Office of Academic Planning and Budget, University of Colorado, Boulder.

Endo, J., & Harpel, R. (1979). *A longitudinal study of attrition.* Boulder: University of Colorado. (ERIC Document Reproduction Service No. ED 174 095)

Endo, J., & Harpel, R. (1980). *A longitudinal study of student outcomes at a state university.* Paper presented at the meeting of the Association for Institutional Research, Atlanta.

Endo, J., & Harpel, R. (1982). The effect of student-faculty interaction on students' educational outcomes. *Research in Higher Education, 16,* 115–138.

Endo, J., & Harpel, R. (1983). *Student-faculty interaction and its effect on freshman year outcomes at a major state university.* Paper presented at the meeting of the Association for Institutional Research, Toronto.

Eniaiyeju, P. (1983). The comparative effects of teacher-demonstration and self-paced instruction on concept acquisition and problem-solving skills of college level chemistry students. *Journal of Research in Science Teaching, 20,* 795–801.

Enos, P. (1981). Student satisfaction with faculty academic advising and persistence beyond the freshman year in college. *Dissertation Abstracts International, 42,* 1985A.

Enwieme, X. (1976). The incidence of formal operations of students in eight subject areas of the Nustep program at the University of Nebraska, Lincoln Campus. *Dissertation Abstracts International, 37,* 2761A.

Enyeart, M. (1981). Relationships among propositional logic, analogical reasoning and Piagetian level. *Dissertation Abstracts International, 41,* 3974A.

Epps, E. (1972). *Black students in white schools.* Worthington, OH: Jones.

Erbring, L., & Young, A. (1980). Individuals and social structure: Contextual effects as endogenous feedback. In E. Borgatta & D. Jackson (Eds.), *Aggregate data analysis and interpretation.* Beverly Hills, CA: Sage.

Erikson, E. (1956). The problem of ego identity. *Journal of the American Psychoanalytic Association, 4,* 56–121.

Erikson, E. (1959). Identity and the life cycle. *Psychological Issues Monograph, 1*(1), 1–171. New York: International Universities Press.

Erikson, E. (1963). *Childhood and society* (2nd ed.). New York: W. W. Norton.

Erikson, E. (1968). *Identity: Youth and crisis.* New York: W. W. Norton.

Erikson, R., Luttbeg, N., & Tedin, K. (1973). *American public opinion: Its origins, content, and impact* (2nd ed.). New York: W. W. Norton.

Erkut, S., & Mokros, J. (1984). Professors as models and mentors for college students. *American Educational Research Journal, 21,* 399–417.

Ernsberger, D. (1976). *Intrinsic-extrinsic religious identification and level of moral development.* Unpublished doctoral dissertation, University of Texas, Austin.

Erwin, T. (1982). Academic status as related to the development of identity. *Journal of Psychology, 110,* 163–169.

Erwin, T. (1983). The influences of roommate assignments upon students' maturity. *Research in Higher Education, 19,* 451–459.

Erwin, T., & Delworth, U. (1980). An instrument to measure Chickering's vector of identity. *NASPA Journal, 17,* 19–24.

Erwin, T., & Delworth, U. (1982). Formulating environmental constructs that affect students' identity. *NASPA Journal, 20,* 47–55.

Erwin, T., & Kelly, K. (1985). Changes in students' self-confidence in college. *Journal of College Student Personnel, 26,* 395–400.

Esposito, D., Hackett, G., & O'Halloran, S. (1987). *The relationship of role model influences to the career salience and educational and career plans of college women.* Paper presented at the meeting of the American Educational Research Association, Washington, DC.

Etaugh, C. (1975a). Biographical predictors of college students' attitudes toward women. *Journal of College Student Personnel, 16,* 273–276.

Etaugh, C. (1975b). Stability of college students' attitudes toward women during one school year. *Psychological Reports, 36,* 125–126.

Etaugh, C. (1986, August). *Biographical and personality correlates of attitudes toward women: A review.* Paper presented to the meeting of the American Psychological Association, Washington, DC.

Etaugh, C., & Bowen, L. (1976). Attitudes toward women: Comparison of enrolled and nonenrolled college students. *Psychological Reports, 38,* 229–230.

Etaugh, C., & Gerson, A. (1974). Attitudes toward women: Some biographical correlates. *Psychological Reports, 35,* 701–702.

Etaugh, C., & Spandikow, D. (1981). Changing attitudes toward women: A longitudinal study of college students. *Psychology of Women Quarterly, 5,* 591–594.

Etaugh, C., & Spiller, B. (1989). Attitudes toward women: Comparison of traditional-aged and older college students. *Journal of College Student Development, 30,* 41–46.

Ethington, C., & Smart, J. (1986). Persistence to graduate education. *Research in Higher Education, 24,* 287–303.

Ethington, C., Smart, J., & Pasacrella, E. (1987). Entry into the teaching profession: Test of a causal model. *Journal of Educational Research, 80,* 156–163.

Ethington, C., Smart, J., & Pascarella, E. (1988). Influences on women's entry into male-dominated occupations. *Higher Education, 17,* 545–562.

Ethington, C., & Wolfle, L. (1986). Sex differences in quantitative and analytical GRE performance: An exploratory study. *Research in Higher Education, 25,* 55–67.

Evans, D., Jones, P., Wortman, R., & Jackson, E. (1975). Traditional criteria as predictors of minority student success in medical school. *Journal of Medical Education, 50,* 934–939.

Evans, J., & Rector, A. (1978). Evaluation of a college course in career decision making. *Journal of College Student Personnel, 19,* 163–168.

Everett, C. (1979). *An analysis of student attrition at Penn State.* University Park: Pennsylvania State University, Office of Planning and Budget.

Ewell, P. (1984). *The self-regarding institution: Information for excellence.* Boulder, CO: National Center for Higher Education Management Systems.

Ewell, P. (Ed.). (1985a). *Assessing educational outcomes* (New Directions for Institutional Research No. 47). San Francisco: Jossey-Bass.

Ewell, P. (1985b). The value-added debate . . . continued. *American Association for Higher Education Bulletin, 38,* 12–13.

Ewell, P. (1988). Outcomes, assessment, and academic improvement: In search of usable knowledge. In J. Smart (Ed.), *Higher education: Handbook of theory and research* (Vol. 4). New York: Agathon.

Ewell, P. (1989). Institutional characteristics and faculty/administrator perceptions of outcomes: An exploratory analysis. *Research in Higher Education, 30,* 113–136.

Eysenck, H. (1978). An exercise in mega-silliness. *American Psychologist, 33,* 517.

Fannin, P. (1977). Ego identity status and sex role attitude, work role salience, atypicality of college major, and self-esteem in college women. *Dissertation Abstracts International, 38,* 7203A–7204A.

Farley, L., & Newkirk, M. (1977). Measuring attitudinal change in political science courses. *Teaching Political Science, 4,* 185–198.

Farr, W., Jones, J., & Samprone, J. (1986). *The consequences of a college preparatory and individual self-evaluation program on student achievement and retention.* Unpublished manuscript, Georgia College, Milledgeville.

Farrell, P., & Fuchs, V. (1982). Schooling and health: The cigarette connection. *Journal of Health Economics, 1,* 217–230.

Faughn, S. (1982). *Significant others: A new look at attrition.* Paper presented at the meeting of the American College Personnel Association, Detroit.

Faust, D., & Arbuthnot, J. (1978). Relationship between moral and Piagetian reasoning and the effectiveness of moral education. *Developmental Psychology, 14,* 435–436.

Feather, N. (1973). Value change among university students. *Australian Journal of Psychology, 25,* 57–70.

Feather, N. (1975). *Values in education and society.* New York: Free Press.

Feather, N. (1980). Values in adolescence. In J. Adelson (Ed.), *Handbook of Adolescent Psychology.* New York: John Wiley & Sons.

Featherman, D., & Carter, T. (1976). Discontinuities in schooling and the socioeconomic life cycle. In W. Sewell, R. Hauser, & D. Featherman (Eds.), *Schooling and achievement in American society.* Orlando, FL: Academic Press.

Featherman, D., & Hauser, R. (1976). Sexual inequalities and socioeconomic achievement in the U.S., 1962–1973. *American Sociological Review, 41,* 462–483.

Featherman, D., & Hauser, R. (1978). *Opportunity and change.* Orlando, FL: Academic Press.

Feldman, K. (1969). Studying the impacts of college on students. *Sociology of Education, 42,* 207–237.

Feldman, K. (1971a). Measuring college environments: Some uses of path analysis. *American Educational Research Journal, 8,* 51–70.

Feldman, K. (1971b). Some methods for assessing college impacts. *Sociology of Education, 44,* 133–150.

Feldman, K. (1972). Some theoretical approaches to the study of change and stability of college students. *Review of Educational Research, 42,* 1–26.

Feldman, K. (1976). The superior college teacher from the students' view. *Research in Higher Education, 5,* 243–288.

Feldman, K. (1984). Class size and college students' evaluations of teachers and courses: A closer look. *Research in Higher Education, 21,* 45–116.

Feldman, K. (1987). Research productivity and scholarly accomplishment

LaCounte, D. (1987). American Indian students in college. In D. Wright (Ed.), *Responding to the needs of today's minority students* (New Directions for Student Services No. 38). San Francisco: Jossey-Bass.

Lacy, W. (1978). Interpersonal relationships as mediators of structural effects: College student socialization in a traditional and an experimental university environment. *Sociology of Education, 51*, 201–211.

Ladd, E., & Lipset, S. (1975). *The dividend academy: Professors and politics.* New York: McGraw-Hill.

Lamare, J. (1975). Using political science courses to inculcate political orientations. *Teaching Political Science, 2*, 409–432.

Lambert, M., Segger, J., Staley, J., Spencer, B., & Nelson, D. (1978). Reported self-concept and self-actualizing value changes as a function of academic classes with wilderness experiences. *Perceptual and Motor Skills, 46*, 1035–1040.

Lamont, L. (1979). *Campus shock: A firsthand report on college life today.* New York: E. P. Dutton.

Land, M. (1979). Low-inference variables of teacher clarity: Effects on student concept learning. *Journal of Educational Psychology, 71*, 795–799.

Land, M. (1980). Teacher clarity and cognitive level of questions: Effects on learning. *Journal of Experimental Education, 49*, 48–51.

Land, M. (1981a). Actual and perceived teacher clarity: Relations to student achievement in science. *Journal of Research in Science Teaching, 18*, 139–143.

Land, M. (1981b). Combined effect of two teacher clarity variables on student achievement. *Journal of Experimental Education, 50*, 14–17.

Land, M., & Smith, L. (1979a). Effects of a teacher clarity variable on student achievement. *Journal of Educational Research, 72*, 196–197.

Land, M., & Smith, L. (1979b). The effect of low inference teacher clarity inhibitors on student achievement. *Journal of Teacher Education, 30*, 55–57.

Land, M., & Smith, L. (1981). College student ratings and student behavior: An experimental study. *Journal of Social Studies Research, 5*, 19–22.

Lando, M. (1975). The interaction between health and education. *Social Security Bulletin, 38*, 16–22.

Lane, R. (1968). Political education in the midst of life's struggles. *Harvard Educational Review, 38*, 468–494.

Lang, D. (1984). Education, stratification, and the academic hierarchy. *Research in Higher Education, 21*, 329–352.

Lang, D. (1987). Stratification and prestige hierarchies in graduate and professional education. *Sociological Inquiry, 57*, 12–31.

Lannholm, G. (1952). Educational growth during the second two years of college. *Educational and Psychological Measurement, 12*, 645–653.

Lannholm, G., & Pitcher, B. (1959). *Mean score changes on the Graduate Re-*

cord Examination Area Tests for college students tested three times in a four-year period. Unpublished manuscript, Educational Testing Service, Princeton, NJ.

Lansing, J., & Mueller, E. (1967). *The geographic mobility of labor.* Ann Arbor: University of Michigan, Institute for Social Research.

Lara, J. (1981). *Differences in quality of academic effort between successful and unsuccessful community college transfer students.* Los Angeles: University of California.

Laufer, R., & Bengston, V. (1974). Generations, aging, and social stratification: On the development of generational units. *Journal of Social Issues, 30,* 181–205.

Laughlin, J. (1976). A sacred cow—class size. *College and University, 51,* 339–347.

Laumann, F., & Rapoport, R. (1968). The institutional effect on career achievement of technologists: A multiple classification analysis. *Human Relations, 28,* 227–239.

LaVoie, J. (1976). Ego identity formation in middle adolescence. *Journal of Youth and Adolescence, 5,* 371–385.

Lawrence, G. (1982). *People types and tiger stripes* (2nd ed.). Gainesville, FL: Center for Applications of Psychological Type.

Lawrence, G. (1984). A synthesis of learning style research involving the MBTI. *Journal of Psychological Type, 8,* 2–15.

Lawrenz, F. (1985). Aptitude-treatment effects of laboratory grouping methods for students of differing reasoning ability. *Journal of Research in Science Teaching, 22,* 279–287.

Lawson, A. (1985). A review of research on formal reasoning and science teaching. *Journal of Research in Science Teaching, 22,* 569–617.

Lawson, A., Nordland, F., & DeVito, A. (1974). Piagetian formal operational tasks: A crossover study of learning effect and reliability. *Science Education, 58,* 267–276.

Lawson, A., & Snitgen, D. (1982). Teaching formal reasoning in a college biology course for preservice teachers. *Journal of Research in Science Teaching, 19,* 233–248.

Lawson, J. (1980). *The relationship between graduate education and the development of reflective judgment: A function of age or educational experience?* Unpublished doctoral dissertation, University of Minnesota, Minneapolis and St. Paul.

Layard, R., & Psacharopoulos, G. (1974). The screening hypothesis and the returns to education. *Journal of Political Economy, 82,* 983–998.

Lazarsfeld, P., & Menzel, H. (1961). On the relation between individual and collective properties. In A. Etzioni (Ed.), *Complex organizations: A sociological reader.* New York: Holt, Rinehart & Winston.

Lazear, E. (1977). Education: Consumption or production? *Journal of Political Economy, 85,* 569–598.

Learned, W., & Wood, B. (1938). *The student and his knowledge: A report to the Carnegie Foundation on the results of the high school and college examinations of 1928, 1930, and 1932* (Bulletin No. 29). New York: The Carnegie Foundation for the Advancement of Teaching.

Learner, R. (1986). *Concepts and theories of human development* (2nd ed.). New York: Random House.

LeBold, W., Thoma, E., Gillis, J., & Hawkins, G. (1960). *A study of the Purdue University engineering graduate* (Engineering Extension Series Bulletin No. 99). West Lafayette, IN: Purdue University.

Lee, L. (1982). Health and wage: A simultaneous equation model with multiple discrete indicators. *International Economic Review, 23,* 199–122.

Leemon, T. (1972). *The rites of passage in a student culture: A study of the dynamics of transition.* New York: Teachers College Press.

Lefcourt, H. (1982). *Locus of control: Current trends in theory and research* (2nd ed.). Hillsdale, NJ: Lawrence Erlbaum.

Lehmann, I. (1963). Changes in critical thinking, attitudes, and values from freshman to senior years. *Journal of Educational Psychology, 54,* 305–315.

Lehmann, I. (1968). Changes from freshman to senior years. In K. Yamamoto (Ed.), *The college student and his culture.* Boston: Houghton Mifflin.

Lehmann, I., & Dressel, P. (1962). *Critical thinking, attitudes, and values in higher education.* East Lansing: Michigan State University.

Lehmann, I., & Dressel, P. (1963). *Changes in critical thinking, ability, attitudes, and values associated with college attendance.* East Lansing: Michigan State University.

Lei, T. (1981). *The development of moral, political, and legal reasoning in Chinese societies.* Unpublished master's thesis, University of Minnesota, Minneapolis and St. Paul.

Lei, T., & Cheng, S. (1984). *An empirical study of Kohlberg's theory and scoring system of moral judgment in Chinese society.* Unpublished manuscript, Harvard University, Center for Moral Education, Cambridge, MA.

Leib, J., & Snyder, W. (1967). Effects of group discussions on underachievement and self-actualization. *Journal of Counseling Psychology, 14,* 282–285.

Leibowitz, A. (1974a). Education and home production. *American Economic Review, 64,* 243–250.

Leibowitz, A. (1974b). Home investments in children. *Journal of Political Economy, 82,* S111–S131.

Leibowitz, A. (1975). Education and the allocation of women's time. In F. Juster (Ed.), *Education, income, and human behavior.* New York: McGraw-Hill.

Leibowitz, A. (1977a). Family background and economic success: A review of the evidence. In P. Taubman (Ed.), *Kinometrics: Determinants of socioeconomic success within and between families.* Amsterdam: North Holland.

Leibowitz, A. (1977b). Parental inputs and children's achievement. *Journal of Human Resources, 12,* 242–251.

Leigh, J. (1981). Hazardous occupations, illness, and schooling. *Economics of Education Review, 1,* 381–388.

Leming, J. (1978). Cheating behavior, situational influence and moral development. *Journal of Educational Research, 71,* 214–217.

Leming, J. (1979). *The relationship between principled moral reasoning and cheating behavior under threat and non-threat situations.* Paper presented at the meeting of the American Educational Research Association, San Francisco.

Lemkau, J. (1983). Women in male-dominated professions: Distinguishing personality and background characteristics. *Psychology of Women Quarterly, 8,* 144–165.

Lenihan, G., & Rawlins, M. (1987). The impact of a women's studies program: Challenging and nourishing the true believers. *Journal of the National Association of Women, Deans, Administrators, and Counselors, 50,* 3–10.

Lenning, O., Beal, P., & Sauer, K. (1980). *Retention and attrition: Evidence for action and research.* Boulder, CO: National Center for Higher Education Management Systems.

Lenning, O., & Hanson, G. (1977). Adult students at two-year colleges: A longitudinal study. *Community/Junior College Research Quarterly, 1,* 271–287.

Lenning, O., Lee, Y., Micek, S., & Service, A. (1977). *A structure for the outcomes of postsecondary education.* Boulder, CO: National Center for Higher Education Management Systems.

Lenning, O., Munday, L., Johnson, O., Vander Well, A., & Brue, E. (1974a). *Nonintellective correlates of grades, persistence and academic learning in college: The published literature through the decade of the sixties* (Monograph No. 14). Iowa City, IA: American College Testing Program.

Lenning, O., Munday, L., Johnson, O., Vander Well, A., & Brue, E. (1974b). *The many faces of college success and their nonintellectual correlates* (Monograph No. 15). Iowa City, IA: American College Testing Program.

Lenning, O., Munday, L., & Maxey, J. (1969). Student educational growth during the first two years of college. *College and University, 44,* 145–153.

Lent, R., Larkin, K., & Hasegawa, C. (1986). Effects of a "focused interest" career course approach for college students. *Vocational Guidance Quarterly, 34,* 151–159.

Lentz, L. (1980). The college choice of career salient women: Coeducational or women's. *Journal of Educational Equity and Leadership, 1,* 28–35.

Lentz, L. (1982). *College selectivity, not college type, is related to graduate women's career aspirations.* Paper presented at the meeting of the American Educational Research Association, New York.

Lentz, L. (1983). Differences in women's freshman versus senior career salience ratings at women's and coeducational colleges. *Review of Higher Education, 6,* 181–193.

Leon, G. (1974). Personality change in the specially admitted disadvantaged student after one year in college. *Journal of Clinical Psychology, 30,* 522–528.

Leslie, L. (1984). Changing patterns in student financing of higher education. *Journal of Higher Education, 55,* 313–346.

Leslie, L., & Brinkman, P. (1986). Rates of return to higher education. In J. Smart (Ed.), *Higher education: Handbook of theory and research* (Vol. 2). New York: Agathon.

Leslie, L., & Brinkman, P. (1988). *The economic value of higher education.* New York: American Council on Education and Macmillan.

Levin, B., & Clowes, D. (1980). Realization of educational aspirations among blacks and whites in two- and four-year colleges. *Community/Junior College Research Quarterly, 4,* 185–193.

Levin, H. (1977a). A decade of policy developments in improving education and training for low income populations. In R. Haveman (Ed.), *A decade of federal antipoverty programs.* Orlando, FL: Academic Press.

Levin, H. (1977b). A radical critique of educational policy. *Journal of Education Finance, 3,* 9–31.

Levin, M. (1967). Congruence and development changes in authoritarianism in college students. In J. Katz (Ed.), *Growth and constraint in college students.* Stanford, CA: Stanford University, Institute for the Study of Human Problems.

Levine, A. (1975). Forging a feminine identity: Women in four professional schools. *American Journal of Psychoanalysis, 35,* 63–67.

Levine, A. (1978). *Handbook on undergraduate curriculum.* San Francisco: Jossey-Bass.

Levine, A. (1980). *When dreams and heroes died: A portrait of today's college student.* San Francisco: Jossey-Bass.

Levine, A., & Associates (1989). *Shaping higher education's future: Demographic realities and opportunities, 1901–2000.* San Francisco: Jossey-Bass.

Levinson, D. (with Darrow, C. N., Klein, E. B., Levinson, M. H., & McGee, B.). (1978). *The seasons of a man's life.* New York: Knopf.

Levinson, D., Darrow, C., Klein, E., Levinson, M., & McGee, B. (1974). The psychosocial development of men in early adulthood and mid-life transition. In D. Ricks, A. Thomas, & M. Roff (Eds.), *Psychopathology* (Vol. 3). Minneapolis: University of Minnesota Press.

Lewin, K. (1936). *Principles of topological psychology.* New York: McGraw-Hill.

Lewin, K. (1951). *Field theory in social science.* New York: Harper & Row.

Lewis, J. (1970). *A study of the achievements and activities of selected liberal arts graduates.* Unpublished doctoral dissertation, University of Iowa, Iowa City.

Lewis, J., & Nelson, K. (1983a). The achievements of university alumni from five academic areas. *Journal of Instructional Psychology, 10,* 163–167.

Lewis, J., & Nelson, K. (1983b). The relationship between college grades and three factors of adult achievement. *Educational and Psychological Measurement, 43,* 577–580.

Lewis, L. (1967). Two cultures: Some empirical findings. *Educational Record, 48,* 260–267.

Liberman, D., Gaa, J., & Frankiewicz, R. (1983). Ego and moral development in an adult population. *Journal of Genetic Psychology, 142,* 61–65.

Liberman, J. (1979). *The rate of return to schooling: 1958–1976.* Faculty Working Paper. Chicago: University of Illinois, Department of Finance.

Lieberman, M., Yalom, I., & Miles, M. (1973). *Encounter groups: First facts.* New York: Basic Books.

Light, R., & Pillemer, D. (1982). Numbers and narrative: Combining their strengths in research reviews. *Harvard Educational Review, 52,* 1–26.

Light, R., Singer, J., & Willett, J. (1990). *By design: Planning research on higher education.* Cambridge, MA: Harvard University Press.

Lillard, L. (1977). Inequality: Earnings vs. human wealth. *American Economic Review, 67,* 42–53.

Lillard, L., & Willis, R. (1978). Dynamic aspects of earning mobility. *Econometrica, 46,* 985–1012.

Lind, G. (1985). Moral competence and education in democratic society. In G. Zecha & P. Weingartner (Eds.), *Conscience: An interdisciplinary view.* Dordrecht, the Netherlands: Reidel.

Lind, G. (1986). Growth and regression in cognitive-moral development. In C. Harding (Ed.), *Moral dilemmas: Philosophical and psychological issues in the development of moral reasoning.* Chicago: Precedent.

Linden, F. (Ed.) (1967). *Market profiles of consumer products.* New York: National Industrial Conference Board.

Linder, F. (1986). *Locus of control and value orientations of adult learners in postsecondary education.* Paper presented at the meeting of the American Educational Research Association, San Francisco. (ERIC Document Reproduction Service No. ED 272 093)

Lindert, P. (1977). Sibling position and achievement. *Journal of Human Resources, 12,* 198–219.

Lindsay, P. (1984). High school size, participation in activities, and young adult social participation. Some enduring effects of schooling. *Educational Evaluation and Policy Analysis, 6,* 73–83.

Lindsay, P., & Knox, W. (1984). Continuity and change in work values among young adults: A longitudinal study. *American Journal of Sociology, 89,* 918–931.

Link, C., Ratledge, E., & Lewis, K. (1976). Black-white differences in returns to schooling: Some new evidence. *American Economic Review, 66,* 221–223.

Linn, R. (1986). Quantitative methods in research on teaching. In M. Wittrock (Ed.), *Handbook of research on teaching* (2nd ed.). New York: Macmillan.

Linn, R., & Slinde, J. (1977). The determination of the significance of change between pre- and post-testing periods. *Review of Educational Research, 47,* 121–150.

Linn, R., & Werts, C. (1969). Assumptions in making causal inferences from part correlations, partial correlations, and partial regression coefficients. *Psychological Bulletin, 72,* 307–310.

Linn, R., & Werts, C. (1977). Analysis implications of the choice of a structural model in the nonequivalent control group design. *Psychological Bulletin, 84,* 299–324.

Linn, R., Werts, C., & Tucker, L. (1971). The interpretation of regression coefficients in a school effects model. *Educational and Psychological Measurement, 31,* 85–93.

Linsky, A., & Straus, M. (1975). Student evaluations, research productivity, and eminence of college faculty. *Journal of Higher Education, 46,* 89–102.

Lipsky, S., & Ender, S. (1990). Impact of a study skills course on probationary students' academic performance. *Journal of the Freshman Year Experience, 2,* 7–15.

Little, A. (1980). *Is education related to productivity?* (Bulletin 11). Sussex, England: Institute of Developmental Studies.

Little, G. (1970). *The university experience: An Australian study.* Carlton, Victoria: Melbourne University Press.

Livingston, M., & Stewart, M. (1987). Minority students on a white campus: Perception is truth. *NASPA Journal, 24,* 39–49.

Lloyd, B. (1967). Retouched picture: Follow-up of a questionnaire portrait of the freshman coed. *Journal of the National Association of Women Deans and Counselors, 30,* 174–177.

Locke, D., & Zimmerman, N. (1987). Effects of peer-counseling training on psychological maturity of black students. *Journal of College Student Personnel, 28,* 525–532.

Locke, E. (1977). An empirical study of lecture note taking among college students. *Journal of Educational Research, 71,* 93–99.

Loeffler, D., & Feidler, L. (1979). Woman—A sense of identity: A counseling intervention to facilitate personal growth in women. *Journal of Counseling Psychology, 26,* 51–57.

Loesch, L., Shub, P., & Rucker, B. (1979). Vocational maturity among community college students. *Journal of College Student Personnel, 20,* 140–144.

Loevinger, J. (1966). The meaning and measure of ego development. *American Psychologist, 21,* 195–206.

Loevinger, J. (1976). *Ego development: Conceptions and theories.* San Francisco: Jossey-Bass.

Loevinger, J. (1979). Construct validity of the Sentence Completion Test of Ego Development. *Applied Psychological Measures, 3,* 281–311.

Loevinger, J., Cohn, L., Redmore, C., Bonneville, L., Streich, D., & Sargent, M. (1985). Ego development in college. *Journal of Personality and Social Psychology, 48,* 947–962.

Loevinger, J., Wessler, R., & Redmore, (1970a). *Measuring ego development: Vol. 1. Construction and use of a sentence completion test* San Francisco: Jossey-Bass.

Loevinger, J., Wessler, R., & Redmore, C. (1970b). *Measuring ego development: Vol. 2. Scoring manual for women and girls* (Vol. 2). San Francisco: Jossey-Bass.

Logan, G. (1976). Do sociologists teach students to think more critically? *Teaching Sociology, 4,* 29–48.

Lokitz, B., & Sprandel, H. (1976). The first year: A look at the freshman experience. *Journal of College Student Personnel, 17,* 274–279.

Long, J., Allison, P., & McGinnis, R. (1979). Entrance into the academic career. *American Sociological Review, 44,* 816–830.

Longino, C., & Kart, C. (1973). The college fraternity: An assessment of theory and research. *Journal of College Student Personnel, 14,* 118–125.

Look, C., & Rolison, G. (1986). Alienation of ethnic minority students at a predominantly white university. *Journal of Higher Education, 57,* 58–77.

Lord, F. (1967). A paradox in the interpretation of group comparisons. *Psychological Bulletin, 68,* 304–305.

Lord, F. (1969). Statistical adjustments when comparing pre-existing groups. *Psychological Bulletin, 72,* 336–337.

Lorence, J., & Mortimer, J. (1979). Work experience and political orientation: A panel study. *Social Forces, 58,* 651–676.

Lorence, J., & Mortimer, J. (1981). Work experience and work involvement. *Sociology of Work and Occupations, 8,* 297–326.

Louis, K., Colten, M., & Demeke, G. (1984). *Freshman experiences at the University of Massachusetts at Boston.* Boston: University of Massachusetts. (ERIC Document Reproduction Service No. ED 242 251)

Loxley, J., & Whiteley, J. (1986). *Character development in college students* (Vol. 2). Schenectady, NY: Character Research Press.

Lucas, R. (1977). Hedonic wage equations and psychic wages in the returns to schooling. *American Economic Review, 67,* 549–558.

Lupfer, M., Cohn, B., & Brown, L. (1982). *Jury decisions as a function of level of moral reasoning.* Unpublished manuscript, Memphis State University, Memphis, TN.

Lutwak, N. (1984). The interrelationship of ego, moral, and conceptual development in a college group. *Adolescence, 19,* 675–688.

Lyle, E. (1958). An exploration in the teaching of critical thinking in general psychology. *Journal of Educational Research, 52,* 129–133.

Lynch, A. (1987). Type development and student development. In J. Provost & S. Anchors (Eds.), *Applications of the Myer-Briggs Type Indicator in higher education.* Palo Alto, CA: Consulting Psychologists Press.

Lynch, M., Ogg, W., & Christensen, M. (1975). Impact of a life planning workshop on perceived locus of control. *Psychological Reports, 37,* 1219–1222.

Lyons, D., & Green, S. (1988). Sex role development as a function of college experiences. *Sex Roles, 18,* 31–40.

Lyson, T. (1980). Factors associated with the choice of a typical or atypical curriculum among college women. *Sociology and Social Research, 64,* 559–571.

Lyson, T. (1984). Sex differences in the choice of a male or female career line. *Women and Occupations, 11,* 131–146.

Maccoby, E., & Jacklin, C. (1974). *The psychology of sex differences.* Stanford, CA: Stanford University Press.

Mackey, J., Blackmon, C., & Andrews, J. (1977). Does academic achievement make a difference in student teaching? *Phi Delta Kappan, 59,* 272–273.

Macomber, F., & Siegel, L. (1957). A study of large-group teaching procedures. *Educational Record, 38,* 220–229.

Madison, P. (1969). *Personality development in college.* Reading, MA: Addison-Wesley.

Magnarella, P. (1975). The University of Vermont's Living Learning Center: A first year appraisal. *Journal of College Student Personnel, 16,* 300–305.

Maier, N., & Casselman, G. (1971). Problem solving ability as a factor in selection of major in college study: Comparison of the processes of "idea getting" and "making essential distinctions" in males and females. *Psychological Reports, 28,* 503–514.

Malinowski, C. (1978). *Moral judgment and resistance to the temptation to cheat.* Paper presented at the meeting of the American Psychological Association, Toronto.

Malinowski, C., & Smith, C. (1985). Moral reasoning and moral conduct: An investigation prompted by Kohlberg's theory. *Journal of Personality and Social Psychology, 49,* 1016–1027.

Malkemes, L. (1972). *An application of Parson's LIGA scheme: The faculty-student system of interaction.* Unpublished doctoral dissertation, University of Colorado, Boulder.

Malkiel, G., & Malkiel, J. (1973). Male-female pay differentials in professional employment. *American Economic Review, 63,* 693–705.

Mallinckrodt, B. (1988). Student retention, social support, and dropout intention: Comparison of black and white students. *Journal of College Student Development, 29,* 60–64.

Mallinckrodt, B., & Sedlacek, W. (1987). Student retention and use of campus facilities by race. *NASPA Journal, 24,* 28–32.

Mandell, L. (1972). *Credit card use in the United States.* Ann Arbor: University of Michigan, Institute for Social Research.

Manis, J. (1985). *Some correlates of self-esteem, personal control, and occupational*

Pfeffer, J. (1977). Effects of an MBA and socioeconomic origins on business school graduates' salaries. *Journal of Applied Psychology, 62,* 698–705.

Pfeifer, C. (1976). Relationship between scholastic aptitude, perception of university climate and college success for black and white students. *Journal of Applied Psychology, 61,* 341–347.

Pflaum, S., Pascarella, E., & Duby, P. (1985). The effects of honors college participation on academic performance during the freshman year. *Journal of College Student Personnel, 26,* 414–419.

Pfnister, A. (1972). *Impact of study abroad on the American college undergraduate.* Paper presented at the meeting of the National Association for Foreign Student Affairs. (ERIC Document No. ED 063 882)

Phares, E. (1973). *Locus of control: A personality determinant of behavior.* Morristown, NJ: General Learning Press.

Phares, E. (1976). *Locus of control in personality.* Morristown, NJ: General Learning Press.

Phelan, T., & Phelan, J. (1983). Higher education and early life outcomes. *Higher Education, 12,* 665–680.

Phelan, W. (1979). Undergraduate orientations toward scientific and scholarly careers. *American Educational Research Journal, 16,* 411–422.

Phillips, M. (1976). The influence of residential setting on the academic achievement of college students: A review. *Journal of College and University Student Housing, 6,* 33–37.

Piaget, J. (1964). *Judgment and reasoning in the child.* Totowa, NJ: Littlefield, Adams.

Piaget, J. (1972). Intellectual evolution from adolescence to adulthood. *Human Development, 15,* 1–12.

Pierce, J., Fiore, M., Novotny, T., Hatziandreu, E., & Davis, R. (1989). Trends in cigarette smoking in the United States: Educational differences are increasing. *Journal of the American Medical Association, 261,* 56–60.

Pierson, G. (1969). *The education of American leaders: Comparative contributions of U.S. colleges and universities.* New York: Praeger.

Pike, G. (1989). Background, college experiences, and the ACT-COMP exam: Using construct validity to evaluate assessment instruments. *Review of Higher Education, 13,* 91–117.

Pike, G., & Banta, T. (1989). *Using construct validity to evaluate assessment instruments: A comparison of the ACT-COMP exam and the ETS Academic Profile.* Paper presented at the meeting of the American Educational Research Association, San Francisco.

Pike, G., & Phillippi, R. (1988). *Relationships between self-reported coursework and performance on the ACT-COMP exam: An analysis of the generalizability of the differential coursework methodology.* Paper presented at the meeting of the Association for the Study of Higher Education, St. Louis.

Pillemer, D., & Light, R. (1980). Synthesizing outcomes: How to use research evidence from many studies. *Harvard Educational Review, 50,* 176–195.

Pincus, F. (1980). The false promises of community colleges: Class conflict and vocational education. *Harvard Educational Review, 50,* 332–361.

Pincus, F., & Archer, E. (1989). *Bridges to opportunity: Are community colleges meeting the transfer needs of minority students?* New York: Academy for Educational Development and College Entrance Examination Board.

Pineo, P., & Porter, J. (1967). Occupational prestige in Canada. *Canadian Review of Sociology and Anthropology, 4,* 24–40.

Plant, W. (1958a). Changes in ethnocentrism associated with a two-year college experience. *Journal of Genetic Psychology, 92,* 189–197.

Plant, W. (1958b). Changes in ethnocentrism associated with a four-year college education. *Journal of Educational Research, 49,* 162–165.

Plant, W. (1962). *Personality changes associated with a college education* (DHEW, Cooperative Research Branch Project 348 [SAE 7666]). San Jose, CA: San Jose State College.

Plant, W. (1965). Longitudinal changes in intolerance and authoritarianism for subjects differing in amount of college education over four years. *Genetic Psychology Monographs, 72,* 242–287.

Plant, W., & Minium, E. (1967). Differential personality development in young adults of markedly different aptitude levels. *Journal of Educational Psychology, 58,* 141–152.

Plant, W., & Telford, C. (1966). Changes in personality for groups completing different amounts of college over two years. *Genetic Psychology Monographs, 74,* 3–36.

Plummer, O., & Koh, Y. (1987). Effects of "aerobics" on self-concepts of college women. *Perceptual and Motor Skills, 65,* 271–275.

Podd, M. (1972). Ego identity status and morality: The relationship between two developmental constructs. *Developmental Psychology, 6,* 497–507.

Pohlmann, J., & Beggs, D. (1974). A study of validity of self-report measures of academic growth. *Journal of Educational Measurement, 11,* 115–119.

Polachek, S. (1978). Sex differences in college major. *Industrial and Labor Relations Review, 31,* 498–508.

Polite, C., Cochrane, R., & Silverman, B. (1974). Ethnic group identification and differentiation. *Journal of Social Psychology, 92,* 149–150.

Polkosnik, M., & Winston, R. (1989). Relationships between students' intellectual and psychosocial development: An exploratory investigation. *Journal of College Student Development, 30,* 10–19.

Pollio, H. (1984). *What students think about and do in college lecture classes* (Teaching-Learning Issues No. 53). Knoxville, TN: University of Tennessee Learning Research Center.

Polovy, P. (1980). A study of moral development and personality relationships in adolescents and young adult Catholic students. *Journal of Clinical Psychology, 36,* 752–757.

Ponsford, R., Alloway, L., & Mhoon, J. (1986). *Self-esteem and moral judgments in a Christian liberal arts college: Class comparisons.* Paper presented at the meeting of the Western Psychological Association, Seattle.

Porter, J. (1974). Race, socialization, and mobility in educational and early occupational attainment. *American Sociological Review, 39,* 303–316.

Porter, J. (1976). Socialization and mobility in educational and early occupational attainment. *Sociology of Education, 49,* 23–33.

Porter, O. (1989). *The influence of institutional control on the persistence of minority students: A descriptive analysis.* Paper presented at the meeting of the American Educational Research Association, San Francisco.

Posthuma, A., & Navran, L. (1970). Relation of congruence in student-faculty interests to achievement in college. *Journal of Counseling Psychology, 17,* 352–356.

Postlethwaite, S., Novak, J., & Murray, H. (1972). *The audio-tutorial approach to learning.* Minneapolis: Burgess.

Pounds, A. (1987). Black students' needs on predominantly white campuses. In D. Wright (Ed.), *Responding to the needs of today's minority students* (New Directions for Student Services No. 38). San Francisco: Jossey Bass.

Powell, J. (1985). The residues of learning: Autobiographical accounts by graduates of the impact of higher education. *Higher Education, 14,* 127–147.

Powers, J. (1976). *An inquiry into the effects of a college education on the attitudes, competencies and behavior of individuals.* Claremont, CA: Claremont Graduate School.

Prager, K. (1982). Identity development and self-esteem in young women. *Journal of Genetic Psychology, 141,* 177–182.

Prager, K. (1986). Identity development, age, and college experience in women. *Journal of Genetic Psychology, 147,* 31–36.

Prather, J., & Smith, G. (1976). *Faculty grading patterns* (Report No. 76-12). Atlanta: Georgia State University, Office of Institutional Planning.

Prather, J., Smith, G., & Kodras, J. (1979). A longitudinal study of grades in 144 undergraduate courses. *Research in Higher Education, 10,* 11–24.

Prather, J., Williams, J., & Wadley, J. (1976). *The relationship of major field of study with undergraduate course grades: A multivariate analysis controlling for academic and personal characteristics and longitudinal trends* (Report OIP-77-3). Atlanta: Georgia State University, Office of Institutional Research.

Presby, S. (1978). Overly broad categories obscure important differences between therapies. *American Psychologist, 33,* 514–515.

Priest, R., Prince, H., & Vitters, A. (1978). The first coed class at West Point in performance and attitudes. *Youth and Society, 10,* 205–224.

Princeton University (1967). *Twenty-five years out.* Princeton, NJ: Princeton University Alumni Office.

Provost, J., & Anchors, S. (1987). *Applications of the Myers-Briggs Type Indicator in higher education.* Palo Alto, CA: Consulting Psycholgists Press.

Psacharopoulos, G. (1972a). Rates of return around the world. *Comparative Education Review, 16,* 54–67.

Psacharopoulos, G. (1972b). The economic returns to higher education in twenty-five countries. *Higher Education, 1,* 141–158.

Psacharopoulos, G. (1973). *Returns to education.* San Francisco: Jossey-Bass.

Psacharopoulos, G. (1985). Returns to education: A further international update and implications. *Journal of Human Resources, 20,* 583–604.

Pugh, R. (1969). Undergraduate environment as an aid in predicting law school achievement. *Journal of Educational Research, 62,* 271–274.

Pugh, R., and Chamberlain, P. (1976). Undergraduate residence: An assessment of academic achievement in a predominantly university community. *Journal of College Student Personnel, 17,* 138–141.

Pyle, K. (1981). Institution cross-cultural service/learning: Impact on student development. *Journal of College Student Personnel, 22,* 509–514.

Quevedo-Garcia, E. (1987). Facilitating the development of Hispanic college students. In D. Wright (Ed.), *Responding to the needs of today's minority students* (New Directions for Student Services No. 38). San Francisco: Jossey-Bass.

Quinn, R., & Baldi de Mandilovitch, M. (1975). *Education and job satisfaction: A questionable payoff.* Ann Arbor: University of Michigan, Survey Research Center.

Quinn, R., & Baldi de Mandilovitch, M. (1980). Education and job satisfaction, 1962–1977. *Vocational Guidance Quarterly, 29,* 100–111.

Quinn, R., & Staines, G. (1979). *The 1977 quality of employment survey.* Ann Arbor: University of Michigan, Survey Research Center.

Quinn, R., Staines, G., & McCullough, M. (1974). *Job satisfaction: Is there a trend?* Washington, DC: U.S. Department of Labor.

Rabinowitz, M., & Glaser, R. (1985). Cognitive structure and process in highly competent performance. In F. Horowitz & M. O'Brien (Eds.), *The gifted and talented: Developmental perspectives.* Washington, DC: American Psychological Association.

Rago, J. (1973). The influence of undergraduate residence upon student personal development. *College Student Journal Monograph, 7.* 11 pp.

Ramirez, A., & Soriano, F. (1981). Causal attributions of success and failure among Chicano university students. *Hispanic Journal of Behavioral Sciences, 3,* 397–407.

Ramseur, H. (1975). *Continuity and change in black identity: A study of black students at an interracial college.* Unpublished doctoral dissertation, Harvard University, Cambridge, MA.

Ratcliff, J. (1988). *Assessment and curriculum reform: Research issues, models, and methods.* Invited symposium presented at the meeting of the Association for the Study of Higher Education, St. Louis.

Ratcliff, J., & Associates (1988). *Development and testing of a cluster-analytic model for identifying coursework patterns associated with general learned abilities of students* (Progress Report No. 6). Ames: Iowa State University, College of Education.

Raudenbush, S., & Bryk, A. (1988). Methodological advances in analyzing the effects of schools and classrooms on student learning. In E. Rothkopf (Ed.), *Review of research in education* (Vol. 15). Washington, DC: American Educational Research Association.

Rawlins, V., & Ulman, L. (1974). The utilization of college-trained manpower in the United States. In M. Gordon (Ed.), *Higher education and the labor market*. New York: McGraw-Hill.

Rayman, J., Bernard, C., Holland, J., & Barnett, D. (1983). The effects of a career course on undecided college students. *Journal of Vocational Behavior, 23,* 346–355.

Raymond, R., & Sesnowitz, M. (1975). The returns to investments in higher education: Some new evidence. *Journal of Human Resources, 10,* 139–514.

Raymond, R., & Sesnowitz, M. (1983). The rate of return to Mexican Americans and Anglos on an investment in a college education. *Economic Inquiry, 21,* 400–411.

Redmore, C. (1983). Ego development in the college years: Two longitudinal studies. *Journal of Youth and Adolescence, 12,* 301–306.

Redmore, C., & Loevinger, J. (1979). Ego development in adolescence: Longitudinal studies. *Journal of Youth and Adolescence, 8,* 1–20.

Redmore, C., & Waldman, K. (1975). Reliability of a sentence completion measure of ego development. *Journal of Personality Assessment, 39,* 236–243.

Reed, R., & Miller, H. (1970). Some determinants of the variation in earnings for college men. *Journal of Human Resources, 5,* 177–190.

Regan, M. (1969). Student change: The new student and society. *NASPA Journal, 6,* 127–135.

Reid, E. (1974). Effects of co-residential living on the attitudes, self-image, and role expectations of college women. *American Journal of Psychiatry, 131,* 551–554.

Reif, R. (1984). The development of formal reasoning patterns among university science and mathematics students. *Dissertation Abstracts International, 45,* 766A.

Reitz, J. (1975). Undergraduate aspiration and career choice: Effects of college selectivity. *Sociology of Education, 48,* 303–323.

Remer, P., O'Neill, C., & Gohs, D. (1984). Multiple outcome evaluation of a life-career development course. *Journal of Counseling Psychology, 31,* 532–540.

Renner, J., & Lawson, A. (1975). Intellectual development in preservice elementary school teachers: An evaluation. *Journal of College Science Teaching, 5,* 89–92.

Renner, J., Paske, W. (1977). Comparing two forms of instruction in college physics. *American Journal of Physics, 45,* 851–859.

Renshaw, E. (1972). Are we overestimating the return from a college education? *School Review, 80,* 459–475.

Rest, J. (1975). Longitudinal study of the Defining Issues Test: A strategy for analyzing developmental change. *Developmental Psychology, 11,* 738–748.

Rest, J. (1976). *Moral judgment related to sample characteristics* (Tech. Rep. No. 2). Minneapolis: University of Minnesota.

Rest, J. (1979a). *Development in judging moral issues.* Minneapolis: University of Minnesota Press.

Rest, J. (1979b). *Revised manual for the Defining Issues Test.* Minneapolis: Moral Research Projects.

Rest, J. (1979c). *The impact of higher education on moral judgment development* (Tech. Rep. No. 5). Minneapolis: Moral Research Projects.

Rest, J. (1981). *The impact of higher education on moral judgment development.* Paper presented at the meeting of the American Educational Research Association, Los Angeles.

Rest, J. (1983a). Morality. In J. Flavell & E. Markman (Eds.), *Handbook of child psychology: Vol. 3. Cognitive development.* New York: John Wiley & Sons.

Rest, J. (1983b). Morality. In P. Mussen (Ed.), *Carmichael's manual of child psychology.* New York: John Wiley & Sons.

Rest, J. (1985). *Moral development in young adults.* Unpublished manuscript, University of Minnesota, Minneapolis and St. Paul.

Rest, J. (1986a). *Discussion of the Sierra Project.* Presentation at the meeting of the Society for Moral Education, Chicago.

Rest, J. (Ed.). (1986b). *Moral development: Advances in research and theory.* New York: Praeger.

Rest, J. (1986c). Moral development in young adults. In R. Mines & K. Kitchener (Eds.), *Adult cognitive development.* New York: Praeger.

Rest, J., Davison, M., & Robbins, S. (1978). Age trends in judging moral issues: A review of cross-sectional, longitudinal, and sequential studies of the Defining Issues Test. *Child Development, 49,* 263–279.

Rest, J., & Deemer, D. (1986). Life experiences and developmental pathways. In J. Rest, (Ed.). *Moral development: Advances in research and theory.* New York: Praeger.

Rest, J., & Thoma, S. (1985). Relation of moral judgment development to formal education. *Developmental Psychology, 21,* 709–714.

Reutefors, D., Schneider, L., & Overton, T. (1979). Academic achievement: An examination of Holland's congruence, consistency, and differentiation predictions. *Journal of Vocational Behavior, 14,* 181–189.

Riahinejad, A., & Hood, A. (1984). The development of interpersonal relationships in college. *Journal of College Student Personnel, 25,* 498–502.

Riccobono, J., & Dunteman, G. (1979). *National longitudinal study of the high school class of 1972: Preliminary analyses of student financial aid.* Arlington, VA: National Center for Education Statistics. (ERIC Document Reproduction Service No. ED 170 303)

Rice, J., & Hemmings, A. (1988). Women's colleges and women achievers: An update. *Signs: Journal of Women in Culture and Society, 13,* 546–559.

Rice, R. (1983). *USC-Lancaster: A retention study for a two-year commuter campus.* Lancaster: University of South Carolina. (ERIC Document Reproduction Service No. ED 231 440)

Rice, R. (1984). *Does University 101 work? You bet: Research documenting the effectiveness of University 101 upon retention and student study habits and attitudes.* Unpublished manuscript, University of South Carolina, Lancaster.

Rich, H. (1976). The effect of college on political awareness and knowledge. *Youth and Society, 8,* 67–80.

Rich, H. (1977). The liberalizing influence of college: Some new evidence. *Adolescence, 12,* 199–211.

Rich, H. (1980). Tolerance for civil liberties among college students. *Youth and Society, 12,* 17–32.

Rich, H., & Jolicoeur, P. (1978). *Student attitudes and academic environments: A study of California higher education.* New York: Praeger.

Richards, E. (1984a). Early employment situations and work role satisfaction among recent college graduates. *Journal of Vocational Behavior, 24,* 305–318.

Richards, E. (1984b). Undergraduate preparation and early career outcomes: A study of recent college graduates. *Journal of Vocational Behavior, 24,* 279–304.

Richardson, J. (1981). Problem solving instruction for physics. *Dissertation Abstracts International, 42,* 3536A.

Richardson, R., & Bender, L. (1985). *Students in urban settings: Achieving the baccalaureate degree* (ASHE-ERIC Higher Education Report No. 6). Washington, DC: Association for the Study of Higher Education.

Ridgeway, C. (1978). Predicting college women's aspirations from evaluations of the housewife and work role. *Sociological Quarterly, 19,* 281–291.

Riffer, S. (1972). Determinants of university students' political attitudes or demythologizing campus political activism. *Review of Educational Research, 42,* 561–571.

Riley, S. (1982). The applicability of undergraduate education in jobs. *Higher Education, 11,* 155–175.

Robbins, R. (1981). Improving student reasoning skills in science classes. *Engineering Education, 72,* 208–212.

Robbins, S. (1976). Outdoor wilderness survival and sociological effects upon students in changing human behavior. *Dissertation Abstracts International, 37,* 1473–A. (University Microfilms No. 76-18,350)

Robertshaw, D., & Wolfle, L. (1982). The cognitive value of two-year colleges for whites and blacks. *Integrated Education, 19,* 68–71.

Robertshaw, D., & Wolfle, L. (1983). Discontinuities in schooling and educational attainment. *Higher Education, 12,* 1–18.

Robin, A. (1976). Behavioral instruction in the college classroom. *Review of Educational Research, 46,* 313–354.

Rock, D. (1972). *The use of taxonomic procedures to identify both overall college effects and those effects which interact with student ability.* Paper presented at the meeting of the American Educational Research Association, Chicago.

Rock, D., Baird, L., & Linn, R. (1972). Interaction between college effects and students' aptitudes. *American Educational Research Journal, 9,* 149–161.

Rock, D., Centra, J., & Linn, R. (1970). Relationships between college characteristics and student achievement. *American Educational Research Journal, 7,* 109–121.

Rodgers, R. (1980). Theories underlying student development. In D. Creamer (Ed.), *Student development in higher education: Theories, practices, and future directions* (ACPA Media Publication No. 27). Alexandria, VA: American College Personnel Association.

Rodgers, R. (1983). Using theory in practice. In T. Miller, R. Winston, & W. Mendenhall (Eds.), *Administration and leadership in student affairs.* Muncie, IN: Accelerated Development.

Rodgers, R. (1989). Student development. In U. Delworth, G. Hanson, & Associates (Eds.), *Student services: A handbook for the profession* (2nd ed.). San Francisco: Jossey-Bass.

Rodgers, R. (1990a). Using theory in practice in student affairs. In T. Miller, R. Winston, & W. Mendenhall (Eds.), *Administration and leadership in student affairs: Actualizing student development in higher education* (2nd ed.). Muncie, IN: Accelerated Development.

Rodgers, R. (1990b). Recent theories and research underlying student development. In D. Creamer & Associates, *College student development theory and practice for the 1990s* (Media Publication No. 49). Alexandria, VA: American College Personnel Association.

Rodgers, R. (1990c). An integration of campus ecology and student development: The Olentangy project. In D. Creamer & Associates, *College student development theory and practice for the 1990s* (Media Publication No. 49). Alexandria, VA: American College Personnel Association.

Roesler, E. (1971). *Community college and technical institute follow-up study of students enrolled during one or more quarters: Fall 1970 to fall 1971.* Washington, DC: U.S. Department of Health, Education, and Welfare. (ERIC Document Reproduction Service No. ED 072 770)

Rogers, R. (1969). Private rates of return to education in the U.S.: A case study. *Yale Economic Essays, 9,* 89–134.

Rogosa, D. (1978). Politics, process, and pyramids. *Journal of Educational Statistics, 3,* 79–86.

Rokeach, M. (1960). *The open and closed mind: Investigations into the nature of belief systems and personality systems.* New York: Basic Books.

Rokeach, M. (1971). Long-range experimental modification of values, attitudes, and behavior. *American Psychologist, 26,* 453–459.

Romano, R. (1986). What is the payoff to a community college degree? *Community/Junior College Quarterly of Research and Practice, 10,* 153–164.

Romig, J. (1972). An evaluation of instruction by student-led discussion in the college classroom. *Dissertation Abstracts International, 32,* 6816A.

Romine, B., Davis, J., & Gehman, W. (1970). The interaction of learning, personality traits, ability, and environment: A preliminary study. *Educational and Psychological Measurement, 30,* 337–347.

Romo, F., & Rosenbaum, J. (1984). *College old-boy connections and promotions.* Unpublished paper, Yale University, New Haven, CT.

Rootman, I. (1972). Voluntary withdrawal from a total adult socializing organization: A model. *Sociology of Education, 45,* 258–270.

Roper, B., & LaBeff, E. (1977). Sex roles and feminism revisited: An intergenerational attitude comparison. *Journal of Marriage and the Family, 39,* 113–119.

Roper Organization. (1974) *The Virginia Slims American woman's opinion poll* (Vol. 3). New York: Author.

Rosen, S. (1975). Measuring the obsolescence of knowledge. In F. Juster (Ed.), *Education, income, and human behavior.* New York: McGraw-Hill.

Rosen, S., & Taubman, P. (1982). Changes in life cycle earnings: What do social security data show? *Journal of Human Resources, 17,* 321–338.

Rosenbaum, J. (1984). *Career mobility in a corporate hierarchy.* New York: Academic Press.

Rosenberg, F., & Simmons, R. (1975). Sex differences in the self-concept in adolescence. *Sex Roles, 1,* 147–159.

Rosenberg, M. (1979). *Conceiving the self.* New York: Basic Books.

Rosenfeld, R. (1978). Women's intergenerational occupational mobility. *American Sociological Review, 43,* 36–46.

Rosenshine, B. (1982). *Teaching functions in instructional programs.* Washington, DC: National Institute of Education.

Rosensweig, M., & Schultz, T. (1982). The behavior of mothers as inputs to child health. In V. Fuchs (Ed.), *Economic aspects of health.* Chicago: University of Chicago Press.

Rosensweig, M., & Seiver, D. (1980). *Education and contraceptive choice: A conditional demand framework.* Unpublished manuscript, University of Minnesota, Minneapolis and St. Paul.

Ross, S., & Rakow, E. (1981). Learner control versus program control as adaptive strategies for selection of instructional support on math rules. *Journal of Educational Psychology, 73,* 745–753.

Rossmann, J. (1967). An experimental study of faculty advising. *Personnel and Guidance Journal, 46,* 160–164.

Rossmann, J. (1968). Released time for faculty advising: The impact upon freshmen. *Personnel and Guidance Journal, 47,* 356–363.

Rossmann, J. (1976). Teaching, publication, and rewards at a liberal arts college. *Improving College and University Teaching, 24,* 238–240.

Rothman, A., & Preshaw, R. (1975). Is scientific achievement a correlate of effective teaching performance? *Research in Higher Education, 3,* 29–34.

Rothman, L., & Leonard, D. (1967). Effectiveness of freshman orientation. *Journal of College Student Personnel, 8,* 300–304.

Rotter, J. (1966). Generalized expectancies for internal versus external controls of reinforcement. *Psychological Monographs, 80* (Whole No. 609).

Rotter, J. (1975). Some problems and misconceptions related to the construct of internal versus external control of reinforcement. *Journal of Consulting and Clinical Psychology, 43,* 56–67.

Rowe, I., & Marcia, J. (1980). Ego identity status, formal operations, and moral development. *Journal of Youth and Adolescence, 9,* 87–99.

Rowe, M., & Deture, L. (1975). A summary of research in science education—1973. *Science Education, 59,* 1–85.

Rubin, D. (1974). Estimating causal effects of treatments in randomized and nonrandomized studies. *Journal of Educational Psychology, 66,* 688–701.

Ruble, D., Croke, J., Frieze, I., & Parsons, J. (1975). A field study of sex-role attitude change in college women. *Journal of Applied Social Psychology, 5,* 110–117.

Rudolph, F. (1956). *Mark Hopkins and the log: Williams College, 1836–1872.* New Haven, CT: Yale University Press.

Rudolph, F. (1962). *The American college and university.* New York: Vintage Books.

Rumberger, R. (1980). The economic decline of college graduates: Fact or fallacy? *Journal of Human Resources, 15,* 99–112.

Rumberger, R. (1981). *Overeducation in the U.S. labor market.* New York: Praeger.

Rumberger, R. (1983). The influence of family background on education, earnings, and wealth. *Social Forces, 61,* 755–773.

Rumberger, R. (1984). The changing economic benefits of college graduates. *Economics of Education Review, 3,* 3–11.

Ryan, F. (1989). Participation in intercollegiate athletics: Affective outcomes. *Journal of College Student Development, 30,* 122–128.

Ryan, J. (1970). College freshmen and living arrangements. *NASPA Journal, 8,* 127–130.

Ryan, T. (1969). Research: Guide for teaching improvement. *Improving College and University Teaching, 17,* 270–276.

Ryder, N., & Westhoff, C. (1971). *Reproduction in the United States, 1965.* Princeton, NJ: Princeton University Press.

Rynes, S., & Boudreau, J. (1986). College recruiting in large organizations: Practice, evaluation, and research implications. *Personnel Psychology, 39,* 729–757.

Rysberg, J. (1986). Effects of modifying instruction in a college classroom. *Psychological Reports, 58,* 965–966.

Sack, A., & Thiel, R. (1979). College football and social mobility: A case study of Notre Dame football players. *Sociology of Education, 52,* 60–66.

St. John, E., Kirshstein, R., & Noell, J. (1988). *The effects of student financial aid on persistence.* Paper presented at the meeting of the American Educational Research Association, New Orleans.

Sakalys, J. (1982). Effects of a research methods course on nursing students' research attitudes and cognitive development. *Dissertation Abstracts International, 43,* 2254A.

Salter, C., & Teger, A. (1975). Change in attitudes toward other nations as a function of the type of international contact. *Sociometry, 38,* 213–222.

Samson, G., Graue, M., Weinstein, T., & Walberg, H. (1984). Academic and occupational performance: A quantitative synthesis. *American Educational Research Journal, 21,* 311–321.

San, G. (1986). The early labor force experience of college students and their post-college success. *Economics of Education Review, 5,* 65–76.

Sanders, C. (1990). Moral reasoning of male freshmen. *Journal of College Student Development, 31,* 5–8.

Sanford, N. (1956). Personality development during the college years. *Personnel and Guidance Journal, 35,* 74–80.

Sanford, N. (1962). Developmental status of the entering freshman. In N. Sanford (Ed.), *The American college: A psychological and social interpretation of the higher learning.* New York: John Wiley & Sons.

Sanford, N. (1967). *Where colleges fail: A study of the student as a person.* San Francisco: Jossey Bass.

Sanford, T. (1979). Residual effects of self-help aid on the lives of college graduates. *Journal of Student Financial Aid, 9,* 3–10.

Sanford, T. (1980). The effects of student aid on recent college graduates. *Research in Higher Education, 12,* 227–243.

Sasajima, M., Davis, J., & Peterson, R. (1968). Organized student protest and institutional climate. *American Educational Research Journal, 5,* 291–304.

SAS Institute (1985). *SAS user's guide: Basics* (Version 5). Cary, NC: Author.

Saunders, P. (1980). The lasting effects of introductory economics courses. *Journal of Economic Education, 12,* 1–14.

Schaie, K., & Parham, I. (1976). Stability of adult personality traits: Fact or fable? *Journal of Personality and Social Psychology, 34,* 146–158.

Schein, L. (1969). Institutional characteristics and student attitudes. *College Student Survey, 3*, 67–70.

Schenkel, S., & Marcia, J. (1972). Attitudes towards premarital intercourse in determining ego identity status in college women. *Journal of Personality, 3*, 472–482.

Schlaefli, A., Rest, J., & Thoma, S. (1985). Does moral education improve moral judgment? A meta-analysis of intervention studies using the Defining Issues Test. *Review of Educational Research, 55*, 319–352.

Schmidt, J. (1983). The intellectual development of traditionally and non-traditionally aged college students: A cross sectional study with longitudinal follow-up. *Dissertation Abstracts International, 44*, 2681A.

Schmidt, J. (1985). Older and wiser? A longitudinal study of the impact of college on intellectual development. *Journal of College Student Personnel, 26*, 388–394.

Schmidt, J., & Davison, M. (1981). Does college matter? Reflective judgment: How students tackle the tough questions. *Moral Education Forum, 6*, 2–14.

Schmidt, J., & Davison, M. (1983). Helping students think. *Personnel and Guidance Journal, 61*, 563–569.

Schmidt, M. (1970). Personality change in college women. *Journal of College Student Personnel, 11*, 414–418.

Schmidt, M. (1971). Relationships between sorority membership and changes in selected personality variables and attitudes. *Journal of College Student Personnel, 12*, 208–213.

Schneider, J. (1971). College students' belief in personal control, 1966–1970. *Journal of Individual Psychology, 27*, 188.

Schoenberg, R. (1972). Strategies for meaningful comparison. In H. Costner (Ed.), *Sociological methodology 1972.* San Francisco: Jossey-Bass.

Schoenfeldt, L. (1968). Education after high school. *Sociology of Education, 41*, 350–369.

Schomberg, S. (1975). *Some personality correlates of moral maturity among community college students.* Unpublished manuscript, University of Minnesota, Minneapolis and St. Paul.

Schomberg, S. (1978). *Moral judgment development and its association with freshman year experiences.* Unpublished doctoral dissertation, University of Minnesota, Minneapolis and St. Paul.

Schonberg, W. (1974). Modification of attitudes of college students over time: 1923–1970. *Journal of Genetic Psychology, 125*, 107–117.

Schrager, R. (1986). The impact of living group social climate on student academic performance. *Research in Higher Education, 25*, 265–276.

Schreiber, E. (1978). Education and change in American opinions on a woman for president. *Public Opinion Quarterly, 42*, 171–182.

Schroeder, C. (1973). Sex differences and growth toward self-actualization during the freshman year. *Psychological Reports, 32*, 416–418.

Schroeder, C. (1980a). Redesigning college environments for students. In F. Newton & K. Ender (Eds.), *Student development practices*. Springfield, IL: Charles Thomas.

Schroeder, C. (1980b). The impact of homogeneous housing on environmental perceptions and student development. *Journal of College and University Student Housing, 10,* 10–15.

Schroeder, C., & Belmonte, A. (1979). The influence of residential environment on prepharmacy student achievement and satisfaction. *American Journal of Pharmaceutical Education, 43,* 16–19.

Schroeder, C., & Freesh, N. (1977). Applying environmental management strategies in residence halls. *NASPA Journal, 15,* 51–57.

Schroeder, C., & LeMay, M. (1973). The impact of coed residence halls on self-actualization. *Journal of College Student Personnel, 14,* 105–110.

Schubert, D. (1975a). A subcultural change of MMPI norms in the 1960s due to adolescent role confusion and glamorization of alienation. *Journal of Abnormal Psychology, 84,* 406–411.

Schubert, D. (1975b). Increase of apparent adjustment in adolescence by further ego identity formation and age. *College Student Journal, 7,* 3–6.

Schuh, J., & Laverty, M. (1983). The perceived long-term influence of holding a significant student leadership position. *Journal of College Student Personnel, 24,* 28–32.

Schultz, T. (1961). Investment in human capital. *American Economic Review, 51,* 1–17.

Schultz, T. (1963). *The economic value of education*. New York: Columbia University Press.

Schultz, T. (1975). The value of the ability to deal with disequilibria. *Journal of Economic Literature, 13,* 827–846.

Schustereit, R. (1980). Team teaching and academic achievement. *Improving College and University Teaching, 28,* 85–89.

Schwartz, A. (1971). On efficiency of migration. *Journal of Human Resources, 6,* 193–205.

Schwartz, A. (1976). Migration, age, and education. *Journal of Political Economy, 84,* 701–720.

Schwartz, E., & Thornton, R. (1980). Overinvestment in college training? *Journal of Human Resources, 15,* 121–123.

Schwartz, J. (1985). Student financial aid and the college enrollment decision: The effects of public and private grants and interest subsidies. *Economics of Education Review, 4,* 129–144.

Schwartz, S., Feldman, K., Brown, M., & Heingartner, A. (1969). Some personality correlates of conduct in two situations of moral conflict. *Journal of Personality, 37,* 41–57.

Scientific American. (1965). *The big business executive, 1964: A study of his social and educational background*. New York: Author.

Scott, R., Richards, A., & Wade, M. (1977). Women's studies as change agent. *Psychology of Women Quarterly, 1,* 377–379.

Scott, S. (1975). Impact of residence hall living on college student development. *Journal of College Student Personnel, 16,* 214–219.

Seabrook, T. (1985). *Attrition and retention of first year students at a college of advanced education.* Unpublished master's thesis, University of New South Wales, Australia.

Sedlacek, W. (1987). Black students on white campuses: 20 years of research. *Journal of College Student Personnel, 28,* 484–495.

Seeborg, M. (1975). The effect of curricular choice on alumni income. *Journal of Behavioral Economics, 7,* 151–172.

Selby, J. (1973). Relationships existing among race, student financial aid, and persistence in college. *Journal of College Student Personnel, 14,* 38–40.

Selznick, G., & Steinberg, J. (1969). *The tenacity of prejudice: Anti-Semitism in contemporary America.* New York: Harper & Row.

Semmes, C. (1985). Minority status and the problem of legitimacy. *Journal of Black Studies, 15,* 259–275.

Serlin, R., & Levin, J. (1980). Identifying regions of significance in aptitude-by-treatment interaction research. *American Educational Research Journal, 17,* 389–399.

Sewell, W. (1971). Inequality of opportunity for higher education. *American Sociological Review, 36,* 793–809.

Sewell, W., Haller, A., & Ohlendorf, G. (1970). The educational and early occupational attainment process: Replications and revisions. *American Sociological Review, 35,* 1014–1027.

Sewell, W., Haller, A., & Portes, A. (1969). The educational and early occupational attainment process. *American Sociological Review, 34,* 82–92.

Sewell, W., & Hauser, R. (1972). Causes and consequences of higher education: Models of the status attainment process. *American Journal of Agricultural Economics, 54,* 851–861.

Sewell, W., & Hauser, R. (1975). *Education, occupation, and earnings: Achievement in the early career.* New York: Academic Press.

Sewell, W., & Hauser, R. (1980). The Wisconsin longitudinal study of social and psychological factors in aspirations and achievements. In A. Kerckhoff (Ed.), *Research in the sociology of education and socialization* (Vol. 1). Greenwich, CT: JAI Press.

Sewell, W., Hauser, R., & Wolf, W. (1980). Sex, schooling and occupational status. *American Journal of Sociology, 86,* 551–583.

Sewell, W., & Shah, V. (1967). Socioeconomic status, intelligence, and the attainment of higher education. *Sociology of Education, 40,* 1–23.

Sewell, W., & Shah, V. (1968a). Parents' education and children's educational aspirations and achievements. *American Sociological Review, 33,* 191–209.

Sewell, W., & Shah, V. (1968b). Social class, parental encouragement, and educational aspirations. *American Journal of Sociology, 73,* 559–572.

Seybert, J., & Mustapha, S. (1988). *Moral reasoning in college students: An evaluation of two curricular approaches.* Paper presented at the meeting of the American Educational Research Association, New Orleans.

Sgan, M. (1970). Letter grade achievement in pass-fail courses. *Journal of Higher Education, 41,* 638–644.

Shaffer, P. (1973). Academic progress of disadvantaged minority students: A two-year study. *Journal of College Student Personnel, 14,* 41–46.

Shand, J. (1969). Report on a twenty-year follow-up study of the religious beliefs of 114 Amherst College students. *Journal for the Scientific Study of Religion, 8,* 167–168.

Sharma, M., & Jung, L. (1984). The influence of institutional involvement in international education on United States students. *International Review of Education, 30,* 457–467.

Sharon, A. (1971). Adult academic achievement in relation to formal education and age. *Adult Education Journal, 21,* 231–237.

Sharp, L. (1970). *Education and employment: The early careers of college graduates.* Baltimore: Johns Hopkins University Press.

Sharp, L., & Weidman, J. (1987). *Early careers of undergraduate humanities majors.* Paper presented at the meeting of the American Educational Research Association, Washington, DC.

Shavelson, R., & Bolus, R. (1982). Self-concept: The interplay of theory and methods. *Journal of Educational Psychology, 74,* 3–17.

Shavelson, R., Burstein, L., & Keesling, J. (1977). Methodological considerations in interpreting research on self-concept. *Journal of Youth and Adolescence, 6,* 295–307.

Shavelson, R., Hubner, J., & Stanton, G. (1976). Self-concept: Validation of construct interpretations. *Review of Educational Research, 46,* 407–441.

Shaver, D. (1985). A longitudinal study of moral development at a conservative, religious liberal arts college. *Journal of College Student Personnel, 26,* 400–404.

Shaver, D. (1987). Moral development of students attending a Christian, liberal arts college and a Bible college. *Journal of College Student Personnel, 28,* 211–218.

Shaycoft, M. (1973). Factors affecting a factor affecting career. *Vocational Guidance Quarterly, 22,* 96–104.

Shea, B. (1974). *Inequality of outcomes: Two-year educations.* Paper presented at the meeting of the Society for the Study of Social Problems, Montreal.

Sheehy, G. (1974). *Passages: Predictable crises of adult life.* New York: E. P. Dutton.

Sheppard, H., & Herrick, N. (1972). *Where have all of the robots gone?* New York: Free Press.

Sherif, M., & Sherif, C. (1970). Black unrest as a social movement toward an emerging self-identity. *Journal of Social and Behavioral Sciences, 15,* 41–52.

Shields, L. (1972). Student maturity in a college of education. *Educational Research, 14,* 101–109.

Shoff, S. (1979). The significance of age, sex, and type of education on the development of reasoning in adults. *Dissertation Abstracts International, 40,* 3910A.

Shostrom, E. (1966). *The Personal Orientation Inventory.* San Diego: Educational and Industrial Testing Service.

Shuch, M. (1975). The use of calculators versus hand computations in teaching business arithmetic and the effects on the critical thinking ability of community college students. *Dissertation Abstracts International, 36,* 4299A.

Shweder, R., Mahaptra, M., & Miller, J. (1987). Culture and moral development. In J. Kagan and S. Lamb (Eds.), *The emergence of morality in young children.* Chicago: University of Chicago Press.

Siegel, L., Adams, J., & Macomber, F. (1960). Retention of subject matter as a function of large-group instructional procedures. *Journal of Educational Psychology, 51,* 9–13.

Siegel, P. (1971). *Prestige in the American occupational structure.* Unpublished doctoral dissertation, University of Chicago.

Silvey, H. (1951). Changes in test scores after two years in college. *Educational and Psychological Measurement, 11,* 494–502.

Simmons, H. (1959). Achievement in intermediate algebra associated with class size at the University of Wichita. *College and University, 34,* 309–315.

Simon, A., & Ward, L. (1974). The performance on the Watson-Glaser Critical Thinking Appraisal of university students classified according to sex, type of course pursued, and personality score category. *Educational and Psychological Measurement, 34,* 957–960.

Simonds, R. (1962). College majors vs. business success. *Business Topics.*

Simono, R., Wachowiak, D., & Furr, S. (1984). Student living environments and their perceived impact on academic performance: A brief follow-up. *Journal of College and University Student Housing, 14,* 22–24.

Simpson, C., Baker, K., & Mellinger, G. (1980). Conventional failures and unconventional dropouts: Comparing different types of university withdrawals. *Sociology of Education, 53,* 203–214.

Sindelar, J. (1979). *Why women use more medical care than men.* Unpublished doctoral dissertation, Stanford University, Stanford, CA.

Singer, J. (1974). Sex and college class differences in attitudes toward autonomy in work. *Human Relations, 27,* 493–499.

Singer, S. (1968). Review and discussion of the literature on personality development during college. In J. Katz (Ed.), *Growth and constraint in college students.* Stanford, CA: Stanford University, Institute for the Study of Human Problems.

Skager, R., Holland, J., & Braskamp, L. (1966). *Changes in self-ratings and life goals among students at colleges with different characteristics.* Iowa City, IA: American College Testing Program, Research and Development Division.

Slade, I., & Jarmul, L. (1975). Commuting college students: The neglected majority. *College Board Review, 95,* 16–21.

Slaney, R. (1983). Influence of career indecision on treatments exploring the vocational interests of college women. *Journal of Counseling Psychology, 30,* 55–63.

Slavin, R. (1984). Meta-analysis in education: How has it been used? *Educational Researcher, 13,* 6–15.

Slevin, K., & Wingrove, C. (1983). Similarities and differences among three generations of women in attitudes toward the female role in contemporary society. *Sex Roles, 9,* 609–624.

Sloan, D. (1979). The teaching of ethics in the American undergraduate curriculum, 1876–1976. *Hastings Center Report, 9,* 21–41.

Sloan, D. (1980). The teaching of ethics in the American undergraduate curriculum, 1876–1976. In D. Callahan & S. Bok, (Eds.), *The teaching of ethics.* New York: Plenum Press.

Smart, J. (1985). Holland environments as reinforcement systems. *Research in Higher Education, 23,* 279–292.

Smart, J. (1986). College effects on occupational status attainment. *Research in Higher Education, 24,* 73–95.

Smart, J. (1988a). College influences on graduates' income levels. *Research in Higher Education, 29,* 41–59.

Smart, J. (1988b). *Life history influences on Holland vocational type development.* Unpublished manuscript, University of Illinois, Chicago.

Smart, J., Elton, C., & McLaughlin, G. (1986). Person-environment congruence and job satisfaction. *Journal of Vocational Behavior, 29,* 216–225.

Smart, J., & Ethington, C. (1985). Early career outcomes of baccalaureate recipients: A study of native four-year and transfer two-year college students. *Research in Higher Education, 22,* 185–193.

Smart, J., Ethington, C., & McLaughlin, G. (undated). *Postsecondary educational attainment and the development of self-concept and career orientation.* Unpublished manuscript, Virginia Polytechnic Institute and State University.

Smart, J., & McLaughlin, G. (1986). *Outcomes assessment and the quality of student involvement.* Paper presented at the meeting of the Association for Institutional Research, Orlando, FL.

Smart, J., & Pascarella, E. (1986a). Self-concept development and educational degree attainment. *Higher Education, 15,* 3–15.

Smart, J., & Pascarella, E. (1986b). Socioeconomic achievements of former college students. *Journal of Higher Education, 57,* 529–549.

Smith, A. (1978). Lawrence Kohlberg's cognitive stage theory of the devel-

Name Index

A

Abraham, K., 433, 434, 436
Abramowitz, S., 363
Abrams, H., 389
Abravanel, M., 278, 287, 312, 333
Acker, J., 482
Adams, A., 522
Adams, D., 266
Adams, E., 497
Adams, G., 164, 165, 169, 177, 178, 180, 188, 189, 196, 210, 216
Adams, J., 87
Adams, W., 533
Adelman, C., 86
Adelson, J., 34, 213
Aderinto, K., 422
Adkins, D., 473, 518
Adler, M., 335
Adorno, T., 265
Agne, R., 117
Agrotes, M., 148
Aiello, N., 90, 91, 93
Ainsworth, C., 161
Aitken, N., 404
Akin, J., 508
Alba, R., 373
Albee, E., 144
Alberti, R., 268
Aldous, J., 278, 287
Aleamoni, L., 112
Alexander, K., 84, 375, 376, 397, 398, 406, 409, 415, 427, 446, 466, 471, 485, 498, 509, 515, 518, 528, 658, 685
Alfert, E., 220
Alishio, K., 212
Allen, R., 125, 143, 161
Allen, W., 210, 212, 380, 645
Allison, P., 448
Alloway, L., 339
Allport, G., 266, 280, 281, 324, 331, 332
Allred, G., 268
Almquist, E., 275, 476, 481, 486
Alterman, E., 639

Alwin, D., 283, 295, 324, 443, 483, 497, 677, 680
Ambrosino, R., 100
Anaya, G., 148
Anchors, S., 38
Andersen, C., 402
Andersen, D., 486
Anderson, C., 658
Anderson, D., 65, 495
Anderson, J., 676, 681
Anderson, K., 275, 300, 308, 309, 332, 373, 375, 378, 381, 388, 400, 407, 408, 409, 440, 507
Anderson, R., 107, 113
Anderson, S., 165, 179, 189, 217
Anderson, W., 422
Andes, J., 391
Andreason, A., 363
Andrews, F., 538, 539, 540
Andrews, J., 305, 497, 690
Andrisani, P., 515, 517
Angle, J., 466, 467, 509, 515, 517, 524, 526, 527
Angrist, S., 275, 283, 476, 481, 486
Anisef, P., 465, 471
Annis, L., 99
Apostal, R., 663
Appel, V., 281
Apprich, R., 425
Arber, S., 282, 294, 295
Arbuthnot, J., 360, 361
Archer, E., 644
Archer, S., 170, 177, 210
Arlin, P., 123
Armstrong, E., 84
Arnold, K., 480–481, 486
Aronson, S., 267
Arrow, K., 505
Arsenian, S., 266, 272, 281, 282, 320, 324, 332, 334
Arvey, R., 439
Astin, A., 5–6, 39, 50–51, 53, 55, 61, 63, 73, 74, 75–76, 77, 78, 80, 86, 98, 102, 103, 111, 147, 172, 173, 174, 175, 176,

Astin, A. (*continued*)
  180, 183, 185, 186, 187, 190, 191, 192,
  194, 210–211, 212, 213, 271, 273, 275,
  277, 278, 279, 281, 289, 290, 293, 295,
  297, 298, 299, 300, 301, 302, 303, 305,
  307, 310, 311, 312, 313, 314, 318, 319,
  327, 367, 370, 372, 373, 374, 375, 376,
  377, 378, 380, 382, 384, 388, 394, 395,
  400, 401, 406, 407, 414, 422, 424, 425,
  444, 445, 448, 449, 453, 456, 457, 458,
  459, 460, 461, 470, 479, 509, 518, 525,
  535, 560, 589, 610, 636, 637, 638, 640,
  641, 642, 646, 647, 651, 654, 656, 657,
  658, 660, 663, 665, 667, 671, 683, 684,
  691
Astin, H., 173, 174, 185, 190, 193, 194,
  213, 278, 311, 313, 322, 373, 381, 424,
  486
Atelsek, F., 402
Atkinson, D., 26
Attiyeh, T., 87
Atwell, C., 372
Aulston, M., 63
Auster, R., 541, 542
Auvenshine, C., 355
Averill, L., 336
Ayala, F., 5, 50
Ayers, J., 220
Ayres, Q., 78–79, 103, 683

B

Babcock, R., 495
Bachman, J., 175, 176, 181, 182, 187, 188,
  198, 200, 275, 278, 279, 285, 287, 310,
  312, 376, 543, 658
Baerwaldt, N., 431, 550
Bailey, D., 504
Bailey, J., 161, 658
Bailey, K., 173, 181, 197
Baillargeon, R., 47
Baird, L., 38, 39, 61, 76, 78, 81, 100, 103,
  172, 173, 174, 191, 298, 380, 389, 395,
  473, 474, 518, 589, 640, 648, 653, 654,
  655, 683
Baker, K., 391, 397
Baker, M., 141
Baker, T., 220, 265
Baktari, P., 534
Baldi de Mandilovitch, M., 437, 439, 497
Baldwin, J., 25, 166, 167
Baldwin, James, 144
Ballou, R., 389
Baltes, P., 72, 163
Bangert-Drowns, R., 92
Banks, J., 25, 166
Banta, T., 67, 137, 140

Banzinger, G., 403
Baratz, J., 457, 514, 639
Barfield, R., 496
Bargh, J., 98, 99
Barker, D., 316
Barker, R., 39, 61, 380
Barker, S., 495
Barlow, R., 555
Barnes, C., 133
Barnes, J., 88, 90, 93, 147
Barnes, M., 63
Barnett, R., 349, 350, 351, 353
Barnhart, R., 211, 306
Barr, M., 60
Barrall, M., 86
Barrows, T., 65
Barton, K., 222, 230, 234
Bartsch, K., 495
Basow, S., 480
Basseches, M., 123
Bassis, M., 63, 172, 184, 187, 685
Bate, W., 390
Bateman, D., 140
Baumann, V., 87
Baumgart, N., 402, 404
Baumgartel, H., 271, 332
Baumol, W., 550
Baumrind, D., 3
Bavry, J., 97, 147, 149, 221, 222, 246, 271,
  278
Baxter Magolda, M., 124, 125, 150
Bayer, A., 172, 174, 271, 275, 278, 282,
  290, 296, 319, 333, 373
Beach, L., 147
Beal, P., 375, 389
Bean, J., 380, 387, 390, 391, 394, 404,
  407, 413–414, 422, 682, 690
Beaton, A., 154, 273, 274, 278, 279, 285,
  287, 321, 323
Beatty, W., 95
Beck, R., 469, 517
Becker, G., 429, 500, 503, 544
Becker, H., 429, 470
Beckham, B., 210
Beckman, L., 283, 294
Beckman, V., 161
Beeken, L., 84
Beggs, D., 100
Behrman, J., 389
Behuniak, P., 176, 194, 215, 241
Belanger, C., 534
Belcher, M., 112
Belensky, M., 60, 212–213
Bell, M., 445–446
Bell, Y., 166, 167
Belmonte, A., 390, 401
Bender, I., 320, 324, 334

Bender, L., 644
Benezet, L., 228
Bengston, V., 292, 333
Bennett, C., 380
Bennett, M., 139
Bennett, R., 78–79, 103, 683
Bennett, S., 219, 222, 225, 226, 227, 245
Bennett, W., 4, 646
Benninga, J., 111, 266
Benson, P., 283, 295
Benton, S., 95
Benware, C., 99
Berdie, R., 83, 100, 267, 683
Berelson, B., 543, 556
Berestiansky, J., 117
Berg, H., 396
Berg, I., 429, 433, 439
Bergen, G., 405
Bergen, M., 405
Berger, R., 363
Bergquist, W., 84
Berliner, D., 690
Berliner, H., 433, 464
Bernstein, A., 643, 644
Bernstein, G., 267
Berry, M., 281
Berry, N., 433
Berson, R., 360
Bertin, B., 352, 354, 355
Best, F., 496
Bidwell, C., 86, 313, 654
Bielby, D., 445, 446, 460, 463, 468, 472, 486, 487
Bielby, W., 427
Bietter, J., 139
Bigelow, G., 277
Biggs, D., 349, 350
Biggs, S., 98
Billigmeier, R., 266, 306
Bills, D., 435, 463
Binnie, A., 495
Bird, C., 202
Birnbaum, R., 80
Bisconti, A., 84, 105, 154, 161, 432, 437, 452, 453, 463, 464–465, 475, 477, 478, 497, 508, 517, 519
Bittner, T., 391, 394
Blackburn, R., 84
Blackmon, C., 497
Blackwell, J., 380
Blai, B., 161, 390
Blake, A., 141
Blake, L., 124
Blalock, A., 112
Blalock, H., 671, 672
Blanc, R., 389
Blanchfield. W., 406

Blann, F., 425, 477
Blasi, A., 338
Blaska, B., 454
Blatt, M., 356, 360
Blau, P., 369, 371n, 415, 658
Blaug, M., 500
Blieszner, R., 72
Blimling, G., 161, 390, 422
Blizard, P., 114
Blocher, D., 43
Block, J., 92, 363
Bloland, P., 211
Blood, R., 543
Bloom, A., 114
Bloom, B., 72, 89, 133, 134, 685
Blumberg, P., 439
Blume, F., 267
Blunt, M., 114
Boaz, R., 112
Bobele, H., 212
Bobo, L., 380
Bode, J., 359–360
Bohrnstedt, G., 658
Bok, D., 114
Bolden, W., 278, 287, 301, 312, 313, 318
Boli, J., 276, 317
Bolus, R., 171
Bond, L., 684
Booth, R., 433
Borders-Patterson, A., 210
Borg, W., 658
Borgers, S., 267
Born, D., 104, 690
Boruch, R., 172, 174
Borzak, L., 212, 266
Bose, C., 426
Boudon, R., 424
Boudreau, J., 442
Bourne, E., 24, 177, 195, 198, 209
Bowen, H., 4, 6, 9, 64, 70–71, 80, 107, 108, 154, 226, 272, 273, 282, 370, 431, 503, 544, 547, 548, 549–550, 554, 555, 557, 563, 564, 573, 575, 588
Bowen, L., 283, 294, 319
Bowen, W., 550
Bowerman, B., 484
Bowles, F., 382
Bowles, S., 369, 406, 439, 500, 527, 658, 672
Bowman, M., 658
Boyd, D., 359, 360
Boyer, E., 393, 646, 652
Brabeck, M., 35, 118, 123, 124, 363
Braddock, J., 380, 421, 467, 658
Bradley, R., 682
Bradshaw, H., 176, 182
Bradshaw, T., 271, 275, 298, 300, 309

Bragg, A., 213
Branch-Simpson, G., 166
Brandt, K., 389, 422
Bransford, C., 355
Braskamp, L., 149, 173, 174, 247, 271, 306
Braungart, M., 278, 318
Braungart, R., 278, 290, 318
Brawer, F., 63, 220, 222, 223, 225, 227, 238, 372, 644
Braxton, J., 83, 133–134, 277, 286, 301, 318, 402, 405, 424, 448, 459, 470, 476, 484
Bray, D., 520, 536
Brazer, H., 415, 555
Brazziel, W., 381
Bredemeier, B., 363
Bredemeier, M., 267
Breneman, D., 372, 373, 440, 442, 507
Bressler, M., 454
Brethower, D., 114
Brier, E., 376, 402, 424, 445, 448, 459, 464, 468, 470, 476, 484
Briggs, K. C., 37
Brigman, S., 404
Brill, A., 288, 292
Brim, O., 55, 369, 658
Brinkman, P., 370, 503, 504, 534, 535
Brint, S., 641, 643
Broadhurst, B., 340
Brogan, D., 480
Bron, G., 389, 403
Brooks, J., 406
Brouillette, J., 312, 318
Brown, D., 210, 217, 220, 222, 225, 227, 242, 244, 245, 246, 247, 248, 271, 277, 305, 310, 311, 322
Brown, J., 349, 350
Brown, L., 339
Brown, M., 363, 383, 444
Brown, R., 5, 60, 161, 244, 246, 247, 267
Browne, M., 120, 129
Bruch, M., 422
Brue, E., 4, 388
Brush, L., 211, 316
Bryan, W., 391
Bryant, F., 539
Bryk, A., 688, 689
Bucklin, R., 426
Bucklin, W., 426
Buebel, M., 210
Buenz, R., 690
Buffington, S., 390
Bumpass, L., 282, 294
Burbach, H., 210
Burke, P., 25, 167
Burlew, A., 486, 498

Burns, R., 92, 139, 658
Burnstein, L., 171
Burrell, L., 380
Burris, V., 439
Burstein, L., 74, 683, 684, 685, 686, 687
Burton, R., 222, 224, 245
Busch, R., 278, 287, 333
Bush, D., 278
Bushey, B., 125
Butler, L., 126
Butler, R., 406
Butts, D., 98
Byrne, B., 171

C

Cabrera, A., 405
Cade, S., 220, 225, 226, 244, 248, 252
Cady, M., 347
Caffey, C., 212
Cahen, L., 9, 690
Cain, G., 672
Calhoon, R., 469, 473, 518, 520, 535
Calvert, R., 431
Camburn, D., 283, 295, 324
Campagna, D., 80, 218, 220, 221, 222, 225, 227, 236, 237, 238, 244, 271, 272, 273, 275, 298, 307, 314, 316, 317
Campbell, A., 113, 438, 439, 538, 539, 540, 541, 543, 544, 545
Campbell, D., 63, 280, 658, 661
Campbell, J., 497
Campbell, L., 267
Campbell, P., 500, 524
Campbell, R., 528
Campbell, T., 141
Candee, D., 363
Canelos, J., 111
Canter, R., 104, 690
Capel, W., 323
Caple, R., 45, 47, 161, 275, 390
Capoor, M., 128
Cappella, B., 388
Capretta, R., 278, 287, 310
Carmichael, K., 92
Carney, P., 217, 242, 267, 277, 278, 307, 311, 317, 318
Carnoy, M., 503, 522, 524
Carp, A., 112
Carroll, C., 405
Carroll, J., 89, 391
Carsello, C., 211, 306
Carter, B., 402
Carter, R., 24, 167
Carter, T., 369, 385, 427, 485
Cartledge, C., 403
Carver, D., 495

Casselman, G., 138
Catlin, J., 289, 310
Cattell, R., 222, 230, 234
Cauble, M., 338, 361
Cebula, R., 425, 516
Centra, J., 76, 77, 78, 79, 81, 82, 95, 112, 161, 210, 683
Chamberlain, P., 61, 389
Chapman, D., 102, 391, 400, 402, 411, 423, 674, 690
Charkins, R., 104
Cheatham, H., 166, 167, 168, 183, 197, 238
Cheek, N., 271
Cheng, S., 341
Chesin, S., 275
Chew, C., 210
Cheydleur, F., 87
Chiappetta, E., 117
Chickering, A., 4, 15, 18, 20–23, 26, 27, 32, 43, 45, 55, 61, 73, 80, 102, 146, 162, 172, 173, 174, 191, 192, 199, 215, 216, 218, 219, 220, 221, 222, 223, 224, 225, 226, 227, 236, 237, 238, 239, 244, 246, 247, 248, 250, 271, 272, 273, 275, 277, 278, 279, 281, 298, 302, 303, 307, 308, 309, 310, 311, 312, 313, 314, 316, 317, 318, 330, 333, 336, 338, 380, 393, 400, 402, 422, 557, 564, 596, 640, 648, 651, 663, 681
Chilson, D., 515–516
Chiswick, B., 506
Christensen, M., 267
Christensen, S., 369, 415
Chistenson, R., 278, 287, 310
Christian, V., 522
Churchill, W., 405, 421
Churchman, C., 122
Clapp, T., 448
Clark, B., 48, 61, 218, 219, 221, 222, 225, 226, 236, 237, 239, 246, 265, 271, 272, 273, 274, 279, 281, 297, 298, 299, 301, 302, 303, 308, 313, 315, 333, 334, 338, 372, 374, 376, 377, 443, 445, 497, 590, 641, 689
Clark, C., 111, 266
Clark, J., 65, 212
Clark, M., 395
Clark, R., 276, 290, 295
Claxton, C., 36, 38
Clemente, F., 539
Clewell, B., 374, 378
Cliff, N., 676
Clinchy, B., 60, 212–213
Cline, H., 534
Cline, M., 92, 111
Clogg, C., 534

Clouse, B., 339
Clowes, D., 373
Cobern, M., 271, 274, 284, 285, 431, 541, 543, 547, 550, 555
Cochran, W., 658
Cochrane, R., 167
Coder, R., 344, 345
Cogan, J., 65
Cohen, A., 63, 65, 66, 372, 644
Cohen, E., 339
Cohen, H., 117
Cohen, J., 80, 658, 660, 666, 667, 668, 691
Cohen, P., 80, 90, 91, 92, 93, 94, 95, 104, 473, 475, 518, 658, 660, 666, 667, 668, 691
Cohn, B., 339
Cohn, E., 503, 504, 523, 534, 536
Cohn, S., 98
Colarelli, S., 443, 448, 450, 452
Colby, A., 337, 341, 342, 344, 346, 361, 659
Coleman, J., 65
Coleman, N., 166, 167, 183, 197, 238
Coles, H., 161
Collins, R., 429, 440, 443
Colten, M., 402, 404
Condran, J., 289
Conrad, C., 84
Constantinople, A., 166, 178, 195–196, 216
Converse, P., 113, 539, 543
Cook, P., 87
Cook, T., 10, 658
Cooker, P., 212
Cooley, R., 312
Cooley, W., 684
Coop, R., 25, 167
Cooper, H., 9
Cooper, R., 363
Cooper, S., 495
Coopersmith, S., 171
Cope, R., 374, 387
Corbett, M., 277, 282, 283, 319
Corlett, D., 388
Corrallo, S., 405
Corsini, D., 338
Coscarelli, W., 161
Cosgrove, T., 690
Costa, A., 402
Costantini, E., 278, 287
Costin, F., 95
Cottle, T., 19
Cowan, C., 286
Cox, G., 658
Cox, S., 266, 271, 281, 317, 320, 324, 332, 334

Craise, J., 218, 221, 233
Crane, D., 447
Crary, L., 504
Crawford, J., 498
Creager, J., 172, 174, 667, 670
Creamer, D., 422
Creaser, J., 211, 306, 402
Crimmel, H., 112
Crockett, H., 279, 280, 288, 291, 333
Croke, J., 316
Cronbach, L., 658, 661, 683, 684, 685, 687, 688, 690
Crook, D., 373
Crooks, L., 497
Cross, K. P., 89, 112, 282, 319, 380–381
Cross, W., Jr., 24–26, 166, 167, 168, 183
Crotty, W., 279, 288, 310
Crouse, J., 427, 446, 499, 500, 508, 510, 511
Crowder, J., 345
Cruickshank, D., 97
Culbert, S., 212
Culler, R., 388
Cunnigen, D., 210, 382
Cunningham, J., 63
Curtin, R., 286
Cutler, N., 292
Czajka, J., 282, 294, 295
Czapski, D., 339

D

Dabrowski, I., 316
Dalgaard, K., 97
Dambrot, F., 283, 294, 295
Daniels, M., 161, 267
Daniels, R., 104, 210, 690
Daniere, A., 508, 526
Dannefer, D., 48, 49
Dark, V., 389
Darkenwald, G., 107, 113
Darlington, R., 668
Darrow, C. N., 199
Datan, N., 199
Dauffenbach, R., 425, 516
Da Vanzo, J., 162, 432
David, M., 415, 533
Davidson, J., 167
Davis, B., 316
Davis, D., 112
Davis, H., 103
Davis, J., 186, 187, 210, 291, 302, 333, 376, 405, 424, 444, 470, 497, 498, 685, 690
Davis, M., 104, 690
Davis, R., 380, 543
Davison, M., 32, 123, 124, 132, 140, 160, 169, 170, 179, 196, 338, 339, 346

Day, R., 63
Daymont, T., 502, 515, 517, 525
Dean, R., 443, 448, 450, 452
Dearman, N., 431
DeBack, V., 434
Debruil, L., 117
De Buhr, L., 389
Deci, E., 99
DeCosta, F., 382
DeCoster, D., 5, 161, 390
Deemer, D., 341, 352, 353, 356, 362, 363
DeFleur, L., 282
de la Vina, L., 519, 528, 535, 536
DeLisi, R., 138, 139
DeLisle, F., 84
Delworth, U., 165, 166, 179, 190
Demeke, G., 402, 404
de Mik, G., 497
Demitroff, J., 388, 426
Denham, M., 96
Dent, P., 112
Deppe, M., 277, 301
Dettloff, J., 117
Deture, L., 90
DeVito, A., 117
de Vries, B., 338, 339
de Wolf, V., 396
Dey, E., 278, 301–302, 313
DeYoung, A., 161, 192, 307
Diamond, M., 267
Dickens, W., 628
Dickstein, E., 210, 339
Didham, J., 84
Diener, E., 539
Dienst, R., 97, 147, 149, 221, 222, 246, 271, 278
Dignan, M., 266
DiMaggio, P., 415
Dimick, K., 425, 477
DiNuzzo, T., 495
Dispoto, R., 355
Disque, C., 404
Dodder, R., 220, 244, 313
Doherty, A., 169, 271, 276, 437
Doherty, W., 338
Dolphin, W., 104, 112, 690
Domhoff, G., 440
Domino, G., 104, 690
Donald, J., 140
Donaldson, G., 72
Donovan, J., 164
Donovan, R., 412, 643, 644
Doren, D., 217, 242, 271, 277, 278, 307, 311, 316, 317, 318
Dortzbach, J., 345
Dougherty, K., 373, 386, 535
Dougherty, T., 519
Douvan, E., 34, 213, 543

Doyle, K., 94
Draper, N., 668
Dreher, G., 519
Dressel, P., 84, 118–119, 120, 130, 136, 137, 140, 144, 338
Drew, D., 172, 174, 187, 376, 444
Dreyer, N., 283, 294
Drum, D., 18, 60, 209
Dubin, R., 87
Dubois, N., 389
DuBois, P., 478, 521
Duby, P., 150, 228, 249, 266, 402, 422
Duffy, J., 340
Dukes, F., 385, 391
Dumont, R., 63, 64, 65, 67, 86, 100
Duncan, B., 210, 370, 385, 426
Duncan, C., 161, 390
Duncan, J., 166, 167
Duncan, O., 369, 370, 371n, 385, 415, 426, 427, 440, 441, 444, 446, 456, 458, 459, 463, 465, 466, 467, 471, 475, 478, 480, 486, 496, 497, 498, 500, 508, 658, 676, 680
Dunivant, N., 363
Dunkelberg, W., 533
Dunkin, M., 88, 90, 93, 147
Dunlop, D., 117, 138
Dunphy, L., 403
Dunteman, G., 405
Duster, M., 405
Dutton, J., 290, 333

E

Easterlin, R., 544
Easton, J., 98
Ebeling, B., 91, 104
Eckland, B., 322, 323, 369, 375, 376, 390, 391, 392, 397, 398, 406, 409, 415, 427, 498, 658, 685
Edmonds, E., 96
Edmonds, G., 380
Edmonson, J., 87
Edwards, H., 210
Edwards, K., 176, 211
Edwards, L., 541, 542
Ehrenberg, R., 407, 508, 518, 521
Eiferman, D., 342, 345
Eigenbrod, F., 268
Eisert, D., 117, 142, 143, 145, 161, 169, 189, 222, 245
Eitzen, D., 312, 318
Elam, S., 428, 500
Elashoff, J., 660
Elfner, E., 149
El-Khawas, E., 382, 453
Ellis, V., 219, 226
Ellison, A., 20, 23

Ellison, R., 498
Elton, C., 220, 222, 243, 390, 422, 464
Ender, S., 389
Endo, J., 101, 149, 150, 160, 194, 271, 305, 306, 391, 394, 404
Englehart, M., 133
Eniaiyeju, P., 111
Enos, P., 404
Enwieme, X., 138
Enyeart, M., 161
Epps, E., 168, 173, 193, 210, 376, 377, 392, 395, 459, 460, 479, 497
Erbring, L., 684
Erikson, E., 15, 17, 19–20, 23, 27, 33, 58, 60, 61, 164, 165, 166, 177, 178, 223, 661
Erikson, R., 278, 287, 313
Erkut, S., 453
Ernsberger, D., 347
Erwin, T., 165, 166, 179, 190, 196, 229, 249
Esposito, D., 396, 453, 480
Etaugh, C., 281, 283, 294, 295, 315, 319
Ethington, C., 55, 63, 70, 173, 175, 176, 180, 181, 182, 184, 185, 186, 190, 193, 194, 197, 198, 199–200, 212, 215, 231, 250, 252, 253, 266, 273, 275, 277, 285, 286, 300, 310, 311, 318, 370, 375, 376, 378, 381, 388, 391, 392, 395, 397, 398, 409, 412, 416, 424, 441, 442, 448, 455, 456, 458, 460, 470, 472, 476, 482, 487, 498, 658, 679
Evans, D., 488
Evans, F., 676
Evans, J., 495
Evans, K., 422
Everett, C., 400
Ewell, P., 5, 239, 240, 657
Eysenck, H., 10

F

Falk, R., 266–267, 312
Fannin, P., 209, 210
Farady, M., 125
Farley, L., 312
Farr, W., 403
Farrell, P., 543
Fast, J., 117
Faughn, S., 391
Faust, D., 360, 361
Fawcett, L., 216, 251, 267
Fay, L., 691
Fazio, F., 117, 138
Feather, N., 270, 271, 281, 284, 304, 314
Featherman, D., 369, 370, 385, 426, 427, 482, 485, 522, 523
Feidler, L., 211, 212

323; religious values studied at, 293; self-esteem studied at, 201

Minnesota, University of, moral development studied at, 350–352

Minority group members: and achieving competence vector, 20; inequalities of, 644–645; psychosocial development of, 26. *See also* Black students

Moral development: aspects of, 335–368; background on, 335–337; and behavior, 363–364, 367; between-college effects on, 347–349, 365; change during college in, 338–344, 364, 562–563; cognitive theory of, 30–32; conditional effects on, 361, 366; design issues in measuring, 343–344; education interventions for, 356–361, 368; history of attention to, 335–336; and individual experiences, 349–355; longterm effects on, 361–363, 366–367, 582–584; and major field, 355; measuring, 337–338, 339–344, 345–347; meta-findings on, 562–563, 573–574, 582–584; net effects on, 344–347, 364–365, 367, 573–574; and residence, 354, 355–356; stages of, 336; summary on, 364–367; within-college effects on, 349–361, 365–366

Moral Judgment Interview (MJI), 337, 338, 341–343, 346, 359, 360, 361–362

Moral Reasoning Experience Checklist, 354

Moratorium identity status, and psychosocial change, 24, 164–165, 178, 199

Morrill Act, 335

Multiple correlation and regression analysis, 668–682

Myers-Briggs Type Indicator (MBTI), 37–38

N

National Center for Education Statistics, 112, 296, 373, 534

National Engineering Career Development Survey, 481

National Fertility Survey, 545

National Institute of Education Study Group, 4

National Longitudinal Study of the High School Class of 1972 (NLS-72): and attitudes and values, 275, 285, 286, 287, 299, 308, 318, 321; and career development, 428, 440–441, 446, 456–457, 458, 465, 466, 475, 485–486; and economic benefits, 501, 507, 511, 513, 514, 521; and educational attainment, 372–373, 375, 381, 397, 408, 409; and

relational system, 215, 231, 235, 241, 250, 252; and self system, 176, 182, 188, 194, 200; and subject matter competence, 69–73; and unit of analysis, 682

National Longitudinal Study of Young Men, 521

National Longitudinal Survey of Labor Market Experience, 441, 507, 524

National Merit Scholarship: and psychosocial changes, 216, 221, 225, 237, 238, 239; and subject matter competence, 74, 75, 80

National Opinion Research Center, 106, 446; General Social Survey of, 291

National Science Foundation, 348

National Teacher Examination (NTE), 79, 82–83, 103, 601

Native Americans, psychosocial development of, 26, 210

NBER-Thorndike data, 508, 511, 524, 525, 528, 542

Need-press model, and person-environment interactions, 41

Nelson-Denny Reading Test, 64

Net effect, concept of, 11–12

Net effects of college: aging, generation, and period effects versus, 290–292, 295–297; assessment issues of, 657–659; on attitudes and values, 283–297, 326–327, 569–570; on authoritarianism, dogmatism, and ethnocentrism, 232–233; on autonomy, independence, and locus of control, 230–232, 266; background on, 566–567; on career choice and development, 426–439, 488–489, 495–497; of causal mechanisms, 504–506; causal model of, 68–69; on cognitive skills, 127–132, 155–156; on communication skills, 127–128; concept of, 7; on consumer behavior, 547–548, 552, 555; on critical thinking, 129–130; on cultural values, 283–284; on earnings, 500–502; on economic benefits, 500–506, 529–530, 534–535, 536–537; on educational and occupational values, 284–286, 333; on ego development, 179–180; on family size, 544–545, 551, 554; on formal operational reasoning, 128–129, 132; on general intellectual and analytic skills, 128; on health, 541–543, 551, 554; on identity development, 177–179; on intellectual orientation, 233–234; on interpersonal relations, 234; on job satisfaction, 437–439, 496–497; on learning and cognitive changes, 567–569; on leisure,

Net effects of college (*continued*)
549–550, 553, 555; magnitude of, 633; on marriage, 543–544, 551; on maturity and general personal development, 235; meta-findings on, 566–573; on moral development, 344–347, 364–365, 367, 573–574; on nurturance of children, 545–547, 552, 554–555; on occupational productivity and success, 433–437, 496; on occupational status, 426–431, 495–496; on personal adjustment and psychological well-being, 234–235; on postformal reasoning, 130–132; on private rate of return, 502–504, 534–535; psychosocial, 569, 571–572; on psychosocial relational system, 230–235, 258–259; on psychosocial self system, 177–182, 203–204; on quality of life, 538–555; on religious values, 292–293; research needed on, 633; on savings and investments, 548–549, 552–553, 555; on self-concept, 180–181, 210–211; on self-esteem, 181–182, 211; on sex or gender role attitudes, 293–297; on social and political values, 286–292; and subject matter competence, 67–73, 108; on subjective well-being, 538–541, 550–551; on work force participation, 431–432, 496

Networks of contacts, and work force participation, 432

New York, educational attainment studied in, 384–385

New Zealand: independence studied in, 230; moral development studied in, 341, 352, 355

Nonmarket benefits. *See* Quality of life

North Carolina, institutional characteristics and student learning in, 78–79

North Carolina, University of, 477

Nurturance of children, and quality of life, 545–547, 552, 554–555

O

Occupational Changes in a Generation Survey, 522–523, 525

Occupational status, and career development, 426–432, 442, 446–448, 465–467, 470–472, 475–476, 482–483, 495–498. *See also* Career entries

Occupational values: between-college effects on, 300; change during college in, 274–276, 332; conditional effects on, 317–318, 333–334; long-term effects on, 321–322; net effects on, 285–286; within-college effects on, 308–309

Office of Civil Rights, 76

Ohio State University Psychological Examination, 63

Older students: cognitive skills of, 120, 130–131; educational attainment of, 414; learning styles of, 112; and moral development, 358; and theories of change, 17, 22, 27

Omnibus Personality Inventory (OPI): anxiety level (AL) scale of, 225, 226, 227, 247, 248; autonomy scale of, 218, 219, 220, 232, 236, 243, 254, 265; complexity (CO) scale of, 221, 222, 233, 237, 245; estheticism scale of, 272, 331; impulse expression (IE) scale of, 225, 226, 227, 239, 247, 248, 255; personal integration (PI) scale of, 225, 226–227, 247, 248; religious orientation scale of, 282; schizoid functioning (SF) scale of, 225, 226, 227; social extroversion (SE) scale of, 223–224, 246, 247, 255; social maturity scale of, 218, 219, 220, 232, 253, 265, 266; theoretical orientation (TO) scale of, 221, 222, 237, 245, 254; thinking introversion (TI) scale of, 221, 222, 233, 234, 237, 245, 254

Operational thought. *See* Formal operational reasoning

Opportunity costs. *See* Private rate of return

Orientation: and educational attainment, 385, 402–405, 419–420, 423; practice issues of, 650–651

Otis Intelligence Test, 64

Outcomes: affective-behavioral, 6; affective-psychological, 6, 162–334; and assessment issues, 657–691; for attitudes and values, 269–334; background on, 1–5, 556–557; and between-college effects, 588–607; of career choice and development, 424–499; certification or screening theory of, 429–430, 435, 438, 442–443, 504–505, 510, 536; and change during college, 557–566; cognitive-behavioral, 6, 369–423, 500–537; cognitive-psychological, 6, 62–161; in cognitive skills, 114–161; conceptual framework for, 5–8; of conditional effects, 626, 628–632; cumulative or specific, 655–656; economic, 500–537; of educational attainment, 369–423; evidence of, 1–14; expected, 1–2; human capital theory of, 429, 442, 504, 505–506, 536; implications of, 636–656; and long-term effects, 573, 575–588; meta-findings on, 556; in moral development, 335–368; and net effects, 566–573; overview of studying, 1–14; for psychosocial relational systems, 214–268; for psychosocial self system, 162–213; on quality of life after college, 538–555; research needed on, 632–635; signaling or labeling theory of, 443; socialization theory of, 429, 442, 456, 495–496; in subject matter competence, 62–113; summary of, 556–635; taxonomy of, 5–6; theories and models of, 15–61; timing of, 634; and within-college effects, 607, 610–626

Overeducation, and job satisfaction, 439

P

Panel Study of Income Dynamics, 446, 508, 510, 522–523

Paragraph Completion Method (PCM), 126–127, 145

Parental education. *See* Intergenerational effects

Path analysis. *See* Causal modeling

Peace Corps, attitudes and behaviors towards, 289, 367

Peers: and attitudes and values, 309, 313, 328; and educational attainment, 384, 390–393; meta-findings on, 520–521; and moral development, 354; teaching or tutoring by, 98–99

Pennsylvania: educational values studied in, 274; religious values studied in, 292–293, 319

Perceptual models, of person-environment interactions, 40–42

Persistence. *See* Educational attainment

Person-environment interaction theories: analysis of, 38–42, 60–61; and educational attainment, 411–414, 422; human aggregate models of, 39–40, 61; perceptual models of, 40–42; physical models of, 39; structural organizational models of, 42

Personal adjustment and psychological well-being: between-college effects on, 238–239; change during college in, 225–227, 266; long-term effects on, 255–256; net effects on, 234–235; within-college effects on, 247–248

Personal Orientation Inventory (POI), 265

Personality development, and moral development, 357, 358, 359

Personalized system of instruction (PSI), and subject matter competence, 89, 91–92, 93, 94, 99, 103–104, 111–112

Philippines, moral development studied in, 340

Physical models, of person-environment interaction, 39

Policy: aspects of implications for, 636–647; on economy, efficiency, and effectiveness, 647; equality issues of, 637–639; inequality issues of, 639–645; on organizational tolerance for individual differences, 645–646

Political attitudes and values: between-college effects on, 301–302; change during college in, 277–279; net effects on, 287; within-college effects on, 311–313

Postconventional stage, in moral development, 31–32. *See also* Moral development

Postformal reasoning: change during college in, 122–126; and instructional approaches, 144–145, 161; net effects on, 130–132

Practice: aspects of implications for, 648–656; for cumulative effects, 655–656; for departmental climate, 652–653; for instructional approaches, 651–652; orientation issues of, 650–651; for psychosocial size, 654–655; for residence units, 653–654; on student and faculty recruiting, 649–650

Preconventional stage, in moral development, 31, 336

Preencounter identity status, and psychosocial change, 25, 167

Press: environmental, 186, 187, 314, 410; and person-environment interactions, 41

Princeton University, 477, 478

Private rate of return, and economic benefits, 502–504, 534–535, 536–537

Productive Americans Survey, 446

Productivity: and career development, 433–434, 449–450; earnings related to, 506

Programmed instruction (PI), and subject matter competence, 89, 91, 93

Progressive conformity, and career choice and development, 461–462, 491, 497

Project on Student Development, 219

Promotions: and academic major, 468–470; and career development, 436; and extracurricular involvement, 477

Protestant institutions, and attitudes and values, 297–298, 300, 303

Proximity. *See* Geographic and social proximity

Psychological Examination, 63

Psychological well-being. *See* Personal adjustment and psychological well-being

Psychosocial development: meta-findings on, 561–562, 569, 571–572, 579, 581–582; principles of, 43–44; and reflective judgment, 32

Psychosocial moratorium, higher education as, 58, 178, 179

Psychosocial relational systems: analysis of changes in, 214–268; authoritarianism, dogmatism, and ethnocentrism in, 218–220, 232–233, 236–237, 243–244, 253–254, 257–258, 259, 265–266, 267; autonomy, independence, and locus of control in, 214–217, 230–232, 235–236, 241–243, 250–251, 252–253, 264–265, 266–267; background on, 214; between-college effects on, 235–241, 259–261; change during college in, 214–230, 257–258; conditional effects on, 250–252, 262–263; intellectual orientation in, 220–223, 233–234, 237, 244–246, 254–255, 260, 266, 267; interpersonal relations in, 223–224, 234, 238, 246–247, 255, 267–268; long-term effects on, 252–256, 263–264; maturity and general personal development in, 227–230, 235, 239–240, 249–250, 251–252, 256; net effects on, 230–235, 258–259; personal adjustment and psychological well-being in, 225–227, 234–235, 238–239, 247–248, 255–256, 260, 266; summary on, 257–264; within-college effects on, 241–250, 261–262

Psychosocial self system: analysis of, 162–213; background on, 162–163, 209; between-college effects on, 183–188, 204–205; change during college in, 163–176, 202–203; conclusions on, 208–209; conditional effects on, 195–198, 207, 212–213; ego development in, 168–170, 179–180, 183, 188–190, 195–196, 198–199, 202–203, 210; identity development in, 163–168, 177–179, 183, 188–190, 195–196, 198–199, 202–203, 209–210; long-term effects on, 198–201, 207–208; net effects on, 177–182, 203–204; self-concept in, 170–175, 180–181, 183–188, 190–194, 197–198, 199–200, 203, 204, 205, 206, 207–208, 210–211, 212, 213; self-esteem in, 171, 175–176, 181–182, 188, 194–195, 198, 200–201, 203, 204, 205, 208, 210, 211; summary on, 201–208; within-college effects on, 188–195, 205–206, 211–212

Psychosocial theories: analysis of, 19–27, 60; of black identity formation, 24–26, 60; ego identity status in, 23–24; maturity model in, 26–27; and vectors of student development, 20–23, 61

Purpose, vector of developing, 22, 216

Q

Qualifying Test, 74, 75, 80

Quality. *See* Institutional quality

Quality of effort: and cognitive skills, 135; involvement in, 99–101

Quality of life: aspects of, 538–555; and causal inference, 553; and consumer behavior, 547–548, 552, 555; and family size, 544–545, 551, 554; and health, 541–543, 551, 554; and leisure, 549–550, 553, 555; and marriage, 543–544, 551; meta-findings on, 584–586; net effects on, 538–555; and nurturance of children, 545–547, 552, 554–555; and savings and investments, 548–549, 552–553, 555; and social class bias, 554; and subjective well-being, 538–541, 550–551; summary on, 550–554

Questing, in identity development, 179

Questionnaire on Student and College Characteristics, 77

R

Racial differences, and economic benefits, 522–523, 536. *See also* Institutional racial composition; Minority group members

Rate of return: private, 502–504, 534–535, 536–537; social, 534

Readiness, and cognitive theory, 44, 59

Reasoning. *See* Formal operational reasoning; Informal reasoning; Postformal reasoning

Recursiveness, and causal modeling, 681–682

Redundancy, and social integration, 380

Reed College, as distinctive, 377

Reference group theory, and psychosocial self system, 186–188, 211

Reflective judgment: change during college in, 123–125; and cognitive theory, 32–33; net effects of college on, 130–132; and teaching/learning context, 140

Reflective Judgment Interview (RJI), 123

Regression analysis: and causality issues, 672–673; hierarchical and stepwise, 673–675; and issue of artifacts, 67

Relational systems. *See* Psychosocial relational systems

Relative deprivation: and educational attainment, 376; and occupational choice, 444; and self-concept, 186, 187

Relativism: change during college in, 126; commitments in positions of, 29–30, 43

Relativism discovered, positions of, 29, 43

Religious attitudes and values: between-college effects on, 303–304; change during college in, 280–282; conditional effects on, 319; long-term effects on, 323–324; net effects on, 292–293; within-college effects on, 313–315

Research methods: analytical approaches for, 663–668; assessment issues for, 657–691; and attributions to college attendance, 659–663; and change scores, 687–688; and conditional or general effects, 689–691; on institutional types and experiences, 663; with multiple correlation and regression analysis, 668–682; and net effects estimation, 657–659; with residual scores, 665–668; resources on, 691; unit of analysis for, 682–687

Residence: and attitudes and values, 307, 309, 310, 311, 314–315, 328; and educational attainment, 378, 389–390, 399–402, 414, 419, 422–423; halls, and cognitive skills, 150–151, 161; and inequalities, 639–640; meta-findings on, 611–613; and practice issues, 653–654; and psychosocial relational change, 244, 245, 246–247, 248, 249, 262; and psychosocial self system, 189, 191–192, 194–195; and within-college effects on moral development, 354, 355–356. *See also* Living-learning centers

Residual scores, use of, 665–668

Retirement patterns, and job satisfaction, 496

Rochester, University of, identity development study at, 166, 178, 195–196

S

SAS Institute, 3

Satisfaction, job, 437–439, 442, 452–453, 474–475, 496–497

Savings and investments, and quality of life, 548–549, 552–553, 555

Scholastic Aptitude Test (SAT): and attitudes and values, 297; and career development, 454; and cognitive skills, 121, 122, 134, 137, 138; and eco-

nomic benefits, 508; and educational attainment, 374, 410; and moral development, 342, 346, 349; and psychosocial relational system, 235, 238, 239, 251; and subject matter competence, 74, 76, 78, 79, 82, 84, 103

Screening. *See* Certification or screening theory; Cooling out function

Self-aware stage, in ego development, 35, 43, 169, 170

Self-concept: academic, 172–174; between-college effects on, 183–188, 211; change during college in, 170–175; conditional effects on, 197–198, 213; definitions and structure of, 170–172; long-term effects on, 199–200; net effects on, 180–181, 210–211; social, 174–175; within-college effects on, 190–194, 212

Self-esteem: between-college effects on, 188, 211; change during college in, 175–176, 210; concept of, 171–172, 175; conditional effects on, 198; long-term effects on, 200–201; meta-findings on, 572, 582; net effects on, 181–182, 211; within-college effects on, 194–195

Self-organization, and developmental theory, 47

Self system. *See* Psychosocial self system

Sentence Completion Test (SCT), 36, 169, 179–180, 196

Sex or gender role attitudes and values: between-college effects on, 304; change during college in, 282–283, 333; conditional effects on, 319–320; long-term effects on, 324–325; net effects on, 293–297; within-college effects on, 315–316

Signaling or labeling theory, 443

Size. *See* Institutional size

Smoking, education and, 542–543

Social and political attitudes and values: of altruism, humanitarianism, and civic responsibility, 227, 286–287, 300–301, 310–311, 332–333; between-college effects on, 300–304; change during college in, 276–280; on civil rights and liberties, 279–280, 287–290, 302–303, 310–311; conditional effects on, 318; long-term effects on, 322–323, 334; net effects on, 286–292; within-college effects on, 310–313

Social charters, and institutional quality, 443

Social climate, and person-environment interactions, 41

Social indicators. *See* Quality of life

Social integration. *See* Student involvement

Social mobility, and educational attainment, 369–371

Social organizations, and developmental theory, 49–50

Social rate of return, and economic benefits, 534

Socialization: anticipatory, 403, 423; for civil rights and liberties, 288–289; and cognitive skills, 149–150; college impact theory of, 55–57; and human capital theory, 429, 442, 504, 505–506, 536; and psychosocial relational change, 246, 249, 254; and psychosocial self system, 190; theory of, 429, 442, 456, 495–496

Socio-Economic Index (SEI): and career development, 426–428, 430, 440–441, 444, 446, 456, 458, 459, 463, 465–467, 471, 475, 478, 480, 486, 496, 497, 498; and economic benefits, 508

Socioeconomic outcomes, meta-findings on, 575–577, 596–597, 628–631

Socioeconomic status, and economic benefits, 524–525

Sororities. *See* Greek society membership

Stanford University: ethnocentrism studied at, 219, 244; occupational values studied at, 276

Status attainment, and educational attainment, 369–371, 390

Structural equations modeling. *See* Causal modeling

Structural organizational models, of person-environment interaction, 42

Student Developmental Task and Lifestyle Inventory (SDTLI), 216, 224

Student Developmental Task Inventory (SDTI-2), 216, 224, 230; mature interpersonal relations (MIR) scale of, 224

Student-faculty interactions: and attitudes and values, 308–309, 311, 313, 315, 328; and career development, 478–480; and cognitive skills, 149–150; and educational attainment, 393–397, 412; involvement in, 101–102; and subject matter competence, 97–98, 112

Student involvement: and attitudes and values, 307–308, 313; and cognitive skills, 147–152, 161; college impact theory of, 50–51; and educational attainment, 379, 380, 390–393, 400–402, 411–413, 414, 418, 420–421; extracurricular, 475–478, 520–521, 624–

625; interpersonal, 620–623; and moral development, 351–352; practices for, 648–649; and psychosocial self system, 192–194, 197; and subject matter competence, 98–102, 110

Student personnel services, and educational attainment, 384–385

Students: characteristics of, and educational attainment, 411–414, 423; and institution effects, 102–103; and instructional approach, 103–105, 112–113; personality characteristics of, 104–105; race and gender of, and institutional characteristics, 409–411, 483–484, 525–526, 536; as unit of analysis, 73–76, 80–81. *See also* Minority group members; Older students

Study abroad, and attitudes and values, 306

Study Group on the Conditions of Excellence in American Higher Education, 646, 651, 654

Study of Values (SOV): aesthetic scale of, 272, 331; economic values scale of, 332; religious scale of, 280, 281–282, 324; social values scale of, 332, 334; theoretical scale of, 266

Subject matter competence: analysis of development in, 62–113; background on, 62–63; between-college effects on, 73–83, 108–109; change during college in, 63–67, 107–108; conditional effects on, 63–67, 107–108; conditional effects on, 102–105, 110–111; long-term effects on, 105–107, 111, 113; net effects on, 67–73, 108; summary on, 107–111; within-college effects on, 83–102, 109–110

Subjective well-being, and quality of life, 538–541, 550–551

Success, and career development, 434–437, 450–452, 472–474, 496, 497–498

Swarthmore College, as distinctive, 377

T

Taiwan, moral development studied in, 341

Targeted education, and economic benefits, 516–517

Teacher behavior: and cognitive skills, 146–147; and subject matter competence, 94–98, 112. *See also* Faculty

Teaching, taxonomy of, 94–95

Teaching/learning context: and cognitive skills, 138–140; research needed on, 634–635; and subject matter competence, 85–87. *See also* Instructional approaches

Team teaching, and subject matter competence, 88

Tennessee, budgetary performance incentives in, 647

Test of Concept Formation, 137–138

Test of Conceptual Complexity, 145

Test of Critical Judgment in the Humanities, 140

Test of Critical Thinking Ability, 119

Test of Logic and Rhetoric, 116

Test of Science Reasoning and Understanding, 140

Test of Thematic Analysis (TTA), 121, 129, 134, 137, 138, 144, 151

Texas, Austin, University of, religious values studied at, 281

Thematic Apperception Test, 121

Theories: analysis of, 15–61; applying, 60; background on, 15–16; categories of, 17–18; of change and development, 16; cognitive-structural, 27–36; college impact, 17–18, 50–57; concept of, 51; conclusions on, 58–60; developmental, 17, 18–50, 60; of person-environment interaction, 38–42, 60–61; psychosocial, 19–27, 60

Thinking. *See* Critical thinking

Tolerance: for individual differences, 645–646; in interpersonal relationships, 21–22

Total effect, concept of, 12

Transactional theory, and person-environment interactions, 41

Transfer between four-year institutions: and career development, 462–463; and economic benefits, 514–515; and educational attainment, 385–387, 409–410, 418; meta-findings on, 607, 609

Transfer to four-year colleges, importance of, 643–644

Triumverate, 18, 28

Two-year or four-year institutions: and career development, 440–442; and economic benefits, 506–507, 535; and educational attainment, 372–373, 414, 417; inequalities of, 640–644; meta-findings on, 590–591

Typologies, of developmental theories, 36–38

U

Undergraduate Assessment Program, 82

Unit of analysis, issues of, 73–82, 682–687

United Kingdom: educational values study in, 273; identity development study in, 179, 183; moral development in, 335

U.S. Army Air Force: educational values studied in, 285; political attitudes studied in, 323

U.S. Bureau of Labor Statistics, 542, 543, 547

U.S. Bureau of the Census, 466, 501, 534

U.S. Commission on Civil Rights, 498

U.S. Department of Education, Higher Education General Information Survey (HEGIS) of, 240

U.S. Military Academy (West Point), social charter of, 443

Utah State University, identity development study at, 177

V

Values. *See* Attitudes and values

Vassar College, authoritarianism study at, 253, 255

Vectors of student development, in psychosocial theories, 20–23, 61

Virginia, moral development studied in, 347

VISTA, attitudes and behavior toward, 289, 367

Visual-based instruction (VI), and subject matter competence, 89, 91, 93

Vocational choice, human aggregate models of, 39–40, 61

W

Watson-Glaser Critical Thinking Appraisal (CTA), 119–120, 129–130, 135–136, 139–140, 143, 146, 148, 158

Well-being: psychological, 225–227, 234–235, 238–239, 247–248, 255–256, 266; subjective, 538–541, 550–551

Wisconsin, status attainment model in, 369, 482, 497, 502

Within-college effects: on academic achievement, 388–390, 421–422, 470–475, 497–498, 517–520, 536, 624, 626–629; and academic experience, 616–620; on academic major, 397–399, 422, 463–470, 497, 515–517, 535, 613–616; on attitudes and values, 304–316, 328; on authoritarianism, dogmatism, and ethnocentrism, 243–244, 267; on autonomy, independence, and locus of control, 241–243, 266–267; background on, 607; on career development, 463–481, 492–493; on class

Within-college effects (*continued*)
size, 87; on cognitive skills, 138–152,
157–159; concept of, 7; and course
work patterns, 84–85; on cultural values, 304–308; on economic benefits,
515–522, 531–532, 535–536; on educational attainment, 387–408, 418–
420, 421; on educational values, 308–
309; on ego and identity development, 188–190; on extracurricular involvement, 475–478, 520–521, 624–
625; of financial aid and work, 405–
408; general conclusions on, 610–611;
and institutional characteristics by college experiences, 414–415; and instructional approaches, 87–94, 141–
146; on intellectual orientation, 244–
246, 267; and interpersonal involvement, 620–623; on interpersonal relations, 246–247, 267–268; on maturity and general personal development,
249–250; meta-findings on, 607, 610–
626; on moral development, 349–361,
365–366; of moral education interventions, 356–361, 368; of orientation and advising, 402–405, 423; of
peer relationships and extracurricular
involvement, 390–393; on personal
adjustment, 247–248; on psychosocial
relational system, 241–250, 261–262;
on psychosocial self system, 188–195,
205–206, 211–212; on religious values, 313–315; of residence, 399–402,
422–423, 611–613; of selective or
general involvement, 626; on self-
concept, 190–194, 212; on self-esteem, 194–195; on sex or gender attitudes, 315–316; on social and political values, 310–313; and student-
faculty interactions, 97–98, 101–102,
112, 393–397, 478–480; and student
involvement, 98–102, 147–152, 161;
on subject matter competence, 83–102,
109–110; and teacher behavior, 94–
98, 112, 146–147; and teacher clarity,

96–97, 112; and teaching/learning
context, 85–87, 138–140; on work
experience, 480–481, 521–522
Within-college experiences: and career
development, 484–485, 498; and
moral development, 349–355
Women: academic major and occupational status for, 466; and achieving
competence vector, 20; authoritarianism among, 236, 254; autonomy development among, 217, 251; career
salience of, 454, 478–479; child care
by, 546; conditional effects on attitudes of, 316–320; contraceptive use
by, 545, 554; cultural values among,
297; different voice of, 33–35, 59, 60;
and economic benefits, 517, 523–524;
educational attainment among, 378–
379, 381, 382–384, 396, 399, 417; ego
development among, 169–170; and
ego identity, 24; general well-being of,
248; and health of family, 554; identity development among, 196, 199; intellectual orientation among, 233–234,
245, 254, 260; job satisfaction by, 452;
occupational values of, 275; political
values among, 301; religious values of,
281; self-concept among, 185, 186,
191, 193, 200; in sex-atypical majors
and careers, 445–446, 448–449, 459,
460, 467–468, 472, 476–477, 482,
486–487, 492, 498; and student-faculty interaction, 308, 311. *See also*
Conditional effects of college; Sex or
gender role attitudes and values
Women's institutions, and career development, 453–456, 490–491, 497. *See
also* Institutional gender composition
Work experience during college: and career development, 480–481; and economic benefits, 521–522; and educational attainment, 405–408, 414–415,
420
Work force participation, and career development, 431–432, 496